# Integrating
# Criminologies

# Integrating Criminologies

**Gregg Barak**
*Eastern Michigan University*

**Allyn and Bacon**
*Boston • London • Toronto • Sydney • Tokyo • Singapore*

*Editor-in-Chief:* Karen Hanson
*Editorial Assistant:* Elissa V. Schaen
*Executive Marketing Manager:* Karon Bowers
*Editorial-Production Administrator:* Rob Lawson
*Editorial-Production Service:* Ruttle, Shaw & Wetherill
*Composition Buyer:* Linda Cox
*Manufacturing Buyer:* Megan Cochran
*Cover Administrator:* Linda Knowles

Copyright © 1998 by Allyn & Bacon
A Viacom Company
Needham Heights, MA 02194

Internet: www.abacon.com
America Online: keyword: College Online

**Library of Congress Cataloging-in-Publication Data**

Barak, Gregg.
    Integrating criminologies / Gregg Barak.
       p.  cm.
    Includes bibliographical references and index.
    ISBN 0-205-16557-5
    1. Criminology.  2. Crime  3. Crime—United States.  I. Title.
HV6025.B26  1997
364—dc21                                    96-53560
                                                CIP

Printed in the United States of America
10  9  8  7  6  5  4  3  2  1      01  00  99  98  97

*In Memory of the Berkeley School of Criminology*

# Contents

# *Preface*

In many ways, this is a very nontraditional criminology textbook. It is truly unique and innovative in its approach. Unlike criminology texts that claim one disciplinary stance, favoring either a single theoretical model or a multiparadigm orientation, *Integrating Criminologies* presents an integrative, interdisciplinary passageway to understanding crime and social control. This is also the first criminology textbook to integrate modernist and postmodernist sensibilities about crime and justice. Moreover, it is the first text of its kind to argue for a paradigmatic shift away from fragmented and toward integrative modes of understanding as a means of transforming both contemporary criminological theory and practice.

This book employs what C. Wright Mills called the "sociological imagination" as a means of connecting personal problems and public issues. However, my objective was not to reinforce sociological ascendancy over the criminological enterprise. On the contrary, one of my purposes for writing this book includes trying to help criminology overcome its historical tendency to succumb to one or the other of the competing social and behavioral sciences. Unfortunately, this state of affairs has contributed to separate bodies of criminological knowledge. Therefore, this book is an attempt to reach out to those estranged bodies of knowledge. It is also an attempt to help unify them. As anybody who does interdisciplinary criminology knows, some of the most promising insights about crime and justice are emerging in the overlapping spaces between disciplinary perspectives. At such sights, there is a convergence of material and spiritual forces; the conscious and the unconscious; the body, the mind, and the environment; and between society as we know it, as it has been, and as it could be.

I maintain that criminology needs more than a rhetoric that simply acknowledges its interdisciplinary nature as fundamental. It needs to begin getting down to the business of filling in the spaces between the different disciplinary perspectives on crime and justice. Criminology also needs to develop theories, methods, and policies based on the principles of integrative knowledge building. As we approach the twenty-first century, the time is well past due for the establishment of alternatives to the traditionally fragmented practices of criminology. These fragmented theories, policies, and methods have failed to ameliorate the crime problem, in part, because they have not told the whole story of crime and justice. More specifically, nonintegrative criminologies, both mainstream and critical, languish culturally because they do not appreciate that each of the major perspectives in criminology has something of value to offer the field. In short, when these perspectives are interwoven, they yield more useful analyses of crime and social control than do the fragmented analyses.

In striving to develop a new paradigm for examining crime and social control, I have found it necessary to depart from the traditional tenets of what constitutes a criminology textbook. For example, although this book provides a comprehensive overview of all of the essentials of criminological study, it does not do so with the same degree of depth found in those criminology textbooks that have artificially restricted their inquiries to comparative reviews of criminology's different component disciplines. Instead, I prefer the domains of breadth that come from uncovering and connecting the important criminological concepts, theories, and methods that have been supported by studies and research and that contribute, regardless from where they are derived, to the totality of criminological thinking, understanding, and acting.

In this sense, I have treated biology, psychology, sociology, law, and economics as equals. Similarly, I have treated as equally significant those bodies of knowledge that revolve around race, class, gender, media, and culture as each interacts with the other and as they all intersect with crime and justice. Different from most textbooks in criminology, rather than assessing or evaluating the merits of one particular theory or discipline over and against the merits of other theories or disciplines, I have, instead, cultivated the links between the various disciplines and theories so as to develop fuller and more complete explanations of crime, criminal behavior, and social order. Moreover, I have written a book that advocates a transcendent criminology based more on integrating criminological knowledges across disciplines than on integrating criminological theories within particular disciplines. I argue that by following the horizontal paths of criminological knowledges a plurality of interdisciplinary wisdom will occur that balances the importance of nature, nurture, agency, and social structure.

In breaking away from the beaten paths of most criminology textbooks, I have engaged in some other nontraditional practices as well. For example, unlike most criminology textbooks, my earnest examination of classical criminology follows rather than precedes my examinations of positivist criminology. In a similar manner, I have moved some of the conventionally located contributions of sociology to psychology. At least from an integrative perspective, I believe that these relocations make more sense than the traditional placements of this material.

Finally, in my attempts both to write a broad-gauged story of criminology and to introduce a new way of practicing criminology, I have departed from the custom of enumerating the basic points addressed at the end of each chapter. Instead, I have written summary and conclusions that identify the key issues or thematic messages that I wish the reader to carry over into the next chapter and beyond. In this way, I have attempted to create a running criminological narrative that situates the construction of crime and justice as it unfolds and merges in both the classroom and the street.

## *Organizational and Pedagogical Features*

This textbook is divided into three major parts, each with four chapters. In the first part, Chapter 1 introduces the reader to the integrative perspective and to the various ways of defining criminology and crime. Chapter 2 provides a comparative examination of both crime and the measurement of crime. Chapter 3 focuses on the historical development and relationship between punishment and criminology since the Enlightenment period. Chapter 4 examines the theoretical and practical implications of the development of criminological inquiry.

The second part of this textbook identifies the range of theoretical explanations and findings that have stood the test of time and that have contributed to the totality of criminological understanding. Chapters 5 through 8, respectively, cover the biological, psychological, sociological, legal, and economic contributions to the study of crime and justice. The aim of these discussions is to extract the most valuable information and analysis from each disciplinary contribution to the study of crime. These chapters are less concerned with evaluating theories than they are with presenting a comprehensive overview of the diversity of the bodies of criminological knowledge.

In the third and final part of this book, the various forms in which integrating (or integration) can be practiced are explored. Chapter 9 provides an overview and critique of integrating criminological theories. Chapter 10 initiates a post-postmodern synthesis for integrating the diverse bodies of criminological knowledge. Chapters 11 and 12 incorporate various contributions from Part II with various contributions from cultural, media, gender, and racial/ethnic studies, in order to illustrate narratively, first, the interdisciplinary nature of crime production, and, second, the interdisciplinary approach to crime reduction. These integrations of crime production and crime reduction serve to construct holistic explanations and analyses of crime and justice. In turn, these integrative approaches to theory and practice can be used to construct more meaningful policies of crime and social control.

Each chapter in this book begins with a general introduction that varies in length and that sets the stage for the topic areas to be discussed. At the end of each chapter are the thematic summaries and conclusions mentioned earlier. Following these and preceding the references contained in each chapter are "discussion" rather than "review" questions. These questions are derived from the material covered in the chapters. However, their answers may require students to go beyond this material. These questions, in other words, are made to highlight the important points discussed in each chapter. In addition, like all good questions that can never be fully answered, the ones developed here demand searches that take the student beyond the pages of this textbook and into the real world.

Finally, although I have tried to make this book clear and interesting, integration is complex and demands that students, and even instructors, venture to places that they may not have been before. To make this journey easier, I have provided a glossary of key terms by chapter at the end of the book. This glossary is also another means of highlighting the material that the student should ideally procure from reading *Integrating Criminologies*.

## *Appropriate Courses*

As an integrative venture, this book is appropriate for a wide variety of programs and courses that study crime and social control. Of course, it is perhaps most useful for programs in criminology, criminal justice, social work, sociology, and legal studies. The book is specifically written for students taking upper-division undergraduate and graduate level courses in criminology and in criminological theory. As an undergraduate or graduate text, it can stand alone or it can be used in conjunction with other texts or readers.

## *Acknowledgments*

Like most books, this was a collaborative effort, even if only one person did the actual writing. I could not have written this textbook without the ideas and support of many people over the years. Some of these persons are aware of their contributions while many others are not. I am grateful to all of these persons whether they are named here or not.

Looking way back, I am first and foremost thankful to the now defunct Berkeley School of Criminology, circa 1967 to 1973. The Berkeley School was not only the first academic unit of its kind in the United States, but, during its demise, also the birthplace of critical criminology in this country. Having completed both my undergraduate and graduate education at the Berkeley School, I would particularly like to acknowledge those criminologists who have left their impact on my thinking to this day. The list of both traditional and radical scholars includes Robert Blauner, Stanley Cohen, Bernard Diamond, Caleb Foote, Vonnie Gurgin, Richard Korn, Barry Krisberg, David Matza, Sheldon Messinger, Gordon Misner, Anthony Platt, Herman Schwendinger, Jerome Skolnick, Lloyd Street, and Paul Takagi. I would also like to acknowledge my cohort of graduate students, which includes Drew Humphries, Dorie Klein, June Kress, Martin Miller, Lynn Osborne, Julia Schwendinger, Richard Spiegelman, Annika Snare, and Joseph Weiss. Although none of these criminologists were "integrationists" per se, in the aggregate they provided an intellectual scene of such enormous range and diversity that it was only a matter of time (twenty years) before I eventually returned to my academic roots as a source for this integrative project.

Over the years, there have been other criminologists who have personally supported and helped to push my criminological thinking. These individuals include, but are not limited to, Bruce Arrigo, Robert Bohm, Susan Caringella-MacDonald, Susan Caulfield, William Chambliss, Lynn Chancer, Francis Cullen, Kathleen Daly, Walter DeKeseredy, Jeff Ferrell, David Friedrichs, Ronald Kramer, Brian MacLean, Coramae Richey Mann, Raymond Michalowski, Dragan Milovanovic, Harold Pepinsky, Richard Quinney, Martin Schwartz, Kenneth Tunnell, and Ronald Vogel. More immediately, there are colleagues from Eastern Michigan University that specifically contributed in one way or the other to this book. They include Liza Cerroni-Long, Deborah DeZure, Stuart Henry, Joseph Rankin, Barbara Richardson, Doug Shapiro, and Marcello Truzzi.

Two individuals deserve special mention. One is Stuart Henry, a colleague, mentor, friend, confidant, and at times my alter ego. Stuart has spent more time sharing ideas in general and critiquing this book in particular than any other person. His intellectual sustenance, conversation, and feedback have provided me with the necessary sense that what I have been up to was important and worth pursuing. The other is Paul Leighton who authored the Instructor's Manual for *Integrating Criminologies*. Paul's efforts have produced a fine pedogogical complement to the textbook.

My friend and wife of more than twenty years, Charlotte Pagni, has also provided me with the emotional and intellectual support that I have required to keep on struggling, as it were. My daughter, Maya Pagni Barak, reveals to me daily why it is important to keep on struggling. Together, they help to make my life enjoyable and the struggle easier.

I would like to recognize Eastern Michigan University for its support and the academic fellowship granted during the fall of 1996 to complete this textbook. I would also like to thank my two graduate assistants, Kerry Horton and Roger Eaton, for assisting me with research and for helping to develop the glossary and the discussion questions for this textbook. As the Department Head of Sociology, Anthropology, and Criminology during the writing of this book, I owe a debt of gratitude to my secretary, Jan Randolph, for her adroit skills and abilities to manage things so I could steal the necessary time to write.

Last but not least, I would like to thank Allyn and Bacon and my editor, Karen Hanson, for her eagerness to become involved in the production of a nontraditional criminology textbook. Allyn and Bacon's recruitment of me through their representative, Mary Beth Chesbrough, and their commitment to this project, even before its fine-tuned inception, were instrumental in my taking on this enterprise. In addition to Karen's fine guidance and coordination, I would like to acknowledge her Editorial Assistant, Elissa Schaen, and Production Administrator, Rob Lawson. I would further like to thank Stephen J. Bahr, Brigham Young University; Karen Baird-Olson, Kansas State University; and Donald H. Smith, Old Dominion University, Allyn and Bacon's reviewers of this manuscript; AnnElise Makin for her fine copyediting job; and project manager, Nadia Blahut. The book has greatly benefited from their comments, criticisms, and suggestions.

G. B.

## About the Author

Gregg Barak is Professor of Criminology and Criminal Justice and former Department Head of Sociology, Anthropology, and Criminology at Eastern Michigan University. Prior to coming to EMU, he was Professor and Chair of the Department of Criminology and Criminal Justice at Alabama State University where he was the recipient of the Dean of the College of Arts and Sciences Award for Excellence in Research and Creativity in 1991. Barak was the Program Chair for the annual meetings of the Academy of Criminal Justice Sciences in 1993 when the theme was "Class, Race, and Gender." He has also been a Deputy Editor of *Justice Quarterly* and the Book

Review Editor for *Social Justice*. Throughout the O. J. Simpson criminal trial in 1995, Barak was an expert commentator for 107.1 FM radio in Ann Arbor. From this has emerged the anthology *Representing O. J.: Murder, Criminal Justice, and Mass Culture* (1996). He is also the editor of three other anthologies: *Crimes by the Capitalist State: An Introduction to State Criminality* (1991); *Varieties of Criminology: Readings from a Dynamic Discipline* (1993); and *Media, Process, and the Social Construction of Crime: Studies in Newsmaking Criminology* (1994). Dr. Barak is also the author of *In Defense of Whom? A Critique of Criminal Justice Reform* (1980) and *Gimme Shelter: A Social History of Homelessness in Contemporary America* (1991), which was selected by the American Library Association for its *Choice* List of Outstanding Academic Books for that year.

*Integrating*
*Criminologies*

*C h a p t e r* *1*

# Criminology and Crime: An Integrative Perspective

Demonstration against the closing of the Berkeley School of Criminology, 1974.

Most criminologists or students of crime and crime control, depending on their background, training, and vocational interests, address questions of criminology or issues of criminal justice from particular perspectives embedded in the disciplines of psychology, sociology, and the law. By contrast, the attempt here is to address crime and justice (criminology) from the perspective of an emerging paradigm of interdisciplinary study. In a nutshell, the argument is that integrative ways of viewing crime and criminals are preferable to nonintegrative or singular ways because the former affords the key to obtaining the fullest possible picture of the nature of crime and social control, whereas the latter provides only partial and incomplete pictures of the phenomenon.

For example, in the 1995 O. J. Simpson criminal trial for the murders of Nicole Brown Simpson and Ronald Lyle Goldman, most people looking at the case did so narrowly. From the average person on the street to the specially trained expert, the mass-mediated consumption of the O. J. case was from one or perhaps two orientations. In reality, however, there were several relevant orientations, including but not limited to legal, scientific, psychological, sociological, philosophical, and cultural spheres (Abramson, 1996; Barak, 1996; Hutchinson, 1996; Rantala, 1996). Each of the available orientations yields sets of issues and questions that are focused on differently by people according to their particular fields and perspectives.

Thus, lawyers and law professors are concerned with issues that are legal in nature, such as the denial of bail or the right to a fair and speedy trial by a jury of one's peers; criminalists or forensic specialists are concerned with issues that are scientific in nature, such as the gathering of physical evidence and the testing of DNA samples; psychiatrists and psychologists are concerned with issues that are emotional in nature, such as the mental capacity or *mens rea* of the accused; sociologists and anthropologists are concerned with issues that are expressive in nature, such as the reactions of the media and of the audiences of mass consumption; pundits and social critics are concerned with issues that are philosophical in nature, such as the questions involving free will and just punishments.

Although some observers, lay or professional, were concerned with more than one set of questions or issues, very few people were concerned with all of the orientations or with an integrated picture of the O. J. Simpson case. What makes matters even more complicated is the fact that underlying this murder trial was a whole range of other behavioral and social perspectives that are relevant to the understanding of crime and crime control that were relatively ignored. For example, very little attention or discussion was given to personality theory, social psychology, and patterns of abusive behavior in general and in relationship to O. J. in particular. These perspectives are derived from such diverse fields as biology, history, cultural studies, psychoanalysis, and political economy, to name some of the more dominant or competitive disciplines in the study of crime and violence.

My point is that the O. J. case is representative of the need for students of crime and justice to develop an integrative approach to the subject matter in order to more fully understand the complex behavioral and environmental processes that are involved in criminality and its control. Toward this objective, *Integrating Criminologies* is both a critique of disciplinary criminology and a synthesis of the emerging paradigm of interdisciplinary criminology. My attempt here is to bring biology, psychology, sociol-

Attorneys Bailey, Cochran, and Shapiro and O. J. Simpson listening to the not-guilty criminal verdict, 1995.

ogy, law, economics, feminist studies, media studies, and ethnic studies to the criminological table. I do this not only for the purpose of facilitating mergers between bodies of criminological knowledge, but so that an integrative-constitutive model of crime and social control is constructed.

## In Search of Criminology

Leon Radzinowicz (1962), in his treatise on the development of criminological thought and penal practice, identified nineteen terms that were in contemporary use in the 1950s describing the field. These were criminology, criminal science, criminal anthropology, criminal biology, criminal psychology, criminal (or forensic) psychiatry, judicial psychology, criminal sociology, penal philosophy, criminal policy, criminal jurisprudence, criminal statistics, penology, prison science, prison law, prison pedagogy, police science, criminalistics, and criminal prophylaxis. As Radzinowicz (1962: 167) observed: "Though these varied titles represent the several emerging lines of a new discipline, it is difficult to justify such a wealth of expressions, and the confusion is increased by the fact that many of them have different meanings for different authors."

My survey of criminological thought some thirty years later (Barak, 1994) revealed twelve criminologies. These were positivist criminology, neoclassical criminology, neofunctionalist criminology, critical criminology, realist criminology, cultural criminology, feminist criminology, peacemaking criminology, biosocial criminology, anarchistic criminology, deconstructionist criminology, and postmodernist criminology. Aside from the many diverse meanings of the subject among today's criminologists, the confusion is perhaps even greater as bodies of knowledge experience exponential growth. I would argue that, even more than in Radzinowicz's day, such a proliferation of criminologies is not warranted and that it diminishes the field's ability to consolidate the various bodies of knowledge and to impact public policy.

The problem is made worse by the fact that today most criminologists typically deny the existence of other criminologies, preferring instead to concentrate on one or perhaps two strands of criminology. As a consequence, most criminological textbooks tend to be one-dimensional, exaggerating the value of one or possibly two perspectives while dismissing the value of virtually all the other perspectives. In the process of writing most criminology textbooks, a paradox occurs. On the one hand, a lot of valuable *breadth* in criminological knowledge is lost or distorted (Andrews and Bonta, 1994); on the other hand, an unnecessary plethora of *depth* is provided from the preferred criminological knowledges.

This textbook is different. It takes an integrative approach whereby the guiding philosophy is that representation and synthesis are more important than an exhaustive explication and criticism of the corpus of existing criminological knowledge. It argues for breadth rather than depth of subject matter. It argues that the time has arrived for criminology not only to set its house in order—assessing the field's development, relevance, and future—but also, in a more ambitious way, to reorder or reconstruct the criminological enterprise to reflect what I refer to as the emerging paradigm of interdisciplinarity.

Historically speaking, although the terminology used to describe crime and criminals has been reduced since Radzinowicz went looking for criminology, the study of criminology has grown tremendously within the curricula of colleges and universities. Moreover, if one compares Edwin Sutherland and Donald Cressey's *Principles of Criminology* (1955), in its fifth edition, with Don Gibbons's *Society, Crime, and Criminal Behavior* (1992), in its sixth edition, then one gets an idea of the expansion of the field. Not only have the theorizing and research activities expanded, but the number of theoretical perspectives has grown considerably as evidenced by the number of criminologies that have emerged over the last quarter of a century.

What distinguishes Radzinowicz's goals from my own is that he was calling for a consensus of definition over the subject matter and boundaries of criminology. I am not calling for a consensus or restriction in the subject matter. On the contrary, I am supportive of an open-ended subject matter where the different analyses and approaches to crime and crime control can be expanded through integration. It is my contention that what is needed is an interdisciplinary criminology that recognizes the value of integrating criminologies. Such a criminology strives to incorporate the social facts of crime with the question "Why do criminals do it?" This commonsense approach appreciates the strengths of the different criminological "knowledges" and their particular theories, methods, interests, and points of view.

An integrative criminology, thus, seeks to bring together the diverse bodies of knowledge that represent the full array of disciplines that study crime. Like other integrative analyses that respect the genuine differences between perspectives, *Integrating Criminologies* still emphasizes the need for both pursuing the interconnectedness between schools of thought and overcoming the isolationism between these same schools. What makes this integrative analysis different from other integrative analyses in sociology (Ritzer, 1981) or in the study of deviance (Orcutt, 1983) is that my integration is a transdisciplinary rather than a disciplinary exercise. It seeks not merely to integrate different frameworks, perspectives, or orientations within particular disciplines, but to do so across disciplines as dissimilar as, for example, biology, sociology, and the law. At the same time, this integrative analysis appreciates that crime and crime control as well as criminology are part and parcel of a cultural and political-economic development that reflects changes in the transforming world order. Finally, this analysis takes into account both the behavioral world represented in human emotions and the world of language and images represented in everyday speech and mass communications.

In today's postmodernist world characterized by the Internet, telecommunications, and virtual reality, I believe that criminology, like the larger American culture, can be described as spinning out of control. Several commentators, such as John Hagan (1989), Clifford Shearing (1989), and Richard Ericson and Kevin Carriere (1994) have referred to "the fragmentation of criminology." The latter have argued in *The Futures of Criminology* that this fragmentation is part of the wider processes of fragmentation in the academy and in other social institutions. Hence, they argue that "it is preferable to engage the fragmentation of criminology for what it is, the inevitable result of academic and institutional change in risk society" (Ericson and Carriere, 1994: 105).

By contrast, Hagan seeks to reestablish order by claiming that his "structural criminology," as part of the sociological-scientific study of social relations, is all that is required for a positivistic studying of crime, rendering alternative methods and disciplines as either insignificant or subservient. Shearing (1989: 176) finds relative security by relegating criminology to the sociological realm in which the "struggle over order, the activity that seeks to guarantee it, and the activity that resists the realization of this guarantee, either in part or whole, is the phenomenon that gives unity to criminological research and teaching." Hagan and Shearing are typical of those criminologists who find their order within the confines of a broadly constructed sociology that is, for the most part, separated from other relevant bodies of criminological knowledge.

Gibbons (1994) believes that the way to criminological order is through more serious theorizing. I also believe like Gibbons (1994: ix) that there is too much "talking about crime" without acknowledging the fact that "much of the time criminologists don't know quite what they are talking about." In fairness, however, the mass media pundits, the public cultural critics, and the professional politicians who are all engaged in the business of talking about crime know far less than the criminologists do. In similar ways, both experts and lay persons suffer from a distorted way of thinking about crime and justice. At the same time, I do acknowledge, as Gibbons contends, that "theoretical flabbiness" is a serious problem, but I think that he overstates the case when he identifies theory construction as the most serious problem confronting criminology. In terms of criminological priorities, for example, I believe that integrating criminologies is more important than developing or integrating criminological theories per se. I also believe that integrating criminologies is a necessary prerequisite for a transformative reordering of the criminological enterprise away from its dominant penal-administrative forms of control and toward its nascent social-democratic forms of regulation.

An integrative transformation of the kind called for here involves both a deconstruction and a reconstruction of the rituals of crime and criminology (Henry and Milovanovic, 1991; 1994; Michalowski, 1993; Pfohl and Gordon, 1986). Stated differently, I believe that the field requires both a critique of disciplinary criminology and a synthesis of interdisciplinary criminologies. I maintain further that in order to bring about these changes in the understanding of crime and crime control, criminology has to confront the social-structural interaction of minds, cultures, and bodies.

For example, with respect to the O. J. Simpson trials, minds refer to the conscious and unconscious thought processes of the accused, the jury, the lawyers, the witnesses, and so on. We could also be referring to the personalities of any of these people. As for cultures, we could reference the backgrounds, the racial-ethnic compositions, the socioeconomic statuses, or the educational levels of the victims, the courtroom participants, and the at-home viewing audiences. References to bodies is even more complex.

By bodies, I refer not only to the physical or constitutional makeup of people, but to bodies of knowledge and to bodies of action. In the context of the O. J. trials, we have particular bodies of knowledge such as law, forensics, logic, and psychiatry. There are also the murdered victims as obvious bodies of action. Moreover, bodies refer to those sites where power comes to life by the ritualistic acts of control and transgression (Foucault, 1977; Katz, 1988). Control and transgression typically identify the bodies' shape, appearance, movement, pleasure, pain, consumption, rejection, resistance, and other functions. Control and transgression can also identify popular, ideological, and intellectual discourses on crime and crime control.

Like crimes and criminologies, societies are composed of minds, cultures, and bodies that are linked in dynamic processes and historical patterns. Whether we are discussing the changing rates of aggregated crimes, the reasons that individuals inflict pain, or the particular forms that harms take, we must take into account several dimensions or levels of social reality that constitute the interconnected world of psychologies, biologies, political economies, and mass-mediated communications. When we talk of the important problem of harm reduction, or crime control, we must similarly link our understanding not only to a systematic study of the spheres of prevention, including the aspects of socialization and role identification, the enactments and enforcements of law and penal sanction, and the methods of treatment, discipline, and punishment, but also to the behavioral strategies and social resources that individuals or groups employ in their competitive struggle for goods and services (Cohen and Machalek, 1988).

Criminologists have traditionally examined crime and crime control by analyzing variations in axes of genetics, class, age, gender, race, personality, population density, and other categories. Although these dimensions of crime, or levels of analysis, have often been examined together, such clustering usually takes a predictable disciplinary form. For example, those looking at *micro* personality factors rarely, if ever, look at *macro* organizational factors, and vice versa. On top of this, most criminologists with their favored criminology have traditionally been in competition with other criminologies.

One of the longest lasting competitions in the study of crime and criminals has been between macro-level sociological criminologies that argue for the importance of structural forces, such as social class, and micro-level psychological criminologies that argue on behalf of the importance of personalities or temperaments. The tendency in criminology to regard such external–internal matters as social class–personality in relatively one-dimensional rather than in multidimensional terms is illustrative of the need for developing an integrative criminology: a criminology that understands that the study of crime, criminals, and law enforcement is not an autonomous disciplinary phenomenon, but is, instead, an interdisciplinary phenomenon involving the combined exchanges of nature and nurture.

The study of the causes, or etiology, of crime and the study of the control, or regulation, of criminals are also not separate but related phenomena. More accurately, they are integrative parts of the whole of crime and social control. Hence, to understand criminals, crime control/prevention, or criminology, criminologists and others must understand each of these not only in relation to the other, but also in relation to other bodies of knowledge such as cultural, media, and gender studies. In turn, these bodies of knowledge need to be combined with legal studies, the more traditional social science disciplines such as psychology, sociology, and anthropology; and the less traditional fields of interdisciplinarity, such as biosociology and social ecology.

By discussing a series of questions related to the integrative approach to criminology, the rest of this introductory chapter is divided into three parts and provides the rationale, or sets the stage, for the kind of interdisciplinary criminology called for in *Integrating Criminologies.* The first part explores the question, "What is criminology?" It claims that despite a relative consensus of what criminology entails, most criminologists have ignored the more fundamental question of whether criminology is first and foremost a discipline, a nondiscipline, or an interdiscipline. The second part explores three questions about the need for integration: "Why should criminology integrate?" "What should criminology integrate?" and "How should criminology proceed?" It claims that the field of study should move from its narrowly based disciplinary focuses on crime and crime control to more broadly based focuses grounded in interdisciplinarity. After addressing the need for criminological integration, the final part of this chapter explores the definitional questions associated with crime and criminals. It exposes the myopic nature of selecting out some criminal behavior (from all the possible harms and injuries) for inclusion in the various legalistic classification schemes. It claims that crime and criminals are more fully dealt with by an integrative perspective that views crime not only as legal but also as social and moral phenomena.

## What Is Criminology?

Although criminologists might agree that criminology entails the study of crime and crime control, crime and punishment, and crime and justice, most criminologists have not resolved the question, "What is criminology?" To do so, criminologists and students of crime and social control should, first and foremost, consider the disciplinary status of criminology. In other words, is criminology a discipline, a multidiscipline, or an interdiscipline? There are, based on the answers to this question, different conceptualizations of what the subject matter of criminology should be. Also flowing from these answers are different approaches to the subject matter as well as different responses to crime and the administration of justice. In short, peoples' fundamental views of the criminological enterprise shape the kind of criminology they practice.

Criminologists have essentially adopted three positions on the nature of the field. I refer to these positions as: (1) sociological traditionalists; (2) multidisciplinary specialists; and (3) interdisciplinary generalists. It is interesting to note that a fourth position, one that could be referred to as "criminological disciplinarians," has not been adopted.

Sociological traditionalists can be traced back to the 1920s and the birth of the Chicago School of sociological and criminological investigation. True to their sociological roots and training, these criminologists subscribe to the belief that criminology is a subsidiary of the discipline of sociology. When identifying the criminological enterprise, they cite Sutherland and Cressey (1978: 3): "Criminology is the body of knowledge regarding juvenile delinquency and crime. It includes within its scope the process of making laws, of breaking laws, and of reacting to the breaking of laws." Gibbons (1992; 1994: 2) has expanded this definition to include "the nature of crime and criminal behavior, the origins of criminal laws, the extent and distribution of criminality, social structure and criminality, the origins and development of criminal acts and criminal careers, and social reactions to crime."

These sociologically oriented criminologists point to the individuals who actually do the work. They argue, for example, as Ronald Akers (1992) does, that because criminologists are trained primarily in sociology, and because much of the theorizing and research on crime and delinquency has been conducted by sociologists, then criminology once again belongs to a subfield of sociology. This sociology-linked definition of criminology regards other disciplines, such as psychology and law, as playing minor or subordinate roles in the study of crime and justice.

The multidisciplinary specialists typically include criminologists from social and behavioral disciplines other than sociology. These criminologists maintain that there are multiple disciplinary paths to the study of crime and criminals. Their roots of inquiry are eclectically based and disciplinary specific; these may be traced to a variety of intellectual and philosophical traditions, such as rationalism, humanism, and empiricism, dating as far back as the Age of Enlightenment in the late seventeenth and eighteenth centuries. Included among this group of criminologists are biologists, economists, legal scholars, historians, political scientists, anthropologists, and others.

These multidiscipline specialists believe that criminology is neither a subsidiary of sociology nor a distinct discipline. Nevertheless, these criminologists tend to elevate their own particular discipline's importance to the study of crime while suppressing the relative importance of other disciplines. Like the sociological traditionalists, the multidisciplinary specialists believe that, unlike economics or political science, the bodies of criminological knowledge are not derived from their own distinctive sets of questions and concepts posed by a single group of scholars:

> There are no distinctively criminological questions; instead, we pose sociological, psychological, economic, or other queries about crime and criminal behavior. Similarly, few if any concepts are unique to criminological inquiry; instead, propositions about lawbreaking and lawbreakers are posed in the conceptual language of the established disciplines, or put another way, sociological, psychological, or economic concepts and propositions are brought to bear upon lawbreaking in the effort to explain it (Gibbons, 1994: 3).

The third group of criminologists are the interdisciplinary generalists. This recently emerging group of criminologists believes that the various knowledges from such diverse fields as the social sciences, natural sciences, and humanities must somehow be connected to the studies of crime and crime control. C. Ray Jeffery made an early case for integration in his textbook *Criminology: An Interdisciplinary Approach* (1990). In that work he argued that criminology has to integrate the various bodies of knowledge from biology, psychology, sociology, law, and other fields. He has subsequently argued that both a theory of crime and a theory of criminal behavior require such integration. To accomplish it, Jeffery (1994: 21) maintains that "we must develop an interdisciplinary theory of behavior and then apply it to the explanations of crime and criminal behavior." Jeffery believes that interdisciplinary criminology represents the next new era in criminology.

As a criminologist who has gradually moved away from a political-economic multidisciplinary approach and toward the interdisciplinary generalist's approach described in the next section, I reject the sociologically linked definition of criminology out of recognition to those from other disciplines who have made, and continue to make, contributions to criminological understanding. This disciplinary approach to criminology is also rejected on the grounds that it is too reductionist, especially with its contemptuous disregard for biology, psychology, economics, and even cultural studies. Similarly, I reject the multidisciplinary specialist's approach because it, too, tends to be disciplinary oriented. Such an orientation typically maintains allegiance to some kind of hierarchical or privileged ranking of knowledges. By contrast, the interdisciplinary approach used here seeks an integration of the varieties of criminological knowledge as equals.

## The Need for Integration

Mass communication allows for knowledge to be generated not only in scholarly disciplinary forms, but also in popular extradisciplinary forms, including such diverse contexts as marketing surveys, court television, public health antiviolence comic books, media discussions, and many others. In other words, the production of criminological knowledge, which was once primarily confined to the writings and research findings of the professionally trained experts or disciplinarians, today, by contrast, includes widely disseminated information propagated by nonexpert criminological sources. Moreover, although knowledge in its disciplinary (specialized) form is only two centuries old and the academy of higher education with its departmental structures and its professionally trained experts has been with us for less than a century, disciplines are commonly regarded as fixed or unalterable. For example, most criminologists usually overlook the field's historical novelty as a discipline that has been coveted by several fields, including medicine, biology, law, psychology, and sociology, to name the most conspicuous. In like manner, students of crime and crime control typically overlook the possibility of alternative ways of producing and organizing criminological knowledge.

The need for integration springs from the historical and contemporary reality in which there are many disciplinary routes to both crime and criminology. Socially and conceptually, as Thomas Kuhn (1961; 1970) first pointed out and as Messer-Davidow, Shunway, and Sylvan (1993: vii) have recently written, "We are disciplined by our disciplines." That is to say, the authors continue, disciplinary structures help produce our world: "They specify the objects we can study (genes, deviant persons, classic texts) and the relations that obtain among them (mutations, criminality, canonicity). They provide criteria for our knowledge (truth, significance, impact) and methods (quantification, interpretation, analysis) that regulate our access to it."

Moreover, disciplines produce students and disciplinarians, in our case, criminologists who are practitioners, orthodox and heterodox; who are specialists and generalists; and who are theoreticians and researchers. Disciplines also produce their own economies of value and manufacture discourses in abundance. Disciplines, of course, produce textbooks. Chapters 5 through 8 in Part II of this book provide a historically oriented and comparative overview of the major contributions from the primary strands of criminological knowledge. Disciplines do other things as well, such as provide jobs, secure funding, and generate prestige. Finally, disciplines produce the idea of progress: "They tell stories of progress, showing how knowledge advances within existing disciplines and by the establishment of new ones" (Messer-Davidow et al., 1993: viii).

One alternative form of producing and organizing knowledge is to embrace interdisciplinarity rather than reentering the now familiar closets of disciplinarity. The interdisciplinary perspective, in other words, chooses integration over differentiation. At the same time, however, it appreciates the tensions and relations between the two. Hence, although the subtext of *Integrating Criminologies* is concerned with the differentiation within and without criminology or with how criminology as a nonintegrative discipline has constructed itself, its primary text emphasizes the reordering and reconstructing of an interdisciplinary criminology that unfolds in Chapters 10, 11, and 12, preceded by an extensive review and critique of theoretical integration in Chapter 9.

Following the insights of both Friedrich Nietzsche (1967) and Michel Foucault (1977), this book recognizes that criminological knowledge has not only been a product of power, but it has itself been a non-neutral form of power. Criminological knowledge is also a product of ethics and notions of justice. In other words, criminology has never been (and cannot be) separated from the prevailing or dominant values of the society of which it is a part. This is especially evident when criminologists tell stories about our historical past or when we try to replace criminological narratives that portray its evolutionary development with those narratives that reveal the contradictions involved in development. For example, Piers Beirne (1993: 1) makes reference to the collective ignorance about the history of concept formation in criminology when he exclaims (borrowing from Karl Marx) "The tradition of the dead generations always weighs like a nightmare upon the minds of the living!" Beirne's (1993: 4) work challenges the alleged "validity of the hallowed distinction drawn between positivist criminology and the dominant discourse about crime that preceded it, namely, 'classical criminology.' "

The point is that there is nothing inevitable about the form of development that criminology has taken. The current state of criminology is the product of a specific history; it has been contingent on the actions of real people and not on some kind of natural or unifying body of knowledge. Its nondisciplinarity, like its history, has emerged because criminology has incorporated certain types of knowledge and has excluded other types. Hence, contemporary criminology is the product of how it has been assembled from bits and pieces of other disciplines. Its legitimation as a body of knowledge has, in part, been established by how expertise was attributed to individuals pursuing certain kinds of study, while those pursuing other kinds were stigmatized as unscientific or unscholarly.

There is still disagreement as to whether, for example, the so-called classical writers such as Beccaria, Voltaire, and Bentham were even engaged in criminology. David Garland (1985) argues that it is more appropriate to regard these men as applying legal jurisprudence to the world of crime and punishment. On the other hand, Beirne maintains that Cesare Beccaria's *Of Crimes and Punishments* (1764) has been misinterpreted as a humanist and volitional work despite the deterministic discourse of its author. He suggests that this book should be understood as an attempt to apply an early understanding of the "science of man" to crime and penal strategies.

Both Garland and Beirne do away with the traditional distinction between classical (eighteenth century) and positivist (nineteenth century) criminology, but for different reasons. Both agree that the conventional distinction made between classical and positivist criminologies is not appropriate, but they differ about why the distinction is inappropriate. Garland, on the one hand, argues that the classical scholars of jurisprudence were not engaged in criminology per se. Beirne, on the other hand, maintains that these classical writers were engaged in a criminology not unlike that of the positivists who came later to criticize them.

Meanwhile, most criminologists and essentially all of the criminology textbooks in print today continue to base their assumptions and instruction on rigidly characterized differences between these two criminologies. For example, in the context of the criminal and civil trials of O. J. Simpson, the classical explanations of his behavior tend to emphasize that his actions were based on a rational and utilitarian calculus that the pleasure lost or the pain inflicted by Nicole Brown Simpson's departure from the relationship became more than O. J. could handle. In response, he acted with free will and malice aforethought, killing Nicole in cold blood. And, surprised by the appearance of

Goldman at the scene of the crime, O. J. killed him as a means of eliminating a potential eyewitness.

By contrast, positivist explanations tend to claim that the murders were the products of internal or external factors (Barak, 1996; Hutchinson, 1996; Rantala, 1996). In these scenarios, it has been suggested that O. J. committed the double murders as an overreaction to Nicole's final rejection and to some combination of psychological and sociological forces that were in the making for some seventeen years or longer. Perhaps, a more complete explanation of Simpson's murders involves the incorporation of classical "free will" and positivist "determinism" (Matza, 1964).

In other words, an integrated approach to the double murders of Nicole Brown Simpson and Ronald Lyle Goldman recognizes that, like most people, O. J. was and is a determining and determined human being. In short, the integrative approach suggests that Simpson could have committed these heinous crimes for a combination of reasons, some rational and some not. For example, an integrative approach offers explanations that tend to emphasize the double murders as acts of temporary insanity induced by a combination of Simpson's need to control, his dependence on Nicole, and his jealous rage that resulted in the reasoning that if he could not have her, then nobody else could either.

## Why Should Criminology Integrate?

My argument is that all disciplines concerned with the study of society and human nature have valuable contributions to make to the study of crime, criminals, and crime control. In turn, the value of these disciplinary contributions are enhanced when they are integrated into an interdisciplinary framework. In other words, interdisciplinarity helps to expose the narrowness and sterility of the answers produced by the psychological, sociological, or juristic approaches to crime and crime control acting alone. I further believe that an integrated criminology will expand the utilitarian knowledge base of social control. In addition, there are primarily two other groups of reasons for why I believe that criminology should integrate. One group revolves around criminological inquiry; the other group revolves around criminological pedagogy.

### Criminological Inquiry

Criminological researchers and instructors, to varying degrees, experience unexamined notions about what constitutes crime and criminals. As I have already suggested, if "disciplinary structures help produce our world," then, similarly, paradigms (or models of intellectual investigation) shape the ways in which we see the world. Kuhn (1970: 175), in his classic work *The Structure of Scientific Revolutions*, defined *paradigm* as "the entire constellation of beliefs, values, techniques, and so on shared by the members of a given community." In short, as disciplines shape students and disciplinarians, paradigms shape the ways in which students or professors of criminology conduct their observations and make their statements of fact. In other words, the different paradigms used by students of crime and criminality influence where they look for facts, the observational instruments they select, and the interpretations they make.

Both disciplines and paradigms are rooted in the historical experiences of their practitioners—proponents and opponents alike. Finally, as Kuhn (1970) has argued, contemporary disciplines cannot operate without paradigms because scientists, natural or social, do not possess neutral languages of observation. The closest that disciplines or scientists can get to neutrality are the paradigms themselves. In effect, one cannot view criminology from a paradigm-free standpoint. Of course, most lay people are unaware not only of the different paradigms (or modes of thinking), but also of the particular paradigm that underpins their own thinking. The same cannot be said of most academicians in general or of criminologists in particular. The problem for most academicians, however, is that most of the time they go about their business acting as though there was only one correct paradigm.

## Criminological Pedagogy

The study, examination, or depiction of crime and deviance occur virtually throughout the disciplines. Students come to criminological inquiry from the humanities, the sciences, and the social sciences, creating a mixture of people with diverse interests and backgrounds. Yet, as a result of mass-mediated education, they typically share some basic beliefs about, perceptions of, and orientations toward crime and criminal justice. This is precisely why courses in criminology and criminal justice are in such high demand in most universities and colleges across the nation. Hence, from a pedagogical perspective, narratives about crime and crime control are utilitarian because most, if not all, students can relate to the phenomenon.

For example, although criminal law constitutes a very small portion of formal and informal legal practices, students are generally aware of crime as a legal phenomenon. In other words, most students typically presumed that O. J. was innocent until such time as the trial process determined that he was guilty or not guilty beyond a reasonable doubt. For most students of criminology the trial was a cut-and-dried depiction of criminal reality. That is to say, neither students nor the general public related to the adjudicated fact that the trial was not the criminal event itself, but rather a reconstructed version of what occurred on the night of the double murders; a product no less of the legally negotiated imaginations of the defense, the prosecution, the judge, and the jury. In short, students and mass audiences alike do not generally appreciate the common distinction between the notions of *legal* and *factual* culpability made by criminologists, attorneys, criminal justice practitioners, and others who are familiar with the day-to-day workings of the legal system.

Students also seem to be interested in or be preoccupied with criminal behavior and to a lesser degree with responses to crime involving both criminal justice and popular culture. At the same time, most students tend to regard criminals as fundamentally different from noncriminals. Finally, students are typically either unaware of or uninterested in the historical and comparative development of crime and crime control, until these relationships are focused on. That is to say, from a pedagogical standpoint, most students are fascinated when domestic violence-related homicides like Nicole Brown Simpson's are placed into historical or comparative perspective.

These contradictions in "student interest in criminology create opportunities for critical thinking and analysis" (Silbey, 1993: 1). Because of the enthusiasm that students bring to criminology, instructors are able to invert "unexamined notions about what constitutes crime and its relationship to social organization and social change" (Silbey, 1993: 1) For example, students interested in and wanting to know more about murder, rape, and, to a lesser degree, environmental pollution and corporate fraud "are immediately confronted by the instability of the concept of crime and invited to examine how the category of crime . . . is created, and how groups of persons are classified as criminals" (Silbey, 1993: 7). In turn, most of these students are then ready to ask, "How do we get the 'crime' and 'criminals' that we have?" Once engaged in this kind of questioning, students are confronted by the need to examine, both historically and comparatively, why only certain forms of injury or particular norm violators become criminalized. As they search for the answers to these questions, inevitably these students find themselves moving back and forth between and across disciplines. In the process, they become ripe for interdisciplinary analysis.

## What Should Criminology Integrate?

After examining what he refers to as the reason and unreason of the conventional and critical goals of criminological inquiry, Bruce DiCristina (1994: 16) observes:

> *The work that has been done within the philosophy of science over the past 250 years has made it acceptable to presuppose that our cognitive apparatus shapes our perceptions of reality at least as much as reality itself. It suggests that interpretation is inseparable from observation and as important as observation. It stipulates that all reality claims are conjectural, and that we should be very cautious whenever we pass judgment. It also suggests that the popular conventional and critical goals of criminology have a utopian quality.*

The conventional and critical goals of criminological inquiry as identified by DiCristina are quite different in content and orientation. The conventional goals include the discovery of causes of crime, the prediction of crime trends and recidivism, the identification of false theories of crime, the discovery of truth about crime, and the identification of means to control crime. The critical goals include mutual understanding, peace, emancipation, the reduction of suffering, and "the greatest happiness shared by the greatest number." Despite all of the problems that DiCristina finds with these goals and despite their "utopian quality," he does not argue that they should be abandoned. Instead, he quotes jurist-sociologist, Max Weber, who noted in a 1913 essay that "the possible is very often achieved only by reaching out towards the impossible which lies beyond it" (quoted in DiCristina, 1994: 16). This means that "we should always be open to new goals, new utopias" (DiCristina, 1994: 16). Simply stated, my argument is that the emerging paradigm of interdisciplinarity as applied to criminology represents the latest goals and the newest utopias that, if not seriously pursued, should at least be carefully paid attention to.

One of the tasks of *Integrating Criminologies* is to accommodate and merge the goals of these allegedly competing criminologies into some kind of synthesized framework. Such a framework, it is argued, is capable not only of addressing the fragmentation in criminology, but also of reestablishing and transforming the current state of criminological affairs. In carrying out the kind of postmodern integrative-constitutive synthesis developed later in this textbook (see Chapter 10), I have assumed that the process of integration will delete, modify, and alter the two original sets of criminological goals. The product of such integrative analysis yields ever newer and never finished goals and utopias for criminology to contemplate. In other words, integrative and interdisciplinary works as conceptualized here represent forms of disequilibrium that unsettle existing assumptions about crime and justice. In this regard, the suitable criteria for criminological integration are not imported intact from one of the participating disciplinary domains, but instead are represented by the cross-fertilization of criteria forged from the interdisciplinary process itself.

Criminological integration should move beyond clarifying and working out disciplinary differences. At the same time, the important differences should remain. There should also be a continuing renegotiation of boundaries across disciplines and among the various criminologies. In this regard, the work of interdisciplinarity becomes corrective, not supplementary. That is, the rhetoric of criminological interpenetration constructs new criteria and replaces, not simply enriches, existing criminologies, thereby altering research procedures, not just the products of research (Klein, 1994).

Comparatively speaking, postmodern forms of integration differ from the more traditional or modern forms of integration. For criminology, the postmodern forms of integration are representative of a broad-gauged approach to crime and justice; the modern forms are representative of a relatively narrow and disciplinarity-based approach. For example, although both types of synthesis call for conceptual integration, the latter emphasize the centrality of theory in scientific endeavors and the construction of "causal models" (Messner, Krohn, and Liska, 1989), and the former emphasize the ever-changing voices of plurality that provide meaning for the local sites of crime, justice, law, and community (Arrigo, 1994; Henry and Milovanovic, 1991).

As Bruce Arrigo (1994: 14) articulates, postmodern integration "refers to its *relational, positional,* and *provisional* function to interpret, re-interpret, validate, and repudiate multiple discourses and their legitimated expression of desire in divergent social arrangements" (Arrigo 1994: 15; emphasis by author). By contrast, modern integration strives for theoretical "linkages among different conceptual arguments as a way of advancing theoretical (scientific) growth precisely because synthetic analyses offer a more cogent explanation for promoting objective science than other strategies." Similarly, in this book I distinguish between postmodern (Chapter 10) and modern (Chapter 9) criminological agendas: the former engaging in synthesis for the purposes of integrating knowledges of crime and social control; the latter engaging in synthesis for the purposes of integrating theories of crime and crime control.

Whereas Part III of this book will differentiate between modern and postmodern forms of criminological integration, presently I want to articulate the ingredients (see Figure 1.1) necessary for a postmodern synthesis. In the next section, I will articulate the disciplinary foundations and interdisciplinary studies necessary for a postmodern synthesis (see Table 1.1). Generally speaking, postmodern integration can be characterized as breadth-oriented rather than depth-oriented. Given the horizontal and vertical directions that knowledge can take, the postmodern synthesis opts for the former. That is to say, postmodern integration chooses its analytic methods, theories, and substantive knowledges from all those fields that are useful for the purposes of criminological unity. Parallel to media, policy, or cultural studies, this kind of synthesis is not fundamentally disciplinarian in nature, but, on the contrary, it is interdisciplinarian.

Interdisciplinary analysis requires that students of crime and crime control become conversant in several areas of inquiry. It requires that criminologists and others become open to what historian and philosopher Karl Popper referred to as the three worlds of everything that exists and can be experienced: World 1—physical objects and states; World 2—levels of consciousness and subjective knowledges; and World 3—cultural heritage and objective knowledges (Popper and Eccles, 1983). Specifically, those individual and social ingredients that an integrative criminology should take into account include the following foci, or levels of criminological analysis: human agency (human nature and consciousness); socialization and identity formation; social structure and institutional orders; discourse, knowledge, and mass communication; and social and cultural change.

Each of these foci, or levels of criminological analysis, are important in their own right. However, when these ingredients of criminological investigation are incorporated, they constitute the complexity of the human condition. For example, whether we are discussing criminals, crime controllers, or the public-at-large, the human mind (agency) as both a physiological and psychological state should be considered. Developmentally, people—criminal and noncriminal—are exposed to and experience fundamental socialization processes such as toilet training and learning right from wrong. Similarly, identities or personalities are not present at birth, but are revealed during the course of early childhood and adolescent development. These individual (micro) ingredients are important in answering the question, "Where do criminals come from?" But, at best, this is only half the story. The social (macro) ingredients are also important, especially in terms of answering the question, "Why do we have the crimes that we do?"

---

Human Agency (human nature & consciousness)
Socialization and Identity Formation
Social Structure and Institutional Order
Discourse, Knowledge, and Mass Communication
Social and Cultural Change

**FIGURE 1.1    Ingredients for an Integrated Criminology**

Put differently, socialization and identity formation do not simply involve significant others, such as parents and teachers, interacting in a social vacuum. Rather, these small-group interactions and experiences occur in the context of political and economic arrangements, as well as in the context of social inequalities in general and of gender and racial–ethnic relations in particular. Finally, none of these societal relationships exist without the power of language and discourse and the ability of mass communications to provide an image medium that precariously balances the social forces of order and the cultural forces of change.

## How Should Criminology Proceed?

The answer to this question is complex. It involves a mixture of both philosophy and pragmatism. In her postmodern text *Reading, Writing, and Rewriting the Prostitute Body,* Shannon Bell (1994) provides a model of sorts. Her book, like this textbook, is interdisciplinary and intertextual, aspiring to combine disciplinary texts in historical and comparative perspective. Bell (1994: 3) specifically combined "the disciplines of political theory, feminist theory, philosophy, comparative politics, literary theory, the politics of new social movements, and aspects of public policy." Similarly, I seek to combine the disciplinary foundations of biology, psychology, sociology, law, and economics with the interdisciplinary studies of mass media, public policy, culture, gender, and ethnicity.

In many ways, *Integrating Criminologies* resembles other criminology textbooks. At the same time, it is radically different from most of these books. Its postmodern integrative approach that strives to bridge both disciplinary boundaries and competing criminologies provides a new criminological synthesis reflective of the emerging paradigm of interdisciplinarity. This postmodern synthesis not only connects the

**TABLE 1.1   Contributions to Criminological Integration**

| Disciplinary Foundations | Interdisciplinary Studies |
| --- | --- |
| 1. Biology<br>Physiological, chemical, neurological, and sexual approaches to criminal behavior and crime control | 1. Crime and Culture |
| | 2. Crime and Gender |
| 2. Psychology<br>Psychoanalytic, psychiatric, behavioral, and cognitive approaches to criminal behavior and crime control | 3. Crime and Ethnicity |
| | 4. Crime and Media |
| | 5. Crime and Policy |
| 3. Sociology<br>Microscopic, mesoscopic, and macroscopic approaches to crime and punishment | |
| 4. Law & Economics<br>Rationalism, justice, and crime control | |

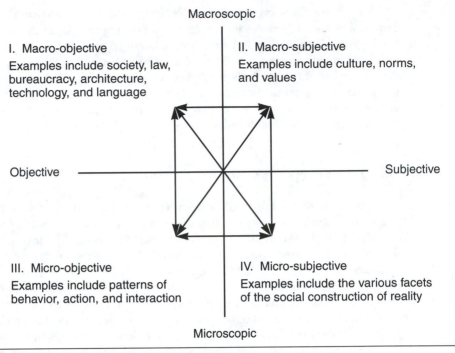

Macroscopic

I. Macro-objective
Examples include society, law, bureaucracy, architecture, technology, and language

II. Macro-subjective
Examples include culture, norms, and values

Objective — Subjective

III. Micro-objective
Examples include patterns of behavior, action, and interaction

IV. Micro-subjective
Examples include the various facets of the social construction of reality

Microscopic

**FIGURE 1.2    Major Levels of Social Reality**

*Source:* George Ritzer, *Toward an Integrated Sociological Paradigm* (1981: 26).

microscopic and the macroscopic depictions of human interaction, but also allows for both objective and subjective interpretations of the social reality of crime (see Figure 1.2). Finally, this textbook invites its readers, students and criminologists alike to join the interpretative action, not merely as a pedagogical exercise, but as a means of helping to transform criminology as we have known it.

Although this criminological inquiry is grounded in both scientific objectivity and textual intersubjectivity, it also proceeds by way of *metaphor*. I will attempt to explain this as straightforwardly as I possibly can in a moment. But first, let me simply say that the "essence of metaphor is understanding and experiencing one kind of thing in terms of another" (Shin, 1994: 10). Let me also note for the record that metaphors have always been a staple of both criminological theory and practice.

More specifically, metaphors can logically describe in an integrated way both personal consciousness and social structure. Morally, discourses as metaphors begin and end with the human authorship of the world. Politically, metaphors serve to reveal the ideological encoding of any particular discourse (i.e., orientation to crime and crime control). Thus, when it comes to the politics of crime, metaphors encourage criticality in policy-making and openness in public debate. In the final chapter of this book I will summarize and depict historically the primary metaphors that have been used in the name of addressing crime and crime control in U.S. society.

Traditionally, the modernist emphasis on scientific (disciplinarian) objectivity, especially in the social sciences, has downplayed the internal workings of the mind as participants in the formation of human knowledge. The major content of knowledge has relied on measurable, observable, and tangible things. This kind of positivist analysis of the order of things became the most important process in the modern scientific search for truth. In the process of truth seeking, things in the world and our knowledge about these things were divided into academic disciplines. As a result, art, science, and technology were regarded as separate entities to be studied in relative isolation (Klein, 1994; Shin, 1994).

Ignored in the modern positivist conceptualization, inside and outside of criminology proper, has been the human mind's mediations of thought, involving most significantly the power of imagination. As Jacob Bronowski (1978a; 1978b) has argued, what makes human beings distinct from other animals is the gift of imagination (artistic or scientific) and the power to work with images and to take sentences apart. To imagine simply means the ability to make images and to create a new meaning by rearranging them.

For example, when millions of O. J. trial observers, not to mention the attorneys on both sides, faced the reality of the adjudication process, they did not (as noted earlier in the chapter) take the criminal reality as it was/is. Instead, they (we) took criminal reality to be that which was reconstructed and renegotiated by the imaginations of people who did not actually observe the events in question. This is not to suggest that observed reality is necessarily better than constructed reality, but to recognize the contributions of both to the study of crime and crime control.

A. C. Cowlings, O. J. Simpson, and the LAPD out for an early evening drive on the San Diego Freeway, June 17, 1994.

Today, both the modern neopositivist and the postmodern interdisciplinary conceptions understand that although a given reality has its inherent properties, its understanding, nevertheless, depends on the perceptual and conceptual systems of human minds. This dependency is no less true for students and criminologists than it is for criminals and victims. The more recent postmodern conceptualizations, in other words, by taking the subjective into account, no longer regard human knowledge as a "total sum of what we learn objectively through analysis of the parts of the objective world, as discipline-oriented objectivists claim" (Shin, 1994: 9).

Hence, the differentiation between modern disciplinarians and postmodern interdisciplinarians is essentially that:

> *Discipline-oriented objectivists are seriously concerned with* what *the given reality is, but they pay very little attention to* how *it is understood. They claim to obtain absolute knowledge of a given reality while interdisciplinarians claim that absolute knowledge of anything is impossible to achieve. At the same time, interdisciplinarians believe that different understandings can be used to make more accurate knowledge possible (Shin, 1994: 10; emphasis in the original).*

The postmodern interdisciplinarian approach adopted here may be characterized as a "middle-of-the-road" postmodernism as it sides with "affirmative" rather than "skeptical" varieties of postmodernism (Cohen, 1993; Henry and Milovanovic, 1996; Rosenau, 1992). Skeptical postmodernists react against the quest for certainty and unitary truth. They maintain, among other things, that the postmodern age is one marked by fragmentation, disintegration, and an absence of moral parameters. These skeptics argue for the impossibility of knowing truth and for the abrogation of the prevailing "order of representation."

Affirmative postmodernists, such as Stuart Henry and Dragan Milovanovic in criminology, react against modernism, but they also reject nihilism or the idea that the world has no meaning. In other words, critical and affirmative criminologists are without the despair, cynicism, and fatalism characteristic of the more skeptical postmodernists. Nevertheless, the affirmatives agree with the skeptics that the daily activities of life may not make sense or be consistent and that there are no final conclusions to be made about human interaction. Both types of postmodernists refrain from trying to wrap up the truth, criminological or otherwise, in simple packages or general theories of crime.

Finally, when it comes to the question of meaning, the two types of postmodernists part company. Unlike the skeptics, the affirmatives do not play the meaning-of-life game by all-or-nothing rules. Instead, the affirmatives honor plurality and multiplicity. They, for example, delight and take pleasure in the partial and inconsistent meanings of *crime* as revealed by disparate forms and alternative ways of knowing. By contrast, skeptics argue that there are no absolutes and that *crime* is always relative and changing. Conversely, traditional modernists (e.g., classical and positivist criminologists) argue for particular kinds of universal notions of crime and criminals. The affirmative postmodernists give credibility, at the same time, to both the positions of relativism and universalism.

To recapitulate, a postmodern integrated criminology, such as the one developed here, draws its strength from established methods, findings, theories, and bodies of knowledge. This criminological integration strives not only to merge the various bodies of knowledge on crime and crime control, but also to reconcile the empirical verifications of pragmatists with the logical persuasions of pluralists. It does so by engaging these two worlds so as to construct a holistic framework for analyzing crime and justice. Moreover, the integrative criminology presented in Part III of this book specifically resists the dichotomizing of knowledge into either/or categories of positivism on the one hand, and of critical, reflexive hermeneutics on the other hand.

Thus, in coming to grips with the various views on knowledge, self, and society, the criminological postmodern synthesis developed in *Integrating Criminologies* emphasizes the importance of both objective-positivist social science and subjective-romantic hermeneutics as interdependent rather than separate phenomena. As Richard Harvey Brown (1992) has argued, there is a need to relativize the positivist approach and thereby invite a broader pluralism of perspectives. He has done so by proposing "an alternative to positivist general theory based on the metaphor of society as a discourse or language rather than an organism or machine" (Brown, 1992: 223). Brown (1992: 224) has suggested that the root metaphor of society as discourse may, in fact, be more adequate logically, morally, and politically than other root metaphors used in theorizing about society (or crime).

In the final section of this chapter, as a means of setting the stage for the comparative analysis of crimes and harms that ensues in Chapter 2, and for the purposes of underscoring the importance of discourse, I turn to a discussion of the differing definitions of crime.

## Definitions of Crime

Defining crime is not an easy task. There are several competing definitions of crime. From an integrative perspective, most of these definitions provide some value, insight, or outlook about the nature of crime. Taken together, these differing definitions of crime are especially useful in understanding how the phenomena of crime and how the discourse about crime have changed and developed over time. By comparatively and historically examining crime and punishment (Chapters 2 and 3), I hope that the student of crime will come to appreciate "how patterns of crime arise from the interplay of political, economic, social, and ideological structures in society" (Beirne and Messerschmidt, 1991: 21). I also hope that the student will come to realize that he or she has agency and can play a role in helping to transform the definition of crime.

Definitions of crime include those that are relatively narrow as well as those that are relatively broad. What is revealing about these definitions is the extent to which crime is somewhat arbitrary and represents a highly selective process of identifying particular behavior as being appropriate for official condemnation. Stated differently, when it comes to defining crime, there are no purely objective definitions; all definitions are value-laden and biased to some degree. This is not to say, however, that all definitions are equally nonobjective or subjective. Nor is this to suggest that all crimes are necessarily relative, subjective, and to be located in the "eyes of the beholder." On the contrary, I argue that it is possible to envision social reality as a rationally constructed hierarchy of both crime and criminal behavior. Finally, although there is considerable consensus over what kinds of individual or institutional behavior should be labeled deviant, if not criminal, "anthropologists have been unable to find any behavior that is universally defined as crime" (Beirne and Messerschmidt, 1991). For example, societies disagree over what constitutes murder, an act that probably best qualifies for the status of universal condemnation.

Crime has been described (defined) by students of crime and deviance as:

1. Form of normal behavior
2. Violation of behavioral norms
3. Form of deviant behavior
4. Legally defined behavior
5. Universally condemned behavior
6. Violation of human rights
7. Social harm
8. Social injury
9. Form of inequality
10. Limit on one's ability to make a difference

As these different perspectives on what crime is are discussed, they should not be thought of as mutually exclusive. In fact, among each other they have several elements in common which overlap between them. Viewed as an eclectic rather than an integrated whole, these definitions portray the social, legal, and moral dimensions involved in the processes of labeling a particular behavior as a crime as well as a particular individual as a criminal.

The late-nineteenth-century French sociologist Emile Durkheim argues that both crime and criminals are normal. Crime as *a form of normal behavior* assumes that the "collective conscience" of a people or that a normative consensus defines what is crime. Durkheim maintains that crime is a normal phenomenon of all societies because it ensures the stability of those societies by identifying and clarifying acceptable and unacceptable standards of behavior. Crime, according to Durkheim, is also *functional* because it serves to strengthen group solidarity by unifying people in disapproval against the violator.

For Durkheim, crime proceeds from both the very nature of humanity and societal order. In fact, crime is the product of the interaction between the two. He, at the same time, argues that while an unspecified amount of crime is normal and healthy for society, at a certain point too much crime becomes abnormal or pathological. Short of that point, however, Durkheim maintains that crime is normal as "it is bound up with the fundamental conditions of all social life; and by that fact it is useful, because these conditions of which it is a part are themselves indispensable to the normal evolution of morality and law" (quoted in Glick, 1995: 17).

Crime as *a violation of behavioral norms* or crime as *a form of deviant behavior* are two other social definitions of crime. Both of these descriptions recognize the relativity of crime. Thorsten Sellin (1938) argues that the basic unit of criminological investigation should be behavioral norms, or what he calls *conduct norms*. Conduct or behavioral norms refer to normal (right) and abnormal (wrong) forms of conduct between social groups. These norms may include custom, tradition, ethics, religion, and rules of criminal law. Sellin argues that violators of any of these conduct norms should be fair game for criminological study, not just those violators of the rules of criminal law. It is Sellin's view that conduct norms, unlike legal norms, are neither the creation of one normative group nor are they confined within political boundaries. In short, conduct norms as contrasted with legal norms are not subject to the biases of powerful interests or the state.

Similarly, the definition of crime as a form of deviant behavior assumes that there is nothing inherent in the nature of a deviant or criminal act that identifies it as deviant or criminal. What becomes deviant or criminal will vary by such factors as age, sex, class, and race. It will also vary from era to era and from society to society. Hence, those acts that become criminal refer to those categories of deviant behavior that ultimately become sanctioned by organized groups of people or the machinery of law (Becker, 1963).

The most popular definitions of crime are those rooted in the criminal law or legal order. This is true for both criminologists and the general public. Of all the definitions of crime, crime as *legally defined behavior* is the most precise definition of crime. It is also the narrowest definition of crime. A classic legal definition of crime is often quoted from Paul Tappan's writings. He argues that "crime is an intentional act in violation of the criminal law (statutory and case law) committed without defense or excuse, and penalized by the state as a felony or misdemeanor" (Tappan, 1947: 100). According to *Black's Law Dictionary* (1979: 334), a crime or public offense is defined as:

> *An act committed or omitted in violation of law forbidding or commanding it, and to which is annexed, upon conviction, either, or a combination of the following punishments: (1) death; (2) imprisonment; (3) fine; (4) removal from office; or (5) disqualification to hold and enjoy any office of honor, trust, or profit.*

The legalistic definition of crime contains several elements or conditions that must be present in order for an act to be a crime. In addition to a crime having to be prohibited and punishable by law, a person found to be guilty or culpable for a crime must have demonstrated that his or her mental state possessed free will or criminal intent (*mens rea*) at the time of the crime's commission and that this intent was linked to the act in question. In other words, a person labeled criminal by law cannot be judged to have been insane at the time of the crime. Nor can a person be labeled criminal if it is concluded that he or she was entrapped by agents working on behalf of the state. In either case, that person could not be found legally guilty of a crime because he or she is said to have lacked criminal responsibility.

Before moving on to the next definition of crime, it should be pointed out that the criminal law makes two noteworthy distinctions: First, it distinguishes between the majority of criminal offenses, *mala prohibita*, and the minority of criminal offenses, *mala in se*. *Mala prohibita* refers to those acts that are prohibited or outlawed by organized society. *Mala in se* refers (allegedly) to those acts that are regarded as evil in themselves, whether or not they have been defined by the law. As a matter of course, however, they typically are outlawed. Examples of the former include burglary, use of illegal substances, and gambling. Examples of the latter include murder, rape, and incest. Second, the criminal law distinguishes between felonies and misdemeanors. Felonies are subject to punishment by either death or imprisonment in a state facility for a term of no less than one year. Misdemeanors are subject to punishment either by fine or by a term in jail of less than one year.

*Universally condemned criminality* is a variation of the legal definition of crime. It refers to "those behavior patterns that are condemned in a criminal sense by the vast majority of people in all societies and outlawed in all societies with legislative bodies" (Ellis, 1990: 19). Universally condemned criminality can be distinguished by five criteria: intentionality, victimization, fellow group member, not in defense of self or property, and nonthreatening to government. In short, these criteria make this definition of crime more exclusive than the more traditional legalistic definition. For example, this definition excludes from criminal behavior those victimless crimes (i.e., smoking marijuana) if there are no injured parties. It also excludes from criminal behavior those acts in which the injured parties or victims are *outsiders*, such as undocumented workers or enemies of war. Comparably, it excludes from criminal behavior those acts that contain political objectives, such as overthrowing a government. In sum, what makes universally condemned criminality a crime is the fact that "it is condemned by the vast majority of people in the world," not that there is universal agreement per se (Ellis, 1990: 20).

During the past twenty-five years or so, coinciding with the development of critical criminology, morally inspired definitions of crime have been introduced. Whether one is talking about crime as a *violation of human rights*, a *social harm*, or a *social injury*, each of these definitions can be characterized as moral ones. Unlike the legalistic definitions of crime in particular, these moral definitions raise higher questions about the fundamental rights that people are entitled to as human beings and members of the world community. These moral definitions of crime recognize that there are acts and behaviors committed by individuals and institutions that deny, harm, injure, victimize, and pain people that are "beyond legal incrimination" (Kennedy, 1970).

Herman and Julia Schwendinger (1970) were the first criminologists to argue that crime should be defined as any behavior that violates an individual's human rights, those rights referring to life, liberty, happiness, and self-determination. In the latter regard, the Schwendingers argue that people have the fundamental right to be free from exploitation, oppression, hatred, racism, sexism, imperialism, and so on. These crimes against humanity raise the question of a person's right to be protected from hunger and homelessness (Barak, 1991a). Crime as a violation of human rights is also grounded in international covenants, treaties, and laws signed by the majority of nations since the end of World War II (Barak, 1991b).

Crime as a social harm or a social injury, like crime as a violation of human rights, refers to behaviors that have not necessarily been prohibited by criminal, regulatory, or civil law. But, nevertheless, in common with such legal classification schemes, these definitions of crime recognize that a social harm has occurred and that by analogy some kind of punishment should occur as well. In other words, any behaviors that harm individuals, even those victimizations that occur with the support of the law, should be treated as criminal (Reiman, 1995 [1979]). Ray Michalowski introduces a concept for the practice of recognizing social harms that are not legally accountable. He calls these "legally permissible acts or sets of conditions whose consequences are similar to those of illegal acts," crimes by "analogous social injury" (Michalowski, 1985: 317). One might think of this as "a crime by any other name."

All students should realize that, to some degree, whatever else crime may be, it is a socially constructed problem. What most people mean by crime is what is normally referred to as legally defined behavior. This is not to suggest that without the social (legal) construction of crime there would be no crime. On the contrary, it suggests, as the moral definitions of crime imply, that there is a lot more victimization and injury occurring than is accounted for by the legal order. Another definition of crime that raises moral concerns is one which argues that crime is a *form of inequality*.

This definition of crime also talks in terms of crime involving pain, conflict, and instances of harm and injury. It argues that people engaged in relations perceived of as crimes are engaged in relations of inequality in which one party exerts its way over another party. Parties do not refer only to individuals in a conflict of some kind. Parties also refer to the social relations of individuals, organizations, and governments. Stuart Henry and Dragan Milovanovic (1993: 12) argue that crime is the power to deny others, whereby "those subject to the power of another suffer the pain of being denied their own humanity, the power to make a difference." This may refer, for example, to a victim of domestic violence and her assailant or to an entire group of people who are discriminated against. Although this definition appears to be rather general, it is actually quite precise and could be wrapped around the three other moral definitions of crime.

Like those moral definitions of crime, however, crime as inequality includes a lot of behaviors that are omitted from the legal codes. In fact, Henry and Milovanovic (1993: 12) argue that a legal definition reflective of their definition of crime would have "to include much of what currently stands for business practices, governmental policies, hierarchical social relations, and a lot of what occurs in family life, since these arenas of power are premised upon the inequality that liberates the expression of the power to create pain." This is not to suggest that the definition of crime as inequality should not be applied to legally defined crime as well. Indeed, it should be.

All of which is to conclude that the different definitions of crime—social, legal, and moral—have more in common than is typically realized. For example, take the similarity in the social definition of crime as normal, as articulated by Durkheim, and in the moral definition of crime as inequality, proffered by Henry and Milovanovic. Despite the roots of the former in positivism and of the latter in postmodernism, both definitions agree that the problem of crime is indivisible from society itself. Moreover, both of these definitions of crime are inclusive of legal and illegal behaviors. Hence, the latter theorists have identified *crimes of repression* and *crimes of reduction* as reflective of the power differentials and hierarchical relations that reinforce both types of harm (Henry and Milovanovic, 1996: Chapter 5).

This integrative approach to the definition of crime allows one to appreciate the commentary of Susan George (1993: x):

> *Earlier societies may have been founded on slavery, but none, until our day, found it necessary to exploit babies (the infant formula scandal), to deprive vast numbers of people of the land they need to feed themselves, to use thousands of women as receptacles for mass 'sexual tourism,' to brand any 'primitive' community standing in the way of profit as sub-human and thus exterminable, or to destroy utterly the environment upon which people depend for their survival in order to extract its natural resources.*

## Summary and Conclusions: A Crime by Any Other Name . . .

As a way of bringing this introduction to a close, I end with several examples of violent crime, the explanations of which would each require elaborate narratives involving the social relations of individuals and their environments. My aim, however, is not to provide these narratives or integrations, but rather to share the many forms that a crime like murder can take in order to elicit a range of emotional reactions from the reader:

> *The people of Texas executed a man [on Jan. 17, 1995] whose functional IQ was 65. According to developmental standards, he was capable of reasoning at about the same level as a five year old. Mario Marquez died at 12:27 A.M. . . . He was a victim of severe child abuse and neglect. He exploded one day in 1984 and killed his niece and her child in what he described as a "fit of jealous rage." About ten years later, officials of the Texas Department of Criminal Justice, Institutional Division, killed him so that justice could be finally satisfied. The circle was completed for many, but for the Marquez family, the circle was left open. The very family that mourned the death of their family members ten years ago were gathered outside the prison to mourn the death of another family member who was to them a child. A child who was being killed by those in power as a symbolic warning to others that the poor and powerless don't really matter (Longmire, 1995: 1).*

> *No one will soon forget the terrible drama that unfolded [in Union, South Carolina, in October of 1994], when after convincing the community that she had been carjacked and her children abducted, Susan Smith confessed that she had, in truth, murdered her babies [by drowning them in John D. Long Lake when she rolled her car with her two boys in their child restraint seats down the boat ramp] (Towle, 1994: 60).*

> *"Fonda [Cecila Moore] loved police work," a friend says. "It was her pride and joy." But prosecutors charge that Moore, the mother of two young boys, moonlighted as a confederate of one of Washington's biggest cocaine dealers. Acquitted of murder and other charges in her first trial, she is awaiting trial on charges of conspiring to commit murder and distribute crack (Morganthau, 1994: 30).*

> *Owners of a Kentucky mine [agreed in February of 1993] to pay a fine for safety misconduct that may have led "to the worst American mining accident in nearly a decade."*

*Ten workers died in a methane explosion, and the company pleaded guilty to "a pattern of safety misconduct" that included falsifying reports of methane levels and requiring miners to work under unsupported roofs (Reiman, 1995: 50; emphasis added).*

*Though John C. Salvi III—the man charged with closing out 1994 by shooting up three abortion clinics, killing two people, and wounding five others—was under lock and key . . . the reverberations of his two-day rampage could be felt from coast to coast [as] the latest abortion-clinic killings—and the support for them—inspired new anxiety on both sides (Simolowe, 1995: 34).*

*On April 19, 1993, FBI tanks began ramming holes into [the Mount Carmel structure near Waco, Texas] in order to pump in CS chemical warfare agent, purportedly because of the threats to the 25 children remaining in the compound. A conflagration broke out, killing most of the estimated 75 persons . . . although [David] Koresh and some of his followers were killed by gunshots rather than fire (Kopel and Blackman, 1994: 4).*

*The medical–industrial complex in this country is not filled entirely with, but is significantly shaped by, outright crooks, bookkeeping tricksters, piratical profiteers, and—though we may be repeating ourselves—doctors, hospital administrators, drug and insurance executives who are robbing taxpayers of perhaps as much as $130 billion a year (a* Consumer Reports *estimate) in providing overpriced, useless and often harmful services. The General Accounting Office . . . predicts that the thieves of corporate medicine will soon be pocketing each year at least $100 billion through fraud and overbilling (Sherrill, 1995: 45).*

## Discussion Questions

1. Discuss the similarities and differences between integrating theories and integrating knowledges.

2. How are the concepts of "mind," "body," and "culture" germane to an integrated understanding of crime and criminology?

3. Criminologists and others have viewed criminology as a subdiscipline of sociology, a multi-disciplinary enterprise, and an interdisciplinary field. What are the implications of each of these approaches to the study of crime and crime control?

4. Compare and contrast disciplinary and either multi- or interdisciplinary analyses of the criminal justice system in general, and in relation to the O. J. Simpson criminal trial in particular.

## References

Abramson, Jeffrey, ed. 1996. *Postmortem: The O. J. Simpson Case.* New York: Basicbooks.

Akers, Ronald L. 1992. "Linking Sociology and Its Specialties: The Case of Criminology." *Social Forces* (September): 1–16.

Andrews, D. A., and James Bonta. 1994. *The Psychology of Criminal Conduct.* Cincinnati: Anderson Publishing Company.

Arrigo, Bruce. 1994. "The Peripheral Core of Law and Criminology: On Postmodern Social Theory and Conceptual Integration." Paper presented at the annual meetings of the American Society of Criminology, Miami.

Barak, Gregg. 1991a. *Gimme Shelter: A Social History of Homelessness in Contemporary America*. New York: Praeger.

———, ed. 1991b. *Crimes by the Capitalist State: An Introduction to State Criminality*. Albany, NY: SUNY Press.

———, ed. 1994. *Varieties of Criminology: Readings from a Dynamic Discipline*. Westport, CN: Praeger.

———, ed. 1996. *Representing O. J.: Murder, Criminal Justice, and Mass Culture*. Albany, NY: Harrow and Heston.

Beccaria, Cesare. 1764 [1986]. *On Crimes and Punishments*. Trans. David Yound. Indianapolis, IN: Hackett.

Becker, Howard. 1963. *Outsiders: Studies in the Sociology of Deviance*. New York: Free Press.

Beirne, Piers. 1993. *Inventing Criminology: Essays on the Rise of 'Homo Criminalis.'* Albany, NY: SUNY Press.

Beirne, Piers, and James Messerschmidt. 1991. *Criminology*. San Diego: Harcourt Brace Jovanovich.

Bell, Shannon. 1994. *Reading, Writing, and Rewriting the Prostitute Body*. Bloomington, IN: Indiana University Press.

Black, H. C. 1979. *Black's Law Dictionary*. St. Paul, MN: West.

Bronowski, Jacob. 1978a. *The Visionary Eye: Essays in the Arts, Literature, and Science*. Cambridge, MA: The MIT Press.

———. 1978b. *The Origin of Knowledge and Imagination*. New Haven, CN: Yale University Press.

Brown, Richard Harvey. 1992. "Social Science and Society as Discourse: Toward a Sociology for Civic Competence." In Steven Seidman and David G. Wagner, ed., *Postmodern and Social Theory*. Cambridge, MA: Blackwell.

Cohen, Lawrence E., and Richard Machalek. 1988. "A General Theory of Expropriative Crime: An Evolutionary Ecological Approach." *American Journal of Sociology* 94 (3, November): 465–501.

Cohen, Stanley. 1993. "Human Rights and Crimes of the State: The Culture of Denial." *Australian and New Zealand Journal of Criminology* 26:97–115.

DiCristina, Bruce. 1994. "Unreason and the Ends of Criminological Inquiry." Paper presented at the annual meetings of the American Society of Criminology, Miami.

Ellis, Lee. 1990. "Conceptualizing Criminal and Related Behavior from a Biosocial Perspective." In Lee Ellis and Harry Hoffman, eds., *Crime in Biosocial, Social, and Moral Contexts*. New York: Praeger.

Ericson, Richard, and Kevin Carriere. 1994. "The Fragmentation of Criminology." In David Nelken, ed., *The Futures of Criminology*. London: Sage Publications.

Foucault, Michel. 1977. *Discipline and Punishment*. New York: Pantheon Books.

Garland, David. 1985. *Punishment and Welfare: A History of Penal Strategies*. Aldershot, Gower.

George, Susan. 1993. "Preface" to *Violence and Democratic Society: New Approaches to Human Rights*, by Jamil Salmi. London: Zed Books.

Gibbons, Don C. 1992. *Society, Crime and Criminal Behavior*. 6th ed. Englewood Cliffs, NJ: Prentice-Hall.

———. 1994. *Talking About Crime and Criminals: Problems and Issues in Theory Development in Criminology*. Englewood Cliffs, NJ: Prentice-Hall.

Glick, Leonard. 1995. *Criminology*. Boston: Allyn and Bacon.

Hagan, John. 1989. *Structural Criminology*. Cambridge: Polity Press.

Henry, Stuart, and Dragan Milovanovic. 1991. "Constitutive Criminology." *Criminology* 29:293–316.

———. 1993. "Back to Basics: A Postmodern Redefinition of Crime." *The Critical Criminologist* 5(2/3): 1–2, 12.

———. 1994. "The Constitution of Constitutive Criminology: A Postmodern Approach to Criminological Theory." In David Nelken, ed., *The Futures of Criminology*. London: Sage Publications.

———. 1996. *Constitutive Criminology: Beyond Postmodernism*. London: Sage Publications.

Hutchinson, Earl Ofari. 1996. *Beyond O. J.: Race, Sex, and Class Lessons for America*. Los Angeles: Middle Passage Press.

Jeffery, C. Ray. 1990. *Criminology: An Interdisciplinary Approach*. Englewood Cliffs, NJ: Prentice-Hall.

———. 1994. "Biological and Neuropsychiatric Approaches to Criminal Behavior." In Gregg Barak, ed., *Varieties of Criminology: Readings from Dynamic Discipline*. Westport, CN: Praeger.

Katz, Jack. 1988. *Seductions of Crime: Moral and Sensual Attractions in Doing Evil*. New York: Basic Books.

Kennedy, Mark C. 1970. "Beyond Incrimination: Some Neglected Facets of the Theory of Punishment." *Catalyst* 5 (Summer): 1–30.

Klein, Julie Thompson. 1994. *Crossing Boundaries: Knowledge, Disciplinarities, and Interdisciplinarities*. Charlottesville, VA: Virginia University Press.

Kopel, David B., and Paul H. Blackman. 1994. "The God Who Answers by Fire: The Waco Disaster and the Necessity of Federal Criminal Justice Reform." Paper presented at the annual meetings of the American Society of Criminology, Miami.

Kuhn, Thomas. 1970. [1961]. *The Structure of Scientific Revolutions*. Chicago: University of Chicago Press.

Longmire, Dennis. 1995. "Comment on the Execution of Mario Marquez." United Nations Criminal Justice Information Network: Internet Communication, January 18.

Matza, David. 1964. *Delinquency and Drift*. New York: Wiley.

Messer-Davidow, Ellen, David R. Shunway, and David J. Sylvan, eds. 1993. *Knowledges: Historical and Critical Studies in Disciplinarity*. Charlottesville, VA: University Press of Virginia.

Messner, Steven F., Marvin D. Krohn, and Allen E. Liska, eds. 1989. *Theoretical Integration in the Study of Deviance and Crime: Problems and Prospects*. Albany, NY: SUNY Press.

Michalowski, Raymond J. 1985. *Order, Law, and Crime: An Introduction to Criminology*. New York: Random House.

———. 1993. "(De)construction, Postmodernism, and Social Problems: Facts, Fictions, and Fantasies at the 'End of History'." In James A. Halstein and Gale Miller, eds., *Reconsidering Social Constructionism: Debates in Social Problems Theory*. New York: Aldine DeGruyter.

Morganthau, Tom. 1994. "Why Good Cops Go Bad." *Newsweek* (December 19): 30–34.

Nietzsche, Friedrich Wilhelm. 1967. *On the Genealogy of Morals*, trans. by Walter Kaufman and R. J. Hollingdale, ed. by Walter Kaufman. New York: Vintage Books.

Orcutt, James D. 1983. *Analyzing Deviance*. Homewood, IL: The Dorsey Press.

Pfohl, Stephen, and Avery Gordon. 1986. "Criminological Displacements: A Sociological Deconstruction." *Social Problems* 33(6): 94–113.

Popper, Karl, and J. C. Eccles. 1983. *The Self and Its Brain: An Argument for Interactionism*. London: Routledge and Kegan Paul.

Radzinowicz, Leon. 1962. *In Search of Criminology*. Cambridge, MA: Harvard University Press.

Rantala, M. L. 1996. *O. J. Unmasked: The Trial, the Truth, and the Media*. Chicago: Catfeet Press.

Reiman, Jeffery. 1995. [1979]. *The Rich Get Richer and the Poor Get Prison: Ideology, Crime, and Criminal Justice*. Boston: Allyn and Bacon.

Ritzer, George. 1981. *Toward an Integrated Sociological Paradigm*. Boston: Allyn and Bacon.

Rosenau, Pauline M. 1992. *Postmodernism and the Social Sciences—Insights, Inroads, and Intrusions*. Princeton, NJ: Princeton University Press.

Schwendinger, Herman, and Julia Schwendinger. 1970. "Defenders of Order or Guardian of Human Rights?" *Issues in Criminology* 5:123–157.

Sellin, Thorsten. 1938. *Culture, Conflict and Crime*. New York: Social Science Research Council.

Shearing, Clifford. 1989. "Decriminalizing Criminology: Reflections on the Literal and Tropological Meaning of the Term." *Canadian Journal of Criminology* 31:169–178.

Sherrill, Robert. 1995. "Medicine and the Madness of the Market." *The Nation* (January 9/16): 45–72.

Shin, Un-Chol. 1994. "The Metaphorical Structure of Interdisciplinary Knowledge." *Association for Integrated Studies Newsletter* 16 (no. 1, March, and no. 2, May: 8–12.

Silbey, Susan S. 1993. "Teaching about Crime: Excursions in Law and Social Theory." *Focus on Law Studies* 8 (3, Spring): 1, 7.

Simolowe, Jill. 1995. "Fear in the Land." *Time* (January 16): 34–36.

Sutherland, Edwin H., and Donald R. Cressey. 1955. *Principles of Criminology*. 5th ed. Philadelphia: Lippincott.

———. 1978. *Criminology*. 10th ed. Philadelphia: Lippincott.

Tappan, Paul W. 1947. "Who Is the Criminal?" *American Sociological Review* 12:96–102.

Towle, Lisa H. 1994. "It Did Happen Here." *Time* (December 19): 60–61.

# Chapter 2

## Crimes and Harms: A Comparative Perspective

The Hague War Crimes Tribunal forensic expert John Gems shows the media the bodies of Moslems killed near the eastern Bosnian village of Nova Kasaba.

In this chapter crimes and harms are placed into comparative perspectives by examining: (1) homicide and genocide; (2) criminal victimization across the historical period from 1970 to 2005; (3) white collar crime; and (4) corporate and state crime. In no way are these comparisons meant to be exhaustive of all the forms of crime and delinquency. Instead, they are meant to be representative of the wide and diverse range of criminality that has existed over time. Moreover, these comparisons are intended to be illustrative of the variations in what has and has not historically come to be regarded as criminal even though the latter may be harmful or injurious, perhaps even more harmful than the former. This comparison is thus, first and foremost, a conceptual comparison of what constitutes crime. It recognizes the comparative importance of appreciating both legal and social (nonlegal) definitions of crime.

More specifically, the comparisons included here are of two fundamental kinds: those that compare crimes and harms over time and those that compare them cross-culturally. Both of these modes of comparison rely on the gathering of statistical data. Unfortunately, "statistics about crime and delinquency are probably the most unreliable and most difficult of all social statistics" (Sutherland and Cressey, 1974: 25). Questions of validity, soundness, or accuracy are always present in comparative discussions because the amount of crime in any given jurisdiction at any particular time is virtually impossible to know because of innumerable inaccuracies in the collection of crime statistics.

There are four basic reasons for the inaccuracy of crime statistics. First, there is always the possibility that people disagree as to what constitutes a particular crime. This may yield two kinds of situations: one where something that should be counted as a crime is not, and one where something that should not be counted as a crime is. Second, there is the large proportion of undetected crimes, or what is often referred to as the *dark figure of crime* that does not become a part of the officially quoted crime statistics. Third, there are those crimes that are detected but not reported to the police by victims or witnesses. Therefore, these, too, are not included as a part of the officially recorded crime statistics. Fourth, there are those crimes that are reported to the police but are not, in turn, recorded and reported by the police as crime statistics to the FBI or to some other governmental counting agency.

When public officials, criminologists, or others compare crime measures, for example, between different cities, states, or countries, what they are actually comparing are rates of crimes (or the number of crimes per unit of population, such as X number of crimes per 100,000 persons). And when these comparisons are made between *crime indexes*, or the estimates of crimes committed rather than by the total number of crimes officially known, the results may actually tell us less about the differences in true crime rates than in the practices and polices of law enforcement, prosecution, and adjudication. The point is that "no index or estimate is a reliable indicator of the actual amount of crime because indexes or estimates vary independently of the true rate of crime" (Bohm and Haley, 1996: 33–34). Thus, crime comparisons over time, for example, do not maintain constant ratios to the true rates of actual crime because these figures are composed of both the unknown dark figures of crime and the specific crime index figures used (see Figure 2.1).

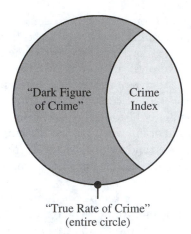

"Dark Figure of Crime"

Crime Index

"True Rate of Crime"
(entire circle)

**FIGURE 2.1    The Dark Figure of Crime**

Relationship among a crime index, the dark figure of crime, and the true rate of crime.

*From:* Robert M. Bohm and Keith N. Haley, *Introduction to Criminal Justice* (New York: McGraw-Hill, 1996), page 34. Reprinted by permission.

In short, before we proceed, it should be recognized that despite what the media often tells us, we do not know, nor can we ever know, what the true rate of crime is. Similarly, we can never know for sure

> *whether crime is increasing, decreasing, or remaining at the same level. The sophisticated student of crime knows only that indexes of crime are very imperfect estimates that vary widely, independently of the true rate of crime, depending on such things as police practices, court policies, and public opinion. Therefore, comparisons of crime measures are an especially dubious exercise (Bohm and Haley, 1996: 34).*

Armed with a healthy skepticism toward official and unofficial estimates of crime and delinquency, I will, nevertheless, attempt to provide a sense of how harms and crimes have generally changed over time. In other words, crime changes, adapts, and develops in response to changes and developments in the conditions of the society as a whole. Crime looks different in agrarian, industrial, and postindustrial society. It also looks different cross-culturally. That is to say, we can compare across cultures and societies at various stages of development, thus locating the uniqueness, for example, of the American crime problem during colonial or postmodern America.

I will also try to provide more of a specific sense about the increasing or decreasing incidences of selected forms of criminality. Although the official statistics on criminal activity in the United States are class-based, the commission of criminal activity is not. Given the class, racial/ethnic, and gender conflicts that are so endemic to American society, we are led to believe that "those who own and control the means of production" often "attempt to secure the existing order through various forms of domination" while "those who do not own and control the means of production" often "accommodate and resist" these various forms of domination (Quinney, 1977: 60). In the course of this domination and accommodation, crimes are frequently and systematically committed both by those at the top and those at the bottom. Richard Quinney has referred to the former as *crimes of control* and the latter as *crimes of survival.* Crimes committed by those in the "middle" have been referred to as "crimes of the public" (Gabor, 1994).

Throughout this book, crimes and harms are viewed as integral parts of social organization so that the saying "A society gets the crime it deserves" applies. This is true in terms of both general and particular social development.

## Official and Unofficial Crime

The primary source of crime statistics in the United States is the Federal Bureau of Investigation's (FBI's) *Uniform Crime Reports (UCR)*. Begun in 1930 by the International Association of Chiefs of Police, the UCR are published annually by the FBI (U.S. Department of Justice, Washington, D.C.) under the title *Crime in the United States*. This is a voluntary national program in which crime and other law enforcement information is collected. Authorized by Congress to serve as the national clearinghouse for crime-related statistical information, the UCR programs involve more than 16,000 city, county, and state law enforcement agencies (Bohm and Haley, 1996).

The Uniform Crime Report contains two major indexes that consist of (1) statistical information about persons arrested and (2) offenses known to the police, discussed earlier. The offenses-known-to-the-police index is divided into Part I and Part II offenses. More is known about Part I as compared with Part II offenses. The former Part I offenses or the *eight index crimes* are murder and nonnegligent manslaughter, forcible rape, aggravated assault, robbery, burglary, motor vehicle theft, larceny theft, and arson. The first four offenses are considered violent offenses; the last four are defined as property offenses. The Part II offenses contain 21 other less serious crimes and *status offenses*, those acts committed by a juvenile that are not crimes if committed by an adult (i.e., curfew, truancy, running away from home). For an inclusive listing of the FBI's Uniform Crime Report for Part I and Part II offenses, see Table 2.1.

**TABLE 2.1   Part I and Part II Offenses of the FBI's Uniform Crime Reports**

Part I Offenses (Index Crimes)

1. Murder and nonnegligent manslaughter
2. Forcible rape
3. Robbery
4. Aggravated assault
5. Burglary—breaking or entering
6. Larceny theft
7. Motor vehicle theft
8. Arson

Part II Offenses

9. Other assaults (simple)
10. Forgery and counterfeiting
11. Fraud
12. Embezzlement
13. Stolen property; buying, receiving, possessing
14. Vandalism
15. Weapons; carrying, possessing, etc.
16. Prostitution and commercialized vice
17. Sex offenses
18. Drug abuse violations
19. Gambling
20. Offenses against the family and children
21. Driving under the influence
22. Liquor laws
23. Drunkenness
24. Disorderly conduct
25. Vagrancy
26. All other offenses
27. Suspicion
28. Curfew and loitering laws
29. Runaways

Barred from these official counts or crime index totals are the true rates of crime because of the *dark side* or hidden figures of crime. Again, crime index totals and rates of crime exclude the Part II offenses from their calculations. They also exclude those harms that are not recognized legally as crimes. These include those acts, legal and illegal, that are harmful but that are ignored, rarely enforced, or leniently punished. They also include those injurious acts in which victims are unaware of their victimization or in which victims choose not to report the harm/crime that they have experienced for various reasons.

Excluded from official sources are the crimes of control such as genocide, price-fixing, and insider trading. Excluded from official records are the crimes of the public such as filing inaccurate income tax returns, making fraudulent insurance claims, and pilfering at work. Excluded from the FBI's eight categories of crime are the number of minor offenses involving such behaviors as driving under the influence, disorderly conduct, and petty shoplifting.

In 1990, for example, there were approximately 9 million arrests, but only one out of five were from the eight crimes listed by the FBI (Felson, 1994: 3). Eighty percent of those arrested were for relatively minor offenses. Again, outside of these official figures on crime are the *crimes of control* and *crimes of the public*. Hence, once one abandons a purely legal definition of crime, it is extremely difficult, if not impossible, to get a real fix on the true rate of crime in the United States.

So the question of "How much crime?" always presents itself as problematic. Nevertheless, when it comes to analyzing the changing times, conditions, and definitions of crime, various sources have proved beneficial in discerning both long-term and short-term trends. There are essentially four sources of crime data collection: *official police reports*, *victim surveys*, *self-reports*, and *archival research*.

The official police reports refer to the crimes reported by local law enforcement departments to the FBI's Uniform Crime Reports. The other major source of crime statistics in the United States is the *National Crime Victimization Survey* (NCVS), which was formerly the National Crime Survey (NCS). Collected by the Census Bureau for the U.S. Department of Justice's Bureau of Justice Statistics, data are derived annually by interviewing a general sample of citizens about their own and their households' victimization experiences and published under the title *Criminal Victimization in the United States*. Typically, the NCVS counts some 40 to 50 percent more crimes in the categories asked about than official police data. Created not only for the purposes of learning more about crime and its victims, the NCVS is also used as a comparative tool for gauging the accuracy of the UCR.

Self-reports, such as the National Youth Survey begun in 1976 or the National Institute on Drug Abuse data collection begun in 1975, refer to interviews or survey questionnaires with selected groups of people, such as youth on their own lawbreaking. These surveys, although involving the reporting of sometimes trivial offenses, such as "cutting classes," nevertheless have found an enormous amount of hidden crime in the United States. These surveys have also "indicated that more than 90 percent of all Americans had committed crimes for which they could have been imprisoned" (Bohm and Haley, 1996: 45–46). Each of the three standard sources of crime reveals that most crime is ordinary rather than dramatic as portrayed in entertainment and news media alike (Barak, 1994).

A fourth source for gathering data, and one not typically noted, is the academic ventures into archival research both in the past and present. Included here is the research of historians, anthropologists, and other social scientists searching out the changing nature and production of crime. Of course, these data and findings are not officially collected and disseminated. They are typically found in the literature of specific disciplines. These data are subject to the same problems of validity as any other official sources of information on crime and victims. They are also subject to the measurement and data collection methods and problems associated with the various independent academicians involved.

Before turning to the comparative examples of this chapter, it is instructive to disclose that just as there were contradictions in the various definitions of crime, there are contradictions in the ordinary sources of data collection as well. This, in part, accounts for the confusion as to whether crime is worse or better than in the past. Compare the data on crime produced by the FBI's Uniform Crime Report with that produced by the Bureau of Justice Statistics' National Crime Victim Survey. The UCR, which relies on police statistics, year after year, usually suggests that crime, at least in absolute numbers, has been on the rise. Although, according to the UCR arrest statistics, as the overall number of arrests for violent crimes has leveled off since 1990, the number of teenage criminals has declined as well. At the same time, however, between 1989 and 1993, the arrests of people under 18 for violent crimes rose 36 percent. On the other hand, the annual report of the NCVS, which relies on victim survey data as well as police reports, usually suggests that the overall rate of known crime is declining. Making matters more unclear is the fact that, for any given year, the two reports may be in the same direction, and both may even be opposite of the *usual* trends just noted.

For example, compare what the FBI revealed about crime in 1993 with what was revealed by the Justice Department's Bureau of Justice Statistics (BJS) for the same year. According to the FBI, "14.1 million violent and property crimes were reported to law enforcement officials, a decrease of 2.1 percent. That included 1.9 million violent crimes, down 0.4 percent, and 12.2 million property crimes, down 2.3 percent" (Skorneck, 1994: A1). But according to BJS, America became a more dangerous place in 1993 with "the incidence of violent crime rising 5.6 percent to 10.9 million" (The Associated Press, 1994a: A1). The difference of 9 million violent crimes between the two reports is significant and is attributed to the latter report's inclusion of crimes not reported to the police as well as the number of attempted assaults, robberies, and sexual attacks totaling 7,633,000.

For a descriptive picture of violent crime, based on a March 1991, U.S. Department of Justice report, see Box 2.1, "Violent Crime in the United States" (*Congressional Digest*, April 1992). For comparative trends on crimes against the person and against property for the worst U.S. cities, based on the UCR for 1990, see Figure 2.2, "Crime in America: Comparing Trends" (Newsweek Education Program, *Newsweek*, Inc., 1992).

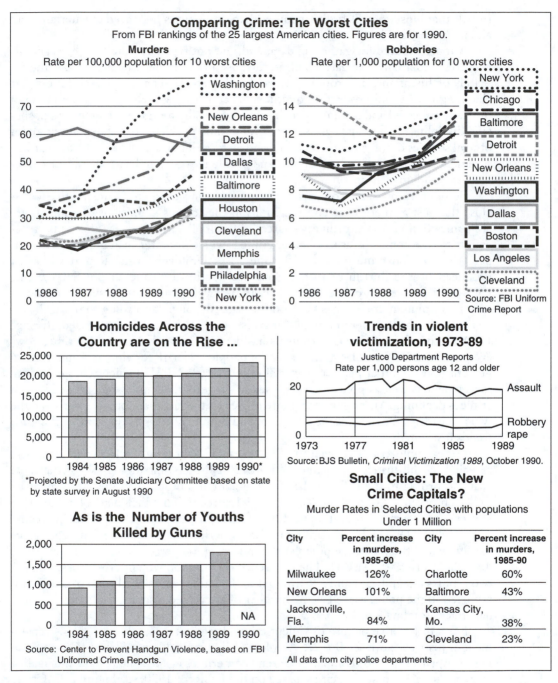

## Comparing Crime: The Worst Cities
From FBI rankings of the 25 largest American cities. Figures are for 1990.

**Murders**
Rate per 100,000 population for 10 worst cities

Washington
New Orleans
Detroit
Dallas
Baltimore
Houston
Cleveland
Memphis
Philadelphia
New York

**Robberies**
Rate per 1,000 population for 10 worst cities

New York
Chicago
Baltimore
Detroit
New Orleans
Washington
Dallas
Boston
Los Angeles
Cleveland

Source: FBI Uniform Crime Report

### Homicides Across the Country are on the Rise ...

*Projected by the Senate Judiciary Committee based on state by state survey in August 1990

### Trends in violent victimization, 1973-89
Justice Department Reports
Rate per 1,000 persons age 12 and older

Assault
Robbery
rape

Source: BJS Bulletin, *Criminal Victimization 1989*, October 1990.

### As is the Number of Youths Killed by Guns

NA

Source: Center to Prevent Handgun Violence, based on FBI Uniformed Crime Reports.

### Small Cities: The New Crime Capitals?
Murder Rates in Selected Cities with populations Under 1 Million

| City | Percent increase in murders, 1985-90 | City | Percent increase in murders, 1985-90 |
|------|------|------|------|
| Milwaukee | 126% | Charlotte | 60% |
| New Orleans | 101% | Baltimore | 43% |
| Jacksonville, Fla. | 84% | Kansas City, Mo. | 38% |
| Memphis | 71% | Cleveland | 23% |

All data from city police departments

**FIGURE 2.2   Crime in America: Comparing Trends**

## BOX 2.1    Violent Crime in the United States

*The following is derived from a March 1991, U.S. Department of Justice report entitled "Violent Crime in the United States."*

### Number of Violent Crimes in the U.S.

Figures from the National Crime Survey (NCS) show that in 1989 there were an estimated 5,861,050 violent victimizations in the United States, including 135,410 rapes, 1,091,830 robberies and 4,633,800 assaults. NCS data are based on interviews with victims and include offenses whether or not the victim reported the crime to the police. In 1989, 45 percent of the violent victimizations were reported to the police.

In addition, according the Uniform Crime Reports (UCR), a nationwide cooperative reporting effort of approximately 16,000 city, county and State law enforcement agencies, in 1989 there were 21,500 murders, and an estimated 4.6 million households (or about five percent of all households nationwide) had a member who experienced one or more violent crimes. Their findings showed that the chance of being a violent crime victim (with or without injury) is greater than that of being hurt in a traffic accident.

### Trends in Violent Crime

NCS data on rape, robbery and aggravated and simple assault show that these crimes increased from 1973 to 1981, dropped between 1981 and 1986, and have increased slightly since then. Nevertheless, 1989 levels were 11 percent below the peak year of 1981.

The UCR Index of criminal incidents reported to law enforcement agencies has evidenced increases in all crime categories since 1985. When violent incidents reported in 1985 and 1989 are compared, law enforcement authorities registered a 24 percent increase in the number of offenses reported to them—from about 1.3 million to 1.6 million nationwide.

Aggravated assaults (up by 32 percent) reflected the largest percentage gain among the index categories of violence, followed by: robbery (up 16 percent); murder and negligent manslaughter (up 13 percent); and forcible rape (up about 7 percent).

In 1985, violent offenses accounted for 11 percent of the total UCR Index offenses (both violent and property offenses) reported by law enforcement agencies and 12 percent of those reported in 1989.

Per capita measures of crime victimization, referred to as victimization rates, take into account population growth over time and allow for comparisons among subgroups in the population. The NCS victimization rate is the number of victimizations per 1,000 residents population age 12 or older. In 1989, about one in 34 persons age 12 or older was the victim of a violent crime. NCS data, based upon the self-reports of crime victims, indicate that:

- From 1973 through 1987, rates of violent victimization for males declined from 48.2 per 1,000 males aged 12 or older to 38.7, while female rates of violent victimization changed little (23.9 in 1973 and 24.0 in 1987).
- The assault rate reached an all-time low in 1986 of 22.3 per 1,000 persons age 12 or older, with a level of 23.0 recorded in 1989.
- The robbery rate reached an all-time low in 1985 of 5.1, with a level of 5.4 in 1989. Even though the robbery rate has been increasing in recent years, it has not yet reached the rates measured in the 10 years prior to 1983.

The percentage of U.S. households with at least one family member who was a victim of violent crime has declined from 5.8 percent in 1975 to 4.9 percent in 1989, staying at levels less than 5.0 percent since 1984.

UCR found that the murder rate peaked in 1980 at 10.2 per 100,000 population, and then dropped to 7.9 in 1984, climbing again to 8.6 in 1986. In 1989, the rate was 8.7. Coroners' reports confirm the UCR trends, and also show that homicide rates have varied substantially since 1900. After dropping from 1933 to 1958, the

**BOX 2.1   *Continued***

homicide rate climbed to an all-time high in 1980. In 1988, however, the homicide rate was 16 percent less than in 1980.

### Characteristics of Violent Crime

#### Where Violent Crimes Occur

Persons who live in central cities are more likely to be violent crime victims than persons who live in suburban or rural areas. Persons who live in cities of 250,000 to 499,999 population have the highest violent victimization rates.

In 1989, 14 percent of violent crime incidents occurred in the victim's home; 8 percent near home; 4 percent on the street near home; and 7 percent near a friend's, relative's or neighbor's home. Twenty-three percent of violent crimes occurred on the street but not near the victim's or a friend's home; 11 percent took place in school or on school property.

In 1989, the West had the highest rate of violent crime (36.4 crimes per 1,000 persons 12 or older), followed by the South and the Midwest. The Northeast recorded the lowest rate of violent crime (23.1 per 1,000 persons).

#### Victims

Although persons of all ages, races and income levels are victims of violent crime, some individuals—specifically males, blacks, teenagers and young adults, persons in low-income families and persons living in central cities—are at a higher risk of experiencing a violent crime than others.

#### Criminals

Of all violent crimes, 55 percent are committed by strangers, 32 percent by acquaintances and 8 percent by relatives. In 1989, persons not known to the victim committed 3.2 million violent crimes.

Of murder victims in 1989, 15 percent were killed by relatives, 39 percent by acquaintances, 13 percent by strangers and 33 percent in circumstances where the relationship was not known.

A few criminals commit many crimes. Studies in Philadelphia, Pennsylvania; Racine, Wis-

consin; and Columbus, Ohio, show that 23 percent to 34 percent of the juveniles involved with crime were responsible for 61 percent to 68 percent of all the crimes committed by juveniles in the cohort. A California study of males born in 1956 showed that a small percentage were responsible for a disproportionate share of all arrests for ages 18 to 29. Specifically, 6.6 percent of the juveniles studied were responsible for 72 percent of all the arrests for index crimes from this group.

Long-term studies show that the more often a person is arrested, the greater the chance of being arrested again. For example, a study of Philadelphia males born in 1945 found the following: 35 percent were arrested at least once; 54 percent of those with one arrest had a second arrest; 65 percent of those with two arrests had three; and 72 percent of those with three arrest had four arrests.

### Firearms and Drugs in Violent Crime

Offenders brandished or used firearms in 11 percent of all violent crimes committed during 1989. Firearms were used to commit:

- 62 percent of all homicides;
- 20 percent of all robberies;
- 10 percent of all assaults; and
- 6 percent of all rapes.

Nearly 12,000 people were murdered with firearms in 1989. Handguns were present in 27 percent of all violent crime incidents involving offenders armed with weapons in 1989. Offenders had a handgun in four out of five of those incidents where a firearm was present.

The actual number of drug-related acts of violence is difficult to measure. Three cities, however, have studied the amount of drug-related homicide in their jurisdictions:

- Of 1,263 homicides reported in New York City in 1984, 24 percent were identified as drug-related.

**BOX 2.1    *Continued***

- Of 1,850 homicides recorded in Miami from 1978 to 1982, 24 percent were classified as drug-related.
- In 1985, 21 percent of the homicides reported in the District of Columbia were identified as drug-related, increasing steadily to 34 percent in 1986, 51 percent in 1987, and to as much as 80 percent in 1988.

Major drug use (cocaine, heroin, PCP, LSD and methadone) is related to the number of prior convictions for state prisoners; the greater the use of major drugs, the more prior convictions the inmate was likely to report.

***Sentences of Convicted Felons***

Convicted violent felons are more likely to be sentenced to incarceration than are other convicted felons. In 1988, state courts imposed incarceration sentences in local jails or state prison in 95 percent of the murder and nonnegligent manslaughter convictions, 87 percent of the rape convictions, 89 percent of the robbery convictions and 72 percent of the convictions for aggravated assaults.

On December 31, 1989, there were 2,250 offenders under sentence of death in 34 States.

Between January 1, 1977 and December 31, 1989, 120 executions altogether were carried out by 13 States.

## Homicide and Genocide

Homicide, according to *Black's Law Dictionary* (Black, 1983: 375), is the killing of one human being by the act, procurement, or omission of another: "A person is guilty of criminal homicide if he purposely, knowingly, recklessly or negligently causes the death of another human being." Homicide is not necessarily a crime, but rather it is "a necessary ingredient of the crimes of murder and manslaughter" (Black, 1983: 375). In fact, there are other cases in which killing (homicide) may be committed without criminal intent and without criminal consequences; hence, the legal classification of "justifiable," "excusable," and "felonious" homicides. In order for someone to be convicted of felonious homicide, there must be intent and evil design absent such circumstances of necessity or duty as to render the act proper, and "relieve the party from any shadow of blame" as when the state lawfully executes a sentence of death upon a malefactor, or "where the killing takes place in the endeavor to prevent the commission of a felony that could not otherwise be avoided, or, as a matter of right, such as self-defense or other causes provided for by statute" (Black, 1983: 375).

Genocide has been defined by the *New Webster's Dictionary of the English Language* (1985: 405) as the "deliberate mass murder of a race, people, or minority group." Nonetheless, the term *genocide* cannot be found in *Black's Law Dictionary*. The same is true for other law dictionaries and for most, if not all, criminology textbooks. Logically, genocide, war crimes, civilian massacres, and other forms of mass killings by the state (or its agents) against groups of people of their own or against peoples of other groups or states may be thought of as homicides, too (Salmi, 1993). Generally, when criminologists discuss homicide, however, this is not the case. As a result, nearly all historical discussions of the changing nature of crime and violence require some kind of asterisk, as we will see shortly.

Murder scene of Nicole Brown Simpson and Ronald Lyle Goldman, 1994.

Without comparing U.S. homicide figures and rates with the figures and rates from other developed nations like ourselves, or without locating these figures or rates in some kind of historical perspective, there is little meaning that can be derived from the raw numbers alone. Steven F. Messner and Richard Rosenfeld (1993) have provided cross-national comparisons of homicide for sixteen developed nations in 1988 (see Figure 2.3). This homicide data in general and their analysis and calculation of nongun homicide rates in particular reveal that homicide is a significant American problem, with or without guns or handguns.

For example, "the U.S. rate of 8.9 homicides per 100,000 population is more than three times Finland's rate of 2.8 per 100,000 population, the next highest among the nations presented" in Figure 2.3; "it is over seven times the rates of most of the other nations" (Messner and Rosenfeld, 1993: 22). Moreover, the "level of lethal violence (3.5 homicides per 100,000 population) committed without a firearm is greater than the overall homicide rates of the other nations displayed in [Figure 2.3] and, in most cases, considerably greater" (Messner and Rosenfeld, 1993: 24).

Historically, between 1900 and 1989, the United States experienced considerable variability in its homicide rates (see Figure 2.4). During the first decades of the century, the levels of homicide more than doubled, peaking at over eight homicides per

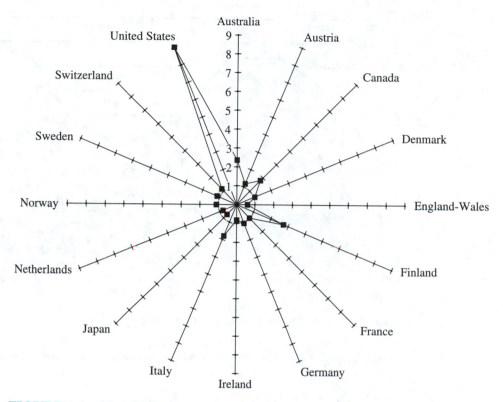

**FIGURE 2.3    Homicide Rates in Sixteen Nations, 1988 (homicides per 100,000 population)**

*From:* Steven F. Messner and Richard Rosenfeld, *Crime and the American Dream* (Belmont, CA: Wadsworth, 1994), Figure 2.2, p. 24. Copyright © 1994 by Wadsworth Publishing Co. Reprinted by permission of the publisher.

100,000 population in the early 1930s. By the 1950s and early 1960s, the homicide rates had declined to just under five per 100,000 population. By the late 1960s, the homicide rates began a pronounced increase, climbing above 9 homicides per 100,000 in the late 1970s. Since then, the U.S. homicide rates have remained fairly stable and high. It should be underscored, of course, that throughout this period, the lowest homicide rates of the United States still exceed the highest rates for any of the other developed nations.

Like other rates of crime, homicide rates should be examined as they vary according to age, race, and gender (see Figures 2.5 and 2.6). Homicide rates, like victimization rates, vary not only by age, race, and gender, but also by socioeconomic status or class. When it comes to official records of homicide like the official records of other UCR crimes, "it is clearly the case that persons *prosecuted* for criminal and delinquent offenses are disproportionately persons of color and reduced economic circumstances.

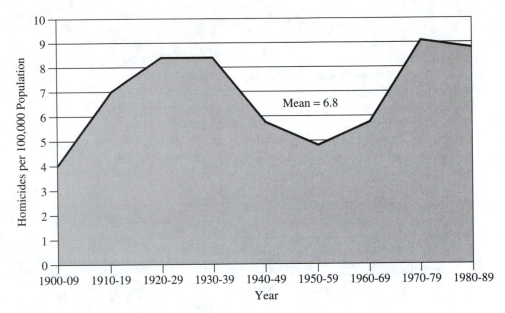

**FIGURE 2.4   U.S. Homicide Rates, 1900–1989**

*From:* Steven F. Messner and Richard Rosenfeld, *Crime and the American Dream* (Belmont, CA: Wadsworth, 1994), Figure 2.3, p. 27. Copyright © 1994 by Wadsworth Publishing Co. Reprinted by permission of the publisher.

It is also clearly the case that some disadvantaged groups are more vulnerable to some kinds of criminal victimization" (Hagan, 1994: 25).

For example, during most of the past half-century, rates of black homicide have ranged from six to seven times those for whites (Hawkins, 1986; Rose and McClain, 1990). In fact, although there have been variations over time in rates by ethnic status and gender, black rates of homicide have exceeded white rates at least since 1910 (Monkkonen, 1993). Similarly, victimization data collected on other felonies by the National Crime Survey in the mid-1980s found that African Americans experience rates of rape, aggravated assault, and armed robbery that are approximately 25 percent higher than those for whites. In addition, when it came to rates of auto theft for black Americans, these exceeded those for whites by about 70 percent. And robbery victimization of black Americans is more than 150 percent higher than for white Americans (Hagan, 1994).

More specifically, homicide rates for African American male youths are highly pronounced. Among the 15 to 19 year olds, for example, the gun homicide rate for black males is more than eleven times the rate for white males, or about 68 and 6 per 100,000 populations respectively (Fingerhut and Kleinman, 1990). And although the late 1980s and early 1990s saw an upward movement in black homicide rates for young men and women, white males and females between the ages of 15 to 24, by contrast, experienced a gradual decline during the same period. Explanations for these different

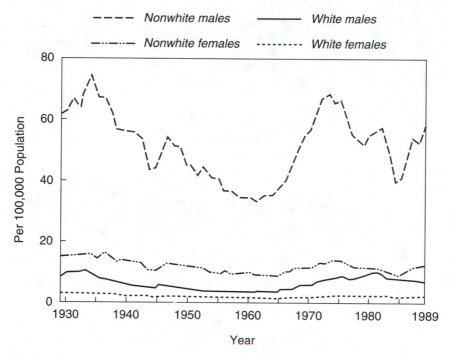

**FIGURE 2.5     Age-Adjusted Homicide Rates, by Sex and Race, United States, 1929–1989**

*Source:* Reprinted with permission from UNDERSTANDING AND PREVENTING VIOLENCE: Copyright © 1993 by the National Academy of Sciences, Courtesy of the National Academy Press, Washington, D.C.

rates in contemporary homicide and other felonious behavior will be discussed in later chapters (see especially Chapter 11).

Thus far, the discussion of homicide trends has been confined to the twentieth century. Although this certainly provides some perspective for comparative purposes, we now turn to a more general history of homicide trends, dating as far back as the fourteenth century. Both historians and criminologists generally agree today that homicide rates were extraordinarily high in Europe during the Middle Ages. Contrary to the basic claim that the city, with its anonymity and crowding, has been in and of itself the factor in causing violence, for centuries it was actually villages rather than cities that experienced the highest rates of homicide and violence (Butterfield, 1994).

Today's research on official homicide rates in England, Australia, France, Italy, and the Netherlands reveals a peaking in the Middle Ages, followed by gradual declines over time to the present. For example, Dutch historian Pieter Spierenburg has shown that the homicide rate in Amsterdam "dropped from 47 per 100,000 people in the mid-15th century to 1 to 1.5 per 100,000 in the early 19th century" (Butterfield, 1994: 10Y). Similarly, Lawrence Stone, a U.S. professor emeritus of history, has estimated that the

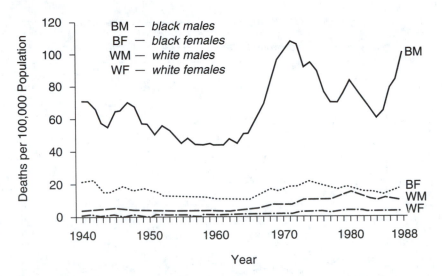

**FIGURE 2.6    Homicide Rates, Persons Ages 15–24 Years, by Race and Sex, 1940–1988**

*Source:* Reprinted with permission from UNDERSTANDING AND PREVENTING VIOLENCE: Copyright © 1993 by the National Academy of Sciences, Courtesy of the National Academy Press, Washington, D.C.

homicide rate in medieval England was on average ten times that of twentieth-century England: "A study of the university town of Oxford in the 1340s showed an extraordinarily high annual rate of about 110 per 100,000 people. Studies of London in the first half of the 14th century determined a homicide rate of 36 to 52 per 100,000 people per year" (Butterfield, 1994: 10Y). Today, the homicide rate of England-Wales is less than 1 per 100,000 population.

In the United States, as previously noted, the homicide rates were higher in the nineteenth century than the twentieth century. Until the 1960s, these rates declined more or less steadily like their earlier European counterparts. For example, the New York City homicide rate declined from about 14 to 4 per 100,000 population between 1860 and 1960. In the City of Brotherly Love, Philadelphia, for example, "the average annual rate of indictments for homicide fell from 4 per 100,000 in the 1850s to 2.2 in the early 1890s," according to research by crime historian Roger Lane (Butterfield, 1994: 10Y). By contrast, in 1993, among cities with a population of over 100,000 people in the United States, the three highest murder rates were found in Gary, Indiana; New Orleans, Louisiana; and Washington, D.C. (Figure 2.7). What is both interesting to observe and consistent with the larger historical trends is the fact that the most populated cities in the nation, New York City, Los Angeles, and Chicago, are not to be found among those cities with the top ten homicide rates.

Explanations for the generally downward historical trend in official homicide rates have been debated. Some argue, following the sociologist Norbert Ellis who intro-

## MURDER RATES

Cities with over 100,000 population with the highest murder rates in 1993 per 100,000 population.

| CITY | Murder Rate |
| --- | --- |
| 1. Gary, Ind. | 89.1 |
| 2. New Orleans, La. | 80.3 |
| 3. Washington, D.C. | 78.5 |
| 4. St. Louis, Mo. | 69.0 |
| 5. Detroit | 56.8 |
| 6. Richmond, Va. | 54.5 |
| 7. Atlanta | 50.4 |
| 8. Baltimore | 48.1 |
| 9. San Bernardino, Ca. | 47.1 |
| 10. Birmingham, Ala. | 45.0 |

**FIGURE 2.7    Murder Rates for 1993**

*Source:* Reprinted with permission of the Associated Press.

duced the idea in the late 1930s, that a "civilizing process" had occurred. Others argue that the civilizing process had more to do with the increase in the coercive power of the state, the centralization of judicial authority, and the concentration of mercantile property and the formation of private militia beginning in the sixteenth and seventeenth centuries (Hay, 1975). A combination of the two is probably correct, but only if one ignores the unofficial millions of indigenous peoples throughout the world that were the victims of capitalist genocide during this same period (Salmi, 1993; Stannard, 1992).

In the mid-1990s, expressions of horror and condemnation over the euphemistic "ethnic cleansing" (genocide) in Bosnia and Herzegovina were routine in the media and mass culture. Because the Bosnians and Croatians were deemed as "worthy victims," cries about "crimes against humanity" could be heard from the United Nations to the capitols of states around the world. By contrast, as far back in time as the late fifteenth century when European explorers set out for the New World, the native peoples of the Americas were never considered worthy victims by the conquering troops who regarded them as subhuman species. Europeans and Americans both, for the most part, have had official and unofficial amnesia when it comes to counting, let alone acknowledging, the widespread exterminations of whole groups of people. These crimes of control are rarely reviewed when criminologists, historians, and others turn to discussions of the downward historical trends in violence.

During the period of merchant capitalism (1500–1750), long-distance trade was the main instrument of profit-making. At the beginning of the capitalist era, the strong nations of Europe, including Spain, Portugal, France, England, and the Netherlands, were dependent for their economic well-being on "the precious mineral ores from Latin America, the sugar from the Caribbean islands, the 'ebony flesh' from Africa, and the spices of Asia" (Salmi, 1993: 27). In short, the gold, silver, tin, and mercury mined in the West Indies, Mexico, Peru, Brazil, and Bolivia; the sugar cultivated in the West Indian, Peruvian, Brazilian, and Javanese plantations; the West African slaves involved in the triangular trade; and Asian spices and textiles "all constituted an enormous source of profits and wealth for the European states, banks, and trading companies" (Salmi, 1993: 27).

For example, on the island of Española, under the governorship of Christopher Columbus, 50,000 native people died within a matter of months after the establishment of the first Spanish colony in the Caribbean. The type of *civilizing process* evidenced by the early explorers included enslaving the native people, "chaining them together at the neck and marching them in columns to toil in gold and silver mines, decapitating any who did not walk quickly enough" (Stannard, 1992: 430). The barbaric cruelty of these early capitalists involved the slicing off of "women's breasts for sport and [feeding] their babies to the packs of armored wolfhounds and mastiffs that accompanied the Spanish soldiers" (Stannard, 1994: 430). Wrote one Spanish eyewitness to the massacres, the soldiers "would test their swords and their manly strength on captured Indians," and they would "place bets on the slicing off of heads or the cutting of bodies in half with one blow" (quoted in Stannard, 1992: 430).

Take the example of Hernando Cortés and his accompanying conquistadors. In November 1519, they became the first Westerners to gaze upon the magnificent Aztec city of Tenochtitlan. This island metropolis was far larger and more impressive than any city they had seen in Europe. At the time, Tenochtitlan's population was five times the population of either London or Seville. Less than two years later that incredible city was a smoldering ruin:

> *Tenochtitlan, with its 350,000 residents, had been the jewel of an empire that contained numerous exquisite cities. All were destroyed. Before the coming of the Europeans, central Mexico, radiating out from those metropolitan centers over many tens of thousands of square miles, had contained about 25 million people—almost ten times the population of England at the time. Seventy-five years later hardly more than 1 million were left. And central Mexico, where 95 out of every 100 people perished, was typical. In Central America the grisly pattern held, and even worsened. In western and central Honduras 95 percent of the native people were exterminated in half a century. In western Nicaragua the rate of extermination was 99 percent—from more than 1 million people to less than 10,000 in just sixty years (Stannard, 1992: 430).*

When the Caribbean holocaust had exhausted itself around 1535, the mass killings, in "number of deaths and proportion of the population affected, vastly exceeded that of any of the hideous genocides that have occurred in the twentieth century against Armenians, Jews, Gypsies, Ibos, Bengalis, Timorese, Cambodians, Ugandans, and others" (Stannard, 1992: 430). The genocide then spread to South America. For example, before the arrival of the Europeans in what are today Peru and

Chile, the population was somewhere between 9 and 14 million. A century later the population had been reduced to a little over 500,000. In Brazil and the rest of the South American continent the same story repeated itself.

All in all, before the seventeenth century had arrived, between 60 million and 80 million Amerindians had perished by the hands of the *civilizing* Europeans. By the time of the Industrial Revolution (1750–1850) in England and the period of imperialist expansion (1850–1950), the mass killings had subsided because what was now desired by capitalist development were cheap sources of labor. As history teaches us, children, women, and slaves provided the labor even as they were subjected to inhuman working and living conditions.

## Criminal Victimization in the United States (1970–2005)

In this section, an overview of the official rates of criminal victimization is presented for the last quarter of the twentieth century. Special attention is given to race, age, and gender in terms of the different rates of victimization. Although homicide remains a focus of this section, the whole category of violent criminality is expanded to include assault, robbery, and rape. These crimes of *accommodation, resistance,* and *alienation* reveal a picture of victimization at the turn of the century in the United States.

In 1992, there were 6.6 million violent victimizations, including 141,000 rapes, 1.2 million robberies, and 5.3 million assaults. In 5 percent of all households, or 4.9 million households, a member had been victimized by violence. In 1992, violent crime rates recorded by the National Crime Victimization Survey (NCVS) were unchanged from 1991. They were 9 percent below 1981, the peak year (see Figure 2.8). Excluding homicide, the percentage of households with a member who had been victimized by violence, 5 percent, was the lowest recorded since the estimates began in 1975. Crime is not decreasing for all groups. For example, in 1992 the violent crime rate for blacks was the highest ever recorded by the NCVS. Finally, the highest violent crime rates have been recorded for young people aged 16 to 24 (U.S. Department of Justice, 1994).

Indeed, one of the more significant and perhaps ominous homicide trends involves American youth. Beginning in the late 1980s, young people killing and being killed have accounted for a disproportionate number of the deaths. For example, "from 1986 to 1991, the homicide rate among those 14 to 24 rose by 62 percent. It jumped 124 percent among those 14 to 17" (The Associated Press, 1994b: 1D). In Baltimore, for example, the 13-to-24 age group accounted for more than half the homicide arrests and nearly 40 percent of the victims in 1993. In Cleveland, for the same year, half the 173 homicides were committed by those younger than 25. Five years earlier, that age group accounted for less than a third of the killings. In short, the pattern of homicide has changed. As Midwest criminologist Scott Decker has stated: "The decreasing age of both offenders and victims is the most profound change in homicide since World War II" (quoted in The Associated Press, 1994b: 1D). What makes the shifting patterns worse is the fact that the increase in violence among young persons comes as the

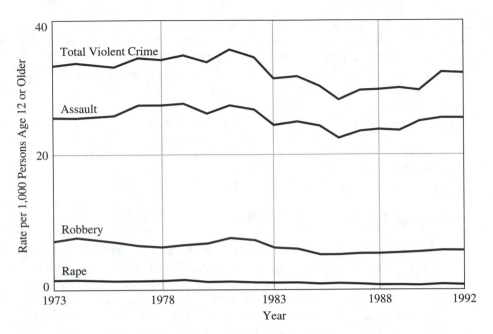

**FIGURE 2.8   The Violent Crime Rate, 1973–1992**

U.S. Department of Justice, Office of Justice Programs, Bureau of Justice Statistics, April 1994.

size of the group has actually decreased. However, by 2005, the 15-to-19 age group is projected to increase by 23 percent. As Decker concludes, "All of the indicators in the demographics are supporting the contention that homicide is only going to increase" (quoted in The Associated Press, 1994b: 1D). Although most recently, during the period from 1994 to 1996, homicide and aggravated assault rates were heading downward for groups of young offenders, especially in such metropolitan areas as New York, Chicago, and Detroit.

Moreover, according to statistics released by the FBI on January 5, 1997, violent crime dropped for the first six months of 1996, continuing a pattern that began in 1991. This 5-year decline is the longest in 25 years. Using the FBI's figures as reported, the aggregated data for the nation as a whole revealed that murders dropped 7 percent, robbery and aggravated assault declined 5 percent, and rape was down 1 percent. During the same period, the only index crime to register an increase was arson at 2 percent (Butterfield, 1997). The recent declines in crimes against the person follow a more sustained period of declines in crimes against property.

Comparatively speaking for the period 1973 to 1992, the victimization trends against property and persons have been uneven (see Figures 2.9 and 2.10), but have generally declined or remained stable. Although violent crime rates did not change significantly during this period, rates of theft, both personal and household, decreased.

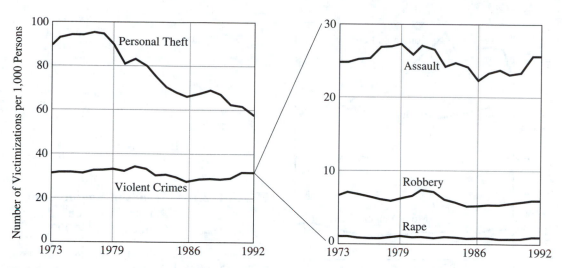

**FIGURE 2.9** Trends in Victimization Rates of Personal Crimes, 1973–1992

U.S. Dept. of Justice, Office of Justice Programs, Bureau of Justice Statistics, April 1994.

The robbery rates in 1992 were down from 1981, the burglary rates were below those of any years in the 1970s and 1980s, and the motor vehicle thefts were fairly average for the period, 1973–1992 (U.S. Department of Justice, 1993). When it came to crimes against the person, some 35 percent of the total personal crimes reported were made up of violent crimes; when it came to crimes against the household, some 55 percent involved household larcenies (see Figure 2.11). The most common of these household larcenies involved lawn furniture stolen from a backyard or a bicycle stolen from the driveway (National Crime Victimization Survey, 1994).

Gender differences in rates of violent victimization, including homicide, are striking within and without the family (see Figures 2.12 and 2.13). For example, 45 percent of family murder victims were female, compared to 18 percent of nonfamily murder victims. A survey of murder cases disposed in 1988 in the courts of large urban areas indicated that 16 percent of murder victims were members of the defendant's family. Among the murder victims, 6.5 percent were killed by their spouses, 3.5 percent by their parents, 1.9 percent by their own children, 1.5 percent by their siblings, and 2.6 percent by some other family member. A third of family murders involved a female as the killer. In murders of their parents, females were 18 percent of the killers, and in sibling murders, 15 percent. In spouse murders, however, women represented 41 percent of killers. Women predominated, accounting for 55 percent of killers, in murders of their offspring. Among black marital partners, wives were just about as likely to kill their husbands (47 percent) as husbands were to kill their wives (53 percent). For white victims, women were the killers of their husbands in 38 percent of the cases, whereas men were the killers of their wives in 62 percent (Dawson and Langan, 1994).

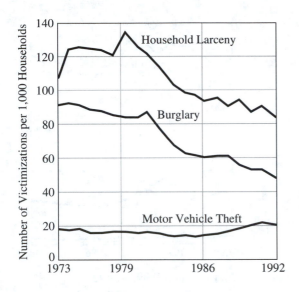

**FIGURE 2.10    Trends in Victimization Rates of Household Crimes, 1973–1992**

U.S. Dept. of Justice, Office of Justice Programs, Bureau of Justice Statistics, April 1994.

Crimes Against Persons: 1992
(Percent of Total Victimizations)

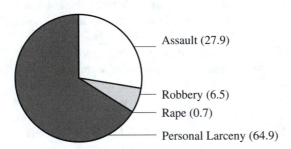

Assault (27.9)

Robbery (6.5)
Rape (0.7)
Personal Larceny (64.9)

Crimes Against Households: 1992
(Percent of Total Victimizations)

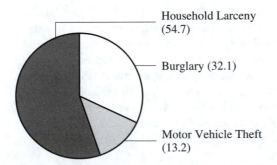

Household Larceny
(54.7)

Burglary (32.1)

Motor Vehicle Theft
(13.2)

**FIGURE 2.11    Crimes Against Persons and Households, 1992**

National Crime Victimization Survey: Fact Sheet, Nov. 5, No. 110.

**FIGURE  2.12     Murder Victims and Defendants in the 75 Largest Urban Counties, by Victim-Assailant Family Relationship, 1988**

| Relationship of victim to assailant | Murder victims | | Murder defendants | |
|---|---|---|---|---|
| | Number | Percent | Number | Percent |
| All | 8,063 | 100.0% | 9,576 | 100.0% |
| Nonfamily | 6,755 | 83.3 | 8,292 | 86.6 |
| Family | 1,308 | 16.2 | 1,284 | 13.4 |
| Spouse | 528 | 6.5 | 531 | 5.5 |
| Offspring | 285 | 3.5 | 258 | 2.7 |
| Parent | 154 | 1.9 | 150 | 1.6 |
| Sibling | 123 | 1.5 | 121 | 1.3 |
| Other | 218 | 2.6 | 224 | 2.3 |

*Source:* U.S. Department of Justice, Bureau of Justice Statistics, July 1994, p. 2.

*Note: Spouse* includes common-law spouse. *Offspring* includes grandchild and step-child. *Parent* includes grandparent and step-parent. *Sibling* includes step-sibling. *Other* includes cousin, in-law, extended family members, and other family members.

Detail percentages may not add to total because of rounding.

Among the largest group of victims of family violence are children. The National Committee for the Prevention of Child Abuse in a report released to *USA Today* for 1993 estimated that there were some 3 million cases of abuse and neglect that year, "including 1,300 children abused and neglected to death," up from 813 in 1985 (Edmonds, 1994: 1A). Studies indicate that 90 percent of the nation's fatal cases involve children 4 years old and younger. A study of the nation's 39 metropolitan areas with populations of more than 1 million (see Figure 2.14) found "death rates of 5.4 to 11.5 for every 100,000 children in the South and 5.2 to 11.2 in the West. The rates were 4.3 to 8.2 for every 100,000 children in the Northeast and 4.6 to 9.8 in the North-Central region" (Leary, 1994: 3C).

Because of the significant problems of wife battering, sexual assault (i.e., rape), and domestic violence more generally, any contemporary discussion of violence in America is inadequate if it does not underscore the prevalence of crimes against women's personhood. The NCVS of some 400,000 women for 1993 revealed the following findings about violence suffered by women in the United States:

- More than 2.5 million women experience violence annually.
- Women are about equally likely to experience violence perpetrated by a relative or intimate, an acquaintance or a stranger.
- Nearly two in three female victims of violence were related to or knew their attacker.
- About one in four attacks on females involved the use of a weapon by the offender.
- About one in three assaults involved a firearm.
- About three out of four female victims of violence resisted the actions of the offender either physically or verbally.

**FIGURE 2.13    Sex, Race, and Age, by the Family Relationship of Murder Victims and Defendants, 1988**

| Relationship of victim to assailant | All | Sex | | Race | | | Age | | | | |
|---|---|---|---|---|---|---|---|---|---|---|---|
| | | Male | Female | White | Black | Other | Under 12 | 12–19 | 20–29 | 30–59 | 60 or older |
| *Victims* | | | | | | | | | | | |
| All | 100% | 77.8% | 22.2% | 43.5% | 54.2% | 2.3% | 4.8% | 10.9% | 35.6% | 41.8% | 7.0% |
| Nonfamily | 100 | 82.2 | 17.8 | 44.4 | 53.3 | 2.3 | 2.1 | 12.2 | 38.5 | 41.1 | 6.1 |
| Family | 100 | 55.5 | 44.5 | 39.0 | 58.6 | 2.4 | 18.8 | 3.9 | 20.3 | 45.3 | 11.6 |
| Spouse | 100 | 40.2 | 59.8 | 41.2 | 56.4 | 2.4 | 0 | 0 | 27.9 | 65.0 | 7.1 |
| Offspring | 100 | 55.8 | 44.2 | 32.6 | 65.6 | 1.8 | 78.5 | 10.9 | 7.7 | 3.0 | 0 |
| Parent | 100 | 57.2 | 42.8 | 54.8 | 45.2 | 0 | 0 | 0 | .9 | 56.7 | 42.4 |
| Sibling | 100 | 73.0 | 27.0 | 33.5 | 64.5 | 2.0 | 8.7 | 2.0 | 43.3 | 42.6 | 3.3 |
| Other | 100 | 74.9 | 25.1 | 34.1 | 61.0 | 4.9 | 4.6 | 8.2 | 19.1 | 47.5 | 20.6 |
| *Defendants* | | | | | | | | | | | |
| All | 100% | 89.5% | 10.5% | 36.2% | 61.9% | 1.8% | .1% | 21.8% | 42.5% | 31.4% | 4.2% |
| Nonfamily | 100 | 93.2 | 6.8 | 35.7 | 62.6 | 1.8 | .1 | 23.1 | 44.4 | 28.4 | 3.8 |
| Family | 100 | 65.5 | 34.5 | 39.7 | 58.0 | 2.3 | 0 | 13.0 | 29.7 | 50.5 | 6.8 |
| Spouse | 100 | 59.3 | 40.7 | 41.8 | 56.1 | 2.2 | 0 | .9 | 21.9 | 66.1 | 11.1 |
| Offspring | 100 | 45.4 | 54.6 | 34.5 | 64.5 | 1.0 | 0 | 17.2 | 36.4 | 40.3 | 6.0 |
| Parent | 100 | 81.6 | 18.4 | 49.8 | 50.2 | 0 | 0 | 38.2 | 30.7 | 29.4 | 1.7 |
| Sibling | 100 | 84.9 | 15.1 | 32.2 | 65.8 | 2.0 | 0 | 16.9 | 36.7 | 46.4 | 0 |
| Other | 100 | 83.5 | 16.5 | 38.1 | 56.1 | 5.9 | 0 | 18.0 | 35.9 | 41.3 | 4.9 |

*Source:* U.S. Department of Justice, Bureau of Justice Statistics, July, 1994. p. 2.

*Note:* See Figure 2.12 note for definitions of the family relationships.

- About a third of female victims of violence were injured as a result of the crime.
- About half the women victimized by violence reported the crime to the police, and among those who didn't, about six in ten said that they considered the matter a private or personal one or that they felt the offense was minor.
- Nearly half the victims of rape perceived the offender to have been under the influence of drugs or alcohol at the time of the offense (adapted from Bachman, 1994a: iii).

When it comes to the two crimes that women fear most—murder and rape—a computerized analysis by *Newhouse News Service* of 1992 showed that the most dangerous places for women in America were small and medium-sized towns (Hallinan and Marchak, 1994). For example, women were more likely to be raped or murdered in areas such as Rapid City, South Dakota; Jackson, Michigan; and Pine Bluff, Arkansas; than in New York, Los Angeles, or Washington, D.C. The rape rate for Rapid City was 137 per 100,000 population. The murder rate for Pine Bluff was 9.2 per 100,000 population. By comparison the national average rate for rape was 46.4 per 100,000 population, for murder it was 1.8.

## DYING YOUNG IN THE CITIES

Estimated range of rates of death for children under 5 due to abuse and neglect, in metropolitan statistical areas with a million people or more. The estimates are annual averages for the years 1979 to 1988, the latest figures available. Lower estimates are officially reported rates, based on sources like death certificates, while the higher estimates include deaths that were apparently the result of unreported abuse.

| City | Range of rates per 100,000 children | City | Range of rates per 100,000 children |
|------|------|------|------|
| 1. Phoenix | 6.6–15.5 | 21. Cincinnati | 4.8–9.7 |
| 2. Orlando, Fla. | 7.5–14.9 | 22. Baltimore | 4.9–9.7 |
| 3. Tampa–St. Petersburg, Fla. | 6.6–14.8 | 23. Norfolk, Va. | 5.1–9.6 |
| 4. Miami | 6.6–13.1 | 24. San Francisco | 4.6–9.6 |
| 5. Chicago | 6.8–13.1 | 25. Cleveland | 4.9–9.3 |
| 6. New Orleans | 6.4–12.5 | 26. Milwaukee | 4.7–9.3 |
| 7. Dallas | 6.7–12.4 | 27. San Antonio | 5.6–9.2 |
| 8. Indianapolis | 6.0–11.6 | 28. New York | 5.2–8.9 |
| 9. Houston | 5.4–11.6 | 29. Charlotte, N.C. | 3.8–8.7 |
| 10. St. Louis | 5.7–11.4 | 30. Washington, D.C.* | 4.8–8.6 |
| 11. Philadelphia | 5.9–11.4 | 31. Buffalo | 4.2–8.0 |
| 12. Kansas City | 5.4–11.1 | 32. Minneapolis–St. Paul | 3.8–7.7 |
| 13. Atlanta | 5.0–10.8 | 33. Sacramento | 4.1–7.7 |
| 14. Seattle | 4.9–10.6 | 34. Providence, R.I. | 4.5–7.6 |
| 15. Los Angeles | 5.1–10.5 | 35. Columbus | 4.5–7.6 |
| 16. San Diego | 5.0–10.4 | 36. Pittsburgh | 3.6–6.9 |
| 17. Salt Lake City | 5.3–10.4 | 37. Rochester | 3.2–6.8 |
| 18. Detroit | 5.0–10.4 | 38. Hartford | 3.5–5.8 |
| 19. Portland, Ore. | 4.6–10.4 | 39. Boston | 2.7–5.5 |
| 20. Denver | 5.1–9.9 | | |

*The District of Columbia alone, without suburban areas, would have the highest rate, at 14.4 to 22.2 deaths per 100,000 people.

*Source:* Copyright © 1994 by The New York Times Co. Reprinted by permission.

**FIGURE 2.14    Dying Young in the Cities**

Of course, not counted or reported are the crimes against women involving sexual harassment, discrimination, and molestation. Numbers are simply not available. U.S. women perhaps can take some solace in the fact that they are not victimized, oppressed, or dehumanized to the extent that women are throughout most of the globe, especially in the regions of the Middle East and South Asia. For example, sexual criminals are a fact of daily life for women commuters on public buses in places like New Delhi. "Eve-teasers" or men who grope, pinch, and molest women on crowded buses turn the daily commute into a battleground for women riders. Eve-teasing "is a peculiarly Indian euphemism for a myriad of sexual harassment offenses ranging from catcalls to assault" (Moore, 1995: A10). In part, as a result of the reluctance of women to report crimes, especially of a sexual nature because of the taboos and stigma, eve-teasing is on the rise. Said one female college student in a self-defense course:

*The buses are very bad. They pack the buses and this gives men total opportunity to misbehave with us. On the streets they make comments, sing songs, whistle. If he is on a motorcycle, he comes close, touches you on your breasts and flees (quoted in Moore, 1995: 10A).*

Moreover, many laws in Pakistan, India, and neighboring countries penalize women crime victims. In Islamic Pakistan, for example, "women frequently are jailed for adultery when they report being raped. In Bangladesh, a 14-year-old girl recently was tied to bamboo canes and beaten eighty times with a broom by village officials because she could not produce a witness to her alleged rape by a village man" (Moore, 1995: A). South Asian newspapers report regularly accounts of women being raped by policemen when they come forward to file sexual complaints.

Before turning to an overview of white collar crime (or crimes by the public), a brief review of the increasing victimization in the workplace is called for. While working or on duty, 1 million individuals become victims of violent crimes each year. According to the NCVS for 1987–1992 (see Figure 2.15), these victimizations account for 15 percent of the over 6.5 million acts of violence experienced by U.S. residents aged 12 or older. These violent victimizations resulted in almost 160,000 injuries annually. In addition, "over 2 million personal thefts and over 200,000 car thefts occur annually while persons are at work" (Bachman, 1994b: 1).

Other findings of comparative interest about victimization at the workplace include the following: (1) Men were more likely than women to experience a violent crime at work; (2) women and men were equally likely to be victims of theft while working; (3) more than a third of those victimized at work faced armed offenders, about the same rate as those victimized while not working; (4) victims of violence at work were less likely to be injured than victims of violence that occurred away from work; (5) although men were more likely to be victimized by strangers at work, women were more likely to be victimized by someone known to them, such as a husband, ex-husband, boyfriend, or ex-boyfriend; and (6) more than half of the victimizations that were sustained at work were not reported to the police (Bachman, 1994b).

## White Collar Crime

Crime by the public, or white collar crime, is highly profitable, relatively risk-free, and almost socially acceptable. White collar crime is also big business, and it appears to be growing, but statistics are few and those that exist are unreliable because many of these

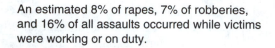

An estimated 8% of rapes, 7% of robberies, and 16% of all assaults occurred while victims were working or on duty.

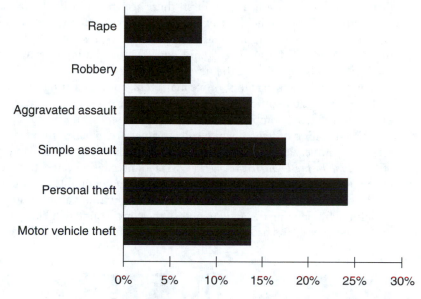

Percentage of the total number of U.S. victimizations that occurred while the victim was working or on duty, 1987-92.

**FIGURE 2.15**    **Victimizations at the Workplace**

U.S. Department of Justice, Office of Justice Programs, Bureau of Justice Statistics, July 1994.

crimes are never reported. The extent seems so great that Dana L. Turner and Richard G. Stephenson (1993: 58), two security management experts, claim: "Significant segments of entire legitimate and criminal industries have been built around white-collar crime." For example, counterfeit goods—knockoffs of well-known prestige products like Rolexes, Gucci bags, Chanel scarves and T-shirts with licensed logos—were conservatively estimated to be a $60 billion to $70 billion industry by a 1988 government report (Glave, 1994).

The range and diversity of white collar criminality is considerable, including but not limited to the following examples: fraud and insider abuse within the savings and loan industry; overcharges and failed product designs within the defense industry; overcharges and inappropriate charges for government-sponsored research within public and private universities; misused post office and banking privileges within the U.S. House of Representatives; embezzlement within the private and public domains; the conversion of nonprofit charitable organizations' dues and donations into political action committees (PACs). A 1986 Bureau of Justice Statistics Special Report has defined white collar crime as nonviolent crime for financial gain committed by deception. Unlike white collar definitions of the past, today's definitions are indifferent as to whether the persons committing such offenses have professional status (white collars) or specialized technical skills, although they often do (U.S. Justice Department, 1987).

White collar crimes may be perpetrated loosely by three types of offenders (Turner and Stephenson, 1993). First, there are the individuals who act against other individuals. These include, for example, crimes of trickery, deceit, or misrepresentation by people in a position of authority and control, such as family members, attorneys, real estate and insurance agents, conservators, and physicians. Second, there are the insiders who act against the interests of their organizations. These internal criminals include business partners, office managers, computer programmers, stockbrokers, and senior executive officers. Third, there are the external criminals who include forgers, counterfeiters, computer hackers, industrial spies, and office supply pirates.

Classification of federal white collar crimes are grouped into five categories: counterfeiting, embezzlement, forgery, fraud, and regulatory offenses. Based on the *Dictionary of Criminal Justice Data Terminology* (1981), counterfeiting refers to "the manufacture or attempted manufacture of a copy or imitation of a negotiable instrument with value set by law or convention, or possession of such a copy without authorization and with intent to defraud by claiming the genuineness of the copy" (quoted in U.S. Justice Department, 1987: 2). Federal laws prohibit counterfeiting of the following: U.S. coins, currency, and

Depositors lining up to collect their money during the Savings and Loan Scandal, 1989.

securities; foreign money; domestic or foreign stamps; and official seals and certificates of federal departments or agencies.

Embezzlement refers to "the misappropriation, misapplication, or illegal disposal of property entrusted to an individual with intent to defraud the legal owner or intended beneficiary" (quoted in U.S. Justice Department, 1987: 2). Fraud refers to "the intentional misrepresentation of fact to unlawfully deprive a person of his or her property or legal rights, without damage to property or actual or threatened injury to persons" (quoted in U.S. Justice Department, 1987: 2). The difference between embezzlement and fraud is that the former involves a breach of trust that existed between the victim and the offender, for example, an army supply officer who sells government property for personal profit.

Forgery refers to "the alteration of something written by another person or writing something that purports to be either the act of another or to have been executed at a time or place other than was in fact the case" (quoted in U.S. Department of Justice, 1987: 2). White collar regulatory offenses refer to "the violation of Federal regulations and laws other than those listed above that meet the definition of white collar crime and that [are] typically classified by U.S. attorneys as white collar offenses" (quoted in U.S. Department of Justice, 1987: 2).

Each federal category of white collar crime includes a number of more specific federal offenses. For a breakdown of white collar crime categories by conviction for 1985, see Figure 2.16, the product of a special report by the Bureau of Justice Statistics, representing the first analysis of federal efforts to prosecute and punish white collar criminals by the Department of Justice. Before sharing some of the findings of this comparative study, it should be underscored that the FBI's official data represents only the very tip of the white collar crime iceberg. For example, according to the FBI's data for 1985 there were approximately 28,000 white collar crimes, including the charged and uncharged cases. When it comes to crime by the public, however, just the two most commonly committed crimes—tax evasion and pilfering from work—are committed by tens of millions of U.S. citizens annually (Gabor, 1994; Touby, 1994; Woodman, 1992).

During 1985, there were 10,733 persons convicted of federal white collar crimes, an increase of 18 percent in the number of while collar convictions since 1980 (U.S. Department of Justice, 1987). The majority of offenders were investigated or prosecuted for fraud. The filing rates, 55 percent, by U.S. attorneys for white collar and nonwhite collar offenses were the same. The filing rate for tax fraud was the highest (79 percent), followed by regulatory offenses (65 percent). The conviction rate for white collar defendants was 85 percent, compared to a rate of 78 percent for all other defendants in federal criminal cases. About 40 percent of white collar offenders convicted in 1985 were sentenced to incarceration, compared to 54 percent for nonwhite collar offenders. Finally, those convicted of white collar crimes received shorter average sentences of incarceration (29 months) than other federal offenders (50 months).

Based on Pretrial Services Agency interviews with federal defendants for 1984 and 1985, which did not reflect the substantial number of corporate defendants in white collar cases, those charged with white collar crimes differed in several respects from those charged with nonwhite collar offenses:

FIGURE 2.16    **Federal White Collar Crime Convictions, 1985**

| Offense | Convictions | |
|---|---|---|
| | Percent | Number |
| Fraud | 100% | 5,972 |
| Tax | 20 | 1,204 |
| Lending and credit | 9 | 540 |
| Wire and mail | 24 | 1,428 |
| Other[a] | 47 | 2,800 |
| Embezzlement | 100% | 1,753 |
| Bank | 48 | 842 |
| Government | 10 | 173 |
| U.S. Postal Service | 18 | 313 |
| Other[b] | 24 | 425 |
| Forgery | 100% | 2,014 |
| U.S. government documents | 79 | 1,594 |
| U.S. Postal Service | 8 | 152 |
| Securities | 13 | 254 |
| Other | 1 | 14 |
| Counterfeiting | 100% | 503 |
| White collar regulatory offenses | 100% | 491 |
| Import and export[c] | 26 | 127 |
| Antitrust | 23 | 114 |
| Transportation | 23 | 113 |
| Food and drug | 17 | 84 |
| Labor | 8 | 37 |
| Agriculture and agricultural materials | 3 | 16 |
| Total white collar convictions | 100% | 10,733 |

*Source:* U.S. Department of Justice, Office of Justice Programs, Bureau of Justice Statistics, Sept. 1987.
*Note:* Data include cases brought by U.S. Attorneys and the Criminal Division of the Department of Justice.
[a]Includes false claims and statements; government program fraud; fraud concerning bankruptcy, commodities, securities, passports, or citizenship; and conspiracy to defraud.
[b]Includes labor organizations, Indian tribal organizations, and other federally protected victims.
[c]Includes customs violations and export of restricted defense materials and information; does not include drug offenses.

*In general, defendants of all types were predominantly male, white, non-Hispanic, and younger than 40 and had not attended college [Figure 2.17]. White collar defendants, however, included higher proportions of women, nonwhites, and persons over 40 than did nonwhite collar defendants. White collar defendants were also less likely to be Hispanic, and they were more likely to have attended college (U.S. Justice Department, 1987: 7).*

More specifically, higher proportions of those charged with tax fraud (93 percent), lending and credit fraud (81 percent), counterfeiting (76 percent), and regulatory offenses (90 percent) were white than were other types of white collar and nonwhite collar defendants. Women represented 26 percent of those charged with white collar crimes overall. The highest proportions of those charged were for embezzlement (41 percent) and forgery (30 percent). Two-thirds of those arrested for tax fraud were

**FIGURE 2.17 Characteristics of Persons Arrested for Federal Crimes, 1984–1985**

| | Percent of Persons Arrested Who Were: | | | | | | | | | |
|---|---|---|---|---|---|---|---|---|---|---|
| | Sex | | Race | | Ethnicity | | Age | | Education | |
| Offense | Male | Female | White | Non-White | Hispanic | Non-Hispanic | 40 and Under | Over 40 | No College | Attended College |
| All offenses | 84% | 16% | 72% | 28% | 21% | 79% | 75% | 25% | 74% | 26% |
| White collar | 74% | 26% | 66% | 34% | 10% | 90% | 66% | 34% | 67% | 33% |
| Tax fraud | 88 | 12 | 93 | 7 | 2 | 98 | 33 | 67 | 56 | 44 |
| Lending and credit fraud | 82 | 18 | 81 | 19 | 5 | 95 | 60 | 40 | 51 | 49 |
| Wire fraud | 83 | 17 | 69 | 31 | 5 | 95 | 59 | 41 | 58 | 42 |
| Other fraud | 75 | 25 | 62 | 38 | 15 | 85 | 64 | 36 | 65 | 35 |
| Embezzlement | 59 | 41 | 68 | 32 | 10 | 90 | 74 | 26 | 60 | 40 |
| Forgery | 70 | 30 | 52 | 48 | 11 | 89 | 80 | 20 | 83 | 17 |
| Counterfeiting | 86 | 14 | 76 | 24 | 9 | 91 | 73 | 27 | 76 | 24 |
| Regulatory offenses | 92 | 8 | 90 | 10 | 11 | 89 | 50 | 50 | 65 | 35 |
| Nonwhite collar | 87% | 13% | 74% | 26% | 26% | 74% | 78% | 22% | 78% | 22% |

*Source:* U.S. Department of Justice, Office of Justice Programs, Bureau of Justice Statistics, Sept. 1987.
*Note:* Data describe 22,580 persons interviewed by the Pretrial Services Agency during calendar years 1984–85.

older than 40, compared to one-third of white collar crime defendants in general, and less than one-fourth of the defendants arrested for nonwhite collar offenses. Finally, those charged with forgery were less likely to have attended college than all other defendants interviewed. In contrast, those charged with tax fraud, lending and credit fraud, and embezzlement were substantially more likely to have attended college than were other types of defendants (U.S. Justice Department, 1987).

Among the most diversified white collar crimes are the well-organized businesses of counterfeit goods. Not only are there the "knockoffs" of well-known clothes and accessories as noted above, but there are the hundreds of thousands of bootleg tapes, CDs, and videos, and who knows how many thousands of copyright violations of books, magazines, and computer software. Most of these crimes by the public are part of the "hidden economy" (Henry, 1978) and are thought to be activities of a relatively harmless nature. In other words, although against the law, they are accepted in society because "everybody does it."

For example, for some tourists, "buying a counterfeit is as much a part of the New York experience as a trip to the Statue of Liberty" (Glave, 1994: 2D). Said one woman from Kokomo, Indiana, "I know it's not real," referring to a $11 fake Guess watch that she haggled a street vendor down from $13, "but it's from New York, you know, it's just the adventure of it all" (quoted in Glave, 1994: 2D). One man who had bought three Power Rangers T-shirts for his grandchildren while visiting New York, figured he wasn't hurting anyone, so why not buy them? After all, "these guys are just trying to make a living like the rest of us" (quoted in Glave, 1994: 2D).

Finally, the most recent, developing, and still emerging form of white collar criminality—computer crime—deserves a brief overview before turning to corporate and state crimes. Computer crime comes in several forms. Some consider today's cyberthief to be the equivalent of the Wild West's rustler of days long gone by. In the brave new world of *cybercrime*, probably among the fastest-growing wrongdoing in America, the bad guys are hard at work. Out there in the electronic ether, cruising the superhighway computer web known as the Internet, are the cybercriminals:

> *Lonely cybersickos are stalking women and kids via PC. Digital bandits are defrauding widows, running securities scams, purloining credit cards and hacking government and industrial secrets for fun or profit. Yet for all the horror stories, there's no reason for hysteria. Cybercrime isn't epidemic. It's just that our excitingly new virtual world, accessible with a few strokes at the keyboard, is coming to resemble the real world—with all its diversity and problems. The trouble is, there are few cops on the Net. Laws that bite here often lack teeth there. "It's the Wild West," says a spokeswoman for Prodigy, the burgeoning online information service. "No one owns it. It has no rules" (Meyer, 1995: 36).*

Because cybercrime is a new area of abuse, reflecting recent and not so recent developments in technology, the law has yet to catch up in order to take a "byte" out of computer crime. The laws, however, will come from interested parties exercising their rights in the legislative process and from test cases that are already starting to emerge. For example, in 1995, there was the charging in federal district court of Jake Baker, a University of Michigan sophomore who posted Internet messages graphically depicting the torture, rape, and slaying of a woman. Baker was charged with communicating threats via interstate commerce, a federal offense that carries a maximum penalty of five years in prison. This case will most likely wind its way up the judicial hierarchy as Baker's attorney, Douglas R. Mulikoff, maintained that his client was exercising his First Amendment right, that it was unclear as to whether or not cyberspace falls under the court's jurisdiction, and that the Internet story file Baker used was "in reality nothing more than words floating in space" (Bridgeforth, 1995: 7A). In his motion filed with the Sixth U.S. Circuit Court of Appeals to overturn a federal district judge's order denying Baker bail while he awaits trial, Mulikoff wrote: "Absent a showing of a tangible threat to another person, these words cannot form the basis of a legitimate prosecution" (Bridgeforth, 1995: 7A). The Sixth Circuit agreed and overturned the lower court.

At an Internet crime conference, set up through the University of Arkansas at Little Rock, that I attended in January, 1995, one of the papers presented was a study of the "Prevalence of Computer-related Abuse in Poland" by Andrzej Adamski. In March 1994, Adamski conducted the first computer-related abuse victimization survey in Poland, using a national sample of 115 computer companies. Among the findings, over three-fourths of all the companies surveyed reported that they had suffered from computer viruses. Illegal copying of computer programs was reported by 52 percent of the respondents, and time theft was reported by 45 percent.

Perhaps most interesting was the fact that the respondents to this survey were asked about acts that did not constitute criminal offenses at the time of the survey. But, as Adamski (1995: 2) reasoned, "some of them have been reported frequently enough to consider their penalization." In all, Adamski surveyed eight forms of abuse. These were unauthorized erasure of important data, damage to computer data or program by the virus, unauthorized access (hacking), unauthorized copying of a protected computer program, computer espionage, unauthorized use of a computer, computer fraud, and vandalism to a computer.

On February 15, 1995, Kevin Mitnick, America's most wanted computer hacker, or online pirate, was arrested for violating his probation and for new charges in computer fraud originating in North Carolina. (For an interesting portrayal of Mr. Mitnick, see Box 2.2.) Despite the relative harmlessness of most hackers as compared with other computer crimes, as the study by Adamski (1995) revealed, most respondents to his survey favored repressive sanctions for these violators and lenient sanctions for the more harmful violations committed by their professional associates. Such attitudes are reflective of the differential sentencing patterns accorded white collar and nonwhite collar offenders in general.

## Corporate and State Crime

Crimes of control or crimes of domination refer to those acts typically committed by powerful organizations or their agents and representatives. Unlike the crimes of survival and the crimes of the public, these acts are not generally perpetrated by isolated individuals against other individuals or their property, but are rather the product of group activities engaged in on behalf of the direct or indirect accumulation of capital. These abuses of power can take a variety of forms including but not limited to the following: antitrust violations, work-related illnesses and deaths, environmental pollution, consumer fraud, restraint of trade, bribes and kickbacks, false and questionable advertising, organized crime and corruption, crimes of law enforcement, crimes of governmental officials and their agents, crimes of the military, and crimes against humanity (Barak, 1991; Ermann and Lundman, 1992; Henderson and Simon, 1993; Michalowski, 1985; Tunnell, 1993).

The victims of these crimes are consumers, workers, and the general public. Although these crimes are commonplace, both domestically and globally, and account for the largest proportion of economic and human losses each year (Cohen, 1993; Reiman, 1995), there are virtually no official or unofficial sources that one can turn to for any accurate statistical information on the injuries inflicted. This situation results, at least in part, from what criminologist Stanley Cohen (1993) refers to as the "culture of denial" that revolves around normal business and normal politics. For example, "when pressed about his company's payment of bribes to Italian political parties in the'80s, the chairman of Olivetti made the [revealing] confession that he personally authorized the payment of bribes and added that he would do it again to protect his company's interests" (Haas, 1994: 507).

## BOX 2.2    High-Tech Search Nabs Most-Wanted Hacker

by John Johnson and Ronald J. Ostrow

WASHINGTON—Kevin Mitnick, America's most wanted computer hacker who evaded authorities in narrow escapes in Los Angeles and Seattle over the past two years, was captured Wednesday morning at his apartment in Raleigh, N.C.

Although authorities were unable to estimate how much damage he wreaked during his years on the run, the cellular telecommunications industry alleges that Mitnick, who used cellular phones to illegally access computers, cost it $1 million a day.

To nab the man who used the code name "Condor," the government brought in an expert from a firm he is suspected of penetrating last Christmas.

"We got him," Tsutomu Shimomura of the San Diego Supercomputer Center said Wednesday morning after the capture, according to Sid Karin, Shimomura's boss.

Mitnick, who grew up in Los Angeles, was arraigned Wednesday on charges of violating the terms of his probation for a 1988 California computer hacking conviction, as well as new charges of computer fraud originating in North Carolina. Assistant U.S. Attorney David Schindler in Los Angeles said the government is looking into additional cases in San Diego, Seattle and Colorado.

"We were up half the night tracking this guy down," said Assistant U.S. Attorney John Bowler in Charlotte, N.C.

The raid was carried out at 1:30 A.M. on an apartment in which Mitnick, 31, was living alone under a false name, authorities said. It ended what the U.S. Department of Justice characterized as an "intensive two-week electronic manhunt."

"His obsession was his downfall," said Deputy U.S. Marshal Kathy Cunningham in Los Angeles. "His obsession to hack using cloned (cellular) phones left us a trail to follow."

The arrest apparently brings an end to the career of a man whose computer escapades began in high school, where he learned to break into the Los Angeles Unified School District's main computers. Eventually, he was able to break into a North American Air Defense Command computer in Colorado Springs, Colo., several years

before the showing of the movie "War Games," about a hacker who nearly starts a war after entering a government computer.

Mitnick also manipulated the telephone system to pull pranks on friends and enemies, authorities said. He disconnected service to Hollywood stars he admired, and a former probation officer said her phone service was terminated just as she was about to revoke his probation.

"He's an electronic terrorist," said a onetime friend who turned him in to authorities in 1988.

Mitnick served a year in prison and was placed on probation. He fled in late 1992, after the FBI showed up at the Calabasas, Calif., private investigations' firm where he was working. The agents were investigating break-ins to Pacific Bell computers.

The California Department of Motor Vehicles also has issued a $1 million warrant for him, accusing him of posing as a law enforcement officer to obtain sensitive DMV information, including driver's licenses and photographs.

The threat that Mitnick posed was described in a recent circular distributed by federal authorities pursuing the fugitive.

"Please be aware that if Mitnick is taken into custody, he possesses an amazing ability to disrupt one's personal life through his computer knowledge," said an advisory from the U.S. Marshal's Service.

On Christmas Day, the San Diego Supercomputer Center, a national laboratory for computer science, was attacked by a hacker using unusually sophisticated techniques.

After the break-ins Shimomura, known as one of the nation's leading specialists in computer security, joined the effort to capture the Condor, who took his nickname from a movie starring Robert Redford as a man on the run from the government.

The Department of Justice cited Shimomura as having offered "significant assistance" in capturing Mitnick, but authorities refused to say exactly what led them to the hacker.

The culture of denial "is not a matter of secrecy, in the sense of lack of access to information, but an unwillingness to confront anomalous or disturbing information" that is simply too distressing to the average person's sense of well-being and reality (Cohen, 1993: 102). Even when people, business and nonbusiness, are willing to confront the practices of corporate wrongdoing, they often acknowledge that the creation of a business culture that promotes ethical behavior is a daily struggle. As Robert D. Haas, Chairman of the Board and Chief Executive Officer of Levi Strauss & Company, put it: "While price fixing conspiracies, bribery, fraud and business collusion are not the norm of contemporary business practice, they occur far more frequently than we care to acknowledge—and clearly more often than is permissible to gain the level of public trust and support that business requires to thrive" (Haas, 1994: 506).

Raymond Michalowski (1985: 324) has defined corporate crimes as those "actions that are either prohibited by law or that knowingly lead to social injury, taken by official representatives of legitimate businesses to facilitate capital accumulation within those businesses." Specifically, these acts seek either to reduce the costs of production or to increase illegally the price or volume of the goods or services marketed:

> *Production costs can be illegally reduced by such actions as failing to make costly changes in known hazardous products, avoiding expenses associated with protecting worker safety or meeting environmental protection requirements, or illegally repressing the organization of labor into effective unions. Price and volume maximization is facilitated through such actions as obtaining monopoly positions in the marketplace, fraudulent or questionable advertising, bribes for favorable contracts offered to governmental or other purchasing agents, or price fixing (Michalowski, 1985: 324).*

Over the past half-century some of the more infamous cases have included the General Electric and Westinghouse conspiracy to fix prices and rig bids (McCaghy, 1976); A. H. Robins Company marketing of the Dalkon Shield, an intrauterine device to prevent pregnancy, that resulted in the deaths of at least seventeen American women and the sterilization of thousands of other women (Dowie and Johnston, 1978); the sale and distribution of the defective gas tank of the Ford Pinto that resulted in the deaths of hundreds of people involved in rear-end collisions (Dowie, 1979); Dow Chemical's marketing of DBCP (a soil fumigant) that resulted in approximately 3,000 of its male workers becoming sterile (Castleman, 1979); E. F. Hutton and Company's pleading in 1985 to defrauding some 400 banks by writing checks in excess of amounts it had on hand by moving funds between banks, and the subsequent pleading of guilt by E. F. Hutton in 1988 to two felony counts for laundering hundreds of thousands of dollars for criminal syndicate figures and respectable business figures alike (Beirne and Messerschmidt, 1991). These and other examples, such as the *Exxon Valdez* oil spill, the Savings and Loan debacle, and the BCCI scandal of the late 1980s are exceptional because they resulted in either successful prosecutions or public exposures (Clinard, 1990; Mokhiber, 1988).

These corporate crimes have not stopped, of course. In the early 1990s it was still business as usual as the following examples illustrate:

Dead sea otters found on the beach at Green Island in the Prince William Sound following the *Exxon Valdez* oil spill, 1989.

- Ontario Air Parts, Inc. and its president and general manager pleaded guilty last week to selling unapproved parts for the General Electric CJ-610 engine used in early Learjets and other aircraft (Dornheim, 1994: 61).
- Executives of American Honda are criminally indicted by Federal prosecutors for accepting bribes from dealers in exchange for franchises and hot-selling cars. Thirteen executives face potential prison terms that total 165 years behind bars;
- Corruption and mismanagement cause Gitano Jeans to lose its largest retail customer. The company's fortunes collapse. It's forced to file for bankruptcy and is ultimately sold;
- Prudential Securities is sued by its investors who allege it inappropriately sold limited partnerships. The scandal costs hundreds of millions of dollars, and the inquiry into possible corporate misdeeds extends into the company's most senior ranks;
- National Medical Enterprises agrees to pay more than $300 million to settle charges of health insurance fraud and patient abuse (Haas, 1994: 506).

State crime refers to both political acts and political omissions. Examples of the former involve illegal surveillance, harassment, and imprisonment; violations of the First and Fourth Amendments; drug and arms trafficking; air piracy; terrorism; and other abuses of state power. Examples of the latter involve public and private policies that result in the victimization of people through the denial of basic needs such as food, clothing, and shelter (Barak, 1991).

These state crimes and others may be conducted for personal gain, but they are generally engaged in on behalf of the prevailing political and economic arrangements. As Michalowski (1985: 379) has maintained, these illegal or socially injurious acts are usually "committed through the usage or manipulation of political power" and are "designed to facilitate the acquisition or maintenance of political power." Moreover, these acts not only rob citizens of effective representation, law enforcement, and public-policy formation, but they also create public cynicism and disillusionment with the government. In turn, the average person retreats from a concern with public affairs, thus enabling corrupt public officials and agents to pursue their nefarious schemes and manipulations.

During the last quarter of the twentieth century, the most sensational and notorious political cover-ups involving the Office of the U.S. presidency have been Watergate, Iran/Contragate, and Iraqgate. Only Watergate, the most innocuous of the three "gates" resulted in any significant revelations or punishments. The other two outcomes were more typical of the cases involving corporate and state wrongdoing. Whether the cases have involved crimes by the police (Armao and Cornfield, 1994), crimes by the presidents and their men, or crimes by businesses in collusion with the U.S. government (see Box 2.3), rarely does anything of criminal consequence occur to these wrongdoers.

Although the records of criminal prosecutions of corporations and executives have increased somewhat at the state level thanks to the creation, for example, of environmental and occupational crime divisions in the state attorneys' general offices of such states as Maryland, California, New York, and New Jersey, at the federal level the record is very poor. In the 1980s, the Justice Department "brought only 44 cases to criminal court and succeeded in producing only three prison sentences" (Barrile, 1992: 3). Moreover, during the entire history of the Occupational Health and Safety Act (OSHA), no one, not one corporate agent, has ever been imprisoned for violating laws that have resulted in the deaths of workers (Barrile, 1993).

Even when the states have tried to act responsibly in such cases as the Film Recovery Systems case in Illinois or the Warner-Lambert chewing gum company case in New York, the appellate courts have intervened so as not to treat corporations and their executives as criminals (Barrile, 1993). In the 1985 Film Recovery case, a landmark in which the first criminal prosecution of a corporation's managers for homicide had succeeded, the Illinois appellate court reversed the trial court's verdict to involuntary manslaughter in the death of one of its workers, Stefan Golab, who had succumbed to cyanide fumes. Similarly, in 1980 when a lower court had indicted Warner-Lambert and four of its agents for negligent homicide and involuntary manslaughter for the deaths of six workers and the injuries of forty-four others, the New York court of appeals reversed the indictments on the grounds that the law itself was unclear (Barille, 1993).

As Barille (1993: 4) has concluded, "The justice department, federal regulatory agencies, and the vast majority of courts would rather exhaust every possible noncriminal strategy against corporate [and state] misbehavior before turning to the criminal justice system." Only when acts of tragic proportion occur, involving such incidents as the Savings and Loan scandal, the Bhopal (India) disaster, or the Alaskan oil spill, does the justice department move into action. And even then, these cases have tended to be ones of negotiation rather than ones of adjudication (Barille, 1993).

## BOX 2.3   Dirty Justice

*Will Clinton clean up the mess
in a department still plagued
by scandal and corruption?*

Alarmed by reports from confidential sources that critical government documents were disappearing into Department of Justice (DOJ) paper shredders, we released our exposé, "Shredded Justice," five weeks before our Jan./Feb. issue hit the streets.

We also sought the help of attorneys at the Government Accountability Project (GAP), who filed on our behalf a formal request that the archivist of the United States fulfill his statutory responsibility to protect government documents.

Finally, we alerted the Clinton transition team to the shredding. They asked Amy Rudnick, a Washington attorney and former Treasury employee, to look into the matter. But when we tried to contact her, we learned that she was on vacation in Florida for the holidays.

After New Year's, we finally reached her and asked how the investigation was going. She couldn't say. "Steve, I used to work at Treasury, and even there I wasn't under the kind of confidentiality requirements we are under on this transition team," Rudnick said. "We can't say anything about anything." When we spoke with another Democratic National Committee official, he told us that Rudnick had mentioned that she'd been in contact with "someone from *Mother Goose* magazine."

We'd gotten a quicker, if not more acceptable, response from Acting Archivist Claudine Weiher. On November 20, the same day we filed our request, we were notified by Weiher that her office "today forwarded your concern to the Attorney General . . . requesting that he initiate an inquiry into the allegations."

So, the archivist had sent the fox our report on missing chickens. By law, then-Attorney General William Barr had little choice but to forward the allegations to the Office of the Inspector General of the Justice Department.

But before the IG could investigate, Barr stripped them of the authority to investigate "allegations relating to entire offices of employees—including secretaries, paralegals, and administrative personnel."

He needn't have bothered. Although IG Special Agent Dwight Colley, who met with us on January 8, refused to discuss details of the ongoing investigation, a source close to the IG's office told us that the investigators had already reached the following conclusions:

Yes, they confirmed, there had been "an enormous amount of shredding" in the days following the November election. But DOJ Head of Security Jerry Rubino, whom we'd identified in our piece as the individual responsible, provided the investigators with a list of what he claimed was shredded and an explanation that they accepted: he had been conducting a long overdue cleaning of his untidy office.

Same song, second verse. At the White House, officials were trying to conduct their own housecleaning. Around the time we released our shredding allegations, the Bush administration announced that they would purge the executive branch computer systems of all electronic files before turning the keys over to the Clinton people.

They should have known better. In 1989, the Bush White House had tried to erase all of the Reagan administration's electronic documents, but they were taken to court by the National Security Archive, a public-interest group that collects declassified government documents. Although the Bush administration eventually agreed to preserve the Reagan records, they did not agree to preserve their own, and near the end of 1992, they informed the court of their plan to wipe the slate clean.

In defending the White House position, the Justice Department claimed that its intentions were purely cordial—after all, if the Bush administration did not remove their material, the Clinton team would not have enough room for their own files.

Federal Judge Charles Richey laughed off the White House's argument, comparing their plan to burning the furniture of an old tenant to make room for a new one. Instead of destroying the records, he said, the White House must do what everyone else who has a computer does— make backup tapes.

It's understandable that the White House would be eager to convert their computer files back into random electrons. Those files contain a

**BOX 2.3**    *Continued*

virtually unedited version of the Reagan/Bush years, including internal memos, drafts of position papers, and executive branch E-mail. They represent not only a valuable adjunct to the documents, positions, and policies released for public consumption, but also a window into the thoughts and rationalizations of the key players in the administration.

The files may also contain the "smoking guns" sought by those investigating the Iran/Contra, BCCI, and Iraqgate scandals.

But the fate and integrity of those files remain in doubt. In the waning days of the Bush administration, Attorney General Barr appointed independent counsel Joseph diGenova to investigate allegations that the White House had been involved in the illegal search of Bill Clinton's passport files.

During the hoopla surrounding Clinton's inauguration, diGenova quietly seized the electronic files. He not only took the tape backups, but also snatched the hard drives from some of the machines the Clinton people were to be using, leaving behind a note saying the disks had been seized "pursuant to this subpoena."

If diGenova grabbed the tapes to get to the bottom of the passport investigation, then all's well. But just in case, the Clinton DOJ should demand that certified copies of the tapes and the material on those disks be delivered to them immediately.

What was Bill thinking? If President Clinton hopes to get to the bottom of a decade's worth of scandals and to confront corruption in his own administration, he needs a Justice Department with a squeaky-clean leader and a serious concern for all injustice and crime—whether committed in the streets or in the suites. With jurisdiction over criminal, civil, anti-trust, environmental, and civil rights laws, the DOJ is central to any president's agenda.

So Clinton's choice of corporate hired gun Zoë Baird for attorney general was truly inexplicable. Reams have been written about the illegal alien scandal that kept her from getting confirmed, but less attention has been focused on her professional life, which alone should have kept her from being considered for the job.

From 1986 to 1990 Baird was the number-two person in the General Electric Corporation's general counsel office. During that time GE ran afoul of the law many times. In his 1992 book, *Who Will Tell the People*, William Greider catalogs the recent criminal and civil record of Baird's former employer:

- cheating the army on a $254 million contract for battlefield computers (GE paid $16.1 million in fines);
- allegedly altering 9,000 daily labor vouchers to inflate its Pentagon billings on jet engines (GE paid a $3.5 million settlement);
- attempting to pay a $1.25 million bribe to a Puerto Rican official for a $92 million power plant contract (three GE executives went to prison);
- defrauding the air force on a Minuteman intercontinental missile contract ($1 million in fines);
- allegedly selling nuclear reactor parts known to be defective (GE agreed to a sealed settlement: amount unknown);
- discriminating against women and minorities ($32 million settlement);
- allegedly, overcharging the army for battle tank parts ($900,000 settlement); and
- bearing responsibility for no fewer than forty-seven of the EPA's Superfund toxic cleanup sites.

Much of GE's legal trouble was the result of information made public by whistle-blowers within the company.

Instead of supporting these people, Baird gained a well-deserved reputation as a foe of anyone who bucked the corporation. In 1989, she lobbied to weaken the False Claims Act, which gives protection to corporate whistle-blowers. She also designed a "self-compliance" program requiring GE employees who suspected fraud to report their suspicions immediately or become liable for the fraud themselves.

The program was a public relations coup for GE, but according to Scott Armstrong of Taxpayers Against Fraud, a public-interest group

**BOX 2.3    *Continued***

supporting corporate whistle-blowers, it actually discouraged employees from reporting corruption. "If an employee suspects their superiors of fraud," Armstrong said, "most are going to wait a while to be absolutely certain. But by the time they are certain, some time has passed since they first suspected the fraud, now making them liable as well."

Furthermore, Armstrong claimed, GE has never rewarded a company whistle-blower.

In any case, Baird's work at GE didn't change their corporate tendency toward corruption. After she left, the company was again caught running with wolves and had to cough up $69 million to settle government fraud charges for false billings made during Baird's tenure.

Perhaps Scott Armstrong came closest to giving voice to the uneasiness that many felt about Baird's nomination. "Look, I'm not saying that a GE or anyone else accused of a crime does not deserve good legal representation," Armstrong said. "That's not the point. The point is that mobster John Gotti's lawyer might be an eth-ical person and a good lawyer, but you certainly would not appoint John Gotti's lawyer head of the Criminal Division of the Department of Justice, would you?"

During his campaign, Bill Clinton's stump speech had a sound bite that always drew applause: "We are going to return Washington to the people in this country who work hard and play by the rules."

What were Clinton and his advisers thinking when they selected Baird? In our last issue, we warned that Clinton might be tempted by the idea of a politicized Justice Department answerable only to him. Insofar as the Baird nomination was indicative of the president's leanings, the omens are not good.

Now that a chastened Clinton is settled in the Oval Office, maybe he should put up a sign that says, "The Principles, Stupid!"

Reprinted with permission from *Mother Jones* magazine, © 1993, Foundation for National Progress.

## *Summary and Conclusions: Our Criminal Society*

In 1969, Edwin Schur, the sociologist and lawyer, published one of his many books entitled *Our Criminal Society: The Social and Legal Sources of Crime in America.* In this book, Schur advanced a number of arguments, including that crime was not only normal in American society, but that it was ubiquitous. In other words, crime could be found anywhere and everywhere in the United States. Nobody had a monopoly on crime in this country. It was neither confined to the urban streets nor to the executive suites. Most of all, crime was not simply a matter of good people versus bad people, but more fundamentally it had to do with the way in which this society had organized its political, economic, and social resources.

Some thirty years later, as this chapter has revealed, we are still living in a criminal society. Only today, we identify many more forms and expressions of criminality than we did then. For example, criminologists and noncriminologists alike recognize a whole new range of antisocial behaviors as we have seen, including domestic violence, crimes of the hidden (or underground) economy, corporate and state crime, and crimes of the criminal justice system. In short, the criminal dangers and the social harms confronting us at the turn of the twenty-first century come not only from those who have been traditionally dominated, the working and underclasses, and from those who have traditionally dominated society, the elite and corporate classes, but they also come from the various groups of professional and nonprofessional classes that constitute everybody else in society.

In response to the question posed at the beginning of the chapter, "Is crime rising or declining?" my answer is that it depends. In general, most Part I offenses have leveled off or declined since 1990. As for Part II offenses, the dark, hidden, or unknown figures of crime are more pronounced than they are for Part I offenses. So it is extremely difficult to say whether these crimes are growing or diminishing in number. Of course, even less can be concluded about the magnitude of corporate and state crimes and the direction in which they are moving.

Having provided a comparative discussion on crime, measurement, and trends in victimization in this chapter, Chapter 3 presents an overview of the historical development of crime and punishment from before the rise of the modern era in Europe until the contemporary period in America. This depiction of the changing practices of penology is meant to provide a more detailed picture of the language and discourse of punishment as it has changed and remained the same over time. As the next chapter reveals, the story of "crime and punishment" has more to do with rationales and justifications for punishment and the status quo than it does with either crime or changing the individual and the environment.

## Discussion Questions

1. Out of the ten definitions of crime discussed in Chapter 1 and elaborated on in the comparative discussion throughout this chapter, which two do you believe are the best and worst definitions? Using historical or contemporary examples of crime to support your answer, explain why.

2. Using any crime data collection source, profile the typical offender and victim for two property offenses and for two person offenses. Are there any similarities between these offenders and victims? If so, what are they?

3. Compare the pros and cons of using the four basic sources of crime data collection: police reports, victim surveys, self-reports, and archival research.

4. Comparatively speaking, has violent crime increased or decreased over the past one hundred years? How would you arrive at this answer? What acts of violence would you consider as being the best indicators? What data sources would you consult?

## References

Adamski, Andrzej. 1995. "Prevalence of Computer-related Abuse in Poland: Preliminary Findings of Victimization Survey." Internet Conference, University of Arkansas at Little Rock (January): 1–15.

Armao, Joseph P., and Leslie A. Cornfeld. 1994. "How to Police the Police." *Newsweek*. (December 19): 34.

Bachman, Ronet. 1994a. "Violence against Women." U.S. Department of Justice Document. *OJP-BJS* (January): 1–14.

———. 1994b. "Violence and Theft in the Workplace." U.S. Department of Justice Document. *OJP-BJS* (July): 1–2.

Barak, Gregg, ed. 1991. *Crimes by the Capitalist State: An Introduction to State Criminality*. Albany, NY: SUNY Press.

———. ed. 1994. *Media, Process, and the Social Construction of Crime: Studies in Newsmaking Criminology*. New York: Garland Publishing Company.

Barrille, Leo G. 1992. "Has the Corporate Veil Really Been Pierced?" *The Critical Criminologist* 4(2, Summer): 3–4.

Beirne, Piers, and James Messerschmidt. 1991. *Criminology*. San Diego: Harcourt Brace Jovanovich.

Black, Henry Campbell. 1983. *Black's Law Dictionary: Definitions of the Terms and Phrases of American and English Jurisprudence, Ancient and Modern.* St. Paul, MN: West Publishing.

Bohm, Robert M., and Keith N. Haley. 1996. *Introduction to Criminal Justice.* New York: Glencoe/McGraw-Hill.

Bridgeworth, Arthur Jr. 1995. "Fantasy writer pleads not guilty to threat charge." *Ann Arbor News* (February 18): A1, A3.

Butterfield, Fox. 1997. "Serious Crime Decreased for Fifth Year in a Row." *The New York Times* (January 5): A8.

———. 1994. "A History of Homicide Surprises the Experts: Decline in U.S. Before Recent Increase." *The New York Times* (October 23): C1, C7–8.

Castleman, Barry. 1979. "The Export of Hazardous Factories to Developing Nations." *International Journal of Health Services* 9(4): 569–606.

Clinard, Marshall B. 1990. *Corporate Corruption: The Abuse of Power.* New York: Praeger.

Cohen, Stanley. 1993. "Human Rights and Crimes of the State: The Culture of Denial." *Australian and New Zealand Journal of Criminology* 26(July): 97–115.

Dawson, John M., and Patrick A. Langan. 1994. "Murder in Families." U.S. Department of Justice Document. *OJP-BJS* (July): 1–13.

Dictionary of Criminal Justice Data Terminology. 1981. 2nd Ed, *Bureau of Justice Statistics*, NCJ-76939.

Dornheim, Michael A. 1994. "California Firm Admits Selling Unapproved CJ-610 Parts." *Aviation Weekly & Space Technology* (May 16): 61.

Dowie, Mark. 1979. "Pinto Madness." In *Crisis in American Institutions*, 4th ed., by Jerome Skolnick and Elliott Currie, eds. Boston: Little, Brown and Company.

Dowie, Mark, and Tracy Johnston. 1978. "A Case of Corporate Malpractice and the Dalkon Shield." In Claudia Dreifus, ed. *Seizing Our Bodies: The Politics of Women's Health.* New York: Vintage Books.

Edmonds, Patricia. 1994. "Maltreatment, neglect cases overwhelming." *USA Today* (April 7): A1.

Ermann, David M., and Richard J. Lundman, eds. 1992. *Corporate and Governmental Deviance: Problems of Organizational Behavior in Contemporary Society.* 4th ed. New York: Oxford University Press.

Felson, Marcus. 1994. *Crime and Everyday Life: Insights and Implications for Society.* Thousand Oaks, CA: Pine Forge Press.

Fingerhut, L. A., and J. C. Kleinman. 1990. "Firearm Mortality among Children and Youth. Advance data from *Vital and Health Statistics, No. 178.*

Gabor, Thomas. 1994. *Everybody Does It: Crime by the Public.* Toronto: University of Toronto Press.

Glave, Judie. 1994. "Counterfeit goods: It's a Booming, well-organized business." *The Ann Arbor News.* Sept 2.

Haas, Robert D. 1994. "Ethics—A Global Business Challenge." *Vital Speeches of the Day.* U.S. Government Printing Office (June).

Hagan, John. 1994. *Crime and Disrepute.* Thousand Oaks, CA: Pine Forge Press.

Hallinan, Joe, and Elizabeth A. Marchak. 1994. "Smaller cities more perilous for women." *Ann Arbor News* (February 13): A1 and A13.

Hawkins, Darnel. 1986. *Homicide among Black Americans.* Lanham, MD: University Press of America.

Hay, Douglas. 1975. "Property, Authority and the Criminal Law." In *Albion's Fatal Tree*, by Douglas Hay, Peter Linebaugh, John G. Rule, E. P. Thompson, and Cal Winslow. New York: Pantheon.

Henderson, Joel, and David R. Simon. 1993. *Crimes of the Criminal Justice System.* Cincinnati, OH: Anderson Publishing Company.

Henry, Stuart. 1978. *The Hidden Economy: The Context and Control of Borderline Crime.* Oxford: Martin Robertson.

Leary, Warren. 1994. "Child-Neglect Deaths Found Highest in Southand West." *The New York Times* (February 6): B3.

McCaghy, Charles H. 1976. *Deviant Behavior: Crime, Conflict, and Interest Groups.* New York: MacMillan Publishing Company.

Messner, Steven F., and Richard Rosenfeld. 1993. *Crime and the American Dream.* Belmont, CA: Wadsworth Publishing Company.

Meyer, Michael. 1995. "Stop! Cyberthief!" *Newsweek* (February 6): 36–38.

Michalowski, Raymond J. 1985. *Order, Law, and Crime: An Introduction to Criminology.* New York: Random House.

Mokhiber, Russell. 1988. *Corporate Crime and Violence: Big Business Power and the Abuse of the Public Trust.* San Francisco: Sierra Club Books.

Monkkonen, Eric. 1993. "Racial Factors in New York City Homicides, 1800–1874." Unpublished paper, University of California at Los Angeles.

Moore, Molly. 1995. "Fighting Sexual Criminals: India takes steps as assaults rise." *Ann Arbor News* (February 16): A10.

*New Webster's Dictionary of the English Language.* 1985. Deluxe Encyclopedia Edition. Delair Publishing Company.

Quinney, Richard. 1977. *Class, State, and Crime.* New York: David McKay Company.

Reiman, Jeffrey. 1995. *The Rich Get Richer and the Poor Get Prison: Ideology, Class, and Criminal Justice.* 4th ed. Boston: Allyn and Bacon.

Reiss, Albert, and Jeffrey Ross. 1993. *Understanding and Preventing Violence.* Washington, D.C.: National Academy Press.

Rose, H., and P. McClain. 1990. *Race, Place and Risk: Black Homicide in Urban America.* Albany, NY: SUNY Press.

Salmi, Jamil. 1993. *Violence and Democratic Society.* London: Zed Books.

Schur, Edwin. 1969. *Our Criminal Society: The Social and Legal Sources of Crime in America.* Englewood Cliffs, NJ: Prentice-Hall.

Skorneck, Carolyn. 1994. "Crime rate falling, but homicides increase." *Ann Arbor News* (December 4):A1.

Stannard, David E. 1992. "Genocide in The Americas: Columbus's Legacy." *The Nation* (October 19): 430–434.

Sutherland, Edwin H., and Donald R. Cressey. 1974. *Criminology.* 9th ed. Philadelphia: J. B. Lippincott.

The Associated Press. 1994a. "Violent crime touches more American lives." *Ann Arbor News* (December 12): A1.

———. 1994b. "As Cities Reach Record Numbers of Killings, Youths Play Grim Role." *The New York Times* (January 1): A3.

Touby, Laurel. 1994. "In the Company of Thieves." *Journal of Business Strategy* (May/June): 24–29.

Tunnell, Kenneth, ed. 1993. *Political Crime in Contemporary America: A Critical Approach.* New York: Garland Publishing.

Turner, Dana L., and Richard G. Stephenson. 1993. "The Lure of White-Collar Crime." *Security Management* (February): 57–58.

U.S. Department of Justice. 1987. "White Collar Crime." *Office of Justice Program Reports. BJS* (Sept.)

———. 1993. "Criminal Victimization: 1992." *A National Crime Victimization Survey Report. NCVS* (110, February).

———. 1994. "Violent Crime." *Office of Justice Programs Report. BJS* (July).

Woodman, Sue. 1992. "Easy Money." *Redbook* (December): 86–89, 112–113.

*C h a p t e r* *3*

# Punishment and Criminology: A Historical Perspective

"The Rock" (Alcatraz) in San Francisco Bay, California.

Placed into historical perspective, the relationship between punishment and criminology is an ambivalent one. At certain times, during particular eras, the relationship between the two seems strong. That is to say, the form or mode of punishment seems consistent with, dependent on, or follows from the specific criminological explanations of crime. At other times, there appears to be no relationship, direct or indirect, between the theories of criminal behavior and the rationales of punishment. In the final analysis, punishment has always been to varying degrees and at different time periods part and parcel of the larger institutional relations involving social structure, culture, labor markets, discipline, and gender.

In the contemporary era of postmodern criminal justice, emphases have moved away from both the individualized and rationalized retribution/deterrence models of classical criminology and the preventive and reintegrative rehabilitative intervention models of positivist criminology. In their place have emerged models of *administrative* criminology based on social utility analysis or actuarial thinking. The older system of criminal punishment, dependent on the modern principles of individual, equal, and public justice, has given way to a newer system of criminal classification, dependent on formal systems, operations research, risk management, and dangerousness. Individual liberty or social justice, if they still matter in postmodern society, do so in the context of a new actuarial criminology. So the primary objective of *actuarial justice* is to reduce the effects of crime not by altering the offender or the social context, but, instead, by rearranging the distribution of offenders in society (Feeley and Simon, 1994).

Historically, regardless of the prevailing relations between punishment and criminology, critics from Jeremy Bentham in the late eighteenth century to David J. Rothman in the late twentieth century have often talked as much about *the crime of punishment* as *the punishment of crime.* After defining punishment, the rest of this chapter, through a five-prong overview, presents the irresolute historical relationship of punishment and criminology: First, I will start with a discussion of the ideology and rationale of punishment. Second, I will reveal that the contemporary state in American punishment (corrections) is in a crisis involving overly determined flat sentencing and overly criminalized drug policy. Third, I will explore the changing explanations for the development of punishment during the premodern, modern, and postmodern periods. Fourth, I will follow with a depiction of the practices of selective enforcement and differential application of the penal law in relation to social status. Fifth, in my summary and conclusion, I will discuss the rhetoric of rights and the "old" penology and the rhetoric of danger and the "new" penology (Feeley and Simon, 1992).

For the purposes of this chapter, punishment in the narrow legal sense refers to any type of criminal sanction applied to those people who have transgressed against the state's rules of order. Punishments usually allude to some kind of loss or deprivation, typically involving a fine or confinement, but they may also embrace death, forced labor, training, treatment, rehabilitation, surveillance, monitoring, or reintegration. Imposing a punishment or the criminal sanction for an adjudicated offense is the state's retaliation against those who threaten its legal or political order. "That sanction, including its administration, is the state's final step in preserving order" (Quinney, 1975: 225). Punishment in the broad social sense transcends the law, criminal or otherwise, and incorporates an array of controls whose sites may be found throughout the larger body politic. Imposing "punishments" in the social realm is the way communities (or cultures) sanction those who threaten their orders of privilege and inequality, serving to preserve social order in the first place.

By bringing the insights of Michel Foucault (1977), David Garland (1990), and Adrian Howe (1994) to this discussion of punishment, we expand the notion of punishment to include not only the penal apparatus, which expresses and affects a whole web of social relations and cultural meanings, but also the specific moral effects of punishment, the power–knowledge mechanisms within the broader strategies of domination and discipline, and the poststructuralist studies of the disciplining of women's bodies. In the broader integrative sense, these analyses help us to understand how the study of punishment needs to blend those views of penality that focus on mechanisms of power and control with those views that focus on moral values and sensibilities.

## Ideology and the Rationale of Punishment

In order to make sense out of the world in general or out of punishment in particular, we need to consult both theories and ideologies. Together, theory and ideology not only influence our views of crime, but they also form the basis for the rationales used to justify punishment. The concern of this chapter as a whole is with the meaning (or lack of meaning) of punishment. For the most part, it addresses the historical importance of ideology in shoring up the rationales for punishment. Although questions of human nature and explanations of crime and criminal behavior will be examined in detail elsewhere in this book (Part II: Criminological Theory), it is worth noting briefly that theories of human nature, if not actually at least allegedly (at times), underpin the justifications of punishment. In other words, it is often stated that the nature of the response to crime is a reflection of "some theory or set of theories about *why* people commit crimes" (Durham, 1994: 16). Traditionally, it has been believed that punishment as a social institution (or penality) has changed in relationship to the prevailing beliefs about humankind in general and about criminals in particular.

For example, the eighteenth-century classical schools of criminology, founded on the utilitarian beliefs of *free will* and the capacity for *rational thought*, viewed crime as the outcome of citizens concluding that the benefits of committing a crime outweigh the risks of significant punishment. The consequence of such criminological thinking called for the imposing of sanctions of sufficient severity to deter real and potential offenders. By contrast, the nineteenth-century positivist schools of criminology, founded on the beliefs of *determinism* and *environmentalism*, viewed crime as the outcome of citizens driven to action by debilitating conditions, individual or social. The consequence of this kind of criminological thinking called for therapy, education, job training, the reform or rearrangement of socioeconomic conditions, and other measures of social intervention.

At the close of the twentieth century, postmodern and modern schools of criminology alike suggest, in contrast to the free-will and determinist theories of the past, that "the methods of modern punishment are neither obvious nor self-evident rational" (Garland, 1990: 5). On the contrary, these methods stand in serious need of explication:

*Their "fit" with the social world and their grounding in the natural order of things begin to appear less and less convincing. It used to be that most criticism of punishment's failures and irrationalities was aimed at the past or at the soon-to-disappear present. Each critique was also, in its hope for penal reform, a kind of hymn to the future. Nowadays, punishment appears to lack a future—or at least a vision of one—which might be different and preferable to that which currently prevails (Garland, 1990: 5).*

Whether one classifies or organizes the world of punishment according to classical, positivist, Durkheimian, Marxian, Foucaultian, feminist, or postmodernist theory or ideology, there are five main rationales that societies have often used to justify punishment. Although not mutually exclusive, these rationales include revenge, retribution, deterrence, incapacitation, and rehabilitation. These rationales for punishment have been distinguished between those that are backward-looking and those that are forward-looking.

The former rationales, such as revenge and retribution, are concerned primarily with *morally* proper responses to offenses committed. These forms of punishment are past oriented in that the nature of the response is tied to the character of the offense perpetrated and not the perpetrator of the offense. The latter rationales, such as deterrence, incapacitation, and rehabilitation, are concerned with the *utilitarian* consequences of punishment on future criminality. Whether focused on the offender or on the general population of potential offenders, these forward-looking rationales view punishment as a means to minimize the likelihood of future crimes. Here it is the character of the offender rather than the character of the offense that matters (Durham, 1994).

As I provide a brief characterization of the five rationales of punishment, keep in mind what David Garland (1990: 3) has concluded after extensive study: "Punishment today is a deeply problematic and barely understood aspect of social life, the rationale for which is by no means clear."

## Revenge

Durkheim (1964) characterized punishment as revenge as consisting of a passionate reaction. Punishment is inflicted for the sake of punishment, making culpable people suffer for the sake of suffering. In other words, revenge occurs without reference to any instrumental objectives such as its impact on the future behavior of offenders. Revenge is, strictly speaking, driven by passion not reason. Revenge is often thought of as "getting even," but, as Durham (1994) points out, it is probably more accurate to talk in terms of "getting back." Hence, revenge is about the punishment of offenders in order to avenge the criminal act of the offender. Finally, "the harm of a revenge-based punishment may be well in excess of the harm created by the original offense. In accord with the lack of measured commensurability, revenge is generally associated with an emotional, unrestrained response, free from well-defined legal constraints and limits" (Durham, 1994: 22).

## Retribution

Immanuel Kant (1965) characterized retribution as punishment as a moral or just necessity. Kant argued that the imposition of punishment restored the moral balance in the universe, a balance upset by the offender's transgression. At its most fundamental level then, retribution is a moral rationale for punishment: "It justifies punishment because morality demands that the harm perpetrated by the criminal be offset by harm imposed on the offender through punishment" (Durham, 1994: 23). In premodern times, the biblical "eye for an eye . . . and tooth for a tooth" was a retributive response because unlike revenge it placed limits on the kinds of punishment that could be imposed. Although modern expressions of retribution do not rely on biblical guidance, they do reflect or operate by a principle of attempting to exact the severity of punishment to the seriousness of the offense.

Retribution is also viewed not only as providing the offended with a sense of satisfaction, but also with annulling the offensive act. The adoption during the last quarter of the twentieth century of the philosophy of *just deserts*, or "let the punishment fit the crime," of the contemporary neoclassical school of criminology exemplifies the modernist model of penal retribution and the ideological attempt to match crime and punishment. Students of crime and punishment often confuse retribution with revenge because both are concerned with affording punishments that derive their form and force from the perpetrated event—the crime. Distinguishing between the two, Durham (1994: 23) comments: "Like revenge, the retributive rationale is not concerned with the impact of punishment on the offender's future behavior or on the future behavior of others. Unlike revenge, however, retributive sanctions attempt to match the severity of the punishment to the seriousness of the crime."

## Deterrence

Cesare Beccaria's *On Crimes and Punishments* (1764) and Jeremy Bentham's *An Introduction to the Principles of Morals and Legislation* (1789) provide the philosophical grounding on which deterrence is based. Both Beccaria and Bentham argued that although punishments should fit their crimes, they more importantly serve the interests or goals of crime prevention. In other words, punishment as deterrence refers to the persuasion or capacity to prevent crime through the threat of punishment. "Punishments based on deterrence are designed to create fear of future punishment in offenders or would-be offenders" (Durham, 1994: 24). Whether discussing *specific deterrence* (of convicted offenders) or the *general deterrence* (of other potential offenders), there is an underlying belief that the fear of future suffering is enough to motivate the rational, free-acting citizen from engaging in criminality.

What is different about deterrence in comparison to revenge and retribution is that only the former takes into account the offender (and potential offenders) as individuals. What is added to the equation of this punishment rationale is a consideration of the deterrent effects to be derived from the appropriate magnitude and nature of the punishment imposed. With deterrence, no longer is punishment solely dependent on the nature of the offense.

## Incapacitation

The rationale of incapacitation during the last quarter of the twentieth century has gained acceptance in a number of postindustrial societies such as the United States (Hudson, 1993). Incapacitation, that is, penal rather than social intervention, is predicated on the claim that crime reduction efficacy occurs by keeping likely reoffenders out of circulation (see Wilson, 1983). Imprisonment or jail is the most obvious form of modern incapacitation. Premodern forms included exile, banishment, cutting off of body parts, and other drastic measures. The goal is simply to disable the offender so that, even if he or she desires to commit a crime, such is not possible, at least not in the free world.

"Incapacitation is an attractive rationale for punishment because it requires little understanding of why individuals commit crimes. . . . Enthusiasts of incapacitation do not have to be concerned with the social conditions that led to an offender's involvement in crime, why the individual freely elected to commit crimes, or what psychological processes operate in the minds of criminals" (Durham, 1994: 25). Two kinds of incapacitation are currently practiced: collective and selective. Collective incapacitation refers to sanctions applied to offenders without regard to their personal characteristics. Belonging to the offending crime categories such as violent offender, drug dealer, or child molester would qualify the offender for a lengthy prison sentence regardless of the circumstances involved in the offense. Selective incapacitation refers to those efforts to identify high-risk offenders and to set them apart from other offenders of the same group. As a result, special groups of offenders have been created by their previous histories of incarceration, drug use, schooling, employment, and patterns of convictions involving particular offenses such as robbery, community and family ties, and so forth. These special groups of individuals are set apart for the stiffest sentencing (i.e., life without parole for three-time felony convicts).

## *Rehabilitation*

Rehabilitation, as the fifth rationale of punishment, focuses on changing the offender so as to reduce his or her preference for further involvement in criminality. Focusing on future outcomes like deterrence and incapacitation, rehabilitation is most similar to specific deterrence in the sense that attention is placed on the individual offender. The emphasis, however, is not on the fear of punishment or the consequences of criminal apprehension and adjudication, but rather on modifying the character of the offender so that he or she finds crime to be morally unacceptable. Under the rationale of rehabilitation, "the punishment deemed appropriate for a particular offender will have less to do with the nature of the offense than with what is perceived to prevent future involvement in crime" (Durham, 1994: 26). As in the case of incapacitation, careful attention is paid to an individual's personality characteristics, attitudes, beliefs, family background, educational experience, occupational history, previous criminal activity, and other factors.

In comparative terms, unlike the other modern rationales of punishment (retribution, deterrence, and incapacitation), rehabilitation is a historically recent development. Rising in the late nineteenth century, the "rehabilitative ideal," if not in practice, was a preeminent ideology in the arsenal of punishment justifications during most of the twentieth century. By the last quarter of this century, the forward-looking rationale of rehabilitation had been largely abandoned. In its place, the backward-looking retributive rationale based on the just deserts model of punishment was resurrected. During this period, the popular retributive rationale was joined by the popular rationales of incapacitation and specific deterrence.

## Punishment at the Turn of the Twenty-First Century

An editorial in *The Nation* (1995: 224) echoed the same sentiments expressed by Garland who has written that punishment appears to lack a future or at least a vision of one that might be different and preferable to what currently prevails:

> *The expanding jailhouse state quite literally condemns America's future. It condemns taxpayers to a never-ending spiral of costly prisons construction. It condemns state governments to making their main function the policing of a permanent prison class. It condemns hundreds of thousands of nonviolent adults to overcrowded, racist, disease-ridden institutions that batter psyche and promote violence, to internal exile that nurtures isolation and anger.*

As a political economy of punishment suggests, "the extraordinary expansion of the U.S. prison system over the past decade represents the regressive socialism of the right" (*The Nation*, 1995: 223). This leaves us with the impression that the only expanding "public housing" in the United States is its prison archipelago. This perspective also maintains that the concomitantly expanding public-sector employment in punishment also represents a part of a larger and an emerging "prison-industrial complex" that controls (or regulates) a "permanent prison class" and that rivals agribusiness as the dominant force in the life of rural America (Davis, 1995).

At the turn of the twenty-first century, the beneficiaries of the prison boom and the "socialism of the right" are pretty clear. As business publications, such as *The Wall Street Journal*, were reporting by the mid-nineties, a new version of the old military–industrial complex has developed. Today, Smith Barney, Merrill Lynch, and other brokerage houses commonly compete to underwrite prison construction with private tax-exempt bonds. Corrections Corporation of America, for example, whose directors and executives read like a Who's Who of rainmakers from both political parties, finds other security firms rushing in to give their highest recommendation.

The Edna McConnell Clark Foundation, the leading private sponsor of programs for prison reform, estimated that in 1992 the United States spent 25 billion dollars on the prison system. Among state government expenditures, growth in prison consumption is second only to Medicaid. For example, New York built twenty-seven new prisons between 1983 and 1990 at the short-term cost of 1.6 billion. Eventually the cost will come to 5.4 billion over thirty years, including the interest payable on the state bonds floated for the construction (Rothman, 1994).

The losers of the prison boom are not only the growing percentage of inmates serving increasingly longer sentences, but also the American people as a whole. The prison-industrial complex, in short, zaps away from the states more and more of the scarce resources and fiscal dollars left for education, housing, health care, and other human services. The quest for penal rather than social dollars deprives those people most in need of assistance and harm reduction from receiving the same. In turn, this helps contribute to the production and reproduction of criminality. We will return to this theme and its policy implications in Chapter 12. But now let us turn to the boom in formal (criminal) punishment.

According to the Sentencing Project of the Bureau of Justice Statistics (see Figure 3.1), the United States leads the world with a rate of 455 incarcerated per 100,000 of population. South Africa is a distant second with 311 per 100,000. By contrast, the Netherlands' rate is 40 per 100,000, Japan's 42, France's 81, and England's 97. Moreover, the U.S. prison population is growing at the fastest rate in the world. At the end of 1994, the Justice Department reported that 1,012,851 people were confined in federal and state prisons designed to accommodate 758,000, representing a quadrupling of the inmate population since 1970. These figures did not count the 500,000 prisoners held in local jails by early 1995. Nor did those figures count the 2.5 million offenders on probation and the 457,000 on parole as of 1990, up from 1.1 million and 220,000, respectively, in 1970 (Rothman, 1994).

In the 1970s it was often noted that a year in jail was as expensive as a year at Harvard. By the 1990s, however, despite the ever-rising costs of higher education, maintaining one inmate for one year in New York City costs $58,000, at least twice the tuition and living expenses at the most elite private universities. Medical costs for an aging prison population are also spiraling out of sight. For example, in 1993 New York State was spending $50 million a year on AZT for inmates with AIDS. A court order had also forced New York City in 1993 to provide eighty-four isolation cells at $450,000 each, to house inmates with tuberculosis (Rothman, 1994).

Despite the increased expenditures over the past twenty-five years, prison construction and capacity have not kept up with the demand created by the increased severities of the penal sanction. By the mid 1990s, federal prisons were on average 46 percent, and state prisons 31 percent, over capacity. "Cells built for one inmate often [held] two or even three. At the start of 1993, forty states and the District of Columbia were under court orders to correct overcrowding and improve substandard conditions" (Rothman, 1994: 34). Many of those orders were never carried out.

Among those groups hurt most by prison expansion are people of color, especially African Americans. Nationwide, blacks who accounted for 13 percent of the population at the end of 1994, constituted 54 percent of those behind bars, up from 35 percent twenty years earlier (Miller, 1992). Rates of confinement per 100,000 were 289 for whites and 1,860 for blacks (Tonry, 1995). It is often noted by students of the "drug war" that the toughening drug laws have accounted for most of the prison population growth and that the two act to reinforce racism in America.

For example, Robert Perkinson (1994: 41) and numerous others have argued that the primary targets of the Reagan–Bush (1980–1992) War on Drugs policy were people of color: "The federal sentence for possessing one gram of crack cocaine carries a one-year prison sentence. The corresponding sentence for its much more expensive counterpart, pure cocaine, is one year probation." Because smokers of crack are more likely to be African Americans than Caucasians, and, conversely, snorters of the white powder tend to be white rather than black, institutional discrimination results from these allegedly neutral penal policies. This racial-class distinction gained national media attention in 1993 when Denver District Judge Jim Carrigan rejected a federal prosecutor's recommendations to give a black defendant eight years for possession of fifty grams of crack. Meanwhile, the same attorney had requested "only 30 months for an Aspen yuppie, in a case involving nearly 2,000 grams of powder cocaine" (Perkinson, 1994: 41).

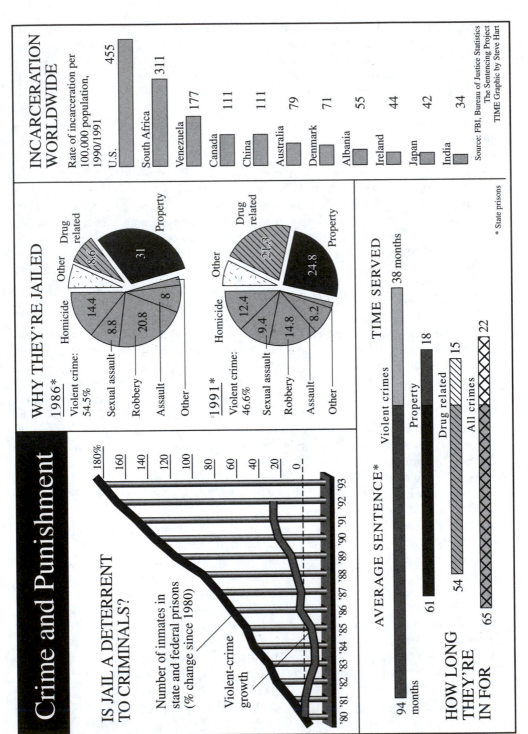

**FIGURE 3.1    Crime and Punishment**

© 1994 Time Inc. Reprinted by permission.

As *The Nation* (1995: 224) editorial expounded, the widening racial gulf as well as the expanding penal apparatus as a whole owes much to the nation's drug laws:

> *From 1986 to 1990, reports the Justice Department, convictions for drug trafficking more than doubled, with no measurable impact on addiction or the drug marketplace. As Harvard Law Professor Philip Heymann has noted, more than 60 percent of the federal prison population have been sentenced for drug crimes and among those a third are "serving longer sentences than violent offenders, have no significant criminal record, have been involved in no violence, and are not involved significantly with any major drug organization."*

Similarly, a 1994 report by the Senate Fiscal Agency studied the cases of sixty-three drug lifers. Forty-seven of these lifers did not have a prior felony on their records. Assuming, on the average, that each of these offenders will spend fifty years in prison, the cost of incarcerating these felons would come to nearly $59 million. In fact, 1,200 persons were sentenced in 1993 for possession of less than two ounces of cocaine. For a third of them, it was their first felony offense (Luke, 1995).

U.S. drug policy is not exclusively responsible for the penal crisis in America. Credit also goes to the philosophy of "just deserts" and the shift away from indeterminate sentencing to the definite-term (or flat-term) sentencing schemes of which "three-time loser acts" are most notorious. Together, the overly determined and longer sentences in general, as well as the reduction or elimination of parole in particular, has, in effect, removed the discretion of judges and parole boards (Glaser, 1994). For an overview of the number of felony convictions, the types of felony sentences by offense, and the lengths of felony sentences imposed by state courts for 1992, see Tables 3.1, 3.2, and 3.3.

## Changing Explanations of Punishment

Explanations and accounts of the changing rationales of punishment over time are diverse and varied, both with respect to their orientations, their points of reference, and their domains of inquiry. During the last three decades of the twentieth century, historical and sociological analyses of punishment have been rich and bountiful. Studies in punishment, discipline, and social control have become central objects of cultural analysis and social theory. My objective is to sketch an overview of the differing perspectives on the development of punishment from premodern to postmodern times.

The implicit argument here is that the competing explanations are not necessarily at odds or incompatible with each other. Furthermore, it is suggested that what is needed by criminologists and others is a pluralistic approach to punishment that integrates the various levels and kinds of analyses. Accordingly, the study of penality should focus on balancing the study of moral values and sensibilities with the study of mechanisms of power and control. More important, a postmodernist synthesis, such as the one articulated in Chapter 10, calls for, among other things, an understanding of punishment supported by a gendered masculinist–feminist interpretation that recognizes the deeply sexed nature of punishment regimes. Theoretically, it requires combining the masculinist project of analyzing "the emergence of punishment regimes in the context of the state's power to punish" with the feminist project of "mapping the differential impact of disciplinary power on live female bodies" (Howe, 1994: 3).

The founding fathers of the study of punishment, represented by Durkheim in the late nineteenth century, by Georg Rusche and Otto Kirchheimer's rediscovered *Punishment and Social Structure* (1939) in 1968, and by Foucault in the late twentieth century, have all shared in common a desire to move away from "idealist philosophy's relentless repetitions of the unholy trinity of retribution, deterrence and reform" (Howe, 1994: 3). In their different ways, these theorists have been historical, constructionist, and materialist. They each have their criminological adherents. But what is missing from these and similar analyses, whether they remain separate and essentialist or whether they are combined in some fashion, is the consistent tendency to ignore feminist intervention into the broad fields of social control (Cain, 1989; Carlen, 1983; Chancer, 1992; Dahl and Snare, 1978; Young, 1990).

Perhaps Durkheim's most significant contributions to the study or explanation of punishment stem from his 1899 essay "The Two Laws of Penal Evolution," which recognized the positive and productive nature of legal controls (Spitzer, 1984). Recall from Chapter 1, Durkheim regarded crime as both normal and functional because it served to strengthen group solidarity by unifying people in disapproval against the violator. In other words, punishment was not just a negative response to crime. It had positive values as well; that is, punishment helped not only to define crime, but also to constitute it. Punishment also had powerful social effects because it reinforced solidarity by symbolically displaying the collective sentiments of society. Not only did Durkheim stress

**TABLE 3.1    Estimated Number of Felony Convictions in State Courts, 1992**

| Most Serious Conviction Offense | Felony Convictions | |
|---|---|---|
| | Number | Percent |
| **All offenses** | 893,630 | 100% |
| **Violent offenses** | 165,099 | 18.4% |
| Murder/manslaughter | 12,548 | 1.4 |
| Murder | 9,079 | 1.0 |
| Manslaughter[a] | 3,469 | .4 |
| Rape | 21,655 | 2.4 |
| Robbery | 51,878 | 5.8 |
| Armed | 13,810 | 1.5 |
| Unarmed | 20,154 | 2.3 |
| Unspecified | 17,914 | 2.0 |
| Aggravated assault | 58,969 | 6.6 |
| Other violent[b] | 20,049 | 2.2 |
| **Property offenses** | 297,494 | 33.5% |
| Burglary | 114,630 | 12.9 |
| Residential | 16,649 | 1.9 |
| Nonresidential | 45,159 | 5.1 |
| Unspecified | 58,822 | 5.9 |
| Larceny | 119,000 | 13.4 |
| Motor vehicle theft | 19,332 | 2.2 |
| Other theft[c] | 99,668 | 11.2 |
| Fraud/forgery[d] | 63,864 | 7.2 |
| Fraud[d] | 30,245 | 3.4 |
| Forgery | 33,619 | 3.8 |
| **Drug offenses** | 280,232 | 31.3% |
| Possession | 109,426 | 12.2 |
| Trafficking | 170,806 | 19.1 |
| Marijuana | 16,376 | 1.8 |
| Other | 125,333 | 14.0 |
| Unspecified | 29,097 | 3.3 |
| **Weapons offenses** | 26,422 | 3.0% |
| **Other offenses[e]** | 124,383 | 13.8% |

*Source:* U.S. Department of Justice, Office of Justice Programs, Bureau of Justice Statistics, Jan. 1995.

*Note:* Detail may not sum to total because of rounding. Data specifying the conviction offense were available for 893,630 cases.

[a]Manslaughter is defined as nonnegligent manslaughter only. Where a case was known to be murder or non-negligent manslaughter, but which of the two was unknown (a small number of cases), the case was classified under manslaughter.
[b]Includes offenses such as negligent manslaughter, sexual assault, and kidnapping.
[c]Includes a small number of convictions with unspecified offenses.
[d]Includes embezzlement.
[e]Composed of nonviolent offenses such as receiving stolen property and vandalism.

the importance of the symbolic significance of penal law, but he appreciated the ideological value as well in which punishment became a "system of signs" (Garland, 1983).

Durkheim's theory of penal evolution proposed that changing modes of punishment were connected to transformations in the nature of the social structure. Durkheim

TABLE 3.2    Types of Felony Sentences Imposed by State Courts, by Offense, 1992

| Most Serious Conviction Offense | Total | Percent of Felons Sentenced to Incarceration | | | Probation |
|---|---|---|---|---|---|
| | | Total | Prison | Jail | |
| **All offenses** | 100% | 70% | 44% | 26% | 30% |
| **Violent offenses** | 100% | 81% | 60% | 21% | 19% |
| Murder[a] | 100 | 97 | 93 | 4 | 3 |
| Rape | 100 | 87 | 68 | 19 | 13 |
| Robbery | 100 | 88 | 74 | 14 | 12 |
| Aggravated assault | 100 | 72 | 44 | 28 | 28 |
| Other violent[b] | 100 | 68 | 39 | 29 | 32 |
| **Property offenses** | 100% | 66% | 42% | 24% | 34% |
| Burglary | 100 | 75 | 52 | 23 | 25 |
| Larceny[c] | 100 | 65 | 38 | 27 | 35 |
| Fraud[d] | 100 | 52 | 31 | 21 | 48 |
| **Drug offenses** | 100% | 70% | 42% | 28% | 30% |
| Possession | 100 | 62 | 33 | 29 | 38 |
| Trafficking | 100 | 75 | 48 | 27 | 25 |
| **Weapons offenses** | 100% | 66% | 40% | 26% | 34% |
| **Other offenses[e]** | 100% | 65% | 35% | 30% | 35% |

*Source:* U.S. Department of Justice, Office of Justice Programs, Bureau of Justice Statistics, Jan. 1995.

*Note:* For persons receiving a combination of sentences, the sentence designation came from the most severe penalty imposed—prison being the most severe, followed by jail, then probation. Prison includes death sentences. Data on sentence types were available for 886,359 cases.

[a]Includes nonnegligent manslaughter.
[b]Includes offenses such as negligent manslaughter, sexual assault, and kidnapping.
[c]Includes motor vehicle theft.
[d]Includes forgery and embezzlement.
[e]Composed of nonviolent offenses such as receiving stolen property and vandalism.

argued that as societies evolved from "mechanical" to "organic" solidarity, penal sanctions became less severe. He claimed that as societies became more complex and differentiated, repressive (penal) law, which corresponded with mechanical solidarity, was replaced by restitutive (civil) law, which corresponded with organic solidarity. Durkheim also claimed that crimes became less collective and more personal as societies grew in complexity. Finally, as societies became more complex, the loss of liberty, which he equated with incarceration, became the dominant sanction (Durkheim, 1964; 1973). Steven Spitzer's (1975) comprehensive study of penal evolution in forty-eight societies revealed that, contrary to Durkheim, greater punitiveness was associated with higher levels of structural differentiation.

By the 1970s, the republication of Rusche and Kirchheimer's *Punishment and Social Structure* had become a classic work in the study of punishment. It certainly has been recognized as a seminal work in the political economy of punishment. As Foucault's assessment concluded, the book's most important contribution was that it taught

**TABLE 3.3   Lengths of Felony Sentences Imposed by State Courts, by Offense and Type of Sentence, 1992**

| Most Serious Conviction Offense | Maximum Sentence Length (in months) for Felons Sentenced to Incarceration | | | |
|---|---|---|---|---|
| | Total | Prison | Jail | Probation |
| **Mean** | | | | |
| **All offenses** | 53 mo | 79 mo | 7 mo | 47 mo |
| **Violent offenses** | 95 mo | 125 mo | 8 mo | 52 mo |
| Murder[a] | 238 | 251 | 10 | 78 |
| Rape | 130 | 164 | 8 | 71 |
| Robbery | 101 | 117 | 11 | 62 |
| Aggravated | 56 | 87 | 7 | 45 |
| Other violent[b] | 55 | 88 | 6 | 52 |
| **Property offenses** | 45 mo | 67 mo | 7 mo | 47 mo |
| Burglary | 56 | 76 | 8 | 55 |
| Larceny[c] | 34 | 53 | 7 | 43 |
| Fraud[d] | 44 | 69 | 6 | 44 |
| **Drug offenses** | 43 mo | 67 mo | 6 mo | 48 mo |
| Possession | 32 | 55 | 4 | 45 |
| Trafficking | 50 | 72 | 8 | 51 |
| **Weapons** | 36 mo | 55 mo | 6 mo | 38 mo |
| **Other offenses[e]** | 32 mo | 53 mo | 6 mo | 42 mo |
| **Median** | | | | |
| **All offenses** | 24 mo | 48 mo | 5 mo | 36 mo |
| **Violent offenses** | 60 mo | 84 mo | 6 mo | 36 mo |
| Murder[a] | 252 | 288 | 10 | 60 |
| Rape | 72 | 108 | 6 | 60 |
| Robbery | 66 | 84 | 9 | 60 |
| Aggravated | 24 | 60 | 6 | 36 |
| Other violent[b] | 24 | 60 | 4 | 36 |
| **Property offenses** | 24 mo | 42 mo | 5 mo | 36 mo |
| Burglary | 36 | 48 | 6 | 36 |
| Larceny[c] | 18 | 36 | 4 | 36 |
| Fraud[d] | 24 | 36 | 3 | 36 |
| **Drug offenses** | 24 mo | 48 mo | 5 mo | 36 mo |
| Possession | 12 | 36 | 3 | 36 |
| Trafficking | 36 | 48 | 6 | 36 |
| **Weapons** | 16 mo | 36 mo | 4 mo | 24 mo |
| **Other offenses[e]** | 12 mo | 28 mo | 4 mo | 36 mo |

*Source:* U.S. Department of Justice, Office of Justice Programs, Bureau of Justice Statistics, Jan. 1995.

*Note:* See note on Table 3.2. Means exclude sentences to death or to life in prison. Sentence length data were available for 854,592 incarceration and probation sentences.

[a]Includes nonnegligent manslaughter.
[b]Includes offenses such as negligent manslaughter, sexual assault, and kidnapping.
[c]Includes motor vehicle theft.
[d]Includes forgery and embezzlement.
[e]Composed of nonviolent offenses such as receiving stolen property.

students of punishment to "rid ourselves of the illusion that penality is above all (if not exclusively) a means of reducing crime" (Foucault, 1977: 24).

> *The bond, transparent or not, that is supposed to exist between crime and punishment prevents any insight into the independent significance of the history of penal systems. It must be broken. Punishment is neither a simple consequence of crime, nor the reverse side of crime, nor a mere means which is determined by the end to be achieved. Punishment must be understood as a social phenomenon freed from both its juristic and its social ends (Rusche and Kirchheimer, 1968: 5).*

The fundamental premise of Rusche and Kirchheimer's materialist conception of the evolution of penality was that "every system of production tends to discover punishments which correspond to its productive relationships" (Rusche and Kirchheimer, 1968: 5). Social forces, economic and fiscal, especially the state of the labor market, they claimed, were central determinants in the origin and fate of penal systems. Accordingly, they divided penal history into three epoch periods, each characterized by different systems of punishment: (1) early Middle Ages dominated by penance and fines; (2) late Middle Ages dominated by a harsh regime of corporal and capital punishments; and (3) the mercantile period from the seventeenth century forward dominated by imprisonment.

Marxist history of penal development as exemplified by the Rusche–Kirchheimer model has undergone severe scrutiny by critics and sympathizers alike. Although most analysts have identified a number of problems with its labor control hypothesis, economism, reductionism, and functionalism, nevertheless, they have not totally abandoned the model. In fact, there have been numerous modifications, refinements, and reformulations in an effort to analyze penal relations within concrete social formations rather than by the more simplistic generalizations about correspondences between penal forms and the economy (for an excellent review, see Howe, 1994).

Foucault's *Discipline and Punish* (1977) has been the most influential revisionist social history of punishment to date. As Garland claimed of this book in 1986, Foucault had fundamentally changed the way in which intellectuals thought about punishment and penal institutions. In effect, Foucault had single-handedly "transformed a field of inquiry that was narrow, technically focused, and of little consequence into a flourishing, interdisciplinary area that has become a central concern for sociologists, historians, and criminologists" (Garland, 1986: 866). Foucault's contributions are many and cannot be adequately covered here.

Briefly, Foucault's critique of early histories of punishment aim at the exaggerated claims of what he called "a process of humanization." The objective for Foucault was to replace the progressivist perspective with a critical account of the "great institutional transformations" of the years 1760–1840, the age when penalties became essentially corrective and individualized, and modern penality and the birth of the prison occurred (Foucault, 1977: 7–17). For Foucault (1977: 30), punishment did not solely revolve around questions of the materiality of the past; it also included questions that revolved around what he called the "political technology of the body" present. Making matters more complicated, Foucault has identified the importance of three interrelated concepts—power, knowledge, and the body—in the study of punishment and other structures of power.

In the process, Foucault reordered the history of punishment as a set of developing relations between power, knowledge, and the body. He did so in order to

> *inscribe the history of punishment within "a history of bodies"—a history, that is, of the "political investment of the body" in power relations. Indeed, in the next to no time, Foucault is speaking not punishment but of "the political technology of the body," the micro-physics of power," "micro-powers," "power-knowledge." Pulling this all altogether, he wants to write "a history of the 'micro-physics' of the punitive power" which will be simultaneously, "a genealogy of the modern 'soul.'" Why? Because the soul is "the effect and instrument of a political anatomy; the soul is the prison of the body" (Howe, 1994: 90).*

Today, following the insights of Rusche and Kirchheimer, Foucault, Garland, and other social historians, punishment (and its relationship to crime and criminology) is no longer viewed as some kind of extension of a fixed social structure. Instead, punishment is conceived of as a complex historical process involving the interacting and changing systems of mass communication, ideological persuasion, and economic and social development. It also involves the social relations of the rich and the poor, of knowledge and power, and of how these intersect with race, ethnicity, and gender. In short, the history of punishment is much more than the alleged independent development of legal or economic institutions.

## Differential Application of the Penal Law

The legal order of differential application of the law refers to at least two related phenomena. First, there is the *cultural meaning* whereby the treatment of others has changed historically as the sensibilities of people have changed, or as the "civilizing process" has occurred, according to Elias (1978; 1982). Second, there is the *social meaning* whereby the treatment of individuals has been related to their status or difference as members of a particular gender, ethnicity, or class (Krisberg, 1975; Howe, 1994). The roles of culture and social status, of course, overlap each other as they unfold in the historically changing political economy.

Most people, experts on crime and punishment as well as the lay public, agree that, to varying degrees, differential application or selective enforcement of the law has always been a staple of the administration of crime control. In popular discourse there is a saying that captures this social reality of punishment: "If you are rich, you pay the fine. If you are not, you do the time." Underlying this simple statement is an appreciation for the dynamic relations of status, power, and wealth and the relationship between these and crime and privilege:

> *In the case of theft there exist rationales that explain the theft of the natural resources of third-world countries or the financial exploitation of the poor, but the taking of*

> *property in a criminal event is portrayed as qualitatively different. Fraudulent business practices might be justified in terms of the vocabulary of motives of the competitive marketplace, or imperialistic exploitation may be defended in terms of the need for industrial growth and development; thus, the offender is placed "beyond incrimination." The petty offender who steals to keep from starving or who burglarizes houses to obtain money to survive in the status system at the bottom of the social structure is not excused because condoning his actions would be to admit to the generality of theft and exploitation in the entire society (Krisberg, 1975: 62).*

As far back as the emergence of early capitalism with the presence of the city–states in Renaissance Italy of the thirteenth and fourteenth centuries, selective enforcement and differential application of the law became institutionalized. With the rise in mercantilism, there was the rationalization of law into civil torts and criminal codes. There were also the social practices of "high" and "low" justice. In a fascinating study of "The Legal Ban in Florentine Statutory Law," Mooney (1976) examined the progression of bankruptcy legislation from a civil offense to a criminal offense and back to a civil offense again. Although this history of a so-called crime is certainly unusual, it nevertheless underscores the difference in the importance of property and economic relations.

As trade and commerce took on increasing importance in thirteenth-century Italy, harsh penalties were passed against the growing number of merchants who were declaring bankruptcy. By the late 1300s, however, the various practices of banning for bankruptcy were rarely enforced because a number of mitigating or less severe punishments had emerged. For example, when the larger banking companies failed, residence in the city was allowed to the families involved in return for partial payment. In other words, full restitution was no longer required before one was permitted back into the community.

In less than a century, the view toward bankruptcy had changed from one associated with a sign of personal instability to one associated with the risks inherent in capitalist speculation. In turn, the crime of bankruptcy became incorporated into those offenses—such as adultery and assault—which were eligible for cancellation. Whether the penalty was originally a fine, a loss of limb, or even death, these offenders (e.g., merchants and bankers) with the economic means could buy the cancellation of their punishments. In the case of the 1994 double homicide of Nicole Brown Simpson and Ronald Lyle Goldman, the accused defendant, O. J. Simpson, a powerful and wealthy African American male with enormous status and popularity, was able to negotiate away the possibility of a death sentence before the actual trial for the murders began.

By contrast, those crimes without class privilege, such as highway robbery, damages to immovable property, or attacks on food supplies, were all offenses for which a reconciliation did not cancel the ban. During this same time period in both England and Germany, where the primitive accumulation of capital was less developed, so too was the rationalization of feudal justice. Nevertheless, as the early English codes of law graphically portray, a high and low justice still prevailed. The amounts of compensation for injury varied in accordance with the rank of the accused and of his victim:

> *A man who "lay with a maiden belonging to the king," for example, had to pay fifty shillings compensation, but if she was a "grinding slave" the compensation was halved. Compensation for lying with a nobleman's serving maid was assessed still lower at twelve shillings and with a commoner's serving maid at six shillings. If a freeman raped the slave of a commoner he had to pay no more than five shillings' compensation, but if a slave raped this same girl he was castrated (Hibbert, 1963: 4).*

Similarly, breaking into the estate of a rich man was a more serious offense than breaking into a peasant's cottage. To a lesser extent perhaps, these kinds of differences in the application of law have carried on over the centuries.

For the most part, punishments for adultery, rape, breaking and entering, robbery, and even murder have remained fairly uncertain and arbitrary. In the distant past, mitigating sentences and acquittals could be easily contrived or purchased. Even after murder, robbery and rape were no longer treated as private torts but, instead, as crimes against the crown or state; both corporal and capital punishments, which the law provided for, were rarely inflicted except on the very poor. The most common form of mitigation, in the past as well as the present, has always been the refusal of officials to execute the prescribed laws and penalties. In the case of O. J., the state, or prosecution, simply exercised its discretionary power to reduce the potential penalty from death to life in prison without the possibility of parole.

When it has come to the selective enforcement or differential application of the law or normative violations in general, the punishment of girls and women has employed a much larger social net. Not restricted to the criminal code, where women have consistently represented only about 5 percent of those formally punished by the criminal law (Durham, 1994), the punishment of females moves across the whole domain of social control to include the closer monitoring of females than males in the areas of domestic, sexual, and social life generally. The outcome of these gendered relations has been that girls/women compared to boys/men have been subjected to more of the informal means of punishment and social control that revolve around both their bodies and their personal freedoms (Cain, 1989; Carlen, 1983; Dahl and Snare, 1978; and Howe, 1994).

## Summary and Conclusions: From Stone Gallows to Intravenous Needles

When discussing social control or the relations of crime, criminal justice, and punishment in relationship to class, race, and gender, the integrative perspective recognizes the importance of both structural and cultural concepts (Sampson and Laub, 1993; Sampson and Wilson, 1993). As noted in the beginning of the chapter, the integrative perspective also explains how the study of punishment benefits from combining the views of penality that focus on mechanisms of power and control with those that focus on moral values and sensibilities. Hence, the revisionist historians and new social theorists of punishment, such as Garland, have concluded that elements of Rusche and

Kirchheimer as well as those of Foucault, Elias, and others can be fused. Rather than punishment and social structure *versus* punishment and cultural sensibilities, these theorists are speaking of social structure *and* cultural sensibility.

Historically, the kind of punitive reactions that have evolved varied according to the forces of production, the changing fiscal and labor relations, and the civilizing processes of cultural development. In other words, the developing relations of punishment at the end of the twentieth century, from individualized criminal justice characteristic of classical and positivist criminology to that of danger management characteristic of actuarial criminology, or the movement away from capital and corporal punishment and toward fines and imprisonment during the eighteenth and nineteenth centuries, have been the outcomes of changing productive relations and cultural sensitivities. In addition to the changes in punitive and productive relations that were brought on by the rise of mercantilism and the subsequent factory system demonstrated by Rusche and Kirchheimer, there were also the changes in cultural relations "where people began to see the animalistic aspects of human life as being crude or uncultivated. Acts of carving animal meat were no longer appropriate for public display and were moved behind closed doors" (Miller, 1994: 2–3). Similarly, acts of violence and punishment came to be viewed as inappropriate for public consumption. Increasingly, these acts too were scorned for being uncultured, uncivilized, and brutish.

For example, Spierenburg (1984) has traced the development of punishment in the Netherlands (Amsterdam in particular) from the seventeenth to the nineteenth century. He identifies several notable changes in punishment during this time period. After 1600, maiming and mutilation began to disappear. During the latter part of the 1600s, the use of torture in prosecution saw a decline. Moreover, by 1770 the old practice of piling up the criminal corpses that had met their fate by the stone gallows at the outskirts of town became outlawed. By the middle of the eighteenth century,

> it can be argued that Enlightenment ideals of humanitarianism led the elites and upper-classes to view such acts of violence as uncivilized and uncultured. As the upper classes prided themselves on their polite and civil treatment of others, they despised those who lacked such culture and civilization. Moreover, it was considered a sign of their uncivilized nature that the lower-class crowds continued to flock to the public executions (Miller, 1994: 4–5).

During the transitions from the ancien régimes of Europe to the new Enlightenment orders, again, the rationalities of economics and the sensitivities of culture were at work. For example, at the time of the French Revolution (1789), the state was faced with the problem of public executions. Prior to this time, the preferred method of execution was beheading with the axe and block. Of course, the axe lacked the precision of its successor, the guillotine. Miscalculations and missed blows, instead of severing the head, merely struck the vertebrae, causing additional pain and mess. In an effort to make the beheading less violent and more accurate, the guillotine was invented.

Two basic arguments for the demise of the axe and the rise of the guillotine have been put forward. One is that the uncertainty of instantaneous death by axe led to the invention of the guillotine. The other argument is, more pragmatically, that throughout the revolution there were simply too many people to kill and not enough jail space to hold them. The guillotine became so efficient, executing as many as sixty-nine people in one day, that "people who made up the audience of the executions, after witnessing the first guillotine execution[s], complained that it was over far too quickly" (Miller, 1994: 1). Today, of course, executions by lethal injection are a little slower than the guillotine, more humane than a firing squad, and certainly as clean and efficient an approach as penology has devised so far in its illustrious history of pain and punishment.

As we move into the twenty-first century, the distinctions between utilitarian and moral justifications for punishment have become more difficult to make as the two may also overlap. For example, take the deterrence (economic) and incapacitative (actuarial) approaches to punishment. As Feeley and Simon (1994: 189) explain, although both are utilitarian, they are also quite different:

> *Deterrence is economic analysis par excellence since it focuses on the behaviour of individuals as rational actors. . . . It treats the offender as a rational economic actor to be influenced by the pricing system of punishments. Incapacitation, in contrast, treats the offender as* inert *from the point of view of influencing decision making. Thus deterrence theory views criminal punishment as only one end of a broad spectrum of incentive signals produced by government and various markets to influence individual decision making (as well as the aggregation of these individual decisions). In contrast, incapacitation theory marks punishment off as a special form of power appropriate to specific categories of people. Its aim is not to influence the decisions of individual would-be criminals, but simply to identify and incapacitate a designated high-risk population.*

Unfortunately, as our cultural sensibilities have developed so far in this country, we are unable to differentiate between individual criminals. Hence, we react to these criminals not as individuals but as members of undifferentiated marginal groups who possess a dangerousness that needs to be controlled or risk-managed according to various administrative and predictive strategies.

## Discussion Questions

1. Barak discusses forward-looking and backward-looking punishment practices. Within this context, compare and contrast the five rationales of punishment.

2. Durkheim, Rusche and Kirchheimer, and Foucault have offered three different explanations of penal evolution. How have each of their insights contributed to our contemporary understanding of punishment?

3. Historically, how has the differential application of penal law been linked to gender, race/ethnicity, and class? Provide present-day examples of the differential impact of these variables on punishment.

4. Discuss the contemporary crisis in crime and punishment as evidenced by an expanding prison system and its relationship to the crisis in the welfare state as evidenced by contracting expenditures on education and human services. What are the implications of this relationship for crime and crime control?

# References

Beccaria, Cesare. 1764 [1986]. *On Crimes and Punishments*. Trans. David Yound. Indianapolis, IN: Hackett.

Bentham, Jeremy. 1789. *An Introduction to the Principals of Morals and Legislation*. London: Pickering.

Cain, Maureen. 1989. *Growing Up Good: Policing the Behavior of Girls in Europe*. London: Sage.

Carlen, Pat. 1983. *Women's Imprisonment: A Study in Social Control*. London: Routledge.

Chancer, Lynn. 1992. *Sadomasochism in Everyday Life: The Dynamics of Power and Powerless*. New Brunswick, NJ: Rutgers University Press.

Dahl, T. S., and Annika Snare. 1978. "The Coercion of Privacy." In Carol Smart and Barry Smart, eds., *Women, Sexuality, and Social Control*. London: Routledge & Kegan Paul.

Davis, Mike. 1995. "A Prison-Industrial Complex: Hell Factories in the Field." *The Nation* 260, no. 7 (February 20): 229–234.

Durham, Alexis M. 1994. *Crisis and Reform: Current Issues in American Punishment*. Boston: Little, Brown and Company.

Durkheim, Emile. 1964. *The Division of Labor in Society*. New York: The Free Press.

Elias, Norbert. [1939] 1978. *The Civilizing Process, i: The History of Manners*. Oxford: Oxford University Press.

———. [1939] 1982. *The Civilizing Process, ii: State Formation and Civilization*. Oxford: Oxford University Press.

Feeley, Malcolm and Jonathan Simon. 1992. "The New Penology: Notes on the Emerging Strategy of Corrections and Its Implications." *Criminology* 30(3): 449–474.

———. 1994. "Actuarial Justice: The Emerging New Criminal Law." In David Nelken, ed., *The Futures of Criminology*. London: Sage.

Foucault, Michel. 1977. *Discipline and Punish: The Birth of the Prison*. London: Penguin.

Garland, David. 1983. "Durkheim's Theory of Punishment: A Critique." In David Garland and Paul Young, eds., *The Power to Punish: Contemporary Penality and Social Analysis*. London: Heinemann.

———. 1986. "The Punitive Mentality: Its Socio-Historical Development and Decline." *Contemporary Crises* 10(4): 305–315.

———. 1990. *Punishment and Society: A Study in Social Theory*. Chicago: The University of Chicago Press.

Glaser, Daniel. 1994. "What Works, and Why It Is Important: A Response to Logan and Gaes." *Justice Quarterly* 11(4, December): 711–724.

Hibbert, Christopher. 1963. *The Roots of Evil: A Social History of Crime and Punishment*. Boston: Little, Brown and Company.

Howe, Adrian. 1994. *Punish and Critique: Towards a Feminist Analysis of Penality*. London: Routledge.

Hudson, Barbara A. 1993. *Penal Policy and Social Justice*. Toronto: University of Toronto Press.

Kant, Immanuel. 1965. *The Metaphysical Elements of Justice*. Trans. John Ladd. New York: Bobbs-Merrill.

Krisberg, Barry. 1975. *Crime and Privilege: Toward a New Criminology*. Englewood Cliffs, NJ: Prentice-Hall.

Luke, Peter. 1995. "Mandatory Minimum Drug Sentences Pack Prisons." *The Ann Arbor News* (February 19): B7.

Miller, Andrew. 1994. "Musical Chairs: Executions and Cultural Sensibilities." Paper presented at the American Society of Criminology, Miami.

Miller, Jerome G. 1992. "Search and Destroy: The Plight of African American Males in the Criminal Justice System." A Report of the National Center on Institutions and Alternatives (August).

Mooney, A. M. C. 1976. "The Legal Ban in Florentine Statutory Law and the *De Bannitis* of Nello da San Gimignano (1373–1430)." Ph.D dissertation: UCLA.

*The Nation* 1995. "The Prison Boom." 260, no. 7: (1995) 223–224.

Perkinson, Robert. 1994. "Shackled Justice: Florence's High-Tech Prison Is the Cutting Edge of Social Control." *Z Magazine* (February): 40–44.

Quinney, Richard. 1975. *Criminology: Analysis and Critique of Crime in America*. Boston: Little, Brown and Company.

Rothman, David J. 1994. "The Crime of Punishment." *The New York Review of Books* (February 17): 34–38.

Rusche, Georg, and Otto Kirchheimer. [1939] 1968. *Punishment and Social Structure*. New York: Russell and Russell.

Sampson, Robert J. and John H. Laub. 1993. *Crime in the Making: Pathways and Turning Points Through Life*. Cambridge, MA: Harvard University Press.

Sampson, Robert J. and William Julius Wilson. 1993. "Toward a Theory of Race, Crime, and Urban Inequality." In *Crime and Inequality*, ed. John Hagan and Ruth Peterson. Stanford, CA: Stanford University Press.

Spierenburg, Pieter. 1984. *The Spectacle of Suffering: Executions and the Evolution of Repression*. Cambridge: Cambridge University Press.

Spitzer, Steven. 1975. "Punishment and Social Disorganization: A Study of Durkheim's Theory of Penal Evolution." *Law and Society* 9(4): 613–637.

———. 1984. "Review Essay—The Embeddedness of Law: Reflections on Luke's and Scull's *Durkheim and the Law*." *American Bar Foundation Research Journal* (4): 859–868.

Tonry, Michael. 1995. *Malign Neglect: Race, Crime, and Punishment in America*. New York: Oxford University Press.

Wilson, James Q., ed. 1983. *Crime and Public Policy*. San Francisco: Institute of Contemporary Studies Press.

Young, Alison. 1990. *Femininity in Dissent*. New York: Routledge.

# Theory and Practice: On the Development of Criminological Inquiry

*Integrating Criminologies* assumes that criminological inquiry consists of three types of questions: logical, aesthetic, and moral. It also assumes that the boundaries separating these kinds of questions, and the bodies of knowledge they represent, are blurred. Criminology as part of the larger constellation of social, cultural, and natural sciences abounds with methods of theory construction and evaluation (Truzzi, 1995). The approaches to the social sciences, for example, have been classified in a variety of ways: positivist, humanist, and postpositivist; quantitative and qualitative; scientific, hermeneutic, and critical. This led Bruce DiCristina (1995: ix) to ask: "But which, if any, are the best for criminologists? Are there any methods that are logically superior for purposes of constructing and evaluating theories of crime?" And another historian of science, I. Bernard Cohen (1952: 508), noted some time ago: "The 'correct opinion' in science may actually be no more than what most of the influential scientists believe." The questions raised by DiCristina above and other questions of the philosophy of science are, nevertheless, neglected, ignored, or downplayed by most criminologists and students of crime and justice.

This chapter locates the theories and practices of criminological inquiry in the wider historical and cultural discussions of science and pseudoscience. More generally, it explores criminology in the contexts of the *study of knowledge* (epistemology) and the *study of existence* (ontology). By raising various questions of epistemology and ontology, Chapter 4 also sets the stage for the articulation developed in Chapter 10 of the relationship between *modernist* and *postmodernist* criminologies, and of the need for a synthesis of the two. At the same time, Chapter 4 attempts to provide an overview of the developing goals of criminology as these have been expounded over the past 250 years. As used below, the goals of criminology refer simply to the stated, legitimated, or official research objectives of the study of crime, including: (1) the discovery of the causes of crime (causation); (2) the discovery of probabilities of association between crime and other phenomena (prediction); (3) the refutation of false theories of crime (falsification); (4) and the identification of strategies to control crime (rational/ technical control).

According to some nominalists, positivist or postpositivist, an approach such as this one is not only contradictory, but necessitates a method of theory construction that combines the *natural* induction and verification of logical empiricists with the *nurtural* approaches of postmodernism and poststructualism. On the other hand, essentialists of the positivist or anarchistic persuasions would say something to the effect that this approach of "integrating criminologies" wants it both ways. Although discussion of the arguments of these nominalists or essentialist critics (Bailey, 1992; Fairlamb, 1994; Seidman and Wagner, 1992) is beyond the scope of this text, they are both partially correct and incorrect.

In defense of the kind of integrative synthesis called for here, I rely on what Kuhn (1978) referred to as the *essential tension* that must "exist in science between keeping the system open to new ideas, and thus to theoretical change, while at the same time conserving the value of the gains already made" (Truzzi, 1995: 13). As Kuhn (1978: 227) contended, "the successful scientist must simultaneously display the characteristics of the traditionalist and of the iconoclast." Marcello Truzzi (1995: 13) also reminds us that we must be cautious about both what we accept and reject.

*Many who use the term pseudoscience, including many working scientists, are mostly ignorant of the history of science. Most of us have been taught what has been called the "Story Book" or "Received View" of science, based on the largely fictional picture drawn by the positivists. As philosopher Pete A. Y. Gunter put it, "We have been conditioned to believe that to be science is to be straight. But after all, we are all a bit kinky, and nothing is more beneficial than to admit the kinky side of science after all these years." He contends that the critical history of science shows "that verification and falsification are arts, and like all arts, require the use of disciplined intuition, and are capable of abuse. Gunter goes on to argue that it is likely "that the sciences are forever in a process of formation, that this process strikes at their essential concepts, and that new sciences (which may turn out to be basic) are being born all the time" (emphasis in the original).*

## Science and Pseudoscience

Science, or the branch of knowledge that deals "with a body of facts or truths systematically arranged and [that reveals] the operation of general laws" (*New Webster's Dictionary of the English Language*, 1985: 859), can be contrasted with pseudoscience, "a pejorative label often used to denounce claims and methods erroneously represented as scientific" (Truzzi, 1995: 1). Issues of pseudoscience focus on debates or controversies concerned with matters of fact, methods, and the social norms of the scientific community. The development of criminological practice, past and present, has to varying degrees been preoccupied with scientific versus nonscientific "facts." Before highlighting these developments in fact and theory, let us first turn to a general discussion of the issues.

### Fact

When discussing the issues of fact in the context of science and pseudoscience, there are questions of both veracity (truth versus fabrication) and validity (accuracy versus error). For the most part, attention has focused not on veracity but on validity. And an emphasis on replication or retesting has short-circuited the debates on what counts as empirical facts. Nevertheless, a long-standing debate especially within the social sciences concerns the sorts of facts that can properly be considered eligible for scientific inquiry.

This debate involves three separate issues: "(1) whether reports of poor reliability or low evidential character, such as anecdotal reports, should be allowed as evidence in scientific debate; (2) whether subjective experiences and human cognition can constitute scientific data; and (3) whether scientific 'facts' can include values and applications as part of what is considered 'science' "(Truzzi, 1995: 3).

Regarding the debate over "evidence with low reliability," there are those who argue that scientists should restrict their examination of evidence to that which conforms to some minimum standards of reliability, such as acceptance by peer-reviewed journals. On the other hand, there are those who argue that evidence is always a matter of degree. Even anecdotal evidence is better than no evidence according to this view-point. The problem then becomes one of finding out how to weight anecdotal and clinical reports, for example, rather than dismissing them altogether.

When it comes to the debate over "subjective experiences as fact," there are the objectivists and positivists who argue that the only appropriate data is yielded from some form of materialism or behaviorism. They have tried to exclude any cognitive phenomena as data. By contrast, the idealists and phenomenologists have argued that social actions involve meanings in the minds of social actors. They argue that these subjective meanings are also data that must be taken into account in order to establish accurate explanations and predictions.

As for the debate over "values and facts," there are the positivists who argue that science must be descriptive and not prescriptive; therefore, facts and values must be separated. In other words, science must deal with what *is* rather than with what *should be*. In the oppositional camp, there are the postpositivists, such as the postmodernists and poststructuralists, who argue that such rigid demarcation between values and facts is not only another fiction of modernity, but also that positivism itself is value-laden in the first place. Further, the notion of a value-free science is actually a myth.

## Methods

The demarcation problem, or the ability to distinguish between authentic and pseu-doscientific knowledge, typically features differing conceptions of the scientific enter-prise, especially those involving methods. Although there are many different approaches taken towards this issue, historians and philosophers of science have tradi-tionally divided into two camps: essentialist and nominalist. The essentialist tradition presumes "that beneath the broad diversity of activity engaged in by the various sci-ences, there is some common denominator of character or method that would allow a solution to the demarcation issue" (Truzzi, 1995: 4). By contrast, the nominalist tradi-tion regards the quest to solve the demarcation problem as futile, not only because it rejects any view of science as coherent, but also because it views "the proposed char-acteristics of science as merely stemming from the definitional practices of the analysts (philosophers, historians or sociologists) themselves" (Truzzi, 1995: 4).

In short, we have the objectivists/positivists who have become essentially pre-scriptive and the idealists/phenomenologists who have become descriptive or even rel-ativistic. On the one hand, the logical positivists principally have dismissed questions of metaphysics as meaningless and therefore as pseudophilosophy. What becomes the hallmark of science, according to the positivists, is the principle of verifiability: Only statements that can be tested, measured, operationalized, and so forth can be scientific. On the other hand, the relative idealists believe scientific laws cannot be validated per se, but rather they can be corroborated. For them, the hallmark of science is the prin-ciple of falsifiability: Only statements that can be refuted or falsified can be scientific (Popper, 1976).

Arguments then ensue, back and forth, between these camps or traditions. It is noted that theories such as Marxism and psychoanalysis, for example, can be opera-tionalizable and verifiable but not falsifiable; that is, both of these theories can point to verifications, but there are no testable means by which they can be proved false. Nevertheless, in scientific practice, some theories are widely accepted, despite the fact that they are not strictly falsifiable. Conversely, when new theories are found to be falsifiable, they may not necessarily be viewed as scientific simply because they are perceived as too outlandish or as too threatening to the status quo. An excellent example was Rupert Sheldrake's 1981 book *A New Science of Life* with its "hypothesis of formative causation." An editorial in *Nature* "condemned it as 'the best candidate for burning there has been in many years' " (Truzzi, 1995: 5).

Suffice it to say, there is a whole lot of philosophical disagreement about what constitutes science and pseudoscience as well as the appropriate methods to incorporate into the searches for knowledge. If there is any agreement in the scientific world, it is the agreement concerning disagreement. Pragmatically, what this means is that scientists and nonscientists alike, based on constructed types or models, typically conclude that there are sciences and nonsciences (pseudosciences, antisciences). But as Truzzi and others have argued, while in theory there may be empirical instances of pure science or pure pseudoscience, in practice, elements of both are contained in the other.

## Social Norms

The social norms of scientific communities have always been integral to the practices of those communities (Kuhn, 1962). Moreover, the facts and values shaped by historical conditions are reflected in the theories and policies that have become articulated in both scientific and popular discourse. The developments in criminological practice have not been an exception to the importance of the role of social norms in the ever-emerging scientific enterprises. Since the rise of rationalism and the demise of demonology in the explanations of crime and its control some 250 years ago, there have been at least three sets of epistemological norms or schools of criminology: classical, positivist, and critical.

In the present as well as in the past, although elements of each of the criminological models or constructs of crime can be discerned, it is helpful to portray each school as I do in the next section as associated with a rough historical period, when one or the other has been the more dominant force in the field's discourse: classical = 1750–1850; positivist = 1860–1960; critical = 1970 to the present. However, please keep in mind that throughout this text it is assumed that although the study and emphases in criminology have changed over the past two centuries, at the same time they have remained essentially modernist in orientation—the focus of each aimed at the rational control of crimes and harms.

Across the disciplines, as part of the postmodern turn in history, we are witness to the contradictory reality that although the nominalists have gained much of their respective fields' attention, the essentialists still retain their hegemony throughout the academy. For example, over the past thirty years, the critical school emerged as the third paradigm in criminology, challenging the dominance of the two mainstream paradigms: classical and positivist. Nevertheless, the official theoretical journals, *Criminology* and *Justice Quarterly*, of the respective professional associations, the American Society of Criminology (ASC) and the Academy of Criminal Justice Sciences (ACJS), are still dominated by positivist contributions. Like the debates between scientific nominalists and essentialists generally, the debates between classical, positivist, and critical criminology are far from over.

As more and more scientists have come to doubt a coherence in the various scientific enterprises, they have rejected the demarcation issue as a pseudoproblem, treating it as a case of description rather than as a case of prescription. Moreover, there are several competing positions among today's nominalists. On the spectrum of nominalism, four standpoints have been described: conservative, liberal, radical, and anarchist (Truzzi, 1995).

At one end of the spectrum are the *conservative nominalists* "who view the sciences as having a common logic of validation . . . but believe there are different standards for precision, evidential criteria and methodological latitude within each science" (Truzzi, 1995: 10). From this standpoint, what is viewed as pseudoscientific in one scientific field might be acceptable practice in another: Astronomers accept unreplicable data whereas zoologists demand multiple sightings; anthropologists accept field reports as an essential methodological tool that experimental psychologists tend to reject as anecdotal. In criminology, positivist criminologists, for example, contend that the causes of criminality must be replicated and that the associated variables, whether grounded in biology, psychology, sociology, or whatever, must be statistically significant in the aggregate to count (Gibbs, 1987).

At the other end of the spectrum are the *anarchistic nominalists*, such as Paul Feyerabend (1975) in philosophy and Bruce DiCristina (1995) or Larry Tifft and Dennis Sullivan (1980) in criminology, who argue that there are no privileged methods of inquiry. Hence, they advocate a methodological anarchy: Any and all methods are problematic, so any and all methods add to the totality of our knowledge and as such are acceptable. Although anarchistic nominalists recognize that innumerable alternative methods of acquiring knowledge exist, they also generally agree that scientific progress is linked both with acts of irrationality and rationality. In a sense, this has yielded an "anything-goes" approach to criminology.

Anarchistic nominalism also includes the intellectual traditions of deconstruction that blend the works of poststructural theorists, such as Jacques Derrida (1973) and Michel Foucault (1977), with the works of postmodernists such as Jean Baudrillard (1981) and Jean-Francois Lyotard (1986). Their standpoints go beyond the methodological relativism of Feyerabend and DiCristina to deny any kind of objective reality. These deconstructive anarchists maintain that knowledge is the product of the historical conditions of its own existence: "All systems of thought are caught in a prison-house of language, and power relationships are encoded in all discourse, including the discourse of scientists" (Truzzi, 1995: 12).

On the spectrum of nominalism the *liberal nominalists* are next to the conservative nominalists. One of the oldest expressions of liberal nominalism has been among those academicians who contend that there are fundamental differences between the "hard" (natural) and "soft" (social) sciences (Schutz, 1967). Present-day humanists within both sociology and psychology, for example, represent such a group of nominalists. Most recently, in the fields of cultural studies, gender studies, legal studies, and media studies, there has been a common recognition that these cultural sciences do not have a logic of validation that is identical with either the natural or social sciences. In criminology, the early works of such critical criminologists as Ian Taylor, Paul Walton, and Jock Young (1973; 1975) are illustrative of this position.

The collective standpoint of the variety of liberal nominalists is captured well by the respective remarks from a philosopher of science, Larry Laudan, and a chemist, Henry H. Bauer: "We have now learned enough about what passes for science in our culture to be able to say quite confidently that it is not all cut from the same epistemic cloth" (Laudan, 1988: 123). "Each science—and to a degree each specialization within science—has come to be an idiosyncratic blend of theorizing and empiricism; and that brings inevitably with it distinct notions about what knowledge (in general!) is and about the degree to which knowledge can be said to be 'certain' " (Bauer, 1992: 26).

Finally, in between the liberal and the anarchistic nominalists on the nominal spectrum are the *radical nominalists*. As with the liberal nominalists, there are also several types of radical nominalists. Each of these positions recognizes that, regardless of discipline, all areas of knowledge involve social negotiation. These areas are not simply logical and objective outcomes. In criminology, those early social constructionists, especially those associated with the "labeling" perspective, such as Howard Becker (1963), Irving Goffman (1963), and Edwin Schur (1971), are representative of radical nominalists. Although all of the radical nominalists are sociocultural relativists to a degree, these theorists do not contend that all scientific knowledge is nothing but a social construct. In varying degrees, each acknowledges some potential input from the empirical world of nature.

## Criminological Construction: Classical, Positivist, and Critical

Criminologists are forever faced with assumptions, conscious and unconscious, about reality and the grounds of knowledge. In turn, these assumptions shape the accumulating knowledge of crime (and justice). These assumptions are essentially of two kinds: *ontological* and *epistemological*. The former assumptions refer to the relationship between the criminologist (or the knower) and crime (or the known). Definitionally, ontology is "the study of the nature of existence and being in the abstract" (*New Webster's Dictionary of the English Language*, 1985: 662). Epistemological assumptions refer to the relationship between theory, method, and practice. Definitionally, epistemology is the "study of the origin, nature, methods, and limits of knowledge" (*New Webster's Dictionary of the English Language*, 1985: 331).

Stated differently, research methods and theories of crime are inextricably linked to the criminologist's notions about the world, about human nature, about social interaction, and about social order (Einstadter and Henry, 1995). As Richard Quinney (1975: 9) put it, "What we know as criminology is formed more by [our] assumptions, including our own values and ideology, than by the concrete methods of research." In other words, in studying crime and the various *modes of inquiry*, it is essential that students realize that "at all stages there is an interplay between theory and research. In fact, it is often the [criminological construction] chosen by the researcher that determines which methods will be used in the research" (Quinney 1975: 9).

In the rest of this section, three criminological constructions are presented in order to provide a sense of each construct's orientation, methodology, theory, and practice. The purpose of this narrative is to characterize the development of criminological practices and to situate them in their historical and social contexts. Its purpose is also to highlight the goals, common and uncommon, to each of these criminological constructions.

## Classical Criminology

Classical criminology, or the rational as opposed to the demonic view of crime and criminals, emerged in the eighteenth and nineteenth centuries during the Enlightenment period in Europe, especially in France and England, with their strong emphases on humanitarian rationalism. As part of a reaction to the turmoil and disorder in many countries across Europe, to the many rebellions and revolutions, and to the harsh and barbaric punishments administered by a highly discretionary state, the classical criminologists set out to study the relationship of citizens to the state's legal structure. Influenced by the Enlightenment's reforming spirit, its widespread philosophical and humanist movement, and the related logic of two new doctrines—the doctrine of the *social contract* and the doctrine of *free will*—classical criminology adopted the view that "reason and experience, rather than faith and superstition, must replace the excesses and corruption of feudal societies" (Beirne and Messerschmidt, 1991: 286).

The doctrine of the social contract was the Enlightenment's answer to Thomas Hobbes's (1588–1679) notion that without some kind of civil society, all citizens would simply pursue their own narrow self-interests in a "war of all against all." Like Hobbes, subsequent philosophers, such as Voltaire, Kant, Hume, and others, asserted that society was held together by a contract between citizens and property owners and that the contract was to be protected not by theology but by the "rule of law." Societies, in short, could not exist without this contract, which required the establishment of government authority to carry it out. In the bargain, "citizens must surrender some measure of their individuality so that government can enact and enforce laws in the interests of the common good; the government, in return, must agree to protect the common good but not to invade the natural, inviolable liberties and rights of individual citizens" (Beirne and Messerschmidt, 1991: 287).

As part of the Enlightenment agenda, the doctrine of free will asserted that men, at least those who were free and who possessed property, rationally and voluntarily chose to engage in the social contract. This doctrine in its utilitarian fashion further claimed that "those who challenged the social contract, those who decided to break its rules, and those who pursued harmful pleasures and wickedness were liable to be punished for their misdeeds" (Beirne and Messerschmidt, 1991: 287). The two most influential classical theorists of the period, Beccaria (1738–1794) and Bentham (1748–1832), applied the doctrines of free will and utilitarianism to the study of crime and punishment.

Reacting against the cruel and inhumane legal practices of the time, these classical criminologists objected to the inequities in the way in which the criminal law was enforced. They proposed reforms (i.e., due process) in the administration of penal justice consistent with their conceptions of human life that allegedly sought to balance the good of society with the rights of the individual. Human beings were to be viewed as responsible for their own actions and consequences. After all, humans were rational and free to engage or not to engage in rightful and wrongful behavior. Accordingly, punishment was to fit the social harm caused by the crime. The focus or object of analysis for classical criminology became, and remains to this day, the crime rather than the criminal. In the classical epistemological scheme of things, the formal or institutionalized reactions to crime are more important in the struggle to reduce crime than are the informal or individualized efforts.

## Positivist Criminology

In the second quarter of the nineteenth century, the emergence of a rationally based criminology was buttressed by the theoretical movement of positivism, which began to study crime as a social phenomenon. Relying on the point of view and methodology of the natural sciences, positivists sought to analyze crime not by speculation, rational or otherwise, but by the collection of observable scientific facts. The positivist analysis of crime, following such disciplines as physics, chemistry, and biology, began its never-ending search up to the present, "to uncover, to explain, and to predict the ways in which observable facts occur in uniform patterns" (Beirne and Messerschmidt, 1991: 295). In short, emphasizing the doctrine of determinism, or the idea that behavior was the result of forces that made people act, the positivist criminologists began their search for the uniformities in the forces of crime and criminal justice.

Reacting in part to the failures of classical criminology to stem the rising tides of criminality through moral reformation and humanitarian intervention (incarceration rather than corporal or capital punishment) and to differentiate between delinquent and pathological inmates (which included syphilitics, alcoholics, idiots, vagabonds, immigrants, prostitutes, and petty and professional criminals), positivist criminology turned its focus away from law and crime and toward the criminal. Positivist criminologists began to assert that the punishment should fit the criminal, based on a variety of determining factors or causal forces. Accordingly, criminal action was not the product of free will; instead, it was the outcome of individuals who were propelled into criminality by biological, economic, psychological, and social forces that were viewed primarily as beyond their control.

One of the most influential early positivists was the Belgian astronomer Adolphe Quetelet (1796–1874). Quetelet set out to develop a *social mechanics* of crime in which he attempted to demonstrate that the same law-like regularity existing in the heavens and the world of nature also existed in society. Quetelet's criminology employed natural science methods, especially statistics, to show the constancy of crime rates, criminal propensities, and the causes of crime. Although Quetelet reasoned that there were many causes of crime that could be divided up into three types—accidental (wars, famines), variable (personality), and constant (age, gender, occupation)—and that society itself caused crime, he ultimately believed that crime had biological causes.

Throughout the rest of the nineteenth century and into the twentieth, positivist criminologists were busy debating *nature* versus *nurture*, or the importance of heredity versus social environment in the origins of crime. The last quarter of the nineteenth century was influenced by three Italian positivists: Cesare Lombroso (1835–1909),

Enrico Ferri (1856–1929), and Raffaele Garofalo (1852–1934). During this period, there was the rise and fall of biological determinism, exemplified by Lombroso's "born criminal"; the emergence of Ferri's sociopolitical criminality that emphasized the interrelatedness of social, economic, and political factors that contribute to crime; and the development of Garofalo's doctrine of "natural crimes," a social Darwinist approach that viewed crimes as offenses "against the law of nature." At the turn of the last century, positivist criminologies were not limited to studying biogenic and sociogenic causes of crime. There were also the psychogenic causes of crime. Influenced by the Viennese psychiatrist Sigmund Freud (1859–1939), the psychologically oriented approaches regarded crime as the symbolic expression of the inner tensions of each person that have failed to be self-controlled.

For most of the twentieth century, the explanatory powers of positivism and the methods of natural science have dominated criminological thinking. Unlike billiard balls on a pool table, however, the criminal does not behave according to certain laws of motion, but to certain sociological, historical, economic, and psychological laws. Therefore the causes of criminality are not immutable laws, because these human conditions are amenable to change. Further, positivists assume, given the changes in the causes of crime that propel individuals into crime, that these criminals can be redirected toward lawful behavior. Crime, in the final positivist analysis, can be reduced through state intervention to cure the causes of individual criminality.

## Critical Criminology

For the last quarter of the twentieth century, the fortresses of criminological positivism have demonstrated that they are not impregnable. As Beirne and Messerschmidt (1991: 314) put it: "If positivist criminology has accurately identified the causes of crime, why do state anticrime policies repeatedly fail? Reflecting the pessimism that seems the obvious answer to this question—they fail because we have failed to grasp the true causes of crime." As a result, many policy analysts, criminal justice practitioners, and others have abandoned the search for causation. As discussed in Chapter 3, these criminologists have returned to the rational-classical calculus of controlling crime, known at the turn of the twenty-first century as *actuarial (administrative) justice*.

On the other hand, reflecting intellectual optimism and idealism has been the emergence and development over the past twenty-five years or so of a *critical criminology*. As critical criminologies reveal, their standpoints can be found in both the positivist and postpositivist camps, their viewpoints have ranged from essentialist to anarchist, and their programs include the agendas of feminist criminology, realist criminology, newsmaking criminology, peacemaking criminology, and postmodern criminology.

Despite the diversity of critical criminologies, there seems to be some epistemological agreement in their critiques of the other constructs, especially those of positivism, which have tended to generally set aside the larger philosophical problem of explanation. In other words, critical criminologists are skeptical of the positivist belief that an orderly universe can be organized by knowledge and by the manipulation of the external world. The problem, in postpositivist terms, is that the critical criminologist does not assume objectivity between the knower and the known. Unlike the positivists, critical criminologists believe that the outside order is inseparable from the observer and his or her cognitive apparatus. Similarly, critical criminologists place their subjective cards on the table, acknowledging that they are part of both a moral and political endeavor. Thus, they do not ascribe to the belief that they are engaged as scientists in a value-free activity as positivists do. Finally, with their rejection of mechanistic conceptions about how social facts are related and gathered, critical criminologists typically present their explanations of crime as having little to do with causality per se.

Unlike classical or positivist criminologists, critical criminologists are reflexive scientists. They have emphasized the questioning of the established order and its whole set of scientific assumptions. They have turned the activity of explanation back upon itself. They have been introspective, preferring not to avoid the whole question of a metaphysics of inquiry. Morally and politically, then, critical criminologists do not blindly endorse any status quo, official reality, or prevailing ideology as the solution to crime control. In short, in response to the bankruptcy of positivist criminology and its promise to cure crime, critical criminology represents alternative modes of inquiry that are searching for new paths to human liberation.

The emergence of a critical criminology in part represents a departure from the traditional practices of criminology that have focused attention on changing the behavior of the lawbreakers either through punishment (classical criminology) or treatment (positivist criminology). As already noted, critical criminology is not some kind of monolithic or prescriptive body of knowledge. On the contrary, there are several prominent perspectives. What these and other critical perspectives share in common is a fundamental opposition to many, but not all, of the modernist assumptions, especially those associated with the instrumentalist knowledges of classicism and positivism (Foucault, 1977). Prior to the rise of feminist social thought, the two most influential perspectives were that of social constructionism and neo-Marxism.

Briefly, the social constructionist perspectives of critical criminology begin with the assumption that crime and other stigmatized behaviors are categories created and imposed on some persons by others (Becker, 1963). Its ontological approach questions the existence of an objective reality apart from the individual's imagination. Hence, any reality that can be perceived can become important. Unable to separate objects or facts of study from their own mental constructions, these critical criminologists acknowledge that crime exists because society has constructed and applied the label *crime*. This is no less true of crime control. As Quinney (1975: 11) has explained: "Criminal law, too, is not separate from society, but is itself a construction created by those who are in power. The administration of justice is a human social activity that is constructed as various legal agents interpret and impose their order on those they select for processing."

By contrast, the Marxist structural criminology perspectives are grounded in a more fundamental materialism and a critique of capitalism. These perspectives argue, among other things, that capitalism is based on the exploitation of labor and on privilege and hierarchy. Critical Marxist theorists, such as Steven Spitzer (1975), William Chambliss (1975), and Julia and Herman Schwendinger (1983), for example, argue, one way or the other, that the causes of human misery, law, and crime are a product of the contradictions of capitalism. In short, the contradictions of the capitalist system constitute the crime problem. The solutions to crime, therefore, call for an eradication of those contradictions.

Following Kant's (1929) distinction between knowing and thinking, critical criminology understands the need both to construct verifiable knowledge and to contemplate the possibilities, including such unthinkable topics as our own existence. Beginning with an examination of the ways in which we understand the world and armed with the understanding that one can never fully separate the objective from the subjective, critical criminologists recognize the indispensable human consciousness involved in the social construction of reality formation. Whether informed by a feminist criminology or a peacemaking criminology, critical criminologists engage in a process of demystification by raising fundamental questions about the official realities of crime and crime control.

In the next section, I provide an integrated perspective on theory and practice that eclectically uses various knowledges from modernism and postmodernism, from science and pseudoscience, and from positivism and postpositivism.

## Theory and Practice: A Post-Postmodern Approach

As Henry and Milovanovic (1996) argue in *Constitutive Criminology: Beyond Postmodernism*, a post-postmodern inspired analysis of crime recognizes three false dualities that have encouraged counterproductive debates between classical, positivist, and critical criminologists. These dualities have revolved around the question of accepting either modernist or postmodernist thought, the issue of clarity versus complexity in discourse use, and the notion of action as privileged over theory. Consistent with their constitutive approach, criminological knowledge need not be modernist or postmodernist. It can be both! In postmodernist fashion, a post-postmodern analysis of crime and its control aspires to integrate the diverse, pluralistic, and subjugated standpoints of modernist and postmodernist experts and nonexperts alike.

Hence, a post-postmodernist perspective represents a synthesis of sorts that consciously infuses more and more bodies of knowledge—theories and practices that cross a wide spectrum of disciplinary boundaries—into the expanding study of crime and crime control. Postmodernism in general, and in relation to the social sciences and criminology in particular, is a movement which attempts to reconceptualize the way criminals, victims, crime fighters, and the public alike, view crime and its reduction. Specifically, postmodernism entertains queries about the way we

> *experience relationships and social structure, and a method to work through how the world around us appears real, thereby questioning that it is real in truth or fact, or that there is any way of making such judgments. Indeed, postmodernism challenges the whole idea of how reality is conceived. It questions the superiority of "science" as a mode of analysis and explanation (just as it questioned high art). It questions all attempts to reduce life to essences or causes. It questions any attempt by communities or individuals as "expert" to prioritize their knowledge over the knowledge of others, and it asserts that no one can claim their knowledge is privileged" (Einstadter and Henry, 1995: 278).*

In contrast, a post-postmodernist perspective in criminology combines principles, facts, and values from both modern empiricism and postmodern interpretation in order to provide an alternative reconstruction of crime and social control. Always in the process of becoming and unfolding, a post-postmodernist integration (see Chapter 10) represents a synthesis of scientific empiricism and affirmative deconstruction. In deconstructionist fashion, this kind of inquiry exposes the underlying assumptions and any contradictions of the theories, methods, and policies of criminology that have stood in the way of addressing the problems of crime and justice (see Chapters 11 and 12). These critiques, not criticisms per se, challenge the institutionalized status quo of crime and justice. They displace established truths, disrupt their smooth passages, and undermine their regimes as they reconstruct policies of crime and social control based on the development of replacement texts and discourses (Henry and Milovanovic, 1991; 1996). In its deconstructionist and reconstructionist (affirmative) modes, an integrative criminology like the one presented in *Integrating Criminologies* seeks to undo all nonintegrative constructions of crime and crime control.

In its post-postmodernist mode, this integrative criminology endeavors to reconcile such paradoxical concepts as nature and nurture, determinism and free will, and objectivity and subjectivity. This kind of contradictory exercise, while dating back to the Hegelian dialectics of the nineteenth century, may perhaps be explained in its contemporary form by the rise of *chaos theory* (Barton, 1994; Gleick, 1987; Prigogine and Stengers, 1984) or to what has been referred to as the "science of contradictions" and the reconciliation of seemingly antithetical phenomena and processes.

> *Whereas Aristotle and his followers were drawn to the separation of opposites, Newton to the mutual neutralization of opposites, and Freud to the conflict that forms between opposites, chaos is concerned with the synthesis of opposites. It is the complementary nature and potential union of opposing forces . . . that stimulates growth and moves the organism toward increased levels of differentiation and adaptability (Walters, 1994: 8).*

For example, take the inability of positivist criminology to deliver on its promises of discovering the laws of criminological causation and prediction. As Glenn Walters (1994: 19) points out, positivists had overly relied on linear models of evaluation to the neglect of "alternative data analytic procedures, nonlinear statistics in particular." Although nonlinear equations may account for the variance commonly overlooked by linear equations, it still remains to be demonstrated that the addition of these statistical methods alone without, for example, a consideration of the cognitive or motivational aspects of situationally experienced behavior, will be enough to improve on the predictive value of tinkering with various criminological indicators as a means of reducing or preventing crime.

## Summary and Conclusions: Integrating the Varieties of Criminology

Theories are narratives or stories that explain why or how things are related to each other, such as poverty and crime. Theories of "crime causation" that assert that *a* or *b* or *c* or *a* and *c*, and so forth are related to criminal behavior, whereby *a*, *b*, and *c* refer to some kind of biological, psychological, or sociological factor ("variable"), have been most closely identified with positivist criminology. Postpositivists, having given up the search for causality, nevertheless are concerned with explaining the interrelationship of concepts such as gender and crime, age and crime, class and crime, race and crime, unemployment and crime, hyperactivity and delinquency, and others. Positivists, post-positivists, and integrationists, therefore, are all free to investigate which relationships are the most compelling when it comes to crime and justice and to subject the various explanations (theories) to empirical tests. As Robert Bohm (1996: 8) writes:

> *When we evaluate theory, then, all we can accurately say is that one theory is more or less compelling, believable, or convincing than another theory. What makes one theory more compelling, believable, or convincing than another theory is that the more compelling theory has successfully withstood more attempts to* falsify *it than has the less compelling theory. It is not accurate to say that a theory is true or false or right or wrong (emphasis added).*

As I noted in the opening chapter of this book, several commentators on crime and justice, such as Hagan (1989), Shearing (1989), and Ericson and Carriere (1994), have referred to the "fragmentation in criminology." This fragmentation or lack of order in criminology has been viewed as part of the wider processes of fragmentation characteristic of postmodern society. In terms of putting criminological inquiry back together again, scholars have suggested a number of alternative paths.

Some have called for direct confrontation with the fragmentation, others have called for a stronger commitment to positivist techniques, and still others have called for more serious theorizing. It is my contention that the reordering of the criminological enterprise can be secured through the integration of the varieties of criminology. It is my conclusion that the field of criminology needs to integrate its diverse knowledges into a practice that moves away from subdisciplinary, disciplinary, and multidisciplinary approaches and toward an interdisciplinary approach. In striving to integrate, in different words, the "social facts of crime" with "why criminals do it," the type of interdisciplinary framework used here does not privilege any particular disciplinary theory or method of criminology. All theories and methods are simply regarded as adding to the criminological whole.

## Discussion Questions

1. Using various disciplines as examples, compare and contrast "science" and "pseudoscience" in relationship to the development of knowledge.

2. In terms of what Truzzi has labeled the "demarcation problem," distinguish between essentialism and nominalism. Would you describe yourself as an essentialist or a nominalist? If the latter, which one of the four nominalist positions best describes your point of view?

3. What are the fundamental differences between "classical," "positivist," and "critical" criminologies? What, if anything, do each of these three schools of criminology share in common with the other two?

4. Do you believe that there could be the development of a paradigm of crime and justice capable of successfully integrating the three major criminological orientations? Make a case for both why it could and could not be achieved.

# References

Bailey, Kenneth D. 1992. *Sociology and the New Systems Theory: Toward a Theoretical Synthesis.* Albany, NY: SUNY Press.

Barton, Scott. 1994. "Chaos, Self-Organization, and Psychology." *American Psychologist* 44:1175–1184.

Baudrillard, Jean. 1981. *For a Critique of the Political Economy of the Sign.* St. Louis, MO: Telos Press.

Bauer, Henry. 1992. *Scientific Literacy and the Myth of the Scientific Method.* Urbana, IL: University of Illinois Press.

Becker, Howard. 1963. *Outsiders: Studies in the Sociology of Deviance.* New York: Free Press.

Beirne, Piers, and James Messerschmidt. 1991. *Criminology.* San Diego: Harcourt Brace Jovanovich.

Bohm, Robert. 1996. *A Primer on Crime and Delinquency Theory.* Belmont, CA: Wadsworth.

Chambliss, William. 1975. "Toward a Political Economy of Crime." *Theory and Society* 2:149–170.

Cohen, I. Bernard. 1952. "Orthodoxy and Scientific Process." *Proceedings of the American Philosophical Society* 96(8, October).

Derrida, Jacques. 1973. *Speech and Phenomena.* Evanston, IL: Northwestern University Press.

———. 1981. *Positions.* Chicago: University of Chicago Press.

DiCristina, Bruce. 1995. *Method in Criminology: A Philosophical Primer.* Albany, NY: Harrow and Heston.

Einstadter, Werner, and Stuart Henry. 1995. *Criminological Theory: An Analysis of Its Underlying Assumptions.* Fort Worth, TX: Harcourt Brace.

Ericson, Richard, and Kevin Carriere. 1994. "The Fragmentation of Criminology." In David Nelken, ed., *The Futures of Criminology.* London: Sage Publications.

Fairlamb, Horace L. 1994. *Critical Conditions: Postmodernity and the Question of Foundations.* Cambridge: Cambridge University Press.

Feyerabend, Paul. 1975. *Against Method.* London: New Left Books.

Foucault, Michel. 1977. *Discipline and Punish.* New York: Pantheon Books.

Gibbs, Jack P. 1987. "The State of Criminological Theory." *Criminology* 25(November): 821–840.

Gleick, James. 1987. *Chaos: Making a New Science.* New York: Viking.

Goffman, Erving. 1963. *Stigma: Notes on the Management of Spoiled Identity.* Englewood Cliffs, NJ: Prentice-Hall.

Hagan, John. 1989. *Structural Criminology.* Cambridge: Polity Press.

Henry, Stuart, and Dragan Milovanovic. 1996. *Constitutive Criminology: Beyond Postmodernism.* London: Sage Publications.

Kant, Immanuel. 1929. *Critique of Pure Reason.* Trans. Norman Kemp Smith. New York: Macmillan.

Kuhn, Thomas. 1962. *The Structure of Scientific Revolutions.* Chicago: University of Chicago Press.

———. 1978. *The Essential Tension.* Chicago: University of Chicago Press.

Laudan, Larry. 1988. "The Demise of the Demarcation Problem." In L. Laudan, ed., *Physics, Philosophy, and Psychoanalysis.* Dordrecht: D. Reidel.

Lyotard, Jean-Francois. 1986. *The Postmodern Condition: A Report on Knowledge.* Manchester: Manchester University Press.

*New Webster's Dictionary of the English Language.* 1985. USA: Delair Publishing Company.

Popper, Karl. 1976. *Unended Quest.* La Salle, IL: Open Court.

Prigogine, Ilya, and Isabelle Stengers. *Order Out of Chaos: Man's New Dialogue with Nature.* New York: Guilford Press.

Quinney, Richard. 1975. *Criminology: Analysis and Critique of Crime in America.* Boston: Little, Brown and Company.

Schur, Edwin M. 1971. *Labeling Deviant Behavior: Its Sociological Implications.* New York: Harper and Row.

Schutz, Alfred. [1932] 1967. *The Phenomenology of the Social World.* Evanston, IL: Northwestern University Press.

Schwartz, Martin D., and David O. Friedrichs. 1994. "Postmodern Thought Criminological Discontent: New Metaphors for Understanding Violence." *Criminology* 32(2, May): 221–246.

Schwendinger, Julia, and Herman Schwendinger. 1983. *Rape and Inequality.* Beverly Hills, CA: Sage.

Seidman, Steven, and David G. Wagner, eds. 1992. *Postmodernism and Social Theory.* Cambridge, MA: Blackwell.

Shearing, Clifford. 1989. "Decriminalizing Criminology: Reflections on the Literal and Tropological Meaning of the Term." *Canadian Journal of Criminology* 31:169–178.

Spitzer, Steven. 1975. "Towards a Marxian Theory of Deviance." *Social Problems* 22:638–651.

Taylor, Ian, Paul Walton, and Jock Young. 1973. *The New Criminology: For a Social Theory of Deviance.* London: Routledge and Kegan Paul.

———, eds. 1975. *Critical Criminology.* London: Routledge and Kegan Paul.

Tifft, Larry L., and Dennis Sullivan. 1980. *The Struggle to Be Human: Crime, Criminology and Anarchism.* Orkney, England: Cienfuegos Press.

Truzzi, Marcello. 1996. "Pseudoscience." In Gordon Stein, ed., *Encyclopedia of the Paranormal.* Buffalo, NY: Prometheus Books.

Walters, Glenn. 1994. "Crime and Chaos: Applying Nonlinear Dynamic Principles to Problems in Criminology." Unpublished paper. Schuylkill, PA.

# Contributions from Biology: "Body and Temperament"

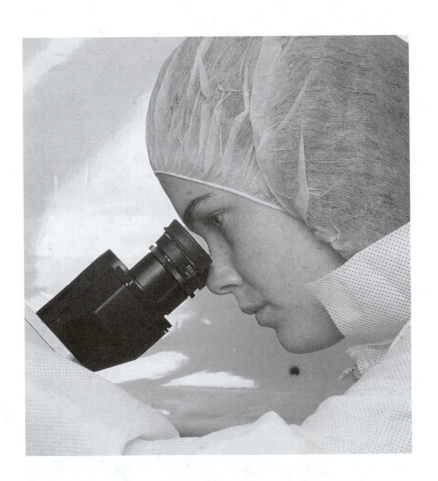

Part II of this textbook discusses criminological theory. In that context, it reviews the contributions that biology, psychology, sociology, law, and economics have brought to bear on theories of crime, criminals, and social control. It is not my intention here to present something approaching a comprehensive, let alone an encyclopedic, overview of the history and development of criminological theories. Nor is it my intention to review the evidence or to evaluate the various theories emanating from the respective disciplines that have come to be accepted or rejected. There are a number of books in the field that provide in-depth reviews of criminological theories, a sample of which include the dissimilar approaches taken by Akers (1994), Curran and Renzetti (1994), Einstadter and Henry (1995), and Gibbons (1994). Instead of pursuing depth, my goals in Part II and Part III are to pursue breadth for the purposes of developing an integrated criminology that connects the various knowledges that cut across the human sciences and the study of crime and justice.

Specifically, my objective is to cull out—from the history of those disciplines and fields that have addressed theoretical issues of crime, from the rhetorics and ideologies that have attached to their various theories, and from all the discussions and controversies that have come and gone—the criminological *knowledges* that have more or less withstood the test of time. In other words, revealed here are those criminological findings (or knowledges) that empirical testing or consensus has granted, at least temporarily, the status of truths. Even this modest objective is easier said than done, especially in those areas such as biology, where nature and nurture are often inseparable, making direct proofs difficult, if not impossible, to derive.

It should be further underscored that although each of the chapters in Part II focuses on a particular discipline and more, and although each of these bodies of knowledge is treated as separate and distinct, the underlying assumption is that these assorted explanations of crime that center on different levels of analysis and on different elements of criminality are related to each other. More important, if we as a society are ever going to develop policies to prevent and reduce crime, then we also need to develop an integrated understanding of the totality of these bodies of knowledge. Without adopting some kind of integrative body of knowledge or integrative criminological paradigm, it is argued that any theory of criminal behavior regardless of its disciplinary base will remain, at best, incomplete. It is similarly argued that policies of crime control, lacking some kind of a holistic approach to criminality, will continue to develop counterstrategic options to crime based on reducing the opportunities for crime and on applying various schemes of deterrence with little or no emphasis paid to the importance of nurturing the early life experiences of child and adolescent development (Currie, 1985; Vila, 1994).

Comparatively speaking, a review of the biological contributions to criminological understanding, thus far, reveals promising lines for conducting biosocial interactive research on the genetic/environmental contributions to the variation in behavior. Specifically, biological knowledge reveals how unlearned neurochemical factors mediate both nature and nurture in the developmental workings of individuals. In the process, these unconscious influences may affect the degree to which a person engages in pro- or antisocial behavior (Eysenck and Gudjonsson, 1989; Ellis, 1990). Beyond this potentially useful line of criminological inquiry, most of the biological explanations for criminality have either proved themselves wrong or yielded mixed findings about some biological condition and its relationship to crime.

From a biologist's perspective, the categories that I am about to describe are far from distinct categories. For example, everything cellular, biochemical, and intracellular is organic in the sense that it is composed of living matter or products of living matter. For the purposes of this review, I have classified biological phenomena into three categories: genetic, biochemical, and body physique and temperament. Genetically, there are those fundamental elements that make the transition from nonliving to living things. These quasi-biological phenomena include the basic amino acids, nucleic acids, and proteins, which constitute the building blocks of life. Particularly important at this level of analysis are the molecules that provide the blueprints for all life forms, namely deoxyribonucleic acid (DNA). At the cellular level where self-contained carriers of a complete set of DNA or genes exist, much biological activity occurs. Although single cells have evolved into large multicellular organisms and typically have taken on specialized functions (e.g., brain, heart, kidney, and so forth) within the organisms, it is the nerve cells (*neurons*) located in the brain and spinal cord that are of particular importance to biosocial scientists. Biochemically, organisms produce complex chemicals that regulate bodily functioning. The three most important biochemicals are *hormones*, *neurotransmitters*, and *enzymes*. Each of these works intracellularly: Hormones are typically produced in one organ of the body and transferred via the bloodstream to another organ for the purposes of exerting effects on bodily (including brain) functioning. Neurotransmitters act to transmit messages from one neuron to another. Enzymes are biochemical agents that transform various other biochemicals, including hormones and neurotransmitters. Finally, in terms of body physique and temperament, physiological attributes exist involving specialized organs of the body such as the genitals and the brain (Ellis, 1990).

## Contextualizing Biological Contributions

When discussing biology and behavior in general or in relation to crime in particular, there are two traditions to draw from. One is relatively old, dating back to at least the early nineteenth century. The other is relatively new, dating back to the 1960s and 1970s. The older tradition tried to establish that criminals were physiologically different from noncriminals. It also attempted to show that not only were criminals structurally different from noncriminals, but also that they were biologically inferior because of certain physical or genetic characteristics that predisposed them to criminality. Basically, the efforts of *physiognomy* (judging character from facial features), *phrenology* (estimating character and intelligence based on an examination of the shape of the skull), *criminal anthropology* (the study of "criminal man"), and *body type* (estimating temperament based on somatotypes characterized as endomorphic, mesomorphic, and ectomorphic) failed to prove any significant difference or variation between criminals and noncriminals.

By contrast, the newer tradition has been trying to establish how biochemical factors "influence the ranges of the form and intensity of emotional responses, the thresholds of arousals, the readiness to learn certain stimuli as opposed to others, and the pattern of sensitivity to additional environmental factors" (Wilson, 1978: 47). Questions of how organs work are questions of proximate causation. Such questions are not directly neo-Darwinian in substance even though answers to those questions may influence the understanding of why a trait evolved, contributing to the ultimate causation questions framed by gene-based evolutionary theory. Although significant gaps remain between these proximate and ultimate bio-evolutionary questions, the newer tradition seeks to understand the relationships between how brains behave and how brains interact with the sociocultural environment to produce behavioral patterns. Expressed in the advances of the late twentieth century's new technologies that are capable, for example, of mapping the neural circuitry of catching the mind in the act of thinking (see Figure 5.1 and photo of brains), these modern methods of measurement are relatively sophisticated compared to those of a hundred years ago (Ellis and Hoffman, 1990; Begley, 1995). Not only are these methods far less crude but the same can be said of the theoretical landscapes surrounding the knowledges of biochemistry and heredity.

The publication of *Sociobiology: The New Synthesis* in 1975 caused a stir, to say the least. Its author, Edward O. Wilson, an entomologist from Harvard University, was pilloried in the 1970s and is still regarded by many social scientists today with scorn for linking biology and behavior. Critics then, and less now, believed that any hypothesis suggesting a biological foundation to human social behavior was, as the Sociobiology Study Group at Harvard put it in a letter to *The New York Review of Books*, "a genetic justification of the status quo and of existing privileges for certain groups according to class, race or sex" (quoted in Fisher, 1994: 15). In trying to explain why people act as they do, Wilson concluded among other things that many human behaviors, including altruism, hypocrisy, and tribalism, may have biological-hereditary underpinnings. Today, such arguments are taken much more seriously by both the natural and social sciences.

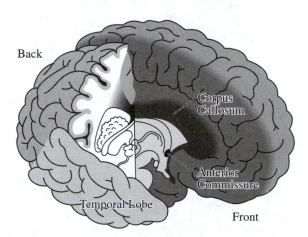

Temporal Lobe: Controls hearing, memory, and sense of self and time.

Corpus Callosum: Carries messages between the left and right brain.

Anterior Commissure: Connects the brain's two hemispheres.

**FIGURE 5.1   Mapping the Neural Scene**

*From: Newsweek,* March 27 © 1995, Newsweek, Inc. All rights reserved. Reprinted by permission.

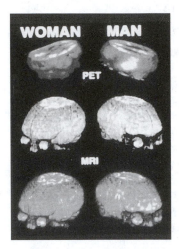

The picture shows the brain of a woman (left column) and a man (right column) studied in 3-dimensions with positron emission tomograhy (PET) for measuring rates of glucose utilization (top row) and magnetic resonance imaging (MRI) for measuring brain anatomy (middle row). The two scans are co-registered or "fused" (bottom row) to enable localization of regions. Men show higher activity in the "old limbic" system, located below the corpus callosum and associated with "instrumental" expression of emotion, i. e., through physical aggression. Women, on the other hand, show higher metabolic activity in the "cingulate gyrus," a part of the limbic system ("the emotional brain") located above the callosum and linked to symbolic and verbally mediated expression of emotions.

Nevertheless, in response to his early cultural critics, Wilson co-authored in 1981 with Charles Lumsden, a theoretical physicist, *Genes, Mind, and Culture*. Using examples such as the universal ways in which children learn language and associate a smiling face with joy, they maintained that the human brain—a vast road map of interconnecting nerve cells—learns in specific patterns that are determined by genes. Wilson and Lumsden argued that although cultures vary enormously, they

> *always converge in fundamental ways that stem from genetic predispositions. Moreover, because cultural forces regularly determine which individuals will survive to reproduce, culture selects for certain human brains and specific human genes. In short, culture and biology share a leash. At the center of their tug-of-war is the architecture and physiology of the brain: both evolve together (Fisher, 1994: 17).*

In another book, *On Human Nature* (1978), Wilson argued that the essential first hypothesis for any serious consideration of the human condition must begin with the Darwinian theory of evolution. This theory holds that humankind evolved by *natural selection* and that over the course of millions of years, genetic chance and environmental influence made the species. Without such a proposition, Wilson (1978: 2) claims, "the humanities and social sciences are the limited descriptors of surface phenomena, like astronomy without physics, biology without chemistry, and mathematics without algebra."

The gist of a Darwinian natural-selection explanation for the emergence of the brain is that the brain (and body) exists because it promotes the survival and multiplication of the genes that direct its assembly. In different words, human behavior or brain (and body) function are devices for maximizing survival and reproduction. Techniques for survival and reproduction are not limited, however, to reason and actions alone. They also encompass "deep emotional centers of the brain, most probably within the limbic system, a complex array of neurons and hormone-secreting cells located just beneath the 'thinking' portion of the cerebral cortex" (Wilson, 1978: 6).

Armed with a more sophisticated understanding of how the brain and nervous systems work in a biochemical environment, today's neuroscientists are advancing propositions on how neurochemistry can contribute to produce excessive anxiety, sadness, or anger. In other words, there may be a basis for the acceptance of inherited temperamental traits and there may be inherited physiologies that make people prone to be melancholic or sanguine (Kagan, 1994). This is not to suggest or imply that there may be *born criminals* or that people inherit criminal propensities. Again, there are no human physiopsychological profiles anyway that are a product of genes alone.

In order to keep biology and evolutionary behavior in perspective, there is another fundamental point that needs to be made before turning to the review of the biological contributions to criminology. It should be kept in mind that the new biology in relation to the new integrated criminology is not about difference per se. Rather, it is about sameness. Just as most biologists and anthropologists have recognized that the conventional categories of racial groups or discrete human races are flawed, the same is true of genetic criminal types. Hence, regarding the human species it makes no evolutionary sense to talk in terms of "atavistic throwbacks" or "biocriminological defects."

To recapitulate: Consistent with neo-Darwinian evolutionary theory, traits of human nature were "adaptive during the time that the human species evolved and that genes consequently spread through the population that predisposed their carriers to develop those traits" that distinguished them from nonhuman animals (Wilson, 1978: 32). But that was a long time ago. For example, the neomammalian age with its developed cortex (cognitive mind) that affects perception, use of symbols, and logic, and that influences culture-specific behavior is some 200 million years old. Even older is the mammalian age (250 million years) with its developed limbic (emotion) systems that affect the senses of smell, memory, health, and vital drives, and that affect aesthetic taste, sexual orientation, displays of affection, and interactive styles. Moreover, it is fairly certain that most of the genetic evolution of human behavior occurred over the past 5 million years when the species consisted of sparse, relatively immobile populations of hunter–gatherers. By comparison, the greater part of cultural evolution has taken place during the past 10,000 years, or since the origin of agriculture and cities. The point is that from an evolutionary perspective, criminal and noncriminal behaviors are essentially derived from the same genetic and cultural pools. This does not rule out, however, the presence of biochemical variations within and between population groups and the fact that such differences may contribute to the pro- or antisocial behaviors of individuals who may be young or old, rich or poor, male or female, black or white.

## Genetic Factors

At the cellular level, there is some evidence to suggest that genes contribute to variation in behavior much as they contribute to physical appearance. A number of literature reviews conclude that this is the case, including Ellis (1982), Cloninger and Gottesman (1987), Mednick, Gabrielli, and Hutchings (1984), Rowe (1986), and Rowe and Osgood (1984). Although the findings are mixed, the strongest evidence linking genes to the variation in people's tendencies to engage in criminal behavior comes from either twin studies (Walters, 1992) or adoption studies (Ellis, 1982).

Studies of identical and fraternal twins, for example, have suggested that genetic factors play some part in the predisposition to engage in criminal behavior (Christiansen, 1977). Research reveals that both male and female identical twins' rates of criminal concordance (association) are approximately three times higher than those for fraternal twins. Studies of adoptees compare persons who have been adopted at or near birth by persons unrelated to them genetically in order to determine whether their criminal behavior resembles the behavior of their biological or adoptive parents. According to Ellis (1990: 9), adoptive studies have "consistently found that the probability of adoptees engaging in criminal behavior (usually operationalized in terms of arrest and/or conviction for felonies) can be predicted with greater accuracy by knowing if one or both of the genetic parents has been similarly arrested and/or convicted than by knowing if one or both rearing parents have been so arrested or convicted."

In sum, those twins with two biological parents who have had criminal dealings or those who have one biological parent and one adopted parent with criminal experiences reveal higher rates of criminal activity than those twins whose parents, biological or adoptive, do not possess such histories. Putting aside a number of methodological considerations, the outstanding weaknesses with both twin and adoptee studies lie in their ultimate inability to theoretically control for the impact of environmental influences. It should also be noted here, especially because of all the media attention, that studies that have tried to link deviant chromosomal complements, such as XXY (Klinefelter's) and XYY (supermale) syndromes as compared to the normal gender-determining pair of chromosomes as female (XX) and male (XY), have not demonstrated a causal relationship between biological factors and crime (Beirne and Messerschmidt, 1991).

## Biochemical Factors

At the biochemical level, various hypotheses have been raised concerning bodily imbalances or abnormal levels of glucose and cholesterol (Virkkunen, 1987); carbohydrates (Lester, Thatcher, and Monroe-Lord, 1982) and diet in general (Fishbein and Pease, 1988); premenstrual syndrome (Taylor and Dalton, 1983); testosterone (Schalling, 1987); and dopamine, epinephrine, and norepinephrine (Iversen, 1983). Although none of these factors has been shown to be significantly associated with crime, testosterone may be an exception. For instance, there are many animal studies that show relationships between testosterone levels and various measures of aggressive behavior. However, studies of humans have not shown a clear relationship between the production rates of testosterone, on the one hand, and aggressive, impulsive, and antisocial behavior, on the other hand.

J. Philippe Rushton in *Race, Evolution, and Behavior: A Life History Perspective* (1995), Harris et al. (forthcoming), and Rushton and Harris (1994) have examined genetic and environmental factors in relationship to levels of testosterone and self-reported violence in male and female twins. Their findings reveal the complexities involved in sociobiological relations. For example, they have found that "salivary testosterone is related to levels of prosocial and aggressive behavior in both men and women" (Rushton and Harris, 1994: 6). Testosterone was also found to "differentiate known group differences in violence including men versus women, teenagers versus older persons, well educated versus those less well educated, and other population differences" (Rushton and Harris, 1994: 6).

Moreover, these researchers have found, as most studies do, that men were more violent than women. Interestingly, they have thus far concluded that male violence is largely genetic in origin, whereas female violence is largely due to specific environmental factors. This difference, they hypothesize, is linked to the sex hormone testosterone. Again, however, the dilemma is the inability of biocriminology to separate the influences of hormones from their interaction with gender roles and sociocultural development.

When it comes to neurotransmitters, the chemical (molecular) messenger *serotonin* seems to be one of several chemical actors associated with antisocial behavior. For example, a study carried out by Maikker Linnoila and his colleagues at the National Institute on Alcohol Abuse and Alcoholism in Bethesda, Maryland, found among a group of "impulsively violent offenders, who [had] killed or attempted to kill in a burst of unpremeditated fury," comparatively low levels of serotonin (Gallagher, 1994: 52). Aggressive and impulsive behaviors also appear to be related to at least one other neurotransmitter system located at the base of the brain.

In the *reticular formation*, as this region of the brain is called, there are dense bundles of nerve cells that "extend upward and forward from the brain stem through the limbic system (an emotion control system), and terminate in a region just above the eyes, called the *frontal lobes*" (Ellis, 1995: 6–7 [in the prepublished chapter numbering]). Like the neurotransmitter serotonin, low levels of three chemically similar neurotransmitters known as *catecholamines* (i.e., *dopamine, epinephrine, norepinephrine*) found in this region of the brain appear to be related to optimal and suboptimal levels of arousal. Low levels of catecholamines have, for example, been at least moderately associated with suboptimal arousal. Low levels of this neurotransmitter have also been linked to hyperactivity and to impulsivity and resistance to punishment (Ellis, 1995).

Lee Ellis (1987: 226) has developed an arousal theory of crime that argues that "criminal psychopathic persons have nervous systems that tend to be suboptimally aroused under 'normal' environmental conditions, and that engaging in criminal behavior is one of a number of 'excitement-seeking' behavioral tendencies that help to raise arousal to preferred levels." As Ellis (1995: 3 [in the prepublished numbering]) points out, *arousal theory* (also called optimal stimulation theory) is actually a general theory of behavior.

> *Arousal theory maintains that much of what motivates human activities can be understood in terms of our attempts to maintain a preferred (or optimal) level of arousal. If we experience too much novel and intense stimulation all at once, we feel anxiety and stress. At the other extreme, if too little is happening in our environment, we feel bored. Arousal theorists assume that our brains function differently with respect to how much of novel and intense stimuli is considered "too much" or "too little." Because of how our brains function, some of us "naturally" prefer much more environmental stimulation than do others.*

The theory has attempted to understand a fairly broad range of behavioral patterns besides criminality and psychopathology, including childhood hyperactivity, sensation-seeking behavior, alcoholism, and extroversion.

More specifically, scientists have come to call people who have suboptimal arousal levels or who thrive on unusually high levels of stimulation *sensation seekers* (Zuckerman, 1979). As Ellis (1995) has shown, there appears to be a relationship between one's sensitivity to incoming stimuli and the frequency with which one engages in illegal behavior. That is to say, those who are very insensitive to stimuli—sensation seekers—have a higher probability of criminality than those who are very sensitive to stimuli. Of course, the former may find his or her need for stimulation satisfied, just as easily, by sky-diving as by criminal behavior.

Similarly, when it comes to criminal motivation, Ellis (1989a and 1989b) has gone so far as to hypothesize that both aggression and property crimes are motivated by a largely unlearned "drive to possess and to control." He hypothesizes further that this drive is directed not only toward inanimate objects but also toward sex partners. Although a few studies from primate and other nonhuman species do suggest such a hypothesis for human behavior, numerous other animal studies of aggression give no reason at all to think that there might be a drive to possess and control. Ellis (1990: 9) argues that if this drive to possess and control exists in human beings, then "many of the techniques involved in committing crime, while entirely learned, are still fundamentally motivated by unlearned brain-functioning patterns." On the other hand, many animal behaviorists prefer not to talk about drives at all.

In sum, if Ellis's theory of arousal and criminality is correct, then biology may not only be a contributor to the variations of sex and age in criminality, but it may also be at the very root of these differences just as it is at "the root of sex differences in sensation seeking, risk taking, hyperactivity, and pain tolerance" (Ellis, 1995: 9) [in prepublished chapter numbering]. When it comes to questions of arousal or impulsivity, however, it should be kept in mind that these biochemical attributes may be viewed as necessary, but not sufficient, conditions of criminality. It should also be noted that these explanations are not restricted to motivations of "street" criminals. They may also be applied to the motivations of "suite" criminals. Evidence of these attributes has been present in both white collar and corporate crime (Wheeler, 1992; Calavita and Pontell, 1990, 1993; Jesilow et al., 1993).

## Body Physique and Temperament Factors

The notion of the "born criminal" was first introduced in 1876 with the publication of *Criminal Man* by the Italian physician Cesare Lombroso. In this book, Lombroso, often referred to as the father of modern or positivist criminology, concluded that

> *many of the characteristics found in savages, and among the coloured races, are also found in habitual delinquents. They have in common, for example, thinning hair, lack of strength and weight, low cranial capacity, receding foreheads, highly developed frontal sinuses . . . darker skin, thicker, curly hair, large or handle-shaped ears, a greater anal-*

Cesare Lombroso

*ogy between the two sexes . . . indolence . . . facile superstition . . . and finally the relative concept of the divinity and morals (quoted in Beirne and Messerschmidt, 1991: 304).*

By the early twentieth century, scientific support for the idea that criminals have a distinct physical appearance had eroded in much of Europe. It would not be until the middle of the century that the relevance of so-called body types to the study of criminality would be more or less put to rest in the United States. Interestingly, the works of an anthropologist, a psychiatrist, and two criminologists from Harvard kept the idea of physical types and crime/delinquency alive. In chronological order, there was Earnest Hooton's *The American Criminal* (1939), William Sheldon's *Varieties of Delinquent Youth* (1949), and Sheldon and Eleanor Glueck's *Unraveling Juvenile Delinquency* (1950) and *Physique and Delinquency* (1956).

Anthropologist Hooton (1939: 300) concluded that "criminals as a group represented an aggregate of sociologically and biologically inferior individuals." Psychiatrist Sheldon introduced the concept of somatotype as an alleged means for accurately measuring variation in body types. He maintained that there were essentially three somatotypes—*endomorphs* (short, well-nourished, soft and rounded body), *mesomorphs* (lean, muscular, and thick-skinned body), and *ectomorphs* (skinny and fragile body)— and each type tended to have a certain temperament. He describes endomorphs as relaxed, convivial, and emotionally constant; mesomorphs as assertive, dominating, competitive, and ruthless; and ectomorphs as secretive, restrained, and unpredictable. Sheldon concluded that delinquency was a product of mesomorphy and that it originated in that part of society that was biologically, intellectually, and spiritually inferior. Finally, the Gluecks, recognizing the influences of nonbiological factors on delinquency, nevertheless confirmed that mesomorphic traits of physical strength, energy, insensitivity, and the tendency to express tensions and frustrations in actions all contributed to temperaments that lent themselves naturally to behavioral aggression.

As we have seen in the two previous sections of this chapter, contemporary biocriminology focuses its energies on genes and on biochemistry. And although the notions of body types and their associated temperaments have been abandoned by all but a few criminologists, such as Wilson and Herrnstein (1985), the search for a more general understanding of human temperaments is very much alive. Today's search, however, is rooted at the molecular or biochemical, rather than at the physical, levels.

Temperament has been described as personality's biological, enduring, and heritable aspect (Gallagher, 1994). It has also been defined as a "set of behavioral predispositions that have physiological substrates *and* experiential components" (Megan Gunnar, quoted in Gallagher, 1994: 52). This means that, although people are predisposed to or possess tendencies toward particular temperaments, these are not fixed or rigidly predictable. In other words, temperaments can bend or adapt; they can also compensate. Moreover, it should be noted that temperament is a polymorphic concept that operates at the cellular, organic, and systemic levels.

Throughout most of history, predating the Enlightenment discovery of the individual, people were regarded more as variations of a few basic types. In the fifth century B.C., for example, Hippocrates described four temperaments: sanguine (optimistic and energetic); melancholic (moody and withdrawn); choleric (irritable and impulsive); and phlegmatic (calm and slow). As quaint as Hippocrates' typology was, today's modern linkages (as we will see later) of biochemisty with behavior find essentially the same types of people.

Temperament, like the mind in the brain, is best glimpsed in action. Temperament refers to something more than personality alone. It is more basic and has something to do with rhythm, reactivity, and emotion. Emotions are simultaneously physiological and psychological processes. Hans Eysenck (1977), a pioneer in the modern biological study of personality, believes that some emotions are so basic and universal that they are nothing less than the lowest common denominators of human experience.

Temperaments can be distinguished by such traits as anxiety, irritability, and impulsivity. In turn, these influence how we react to such stresses as intimidation or danger. As Gallagher (1994: 42) points out: "Physical or emotional, real or perceived, danger lurks everywhere, and from an evolutionary perspective our species' great asset and, sometimes, liability is an extremely sensitive emotional and physiological arousal system that detects and reacts to it." Most people have heard about two of the more common stress responses: flight or fight. There are actually three fundamental behavioral reactions to danger. According to Eysenck and Gudjonsson (1989), people can basically express behavior through *fear*, which helps us to engage in flight; *aggression*, which allows us to fight; and *sociability*, which permits us to act with equanimity.

Neuroendocrinologists further believe that our individual human natures are organized around habituated reactions to threats, ranging from physical danger to social change. Developmentally, each of us creates in interaction with those around us, especially during early childhood, patterns of behavioral expression. There are the stable people whom modern researchers describe variously as uninhibited, bold, or relaxed. These people can better cope with life's vicissitudes—from a snake in the desert to a barking boss—by being a bit more philosophical or existential about things; that is to say, the stress responses of these people are not triggered by every little thing nor are they on "red alert" for any longer than is necessary. Philip Gold, a research psychiatrist and chief of neuroendocrinology at the National Institute of Mental Health (NIMH), maintains with perhaps too much hyperbole that resilient people are innately disposed "to celebrate the beauty of existence and the wonders of an interior life and external connections despite being surrounded by unanswerable questions, ambiguous dilemmas, and the certainty of loss and death" (quoted in Gallagher, 1994: 42–43).

On the other hand, those less stable people will naturally react to threatening or merely unfamiliar situations with stress responses grounded in an excess of either flight or fight. These people will potentially find themselves in more trouble than their stable brothers and sisters. Today's anxious, inhibited, or reactive types (Hippocrates' melancholics) are apt to behave in depressive and, sometimes, in angry ways. Today's aggressive, impulsive, or irritable types (Hippocrates' cholerics) are apt to respond to stress by going into a fighting mode. Researchers argue that the possibility of pain or defeat is so intense for these people that they cannot bear to be accountable for it in a depressive way. Instead, blaming misfortune on others, they tend to react by striking out (or back).

Before proceeding with the evidence for these observations and descriptions, some perspective is called for. First, very few people are colored by a single emotional tone that equates to inhibited, uninhibited, aggressive, and other types. Most temperaments, in other words, are not primary yellow, blue, or red, but rather a combination of subtle shades or tones that include greens, oranges, and violets blended from lots of genetic proclivities. Second, scientists do not agree about the ultimate number of traits and temperaments they color. As we have already discussed, research to date has focused on the three most obvious qualities: fearlessness, boldness, and aggressiveness. Third, there is the case, once again, of the interaction between nature and nurture. Hence, a person's temperament is a product of the way one "has learned what he [or she] has to be in order to be loved" and the "genetic factors that biologically predispose him [or her] to respond in a certain way to the paradigmatic human situations of pleasure and opportunity, danger and loss" (P. Gold quoted in Gallagher, 1994: 43).

As this chapter implies, biochemistry and endocrinology are in the early stages of using a developing technology that not only allows them to trace the movement of neurotransmitters, the brain's chemical agents of communication, but that also permits their understanding of how these are translated into modulations of behavior. Jerome Kagan, author of *Unstable Ideas: Temperament, Cognition, and the Self* (1989) and *Galen's Prophecy: Temperament in Human Nature* (1994), has demonstrated, regarding infancy, what every parent knows: Each baby is born with a characteristic mood and style of responding.

By periodically measuring the behavioral and physiological responses (e.g., heart rate, blood pressure) of his infant subjects to mild stressors, such as noise, sour tastes, unfamiliar objects and people, including Mom's frowns, Kagan has demonstrated that by the second or third year of life, many babies clearly express one of two great temperamental extremes. About 15 percent of his samples are plainly inhibited and some 30 percent are uninhibited. The former differ from other children in many ways. They have greater incidences of allergies and constipation. They also have higher heart rates and levels of cortisol, a stress-related hormone. Slightly more than half of the inhibited types are girls and tend to have blue eyes and narrow faces. Psychologically, this group of subjects is "constrained and fretful, and have unusual fears—fears say of kidnapping rather than of monsters. The stimuli that swamp their sensitive nerves barely stir those of another group of children" (Gallagher, 1994: 44).

By contrast, the uninhibited types are said to demonstrate bold and aggressive personality. The majority of this group are boys. Their physiological stigma is their very low heart rate. Their behavior is characterized both by high energy and spontaneity.

Evidence from twin studies and Kagan's subject family histories have convinced him that inhibited and uninhibited natures begin with genes. Kagan, of course, is left asking himself as we should be asking ourselves: "How much of the temperament variation among individuals is due to biology and how much is due to learning?" What scientists do know is that the distinctive behavioral characteristics of anxious and bold children are associated neurochemical differences in the functioning of the *amygdala*—a brain structure that assigns emotion to experience—and its connections. The result is that the same loud noise that scares the inhibited child intrigues the uninhibited one.

Let us now turn to the temperament that Hippocrates called choleric and that his modern successors call "irritables." Hagop Akiska, a senior science advisor at the NIMH, says that although the irritable temperament is the hardest to define, it is the easiest to see. Irritables are said to possess hot-blooded temperaments. Their character types are quite popular at the movies, where actors often portray people who "express intense unmodulated emotion that, seemingly out of nowhere, comes on like an avalanche, striking one" (Akiska quoted in Gallaher, 1994: 48).

Irritability—the tendency to be easily annoyed—is not the same as aggressiveness, although the two are often observed together. Some scientists not only believe that irritability and aggressiveness overlap, but they also contend that the latter represents a combination of several traits. Unlike inhibition or boldness, the genesis of aggressiveness is believed to be more complex. Unfortunately, because irritability and aggressiveness evoke a lot of negative feelings in people, these temperaments have not been studied as much as the other temperaments.

For practical reasons, much of the research on aggressiveness has involved people who have committed violent crimes. "Although they are by no means a homogeneous group, many of the imprisoned have a few sad biographical features in common, including a history of inappropriate aggression from early childhood, an impulsive, angry personality, and a lower-than-average verbal IQ" (Gallagher, 1994: 49). At the same time, these "bad asses" are inhibited sorts. The evidence also suggests that at least one type of aggressive or violent behavior, namely that which evokes hot, or impulsive, rather than cold, or premeditated action, tends to be associated with low levels of serotonin and high levels of norepinephrine. Such persons have a tendency to act first and reflect later.

Kagan and others question the notion that there is an aggressive tendency per se. Instead, they contend that aggressive children are "fundamentally characterized by fearlessness: they're bold but badly brought up, so that they become bullies" (Gallagher, 1994: 48). Young research subjects who have been characterized as unruly and as having conduct problems, for example, have been described by their mothers as inhibited or anxious children. Clearly, all this mixture in temperaments rules out the possibility of a single gene for aggressiveness, let alone a gene for crime.

## Summary and Conclusions: Looking for a Molecular Knowledge of Crime

The study of biology and its relation to crime has, at the turn of the twenty-first century, gained new credibility. As Beirne and Messerschmidt (1991: 489) write: "For the first time in several decades, recognition of biological factors is gaining importance among criminologists, especially among those with training in psychiatry, psychology, or forensic medicine," as we will discover in Chapter 6. Many people, of course, are lulled by the undeniable accomplishments of the biomedical revolution and are hoping for a quick cure to the crime problem.

More realistically, however, what we have are neurotransmitters that have been linked to some forms of impulsive and aggressive behavior. Contemporary biocriminology has moved from those analyses that argued that biology caused crime to more complex theoretical analyses that view crime as a product of sociobiology. Whether biology is the first stage in a causal sequence leading to crime that requires the subsequential intervention of psychological and sociological variables (Rowe and Osgood, 1984; Cohen and Machalek, 1988), or biology is part of a more developmental, interactive, sociocultural and biochemical integration (Ellis and Hoffman, 1990; Vila, 1994), the study of the molecular correlates of behavior is still in a relatively embryonic stage, far from producing any immediate, short-term payoffs. Nevertheless, much of this work is provocative and promising, and, I believe, certainly worth pursuing.

Of course, it still remains to be seen how exactly these internal biochemical predispositions contribute to theories of criminal behavior. In the meanwhile, it seems to make sense that we begin by taking the production of temperament into account, not only exclusively at the obvious individual level, but also at the more subtle aggregate level of social and institutional interaction. In the next chapter, we turn to a review of the contributions from psychology. These have identified other internal traits or "kinds-of-people theories" of criminality.

## Discussion Questions

1. What are the primary differences between the "older" and "newer" biological approaches to criminal behavior?

2. While paying attention to the research methodologies, units of analysis, and basic premises, compare and contrast twin studies, testosterone studies, and somatotypic studies.

3. What are the hypothesized relationships between "body temperament," "character traits," and crime?

4. What do you find most and least compelling about biological explanations of crime?

# References

Akers, Ronald L. 1994. *Criminological Theories: Introduction and Evaluation.* Los Angeles: Roxbury.

Begley, Sharon. 1995. "Gray Matters." *Newsweek* (March 27): 48–54.

Beirne, Piers, and James Messerschmidt. 1991. *Criminology.* San Diego: Harcourt Brace Jovanovich.

Calvita, Kitty, and Henry N. Pontell. 1990. " 'Heads I Win, Tails You Lose': Deregulation, Crime and Crisis in Savings and Loan Industry." *Crime and Delinquency* 36: 309–341.

———. 1993. "Savings and Loan Fraud as Organized Crime: Toward a Conceptual Typology of Corporate Illegality." *Criminology* 31:519–548.

Christiansen, Karl O. 1977. "A Preliminary Study of Criminality among Twins" and "A Review of Studies of Criminality among Twins." In Sarnoff A. Mednick and K. O. Christiansen, eds., *Biosocial Bases of Criminal Behavior.* New York: Gardner.

Cloninger, C. R. and I. I. Gottesman. 1987. "Genetic and Environmental Factors in Antisocial Behavior Disorders." In S. A. Mednick, T. E. Moffitt, and S. A. Stack, eds., *The Causes of Crime: New Biological Approaches.* Cambridge: Cambridge University Press.

Cohen, Lawrence E., and Richard Machalek. 1988. "A General Theory of Expropriative Crime." *American Journal of Sociology* 94:465–501.

Curran, Daniel J., and Claire M. Renzetti. 1994. *Theories of Crime.* Boston: Allyn and Bacon.

Currie, Elliot. 1985. *Confronting Crime: An American Challenge.* New York: Pantheon.

Einstadter, Werner, and Stuart Henry. 1995. *Criminological Theory: An Analysis of Its Underlying Assumptions.* Fort Worth: Harcourt Brace.

Ellis, Lee. 1982. "Genetics and Criminal Behavior: Evidence Through the End of the 1970s." *Criminology* 20: 43–66.

———. 1987. "Neurohormonal Bases of Varying Tendencies to Learn Delinquent and Criminal Behavior." In E. K. Morris and C. J. Braukmann, eds., *Behavioral Approaches to Crime and Delinquency.* New York: Plenum.

———. 1989a. *Theories of Rape: Inquiries into the Causes of Sexual Aggression.* New York: Hemisphere Publications.

———. 1989b. "Evolutionary and Neurochemical Causes of Sex Differences in Victimizing Behaviour: Toward a Unified Theory of Criminal Behaviour and Social Stratification." *Social Science Information* 28:605–636.

———. 1990. "Introduction: The Nature of the Biosocial Perspective." In L. Ellis and H. Hoffman, eds., *Crime in Biological, Social, and Moral Contexts.* New York: Praeger.

———. 1995. "Arousal Theory and the Religiosity-Criminality Relationship." In L. Siegel and P. Cordella, eds., *Contemporary Criminological Theory.* Boston: Northeastern University Press.

Ellis, Lee, and Harry Hoffman, eds. 1990. *Crime in Biological, Social, and Moral Contexts.* New York: Praeger.

Eysenck, Hans. J. 1977. *Crime and Personality.* London: Routledge and Kegan Paul.

Eysenck, H. J., and G. H. Gudjonsson. 1989. *The Causes and Cures of Criminality.* New York: Plenum.

Fishbein, D. H., and S. E. Pease. *The Effects of Diet on Behavior: Implications for Criminology and Corrections.* Boulder, CO: Rand Corporation and National Institute of Corrections.

Fisher, Helen. 1994. " 'Wilson,' They Said, 'You're All Wet!': A Review of the *Naturalist* by E. O. Wilson." *The New York Times Book Review* (November): 15–17.

Gallagher, Winifred. 1994. "How We Become What We Are." *The Atlantic Monthly* (September): 38–55.

Gibbons, Don C. 1994. *Talking About Crime and Criminals: Problems and Issues in Theory Development in Criminology.* Englewood Cliffs, NJ: Prentice-Hall.

Glueck, Sheldon, and Eleanor Glueck. 1950. *Unraveling Juvenile Delinquency.* New York: The Commonwealth Fund.

———. 1956. *Physique and Delinquency.* New York: Harper.

Harris, J. A., E. Hampson, J. P. Rushton, and D. N. Jackson. n. d. (submitted for publication) "Salivary Testosterone and Self-Report Personality: Aggression and Prosocial Dimensions."

Hooton, Ernest A. 1939. *The American Criminal: An Anthropological Study.* Cambrdige, MA: Harvard University Press.

Iversen, Susan. 1983. "Brain Endorphines and Reward Function: Some Thoughts and Speculations." In J. E. Smith and J. D. Lane, eds., *The Neurobiology of the Opiate Reward Process*. Amsterdam: Elsevier.

Jesilow, Paul, Henry N. Pontell, and Gilbert Geis. 1993. *Prescription for Profit: How Doctors Defraud Medicaid*. Berkeley: University of California Press.

Kagan, Jerome. 1989. *Unstable Ideas: Temperament, Cognition, and the Self*. Cambridge, MA: Harvard University Press.

———. 1994. *Galen's Prophecy: Temperament in Human Nature*. New York: Basic Books.

Lester, M. L., R. W. Thatcher, and L. Monroe-Lord. 1982. "Refined Carbohydrate Intake, Hair Cadmium Levels and Cognitive Functioning in Children." *Journal of Nutrition and Behavior* 1:1–14.

Mednick, S. A., W. F. Gabrielli, and B. Hutchings. 1984. "Genetic Influences in Criminal Convictions: Evidence From an Adoption Cohort." *Science* 224:891–94.

Rowe, David C. 1986. "Genetic and Environmental Components of Antisocial Behavior: A Study of 265 Twin Pairs." *Criminology* 24:513–532.

Rowe, David C., and D. Wayne Osgood. 1984. "Heredity and Sociological Theories of Delinquency: A Reconsideration." *American Sociological Review* 49:526–540.

Rushton, J. Philippe. 1995. *Race, Evolution, and Behavior: A Life History Perspective*. New Brunswick, NJ: Transaction.

Rushton, J. Philippe, and Julie Aitken Harris. 1994. "Genetic and Environmental Components to Self-Report Violence in Male and Female Twins." Paper presented at the annual meetings of the American Society of Criminology, Miami (November).

Schalling, Daisy. 1987. "Personality Correlates of Plasma Testosterone Levels in Young Delinquents: An Example of Person-Situation Inter-

action?" In S. A. Mednick, T. Moffitt, and S. A. Stack, eds., *The Causes of Crime: New Biological Approaches*. Cambridge: Cambridge University Press.

Sheldon, William H. 1949. *Varieties of Delinquent Youth*. New York: Harper.

Taylor, Lawrence, and Katharina Dalton. 1983. "Premenstrual Syndrome: A New Criminal Defense?" *California Western Law Review* 19: 269–287.

Vila, Bryan. 1994. "A General Paradigm for Understanding Criminal Behavior: Extending Evolutionary Ecological Theory." *Criminology* 32: 311–359.

Virkkunen, Matti. 1987. "Metabolic Dysfunctions Among Habitually Violent Offenders: Reactive Hypoglycemia and Cholesterol Levels." In S. A. Mednick, T. Moffitt, and S. A. Stack, eds., *The Causes of Crime: New Biological Approaches*. Cambridge: Cambridge University Press.

Walters, Glenn D. 1992. "A Meta-Analysis of the Gene Crime Relationship." *Criminology* 30: 595–613.

Wheeler, Stanton. 1992. "The Problem of White-collar Motivation." In *White Collar Crime Reconsidered*. Boston: Northeastern University Press.

Wilson, Edward O. 1975. *Sociobiology: The New Synthesis*. Cambridge, MA: The Belknap Press of Harvard University Press.

Wilson, Edward O. 1978. *On Human Nature*. Cambridge, MA: Harvard University Press.

Wilson, Edward, and Charles Lumsden. 1981. *Genes, Mind, and Culture*. Cambridge, MA: Harvard University Press.

Wilson, James Q., and Richard Herrnstein. 1985. *Crime and Human Nature*. New York: Simon and Schuster.

Zuckerman, M. 1979. *Sensation-Seeking: Beyond the Optimal Level of Arousal*. Hillsdale, NJ: Erlbaum.

Chapter *6*

# Contributions from Psychology: "Mind and Nature"

Jeffrey L. Dahmer, Milwaukee, 1991

When it comes to bodies of knowledge, with the possible exception of sociology, perhaps no field or discipline is as broad and diverse, or as eclectic and divided, as psychology. The contributions that psychology has brought to bear on explaining general behavior and criminal behavior spring from a number of orientations: behavioral, cognitive, evolutionary, humanistic, social-psychological, and psychoanalytic. As different as these psychologies are, they share in common an attempt to formulate theories of behavior that "rise above the culturally and historically particular so as to capture something more lasting and basic" (Daly and Wilson, 1994: 256). That is to say, whether psychologists are discussing retrieval mechanisms, self-esteem, group dynamics, or oedipal conflicts, they tend to focus their examinations on basic components of human nature, such as appetites and aversions, motives, and emotions that are viewed as characteristic of the human species (or of one sex or life stage).

As for the psychological theories of antisocial behavior or criminal offending, there are many common features that prevail. Most of these explanations of criminal behavior assume that: (1) there are consistent individual differences, such as an underlying criminal potential or antisocial personality; (2) the pursuit of pleasure is the main energizing factor; (3) there are internal and external inhibitors involved in processes of socialization; (4) the violations are the result of rational decisions involving cost-benefit type analyses; and (5) that "impulsivity, or a poor ability to take account of and be influenced by the possible future consequences of offending, is an important factor, often linked to a poor ability to manipulate abstract concepts and low intelligence" (Farrington, 1994a: xxxi). Certainly, some of these assumptions have been supported whereas others have not.

When it comes to the empirical evidence or to proofs based on natural science criteria, psychology has been successful in only some of its subfields. For example, among the most successful subfields of psychology have been those associated with biology, such as the study of sensation and perception. More generally, the problem of psychological validation has to do with the fact that the primary object of study is the mind rather than the body. Hence, until the time when neuroscience advances in its understanding of the structural and functional complexity of the brain, some of the proofs regarding the public verifiability of the privacy of minds will have to wait.

For the purposes of this chapter, however, the demands of the scientific method will not delimit the discussion of those psychological insights that stem, for example, from psychoanalytic theories. Hence, it is assumed that the data of psychological science consists of more than the mind's behavioral manifestations. It also consists of those psychological hypotheses that are necessarily claims about the processes and mechanisms that produce individual behavior. Comprised in a person's *psyche*, then, are both conscious and unconscious components of the mind, which can become subjects of criminological examination.

Before turning to the contextualization of the psychological contributions to criminology, it should be pointed out that like the theories of a "born criminal" the theories of a "sick criminal" are just as fallacious. This theory has two null hypotheses. First, mentally ill persons are not any more likely to engage in offending behavior than mentally healthy persons. Second, most offenders are not necessarily suffering from a

Theodore Bundy, Florida, 1978

diagnostic mental illness of any abnormal consequence. As Paul Tappan (1951: 11) concluded some fifty years ago, "the prevalent idea of criminal illness is highly misleading. Criminals are not generally neurotic, psychotic, or psychopathic." Although the conceptions of a criminal as a fundamentally sick person or of a criminal personality type are rejected here, the conceptualization of a "psychology of criminal conduct" (Andrews and Bonta, 1994) is not. With this in mind, the focus of Chapter 6 is more about mental adaptation than mental pathology.

## Contextualizing Psychological Contributions

Trying to contextualize the contributions of psychology to the understanding of human behavior in general and to criminal behavior in particular is not easy. This is due, in part, to the overlapping identification of some criminological theories, such as Tarde's "imitation," Sutherland's "differential association," Reckless's "containment," Hirschi's "control," and Jeffery's "differential reinforcement," as belonging to both sociology and psychology. As applied to theories of crime, the psychological contributions included in this chapter are inclusive of what other textbooks would typically classify as contributions belonging in the sociological traditions. For example, although most criminologists classify theories of social control and theories of social learning as sociological, I prefer to think of them as psychological because of the way in which human nature interacts with desire, translated as appetites and aversions, motives and emotions.

The variation in psychological contributions spans the late nineteenth and early twentieth centuries to the present day. During the nineteenth century there were developments in biological and psychiatric approaches to criminal behavior. Parallel to the work of Darwin on evolution and Lombroso on the "born criminal," there was

Issac Ray (1807–1881) in the United States, who "carried out studies in forensic psychiatry, which led to separate treatments for the mentally ill offender. Shortly after the turn of the century, the development of scales of intelligence by Binet enabled studies of a possible link between crime and intelligence" (Feldman, 1993: xii). By the 1920s, there was the emergence of both the psychoanalytic and sociopsychological traditions.

The next seventy years or so gave rise to an evolving concept of *social control* that had two meanings: one for sociologists and one for psychologists. Sociologists, such as Ross (1901) and Park and Burgess (1925), thought of social control in a broad sense, including all institutions and processes engaged in preserving social order. Social psychologists, such as Cooley (1902) and Mead (1934), picking up on the earlier works of Tarde, proceeded to narrow the concept of social control to the way in which significant others socialized members into their groups. The two best-known criminological versions of social control have been Reckless (1961) and Hirschi (1969). As discussed later in the chapter, Hirschi's work was in the narrower traditions of childhood socialization whereas Reckless's work was in the broader sociopsychological tradition. Sutherland's work also falls into the broader tradition as he stresses social, cultural, and organizational features involved in learning to "become a criminal."

The middle of the twentieth century saw the rise of behaviorism (Skinner, 1953) and the elaboration of social learning theory. This theory maintains that "social behavior is a cognitive process in which personality and environment engage in a continuous process of reciprocal interaction" (Beirne and Messerschmidt, 1991: 435). Most of these formulations claim that crime is a product of one's past conditioning history or a response to reinforcing stimuli. Another development that occured during the middle of this century was the influence of a post-Freudian (and neo-Freudian) humanistic psychology (Maslow and Murphey, 1954; Maslow, 1959; Halleck, 1967) that assumed human beings are essentially good and that they respond to basic needs and feelings. Crime, according to these developmental schemata, is either a way to satisfy basic needs or a way of adapting to feelings of helplessness.

The most recent development in the discipline of psychology is the body of knowledge referred to as evolutionary psychology. Like evolutionary biology, evolutionary psychology argues that many of the impulses created by natural selection's genetic self-interest are not necessarily or directly selfish. These impulses also involve the machinery of what evolutionists call reciprocal altruism. Besides the genetic heritage of aggressive and sexual behavior, there are the genetic inheritances, for example, of affiliative impulses such as love, pity, generosity, remorse, friendly affection, and enduring trust. "Because social cooperation improves the chances of survival, natural selection imbued our minds with an infrastructure for friendship, including affection, gratitude and trust" (Wright, 1995: 53).

Contemporary biopsychologists argue further that it is the structures of modern society that have created unknown stresses and tensions as some of the affiliative impulses are increasingly frustrated. The problems of modern life, in other words, are connected to a social reality of under- rather than oversocialization. In short, "too little of our 'social' contact is social in the natural, intimate sense of the word" (Wright, 1995: 56).

Before turning to my review of the psychological contributions to criminology, a couple of points concerning mental health and psychopathology are in order. First, most psychologists are inclined to say that early familiar nurturing is key in the formation of deviant and nondeviant behavior. Second, throughout the history of psychology, psychoanalysis, and psychiatry, there have been the implicit, if not explicit, arguments that there are criminal personalities or that criminals are mentally defective in one way or another.

However, the extreme case of Jeffrey Dahmer, for example, reveals the complexities of the mind and the facile approaches that often attempt to diagnose the motivation of such conditions. Dahmer, who was 34 and serving 936 years at the Columbia Correctional Institution in Portage, Wisconsin, for the grisly murders and dismemberment of sixteen young men, was himself the victim of a brutal homicide on November 28, 1994.

Dahmer was beaten to death with a broom handle by a "psychotic" inmate who had been previously sentenced for an execution-style murder during a robbery in 1990. Dahmer did not put up a fight. It was believed that he looked forward to death. Thus, he said to the judge at his sentencing in 1992, "Your honor, it is over now. This has never been a case of trying to get free. I didn't ever want freedom. Frankly, I wanted death for myself" (quoted in Gleick, 1994: 129). In a 1994 interview that Dahmer gave *Dateline NBC*, he said that he needed to live in a world where he "could completely control a person—a person that I found physically attractive, and keep them with me as long as possible, even if it meant just keeping a part of them," referring to the freezers and lobster-cooking pots full of human body parts (quoted in Gleick, 1994: 129).

As an exceptional member even within the highly select grouping of serial killers, Dahmer exhibited what appeared to be an unusual quality of honesty. This honesty, however, may simply have been a lack of insight or a case of denial. Nevertheless, most serial killers are thought to be pathological liars (Leyton, 1986). Dahmer admitted his guilt and shared his experiences of murder, or at least his interpretations of these experiences. He was also allegedly interested in getting to the roots of his behavior, to its motivation, and to explaining why he did what he did. Dahmer (a Caucasian) was driven to pick up young, gay (mostly African American) men, bring them home, drug them, strangle them, have sex with their corpses, and perhaps cannibalize them.

Nobody would exactly call this "normal" behavior. In fact, most people, regardless of their psychological persuasion, would call this behavior pathological. Nevertheless, Dahmer's attorney was unable to persuade the jury of his client's innocence by reason of insanity. He was found guilty of murder, which certainly raises the questionable legal value of such labels as "psychopathic" and "sociopathic" when it comes to diminished capacity or *mens rea* (guilty mind).

The "old compulsions," as Dahmer called them, took control when he killed sixteen times. Still, Dahmer was liked by prison guards and inmates alike. He was said to have a good sense of humor, once posting a sign on the prison bulletin board for a "Cannibals Anonymous" meeting. While spending time in prison in the early 1990s before his death, Dahmer would smoke cigarettes, read religious materials, and listen to tapes of classical music, Gregorian chants, and humpback whales. Dahmer thought that he deserved to die and that his living was a sin against God. At the same time, he was willing to accept responsibility for his actions. He did not blame a lonely, alienated childhood nor his parents' bitter divorce in 1978. He didn't believe, as his chemist father did, that his behavior was the product of the medication his mother had taken during pregnancy. Similarly, he maintained that parents, society, pornography, and so on were excuses and not the causes for what he did. At the same time, Dahmer didn't feel that he was born that way, but rather that his mind acquired compulsive habits and behaviors in early childhood and that these eventually overpowered him and took control.

It is precisely in the relationship between mind and nature that the different psychological orientations cross paths. Each orientation features different factors of abnormal characterological development. Some stress desires, others emphasize needs, but all orientations are shaped by the developmental processes that occur during the formative years of socialization. Moreover, several of the psychological theories "posit a mechanistic and deterministic relationship between the unconscious mind and behavior. Others locate the causal agency in social relationships" (Einstadter and Henry, 1995: 109–110). Still other theories "give priority to distorted but limited cognitive processes that exercise 'free' will in carrying out goal-directed behavior" (Einstadter and Henry, 1995: 110).

All in all, the breadth and diversity of psychology helps to centralize its place—between biology and sociology—in the process of integrating criminologies. The rest of this chapter divides and groups psychological factors and explanations of crime and delinquency into five categories: biopsychological, psychoanalytic, antisocial personality, social-psychological, and humanistic-psychological. Each of these categories will, in turn and where appropriate, be further subdivided.

## Biopsychological Approaches to Criminal Behavior

One of the oldest strands of biopsychology involves the relationship between intelligence (IQ) and crime. Popular during the late teens and 1920s, the idea of crime as a product of *low intelligence* was also resurrected in the 1970s. In 1914, H. H. Goddard published *Feeblemindedness: Its Causes and Consequences*. He argued that criminals were *feebleminded*, a term that has been replaced by the more modern label *mentally retarded*. In a schema such as Goddard's, the idea that criminals are mentally inferior is substituted for the idea that criminals are biologically inferior. By the 1930s, based on hundreds of studies, it was concluded that the distribution of intelligence scores of delinquents and criminals was very similar to the distribution of intelligence scores of the general population (Sutherland and Cressey, 1978).

More recently, Hirschi and Hindelang (1977) and Gordon (1987) found a not very strong negative correlation between IQ (intelligence quotient) and delinquent behavior, which was not significantly diminished when class, race, and other factors were controlled for. The difference in intelligence between delinquents and nondelinquents had appeared to stabilize at about eight IQ points. Such a difference, however, is generally considered within the normal range for both groups and could easily be explained by variations in socialization and educational training rather than in raw, or genetic, intelligence. As for adult criminals, most are not feebleminded. Finally, because correlation is not causation, even a low negative association between IQ and crime does not explain the distribution of crime, especially when white-collar and corporate crimes are factored in (Bohm, 1996).

Modern research has expanded its study of intelligence to include the detailed study of patterns of cognitive and *neuropsychological deficit*. This neuropsychological research is concerned with examining the link between brain functioning and behavior. It specifically explores the frontal lobes of the brain where the executive functions are located. These functions include sustaining attention and concentration, abstract reasoning and concept formation, anticipation and planning, self-monitoring of behavior, and inhibition of inappropriate or impulsive behavior (Moffitt, 1990). Studies of children and young adolescents have found, for example, neuropsychological deficits in these executive functions, especially for delinquents who were both antisocial and hyperactive (Moffitt and Henry, 1989). Studies have also found that verbal, memory, and visual-motor integration deficits, independent of social class and family adversity, were related to self-reported offending (Moffitt and Silva, 1988).

The point is that "deficits in these executive functions are conducive to low measured intelligence and to offending" (Farrington, 1994a: xix). Moreover, developing intelligence is clearly related to other psychological theories of offending, such as the moral development theory of Lawrence Kohlberg (1976). This theory argues that as people get older, they progress through different stages, "from the preconventional stage (where they are hedonistic and only obey the law because of fear of punishment) to the conventional stage (where they obey the law because it is the law) to the postconventional stage (where they obey the law if it coincides with higher moral principles such as justice, fairness, and respect for individual rights)" (Farrington, 1994a: xix).

Developing *moral reasoning*—moving from the preconventional concrete level of thinking to the postconventional abstract level of thinking, in other words, is related to developing intelligence. Moral reasoning is also related to the abilities of manipulating abstract concepts, of empathizing with the feelings of victims, and of foreseeing the consequences of negative actions. Hence, moral reasoning becomes the precursor for moral actions.

Offenders are presumed to have retarded powers of moral reasoning and to be stuck mainly in the preconventional state (Kohlberg and Candee, 1984). Evidence that young offenders demonstrate lower levels of moral reasoning than nonoffenders has been amply presented (Smetana, 1990; Thornton, 1987). However, it is suspected that if studies of the moral reasoning of white collar and corporate offenders were factored in, the distribution in the orders of moral reasoning would change considerably. Even if the relationships were upheld, this would not prove, for example, whether moral reasoning was the cause or merely another symptom of an underlying antisocial personality.

*Impulsivity* and its typically associated behaviors of restlessness, hyperactivity, and short attention span are part of another important biopsychological construct that has predicted delinquency (Taylor, 1986). HIA (hyperactivity-impulsivity-attention deficit) syndrome usually begins before age 5 and often before 2, and tends to persist into adolescence. Related behavioral constructs, such as conduct disorders and sensation seeking or risk taking, as well as poor concentration or restlessness, were all predictors of delinquent and early adult offending (Farrington et al., 1990; Farrington 1994b; White et al., 1985).

Some of these biopsychological constructs are also related to low levels of physiological arousal as discussed in Chapter 5. For example, it has been suggested that HIA might be a behavioral consequence of a low level of arousal. As Farrington (1994: xvii) writes; "Offenders have a low level of arousal according to their low alpha (brain) waves on the EEG, or according to autonomic nervous system indicators such as heart rate, blood pressure or skin conductance; also, they show low automatic reactivity."

The final biopsychological construct to be discussed is that of *evolutionary psychology*. Like physiological psychologists who study feeding (i.e., eating disorders), or students of sensation and perception, memory, and motor control, evolutionary psychologists assume that the mechanisms under study are adaptively designed. Evolutionary psychologists, like their counterparts, don't assume that biology is the study of some kind of innate invariant. Nor do they believe that biology is mute on the subjects of sociality and behavior manifesting developmentally, experientially, and circumstantially contingent variations. On the contrary, these domain-specific models (rather than domain-general models of behavioral learning) of contingent variation are "precisely what evolutionary biological theories of social phenomena are about" (Daly and Wilson, 1994: 261).

The argument is made that the apparent purpose in organismic design depends not only on the persistence of essential features of past environments, but also on the adaptive abilities of organisms to find solutions to those problems that have been sufficiently tenacious across generations. For example, a central proposition in the often vilified 1966 book *On Aggression,* by Nobel Prize-winning ethologist Konrad Lorenz, was that aggressive behavior is an instance of evolved adaption rather than pathology. In other words,

> *Animals (including people) react violently to usurpation of essential resources by rivals, and they direct their violence against those rivals. Moreover, those who initiate violence typically do so where there is some means to the end of fitness to be gained. Aggression occurs where territories are limited, when one's own offspring are under threat, when food is scare, and in the context of mating competition (Daly and Wilson, 1994: 265).*

The point is that the evidence for a functional design of violence is multifarious. Martin Daly and Margo Wilson (1994: 265), who have examined violence as a complex adaptation of evolutionary psychology involving motivational states of readiness for violence (anger arousal), psychophysiological mobilization for effective agonistic action (battle), and morphological structures that function in intraspecific ways (i.e., the ability of men to totally disregard a woman's unwillingness to have intercourse as evidenced by their sustained erections and coerced copulations), argue that the prevalence of male violence compared to that of female violence is inseparable from the "potency of natural and sexual selection in shaping the anatomy and psychology of intrasexual aggression."

When it comes to sexual conflict between men and women or to intersexual aggression, violence by men against their wives, lovers, and other females is a rather ubiquitous phenomenon cross-culturally. However, there are only a few contexts in which men typically engage in such violence (Campbell, 1992; Dobash and Dobash, 1979; Daly et al., 1982; Polk and Ranson, 1991; and Wilson and Daly, 1992). Men will, for example, assault wives or lovers in response to real or perceived sexual infidelity. They will also do so when a wife or lover either threatens to terminate or appears to be terminating a relationship. Men will also respond with violence as a means of disciplining women who are perceived as too independent.

Arguing from the point of view of evolutionary psychology, Daly and Wilson put forward related explanations for male violence against intimates and against strangers. When it comes to intimates, they "propose that the particular cues and circumstances which inspire men to use violence against their partners reflect a domain-specific masculine psychology which evolved in a social milieu in which assaults and threats of violence functioned to deter wives from pursuing alternative reproductive opportunities, which would have represented substantial threats to husbands' fitness by misdirecting parental investment and loss of mating opportunities to reproductive competitors" (Daly and Wilson, 1994: 269). They also discuss a domain-specific psychology of women reflecting "the past costs and benefits of accepting or rejecting particular sexual partners" (Daly and Wilson, 1994: 269–270).

Throughout history one of the most costly threats to a woman's personhood has been the loss of opportunity to choose who is likely to sire her offspring (Thornhill and Thornhill, 1983; 1990). Without that choice, women are deprived of the opportunity to have their children sired by desirable phenotypes. In the case of rape in particular, children are similarly deprived of the time, energy, and resources of a father selected by the mother. In any case, it is reasonable to assume that undesired sexual encounters have been resisted by women and that the "use of violence by men [would have been] a very effective means of controlling the reluctant victim" (Daly and Wilson, 1994: 270). As Daly and Wilson (1994: 270) contend, "the fitness costs of any single act of sexual intercourse have always been less for men than for women, which suggests that the evolved sexual psychology of men is likely to be less discriminating regarding choice of partner for a single sexual opportunity than that of women."

## Psychoanalytic Views of Criminal Behavior

By the 1920s and 1930s, to the extent that individual personality was considered a factor in behavior, it was the psychoanalytic approach that interpreted crime as the expression of tensions and conflicts within the individual. Along with the dominant sociological views of the period that stressed social environment, the dominant perspective in the psychology of crime was psychoanalytic. It is basic to Freudian theory, both in general and as applied to crime, "that all human behaviors are motivated, with latent meanings to all actions, meanings which remain unconscious. An understanding of behavior, delinquent or otherwise, requires the analysis of the individual, whether patient or offender" (Feldman, 1993: 165).

All of the Freudian-related theories of crime assume that at the root of antisocial or criminal behavior are patterns of emotional disturbances brought about by experiences, real and imaginary, that inhibit children from developing in healthy ways. These theories linking childrearing and criminal behavior all assume that the personality consists of three major mechanisms identified by Sigmund Freud (1923): the id, ego, and superego. The id contains the instinctual, unconscious desires, such as sex and aggression, with which a child is born. It functions according to the *pleasure principle*, avoiding pain and seeking gratification. The ego, by contrast, functions according to the *reality principle* and is said to develop out of the id by age 3. Herein lies the seat of consciousness wherein the individual tries to negotiate the desires of the id with the accounts of the reality of social conventions. By the age of five, the superego has developed out of the ego in order to perform the tasks of (1) suppressing or diverting instinctual desires that violate social rules (conscience) through the process of *sublimation* and (2) representing or internalizing the parents' standards (ego-ideal) through the process of *identification*.

Systemically speaking, Freud believed that humans possess minds, or psyches, for the purposes of adapting to their environments, good or bad. More fundamentally, he assumed that the psychic processes of the mind were preceded by physiological processes and were dependent on the brain's biological processes. Based on this assumption, no matter how information reaches the mind, whether from the outer world through the sense organs or from the body through the chemical stimuli it provides, the psyche must begin as a physical excitation (Jones, 1953).

More specifically, psychoanalysis argues that the psychopathology of delinquents or of emotionally disturbed nondelinquents is essentially the same since they have all proceeded unsuccessfully through Freud's (1923, 1930) five stages of *psychosexual development:* oral, anal, phallic, latent, and genital. It is assumed, then, that problematic behavior is the result of individuals fixating at one or more stages of their development. In other words, the development of a child with a strong ego depends on a close emotional relationship with its parents. Moreover, in the formation of the ego-ideal, healthy children, through a process of *introjection* (itself dependent on loving parental

Sigmund Freud

relationships), incorporate not only the verbal prohibitions of their parents, but also the "emotionally charged images of their parents—thinking, feeling, and acting like them" (Farrington, 1994a: xxv).

According to psychoanalytic theories, healthy egos and normal development allow individuals to adapt to the realities of social convention that they confront. For example, the ego-ideal can delay immediate gratification in deference to long-term goals, think ahead and plan, and reduce the desires of the id through fantasy. By contrast, the inadequate development of the ego or superego, a product of unloving or deviant parents, will result in emotionally disturbed, if not criminal, behavior. In short, psychodynamically oriented theories assume that humans are formed by being "adequately socialized through a series of normal developmental stages to develop moral and social selves" (Einstadter and Henry, 1995: 103).

Psychoanalytic approaches to criminal behavior can be broken down into four camps. One camp sees criminal acts as being undertaken to maintain psychic balance or to rectify psychic equilibrium, which may even stem from an unconscious desire for punishment. A second camp views crime as a form of neurosis expressed not through psychiatric symptoms but rather through overt acts. A third group claims that crime is a substitute form of gratification for other needs blocked or left unsatisfied. A fourth group talks of crime as a means of compensation for repressed feelings of inadequacy (Feldman, 1993).

A myriad of psychoanalytically oriented theories of criminal behavior has been put forward that does not necessarily fit neatly into one of the above categories. Three examples will have to suffice here. First, there is the general concept of psychopath and its parallel in sociology the sociopath, both of which have come to be called the *antisocial personality*. According to psychosexual developmental theory, between the ages of 3 and 6, the child develops a monopoly feeling for the opposite-sex parent. For Freud, this is a normal, universal phenomenon expressed in boys by the Oedipus complex and in girls by the Electra complex. If the conflict between the child and the same-sex parent for the attentions of the opposite-sex parent is not resolved through normal development, the result is the formation of a weak superego. In the case of psychopathic personality profiles, there is the alleged lack of remorse or shame, the general poverty in major affective reactions, the untruthfulness and insincerity, the superficial charm and good intelligence, and the absence of delusions and other signs of irrational thinking, among a much larger list of characteristics (Cleckley, 1955).

Second, there are the *psychic-need* theories, which argue that the developing child requires care and affection from adults and the ability of self-realization (Bowlby, 1946). In order for the growing child to self-realize or to cope with reality, he or she needs to be not only loved by an adult, but also to be valued by his or her peers. When either or both of these psychic needs are denied, the result is first discomfort and subsequently anxiety. If these are severe enough, they can trigger delinquent behavior aimed at restoring emotional (not material) equilibrium. The ends typically sought include: "a search for excitement in order to avoid anxiety; retaliation against parents; attention-seeking from parents; and seeking removal from home and compensation for inferiority by adopting a pose of bravado" (Feldman, 1993: 166).

The third, and probably the best-known Freudian application to delinquent behavior, is the *techniques-of-neutralization* theory advanced by Gresham Sykes and David

Matza (1957) some forty years ago. Applying Freud's various *defense mechanisms*, such as projection and rationalization, they argued that "much of delinquency is based on what is essentially an unrecognized extension of defenses to crimes, in the form of justifications for deviance that are seen as valid by the delinquent but not by the legal system or society as large" (Sykes and Matza 1957: 666). For Sykes and Matza it was by learning the techniques of neutralization that juveniles become delinquent. They described five such defense mechanisms: (1) denial of responsibility, such as "I didn't mean to do it"; (2) denial of injury, such as "nobody got hurt"; (3) denial of victim, such as "they had it coming to them"; (4) condemnation of the condemners, such as "everybody does it"; and (5) appeal to higher loyalties, such as "I only did it for the gang." For Sykes and Matza, it was not the learning of attitudes, values, or laws per se that facilitated delinquency, but rather the ability of juveniles to justify their delinquent behavior. Without the justification, they contended, youth would not engage in offending behavior.

Contributions to understanding the psychology of behavior in general and personality disorders in particular have also been made by such neo-Freudians as Alfred Adler ([1931]1960), Karen Horney (1937), Erik Erikson (1950), and Erich Fromm (1955). With the exception of Fromm, these theorists did not address criminality per se, but they have provided a basis on which criminological knowledge can build. Questioning many of Freud's concepts, such as libido theory or his notions about fixation and regression, these theorists parted company with the individual's irrationality and continual battle with socially disapproved instincts. Instead of resistance or repetitive compulsions, these theorists were talking about "blockages of development" (Coleman, 1964; Kelman, 1967). Moving away from Freud's "Man is wolf to man" and from his strict determinism, these neo-Freudians maintained that people are fundamentally social beings and that their most basic motivation is to participate in a group. Compared to Freud's male-oriented psychology, their psychoanalytic work incorporated social and cultural meanings that were holistic and existential, phenomenological and humanistic. Together, these theorists talk about a potentially hostile world and basic human needs to overcompensate for feelings of insecurity, inferiority, isolation, and helplessness. They also discuss the fundamental needs both to belong and to be free. Hence, delinquent and criminal behavior becomes a means for satisfying basic emotional needs.

Freudian and neo-Freudian models of criminal behavior are not limited to psychoanalytic approaches to problematic behavior. As the rest of this chapter reveals, psychoanalytic ideas spill over into other psychologies as well. Whether reviewing antisocial, social, or humanist psychologies, there are various psychoanalytic assumptions that often underscore these schools of thought.

## Antisocial Personality Approaches to Criminal Behavior

In general, the "antisocial child tends to become the antisocial teenager and the antisocial adult, just as the antisocial adult then tends to produce another antisocial child" (Farrington, 1994: xv). In other words, psychological theories assume a high degree of consistency in the relative ordering of any cohort of individuals regarding criminal potential or antisocial tendency over time. In reviewing the predictors of male offending, the most significant ones have been childhood problem behavior, including troublesome or disruptive classroom conduct, aggressiveness, lying and dishonesty (Loeber and Dishion, 1983; Loeber and Stouthamer-Loeber, 1987). Other predictors of offending behavior were poor parental child management techniques, offending by parents and siblings, low intelligence and educational attainment, and separation from parents (Feldman, 1993).

Juvenile delinquents and career criminals, for example, have been routinely diagnosed as having an antisocial personality (Robins, 1979; Moffitt, 1990). The diagnostic classification includes a history of conduct disorder, attention-deficit-hyperactive disorder prior to age 15, and a pattern of irresponsible and antisocial behavior into adulthood (American Psychiatric Association, 1987). Specifically, it is argued that a number of reliable risk factors associated with antisocial personality, such as poverty, maleness, early maturity, poor school performance, parental criminal history and psychopathology, and lone mother *in loco parentis* (Schonfeld et al., 1988; Robins and Rutter, 1990; Tonry et al., 1991; Tremblay et al., 1992), largely overlap the risk factors for juvenile delinquency and violent crime (Messner and Tardiff, 1986; Sampson, 1987; Hagan, 1990; Messner and Sampson, 1991).

The antisocial personality is associated with a likelihood of engaging in violent aggressivity. However, facultative violence is not in everyone's repertoire, although all human beings share a potential for violence. Seen from the perspectives of an evolutionary psychological as well as from an interpersonal, developmental, and experientially based approach to personality, "it would seem that prior effective experience in the use of threats and assaults increases the expected utility and hence the probability of using violence again" (Daly and Wilson, 1994: 272). Situated within a socially contingent psychology, a "universal human psychology which uses violence in response to cues of its utility may then develop into the 'antisocial personality' type in those circumstances where there is intense competition amongst rivals who have a limited number of effective alternatives to compete" (Daly and Wilson, 1994: 273).

David Berkowitz, New York, 1977

Hans Eysenck's theory of *personality and crime* is probably the best-known comprehensive attempt to link personality and offending. Eysenck (1977; 1987), assuming that humans are basically hedonistic animals, views offending as natural and rational. In brief, crime is pleasurable. He argues that the hedonistic tendency to commit crimes is opposed by the development of the conscience. Eysenck views the conscience as a conditioned fear response and argues, therefore, that the likelihood of people committing crimes depends on the strength of the conscience. Children who refrain from offending have sufficiently developed consciences so that they subjectively experience guilt if they transgress approved boundaries. Conversely, children who engage in offensive behavior have not built up strong consciences.

Eysenck argues further that offenders have inherently "poor conditionality" as linked to his three dimensions of personality: extraversion (E); neuroticism (N); and psychoticism (P). According to Eysenck, people who are high on E have low levels of cortical arousal and build up conditioned responses less well. Similarly, people who are high on N condition less well because their anxiety interferes with conditioning. Finally, people who are high on P also seem to correlate with official offending, whereas both groups tend to be emotionally cold, low on empathy, high on hostility, and inhumane.

Reviews by Feldman (1977) and by Farrington, Biron, and LeBlanc (1982) find equivocal results for E, and some support for N and P. Those relationships also held independently of other variables such as low family income, low intelligence, and poor parental childrearing behavior. Basically, Eysenck's theory has found strong support for a link between impulsivity and offending as E actually consists of two semi-independent components, impulsiveness and sociability. As is pointed out in the last chapter, genetic factors do seem to contribute to all three dimensions, but even the variation in relationship to the differences in cortical arousal levels between sociopaths and controls is not significant.

## Social-Psychological Views of Criminal Behavior

Social-psychological perspectives on criminal conduct embody the diversity of psychological perspectives in general. Although the social-psychological approaches maintain that "the analysis of criminal behavior considers biological, personal, interpersonal, familiar and structural/cultural factors" (Andrews and Bonta, 1994: 10–11), their focus is on the behavior of individuals rather than on bodily systems, social structures, or political economies of law and criminal justice. As a subfield of human psychology, the psychology of criminal conduct (PCC), for example, focuses its primary attention on human development, sensation and perception, motivation and emotion, learning and cognition, memory and information processing, and personality and individual differences as these apply to illegal behavior. In short, as D. A. Andrews and James Bonta (1994: 1) explain, the PCC "seeks a rational and empirical understanding of variation in the occurrence of criminal acts and, in particular, a rational empirical understanding of individual differences in criminal activity."

It is important to underscore that social psychologies of criminal behavior assume that criminal acts are but one constituent of a more general category of antisocial acts. In other words, the "same psychological principles that account for criminal acts will also account for noncriminal antisocial behavior, and, indeed, for prosocial behavior" (Andrews and Bonta, 1994: 20). At the same time that these theories focus attention on the individual, they also emphasize family influences (Farrington, 1994). Numerous studies, for example, have examined family factors as correlates and predictors of both juvenile conduct problems and delinquency (McCord, 1979; Robins, 1979; Wilson, 1980; Riley and Shaw, 1985; and Loeber and Stouthamer-Loeber, 1986). Together, these studies demonstrate that poor parental supervision, erratic or harsh disciplinary practices, marital disharmony, parental rejection (or neglect) of the child, large family size, and antisocial parents are predictors of offending. Other factors, such as teenage childrearing combined with single-parent female households (Morash and Rucker, 1989) or the abuse of children up to the age of 11, are also significantly predictive of antisocial behavior (Widom, 1989).

Most contemporary psychological theories that attempt to explain the bond between childrearing methods and criminal offending are social learning theories. These theories assume that children are naturally selfish and hedonistic and that stealing and fighting or becoming delinquent in order to get what they want comes naturally, too. Accordingly, "children learn to rein in their antisocial tendencies and build up internal inhibitions against offending in a social learning (socialization) process as a result of the way their parents react to their transgressions" (Farrington, 1994a: xxiii–xxiv). In classical conditioning terms, the parent's responses to a child's transgressions produce over time anxiety reactions that block the tendency to commit the punished acts (Trasler, 1965). These unpleasant states of physiological arousal also generalize to similar acts of transgression. In psychoanalytic terms, through the processes of introjection, the verbal prohibitions of the parents become internalized as the child's superego.

Childhood development and cognitive development in general rely on two major descriptions of moral development, one by Jean Piaget (1932) and the other by Kohlberg (1964). Both theories assume naturalistically that moral development will occur within normal or optimal parenting situations. Both of these descriptive systems also present sequential stages roughly correlated with age as the young mature. Without supporting biological evidence, these theories argue that developmental changes are largely independent of specific learning experiences. Furthermore, they contend that these developments in thinking reflect the inherent structure of human cognitive functioning.

Piaget argues that there are three principal stages in cognitive development. He characterizes "the first stage as one in which the rules are given by powerful others, the second in which children perceive that they can invent and modify rules, and the third in which they perceive the primacy of abstract rules over the particular situation" (Feldman, 1993: 185). Consistent with the general view of modern behaviorists such as Albert Bandura (1973; 1986), behavior (or "practical morality") precedes attitude (or "theoretical morality"). Kohlberg has postulated a more complex six-staged system in three blocks of two each: (1) the pre-moral period, in which conformity depends on avoiding punishment; (2) the period of conventional conformity, in which the individual does not want to be thought of badly and in which he or she defers out of respect or duty to authority; finally, (3) the period of autonomy, with a morality of self-accepted principles of human rights and social justice.

The earliest expression of a social psychology of crime was provided by Gabriel Tarde (1890). Analyzing the sociopsychological level of individual interaction, Tarde introduced the concept of *imitation* as a means of explaining the alleged statistical constancy of rates of crime in nineteenth-century Europe. Like all social phenomena, Tarde (1890: 322) reasoned that crime was influenced by the mental processes of imitation or by "the powerful, generally unconscious, always partly mysterious, action by means of which we account for all the phenomena of society." Tarde argued that in order for individuals to resolve endless conflicts in their social lives, they do so for both logical reasons (e.g., rational calculation of costs and benefits) and extra-logical reasons (e.g., imitation of a superior by an inferior). In his analysis of recidivism, Tarde (1890: 263–264) suggested that subsequent criminality was caused not only by processes of self-imitation and self-fulfilling prophecy, but also by the fault of society and the reactions of the external world.

Tarde did not limit, in other words, the processes of imitation to the individual level. He also emphasized the fact that these processes were always present in the context of particular social and historical developments. For example, factors such as urbanism and mass collective behavior were important constituents of the imitation process. With that constellation in mind, Tarde certainly became a broad-gauged social psychologist who also engaged in sociological demography.

Recent social learning theories vary in the extent to which they emphasize internal and external aspects. For example, Clarence Ray Jeffery's (1965: 295) theory of *differential reinforcement* claims that "a criminal act occurs in an environment in which in the past the actor has been reinforced for behaving in this manner, and the aversive consequences attached to the behavior have been of such a nature that they do not control or prevent the response." In a direct application of Skinnerian theory, Jeffery argues that crime is a response to reinforcing stimuli. In a more complex, less determining, and more interactive learning theory application, there is the work of Robert Burgess and Ronald Akers (1966) and of Akers (1973). Herein, differential reinforcement is not only a matter of learning to act, but also of learning whether the act is defined as good or bad according to Sutherland's *differential association.* Moreover, present as well as past reinforcements (i.e., rewards and punishments) are important both for the act as well as for alternative acts.

*Control theories* of criminal behavior represent another variant within social psychology. These theories contend that crime is likely to occur when the social bonds between an individual and society are weakened or severed. Two prominent sociological applications of social control are *containment* theory (Reckless, 1961) and *control/bonding* theory (Hirschi, 1969). Walter Reckless suggested that the variation in the crime rates of different social groups in the United States had to do with the ability to contain norm-violating behavior in the face of social change and cultural conflict. Travis Hirschi suggested that criminologists needed to look for the causes of conformity rather than the causes of delinquency. In terms of empirical proofs, although the concepts of both containment and control theories are rather vague and difficult to test, the latter continues to have influence on criminological thinking.

Relying on a number of sociological studies of delinquency (Redl and Wineman, 1951; Reiss, 1951; Nye, 1958) that revealed that delinquents came from homes where there was inadequate control and socialization by significant others, Reckless argued that crime was generally contained (or prevented) by two processes. One process operated at the level of the individual, the other at the level of social organization. Reckless's theory involves inner and outer barriers of deviance containment. "Inner containments" refer to an individual's consciousness, "outer containments" refer to functional families and supportive groups. For Reckless, "inner and outer containments occupied a position between the pressures and pulls of the social environment and inner pushes of the individual personality" (Beirne and Messerschmidt, 1991: 427). Accordingly, if a person's outer containment is weak, then the individual is susceptible to social pressures (e.g., poverty, family conflict, social inequality) and pulls (e.g., bad company, propaganda/media, delinquent subcultures). Similarly, those with a weak inner containment possess some combination of vulnerable ego, bad self-concept, low frustration tolerance, lack of a sense of responsibility, and so on that results in psychological pushes (e.g., hostility, aggressiveness, guilt reactions, feelings of inadequacy and inferiority, and suggestibility). Finally, the weaker the inner and outer containments, the more likely one is to engage in deviant activity.

Hirschi argues that his *control* theory rather than *subcultural* theory (see Chapter 7) explains the factors that lead to delinquency. Hirschi's theory, like Freud's, assumes that all human beings are born with antisocial tendencies. However, these tendencies only materialize when various kinds of social controls are relaxed. Hirschi postulates that four interrelated factors are critical in bonding individuals to society: attachment, commitment, involvement, and belief. Whether young persons become law-abiding or deviant depends on how strong or weak their attachments are to parents, school, and peers; their commitments are to conventional lines of action; their involvements are in conventional activities; and their beliefs are in conventional values.

## Humanistic-Psychological Approaches to Criminal Behavior

Humanistic-psychological approaches to criminal behavior are influenced by neo-Freudian psychoanalytic theories. They assume that humans are essentially good even though, at times, people can be constrained by society to act badly. Two theorists are particularly relevant, Abraham Maslow and Seymour Halleck. Only the latter, however, has applied his theory directly to crime.

Maslow's theory of *need hierarchy* is composed of what he argued were the five basic need groups of human beings. First, there are the basic physiological needs such as food, shelter, and procreational sex. Second, there are the safety needs such as security and stability or freedom from fear, anxiety, and disorder. The third and fourth sets of needs are very closely related; they are, respectively, the needs to belong and to be loved, and the needs for esteem from self and others. Finally, there is the need for self-actualization, or the need for people to become everything that they are capable of becoming by being true to their nature (Coleman, 1964). Within a hierarchy-of-needs framework, then, criminal behavior may be the means by which individuals satisfy their basic human needs. Blocked, for whatever reasons, personal or social, from obtaining their basic needs in a prosocial fashion, people may then consciously or unconsciously resort to antisocial means as a way of meeting their fundamental human needs.

Building on the Adlerian *individual psychology* variant of psychoanalysis that saw mental disturbance and criminality arising from goal-directed behavior whereby individuals sought to satisfy unfulfilled longings of infantile inferiority, on the one hand, and the more traditional Freudian interpretation of crime as displaced sublimation, on the other hand, Halleck argues that criminal behavior "provides people with the opportunities for creativity and autonomy denied them by conventional society as well as the excuses necessary to rationalize their guilt" (Einstadter and Henry, 1995: 111). Halleck (1967) specifically discusses fourteen psychological advantages provided by crime: for example, crime involves activity; crime promises a change in a favorable direction; crime allows for expression and freedom; crime provides excitement; and others. For Halleck, criminal behavior represented one of six possible adaptations to the helplessness caused by oppression.

According to Halleck, there are two general types of oppression, objective and subjective, with each having two subtypes. Objectively, oppression can involve two-person interactions or it can be social. The former consisting, for example, of parents unfairly punishing their children; the latter consisting, for example, of sexual or racial discrimination. Subjectively, oppression can come from within or it can result from false projections. In the first case, oppression may be the guilt experienced from an overactive superego. In the second case, people's perceptions tell them that they are oppressed when, in fact, they are not.

Finally, Halleck maintains that the subjective emotional experience of either type of oppression is one of helplessness. People may react or adapt to their helplessness through conformity, through prosocial or antisocial activism, through a combination of conformity and activism, through mental illness, or through criminality. The criminal adaptation, or the attempt to change the environment by breaking society's rules or creating alternative (illegal) rules, becomes more likely as the other avenues of adaptation are blocked by people or circumstances.

## Summary and Conclusions:
## Personality and Interpersonal Development

A general personality and social psychology of crime, particularly the social learning and cognitive-behavioral bodies of that knowledge, reveals basic empirical, theoretical, and practical findings that address individual differences in criminal conduct. As a means of extracting the more useful information about risk factors and crime, Andrews and Bonta (1994) have reviewed this material in detail. For example, a rationally, empirically based psychology of crime finds that "people differ in their frequency of criminal activity and in the manner, type, and variety of criminal acts in which they engage. In addition, although accounting for a disproportionate amount of the total criminal activity, the more criminally active offenders tend not to be specialists" (Andrews and Bonta, 1994: 230).

Andrews, Bonta, and colleagues, after examining the classification and treatment literature, and after having conducted their own cross-sectional and longitudinal studies of the risk factors associated with criminal behavior, have created a table of reasonably well-established correlates of criminality (Figure 6.1). They have also ordered these factors into categories of major and minor risk factors (Figure 6.2). "The average correlation coefficients for the weakest of the tabled risk factors is estimated to be in the .05 to .10 range. The average coefficients for the stronger of the tabled risk factors are estimated to be in the .20 to .30 range" (Andrews and Bonta, 1994: 230). Moreover, when a number and variety of risk factors are sampled, the multiple correlations with crime reach the .70 level.

1. LOWER-CLASS ORIGINS,
   as measured by neighborhood characteristics,
   or indices of parental education/occupation.

2. FAMILY OF ORIGIN
   Long-term reliance on welfare (as opposed to
   occasional use of welfare services).
   Criminality in family of origin (parents, siblings, other relatives).
   Multiple psychological handicaps (low verbal
   intelligence, emotional instability, alcoholism, parenting skill deficits).
   Antisocial attitudes.

3. PERSONAL TEMPERAMENT, APTITUDE
   AND EARLY BEHAVIORAL HISTORY
   Restlessly energetic, impulsive, adventurous
   pleasure-seeking, a taste for risk.
   Below-average verbal intelligence.
   Response to frustration more likely to involve
   resentment and anger rather than compo-
   sure or anxiety/guilt/depression.
   Lack of conscientiousness.
   Egocentricism (below age-based norm for per-
   spective-taking).
   Moral immaturity (below age-based norm for
   moral thinking).
   Poor problem-solving/coping skills.
   If diagnosed as a child, more likely to be
   diagnosed externalizing (conduct disorder)
   than internalizing
   (neurotic/depressive/withdrawn).
   Early and generalized misconduct (lying, stealing, aggression, early experimentation with
   sex and drugs—including tobacco).

4. EARLY AND CONTINUING
   FAMILY CONDITIONS
   Low levels of affection/cohesiveness within
   home.
   Low levels of supervision and poor discipline
   within home.
   Neglect/abuse.

5. SCHOOL-BASED RISK FACTORS
   Below-average effort.
   Lack of interest/being bored.
   Not worrying about occupational future.
   Conduct problems (truancy).
   Poor schools.

6. PERSONAL EDUCATIONAL/
   VOCATIONAL/SOCIOECONOMIC
   ACHIEVEMENT

   Low level of achieved education.
   Long periods of unemployment (rather than
   low levels of occupational prestige).
   Reliance on welfare (as opposed to occasional
   use of welfare services, and rather than low
   income).

7. INTERPERSONAL RELATIONSHIPS
   Generalized indifference to opinion of others.
   Unstable marital history.
   Rejected/rejecting.

8. SOCIAL SUPPORT FOR CRIME
   Association with antisocial others.
   Isolation from noncriminal others.

9. PERSONAL ATTITUDES/VALUES/
   BELIEFS SUPPORTIVE OF CRIME
   High tolerance for deviance in general.
   Rejection of the validity of the law in particular.
   Applies rationalizations for law violations to a
   wide variety of acts and circumstances.
   Interprets a wide range of stimuli as reasons
   for anger.
   Thinking style and content is generally anti-
   social.

10. BEHAVIORAL HISTORY
    Criminal history, juvenile and adult (look for
    an uninterrupted history, beginning at a
    young age, including a variety of different
    types of offenses, and violations that con-
    tinue even while under sentence).
    Alcohol and drug abuse.
    Aimless use of leisure time.
    Disorganized lifestyle.

11. PSYCHOPATHOLOGY
    High scores on measures of "antisocial person-
    ality/psychopathy." Many forms of emo-
    tional/behavior disturbance when combined
    with a history of antisocial behavior (e.g.,
    conduct problems plus shyness).

12. OTHER RISK FACTORS
    Being male.
    Being a member of some minority groups.
    Being young (16–22 years).
    A host of apparent biological anomalies that as
    yet have not been pulled together in a theo-
    retically interesting, empirically convincing
    or practically useful way.
    Other risk factors, as yet undiscovered or
    completely missed in our reviews of the
    literature.

**FIGURE 6.1   A Brief Survey of Risk Factors from the Cross-Sectional and
Longitudinal Studies**

*From:* D. A. Andrews and James Bonta, *The Psychology of Criminal Conduct* (Cincinnati, OH: Anderson Publishing, 1994),
page 232. Reprinted with permission.

**The Major Factors:**

1.  Antisocial/procriminal attitudes, values, beliefs and cognitive-emotional states (i.e., personal cognitive supports for crime).

2.  Procriminal associates and isolation from anticriminal others (i.e., interpersonal supports for crime).

3.  Temperamental and personality factors conducive to criminal activity including psychopathy, weak socialization, impulsivity, restless aggressive energy, egocentrism, below-average verbal intelligence, a taste for risk, and weak problem-solving/self-regulation skills.

4.  History of antisocial behavior evident from a young age, in a variety of settings and involving a number and variety of different acts.

5.  Familial factors that include criminality and a variety of psychological problems in the family of origin and, in particular, low levels of affection, caring and cohesiveness; poor parental supervision and discipline practices; and outright neglect and abuse.

6.  Low levels of personal educational, vocational or financial achievement and, in particular, unstable employment.

**The Minor Factors:**

7.  Lower-class origins as assessed by adverse neighborhood conditions and/or parental education/vocational/economic achievement.

8.  Personal distress, whether assessed by way of the sociological constructs of anomie, strain and alienation or by way of the clinical constructs of low self-esteem, anxiety, depression, worry or officially labeled "mental disorder."

9.  A host of biological/neuropsychological indicators that have yet to be integrated in a convincing manner by way of either theory or the construction of practical risk/need assessment instruments.

---

**FIGURE  6.2    Risk/Need Factors within the General Personality and Social Psychology of Criminal Conduct**

*From:* D. A. Andrews and James Bonta, *The Psychology of Criminal Conduct* (Cincinnati, OH: Anderson Publishing, 1994), page 232. Reprinted with permission.

Keeping in mind that the vast majority of illegal conduct is not of a predatory nature (e.g., violent or sexual acts), but rather of an economic or acquisitive nature, Andrews and Bonta (1994: 231) contend that the "same sets of risk factors appear to be involved within categories of geography, class, age, gender and ethnicity." They argue further that the correlations of crime with biological and social variables are "reduced, if not eliminated, when controls are introduced for the stronger of the personal, interpersonal and familiar risk factors" (Andrews and Bonta 1994: 231).

At odds with this characterization of crime are the sociological analyses with their implicit understanding that these environments act differently on those predisposed to criminality. In effect, even though the personal, interpersonal, and familiar conditions may be arguably more important than the biological and social, this does not mean that the perspectives of sociology, for example, are without their contributions. Quite to the contrary, the range and diversity of the contributions of sociology to the study of crime and justice, from small-group behavior to community-oriented models of criminal behavior, from community-based models of criminality to structurally oriented models of crime and social control, have been impressive.

## Discussion Questions

1. Explain why Barak views psychology as a centralized component for integrating criminologies.

2. Characterize the underlying assumptions, primary hypotheses, and basic approaches of the five bodies of psychological knowledge as these have been applied to crime.

3. Compare and contrast three of the more popular psychological theories of crime and delinquency: antisocial personality, psychic needs, and techniques-of-neutralization.

4. What do you find to be the strengths and limitations of the various psychological approaches to crime?

## References

Adler, Alfred. [1931] 1960. *What Life Should Mean to You*. London: Allen and Unwin.

Akers, Ronald L. 1977. *Deviant Behavior: A Social Learning Approach*. 2nd ed. Belmont, CA: Wadsworth.

American Psychiatric Association. 1987. *Diagnostic and Statistical Manual of Mental Disorders*. 3rd ed. Washington, DC: American Psychiatric Association.

Andrews, D. A., and James Bonta. 1994. *The Psychology of Criminal Conduct*. Cincinnati, OH: Anderson.

Bandura, Albert. 1973. *Aggression: A Social Learning Analysis*. Englewood Cliffs, NJ: Prentice-Hall.

———. 1986. *Social Foundations of Thought and Action: A Social Cognitive Theory*. Englewood Cliffs, NJ: Prentice-Hall.

Beirne, Piers, and James Messerschmidt. 1991. *Criminology*. San Diego, CA: Harcourt Brace Jovanovich.

Bohm, Robert. 1996. *A Primer on Crime and Delinquency Theory*. Belmont, CA: Wadsworth.

Bowlby, John. 1946. *Forty-Four Juvenile Thieves: Their Characters and Home-Life*. London: Bailliere, Tindall and Cox.

Burgess, Robert L., and Ronald L. Akers. 1966. "A Differential Association-Reinforcement Theory of Criminal Behavior." *Social Problems* 14:128–147.

Campbell, J. C. 1992. "If I Can't Have You, No One Can: Issues of Power and Control in Homicide of Female Partners." In J. Radford and D. E. H. Russell, eds., *Femicide: The Politics of Woman Killing*. New York: Twayne.

Cleckley, Hervey. 1955. *The Mask of Sanity*. St. Louis, MO: Mosby.

Coleman, James C. 1964. *Abnormal Psychology and Modern Life*. 3rd ed. Glenview, IL: Scott, Foresman.

Cooley, Charles H. 1902. *Human Nature and the Social Order*. New York: Scribner's.

Daly, Martin, and Margo Wilson. 1994. "Evolutionary Psychology of Male Violence." In J. Archer, ed., *Male Violence*. London: Routledge.

Daly, M., M. Wilson, and S. J. Weghorst. 1982. "Male Sexual Jealousy." *Ethology and Sociobiology* 3:11–27.

Dobash, R. E., and R. P. Dobash. 1979. *Violence Against Wives: A Case Against Patriarchy*. New York: Free Press.

Einstadter, Werner, and Stuart Henry. 1995. *Criminological Theory: An Analysis of Its Underlying Assumptions*. Fort Worth, TX: Harcourt Brace.

Erikson, Erik. 1950. *Childhood and Society*. New York: W. W. Norton.

Eysenck, Hans J. 1977. *Crime and Personality*. 2nd ed. London: Routledge & Kegan Paul.

———. 1987. "Personality Theory and the Problem of Criminality." In B. J. McGurk, D. M. Thornton, and M. Williams, eds., *Applying Psychology to Imprisonment*, 29–58. London, HMSO.

Farrington, David P., ed. 1994a. *Psychological Explanations of Crime*. Aldershot, England: Dartmouth.

———. 1994b. "Childhood, Adolescent and Adult Features of Violent Males." In L. R. Huesmann, ed., *Aggressive Behavior: Current Perspectives*, 215–40. New York: Plenum.

Farrington, D. P., L. Biron, and M. LeBlanc. 1982. "Personality and Delinquency in London and Montreal." In J. Gunn and D. P. Farrington, eds., *Abnormal Offenders, Delinquency, and the Criminal Justice System*, 153–201. Chichester: Wiley.

Farrington, D. P., R. Loeber, and W. B. Van Kammen. 1990. "Long-term Criminal Outcomes of Hyperactivity-Impulsivity-Attention Deficit and Conduct Problems in Childhood." In L. N. Robins and M. Rutter, eds., *Straight and Devious Pathways from Childhood to Adulthood*, 62–81. Cambridge: Cambridge University Press.

Feldman, Philip. 1977. *Criminal Behavior.* London: Wiley.

———. 1993. *The Psychology of Crime.* Cambridge: Cambridge University Press.

Freud, Sigmund. 1923. *The Ego and the Id.* Trans. J. Riviere. London: Hogarth Press.

———. 1930. *Civilization and Its Discontents.* Garden City, NY: Doubleday.

Fromm, Erich. 1955. *The Sane Society.* New York: Rinehart.

Gleick, Elizabeth. 1994. "Death of a Madman: The Final Victim." *People* (December 12): 126–132.

Gordon, Robert A. 1987. "SES versus IQ in the Race-IQ-Delinquency Model." *International Journal of Sociology and Social Policy* 7(3): 30–96.

Hagan, John. 1990. "Destiny and Drift: Subcultural Preferences, Status Attainments, and the Risks and Rewards of Youth." *American Sociological Review* 56:567–582.

Halleck, Seymour L. 1967. *Psychiatry and the Dilemmas of Crime.* New York: Harper and Row.

Hirschi, Travis, 1969. *Causes of Delinquency.* Berkeley: University of California Press.

Hirschi, Travis, and Michael J. Hindelang. 1977. "Intelligence and Delinquency: A Revisionist Review." *American Sociological Review* 42(4): 571–587.

Horney, Karen. 1937. *The Neurotic Personality of Our Time.* New York: W. W. Norton.

Jeffery, C. Ray. 1965. "Criminal Behavior and Learning Theory." *Journal of Criminal Law, Criminology, and Police Science* 56:294–300.

Jones, Ernest. 1953. *The Life and Work of Sigmund Freud.* New York: H. Wolf.

Kelman, Harold, ed. 1967. *Feminine Psychology: Karen Horney, M.D.* New York: W. W. Norton.

Kohlberg, Lawrence. 1964. "The Development of Moral Character." In M. C. Hoffmann, ed., *Child Development.* New York: Russell Sage.

———. 1976. "Moral Stages and Moralization: The Cognitive-Developmental Approach." In *Moral Development and Behaviour*, 31–53. New York: Holt, Rinehart and Winston.

Kohlberg, L., and D. Candee. 1984. "The Relationship of Moral Judgment to Moral Action." In L. Kohlberg, ed., *The Psychology of Moral Development.* San Francisco: Harper and Row.

Leyton, Elliott. 1986. *Hunting Humans: Inside the Minds of Mass Murderers.* New York: Pocket.

Loeber, R., and T. Dishion. 1983. "Early Predictors of Male Delinquency: A Review." *Psychological Bulletin* 94:68–99.

Loeber, R., and M. Stouthamer-Loeber. 1986. "Family Factors as Correlates and Predictors of Juvenile Conduct Problems and Delinquency." In M. Tonry and N. Morris, eds., *Crime and Justice*, vol. 7, 29–49. Chicago: University of Chicago Press.

———. 1987. "Prediction." In H. C. Quay, ed., *Handbook of Juvenile Delinquency*, 325–382. New York: Wiley.

Maslow, A. H., and G. Murphy. (eds.) 1954. *Motivation and Personality.* New York: Harper.

Maslow, Abraham H. (ed.) 1959. *New Knowledge in Human Values.* New York: Harper.

McCord, Joan. 1979. "Some Child-rearing Antecedents of Criminal Behavior in Adult Men." *Journal of Personality and Social Psychology* 37:1477–1486.

Mead, George H. 1934. *Mind, Self and Society.* C. W. Morris, ed. Chicago: University of Chicago Press.

Messner, Steven F., and Ronald J. Sampson. 1991. "The Sex Ratio, Family Disruption, and Rates of Violent Crime: The Paradox of Demographic Structure." *Social Forces* 69:693–713.

Messner, S. F., and K. Tardiff. 1986. "Economic Inequality and Levels of Homicide: An Analysis of Urban Neighborhoods." *Criminology* 24:297–317.

Moffitt, T. E. 1990. "Juvenile Delinquency and Attention Deficit Disorder: Boys' Developmental Trajectories from Age 3 to Age 15." *Child Development* 61:893–910.

Moffitt, T. E., and P. A. Silva. 1988. "IQ and Delinquency: A Direct Test of the Differential Detection Hypothesis. *Journal of Abnormal Behavior*, 97:330–333.

Moffitt, T. E., and B. Henry. 1989. "Neuropsychological Assessment of Executive Functions in Self-Reported Delinquents." *Development and Psychopathology* 1:105–118.

Morash, M., and L. Rucker. 1989. "An Explanatory Study of the Connection of Mother's Age at Childbearing to her Children's Delinquency in

Four Data Sets." *Crime and Delinquency* 35:45–93.

Nye, Ivan F. 1958. *Family Relationships and Delinquent Behavior*. New York: Wiley.

Park, Robert E., and Ernest Burgess. 1925. *The City*. Chicago: University of Chicago Press.

Piaget, Jean. 1932. *The Moral Judgment of the Child*. London: Kegan Paul.

———. 1952. *The Origins of Intelligence in Children*. New York: International University Press.

Polk, K., and D. Ranson. 1991. "The Role of Gender in Intimate Violence." *Australia and New Zealand Journal of Criminology* 24:15–24.

Reckless, Walter C. 1961. "A New Theory of Delinquency and Crime." *Federal Probation* 25:42–46.

Redl, Fritz, and David Wineman. 1951. *Children Who Hate*. New York: Free Press.

Reiss, Albert J. 1951. "Delinquency as the Failure of Personal and Social Controls." *American Sociological Review* 16:196–207.

Riley, D., and M. Shaw. 1985. *Parental Supervision and Juvenile Delinquency*. London: HMSO.

Robins, L. N. 1979. "Sturdy Childhood Predictors of Adult Outcomes: Replications from Longitudinal Studies." In J. E. Barrett, R. M. Rose and G. L. Klerman, eds., *Stress and Mental Disorder*, 219–35. New York: Raven Press.

Robins, L. N., and M. R. Rutter, eds. 1990. *Straight and Devious Pathways to Adulthood*. Cambridge: Cambridge University Press.

Ross, E. A. [1901] 1922. *Social Control*. New York: Macmillan.

Sampson, Robert J. 1987. "Urban Black Violence: The Effect of Male Joblessness and Family Disruption." *American Journal of Sociology* 93:348–382.

Schonfeld, I. S., D. Shaffer, P. O'Connor, and S. Portney. 1988. "Conduct Disorder and Cognitive Functioning: Testing Three Causal Hypotheses." *Child Development* 59:993–1007.

Skinner, B. F. 1953. *Science and Human Behavior*. New York: Macmillan.

Smetana, J. G. 1990. "Morality and Conduct Disorders." In M. Lewis and S. M. Millers, eds., *Handbook of Developmental Psychopathology*, 157–179. New York: Plenum.

Sutherland, Edwin H., and Donald R. Cressey. 1978. *Principles of Criminology*. Philadelphia: Lippincott.

Sykes, Gresham M., and David Matza. 1957. "Techniques of Neutralization: A Theory of Delinquency." *American Sociological Review* 22:664–670.

Tappan, Paul. 1951. *Crime, Justice, and Correction*. New York: McGraw-Hill.

Tarde, Gabriel. [1890] 1903. *The Laws of Imitation*. Translated by E. Parsons. New York: Henry Holt.

Taylor, E. A. 1986. "Childhood Hyperactivity." *British Journal of Psychiatry* 149:562–573.

Thornhill, N. W., and R. Thornhill. 1990. "Evolutionary Analysis of Psychological Pain of Rape Victims: The Effects of Victim's Age and Marital Status." *Ethology and Sociobiology* 11:155–176.

Thornhill, R., and N. W. Thornhill. 1983. "Human Rape: An Evolutionary Analysis." *Ethology and Sociobiology* 4:137–173.

Thornton, D. M. 1987. "Moral Development Theory." In B. J. McGurk, D. M. Thornton, and M. Williams, eds., *Applying Psychology to Imprisonment*, 129–150. London: HMSO.

Tonry, M. H., L. E. Ohlin, and D. P. Farrington. 1991. *Human Development and Criminal Behavior*. New York: Springer-Verlag.

Trasler, G. B. 1965. "Criminality and the Socialization Process." *Advancement of Science* 21:545–550.

Tremblay, R. E., B. Masse, D. Perron, M. Leblanc, A. E. Schwartzman and J. E. Ledingham. 1992. "Early Disruptive Behavior, Poor School Achievement, Delinquent Behavior, and Delinquent Personality: Longitudinal Analyses." *Journal of Consulting and Clinical Psychology* 60:64–72.

White, H. R., E. W. Labouvie, and M. E. Bates. 1985. "The Relationship Between Sensation Seeking and Delinquency: A Longitudinal Analysis." *Journal of Research in Crime and Delinquency* 22:197–211.

Widom, C. S. 1989. "Does Violence Beget Violence? A Critical Examination of the Literature." *Psychological Bulletin* 106:3–28.

Wilson, H. 1980. "Parental Supervision: A Neglected Aspect of Delinquency." *British Journal of Criminology* 20:203–235.

Wilson, Margo, and Martin Daly. 1992. "The Man Who Mistook his Wife for Chattel." In J. H. Barkow, L. Cosmides, and J. Tooby, eds., *The Adapted Mind*. New York: Oxford University Press.

Wright, Robert. 1995. "The Evolution of Despair." *Time* (August 28): 50–57.

### Chapter 7

# Contributions from Sociology: "Environment and Structure"

Los Angeles looters protest acquittal of officers for beating of Rodney King, 1992.

During the twentieth century few would disagree with the assertion that no other discipline has conducted more research and produced more studies and scholarship on crime and delinquency than sociology. Both the empirical findings on crime and criminals as well as the models of crime causation and its control have been deeply influenced by and, perhaps, too heavily dominated by sociological inquiry. As most authors of criminological works have been primarily schooled in sociological theories of crime, their textbooks have tended to reflect their sociological roots. In most crime texts, for example, not only is there more sociological material presented, debated, and evaluated than there is of the other disciplines, but the other disciplines are also dismissed as relatively unimportant to the understanding of crime and justice.

Given the vast amount of relevant sociological research and theorizing on crime over the past seventy-five years, this chapter attempts to cover the range of criminological perspectives derivative of sociology. Excluding the social psychological factors that are often addressed within discussions of sociology, I have elected to provide summative rather than meticulous discussions of the sociological contributions. Having examined social psychology in the previous chapter, I have grouped the sociological contributions that remain into three unorthodox frameworks: (1) crime and social organization (CSO); (2) crime and social process (CSP); and (3) crime and social structure (CSS).

Despite their differences, all of these sociological theories share at least one proposition in common. Each seeks the explanation of crime in factors that are external to or beyond individual control. By comparison, biology and psychology are focused more on the internal geography of individuals. As a matter of degree, then, in terms of balancing internal and external factors, theories of social psychology can be located within psychology or sociology, for they are natural integrative parts of both. As for my decision to classify psychological and sociological contributions to criminology as I have: If the ultimate influence of a theory is individual, then I label it psychology; if the ultimate influence is environmental, then I label it sociology. From an integrative or interdisciplinary perspective of crime and justice, the location of social psychology makes little difference. At the same time, the former explanations tend to regard criminal actions more as the outcome of individual anomalies or as residing inside the person. The latter explanations tend to regard crime more as an environmental thing or as residing outside the person. In biological and psychological versions, crime results from criminals doing what comes natural for them. In the sociological version, crime results from social forces acting on human behavior. From a constitutive-integrative perspective, crime and social control are coproducts of the interaction of the natural and social forces coming together in time and space.

The objectives of Chapter 7 are to discuss the three sociological frameworks both in terms of the common assumptions and perspectives held, and in relationship to the particular variations found within each framework. As treated below, those theories grouped as CSO include social ecology, anomie or strain, and the subcultural; those theories grouped as CSP include differential association, labeling, and social constructionism; and, those theories grouped as CSS include conflict, Marxist, and feminist. It should be recalled that in the previous chapter on psychological contributions, I chose to incorporate learning, bonding, and control theories, acknowledging that most textbooks traditionally deal with this material as sociological in nature.

## Crime and Social Organization (CSO)

The common theme found among those theories grouped as CSO is that "social order, stability, and integration are conducive to conformity, while disorder and malintegration are conducive to crime and deviance" (Akers, 1994: 141). On the one hand, communities are considered to be socially organized and well integrated if there is a consensus about their norms and values that allow for social interaction in an orderly fashion. These communities are regarded as possessing social cohesion among their members. Communities, on the other hand, are considered to be socially disorganized or anomic if there is conflict about norms and values and a malintegration among their elements. In these communities, there is also said to be a disruption in social cohesion or a lack of continuity as well as conformity. As social cohesion or solidarity among community members breaks down, the rates of crime and deviance go up.

According to the Chicago School of the 1920s, also known as the Ecological School or the School of Human Ecology, because it applied the principles of plant and animal ecology to the task of explaining social deviance, the sources of crime were to be found in the physical, social, and cultural context of human activity. The social ecologists, for the most part, argued that crime was the result of the *social disorganization* that characterized the inner-city areas. They argued further that social disorganization was caused by rapid social change whereby dominant legitimate values and norms compete with each other as well as with the illegitimate norms and values. In turn, various subcultures engage in conflict, young generations clash, and social cohesion dissolves as otherwise normally operating social systems or communities experience social deviance and disruption.

The *social ecology* framework has been heavily influenced by human geography and biology, viewing environment as the structuring of space mediated by culture or subculture. One of the outcomes of such structuring is the patterned distribution of crime. Among the notable early theorists of this group were Robert Park and Ernest Burgess (1925), Frederick Thrasher (1927), Clifford Shaw and Henry McKay (1931; 1942). Among contemporary theorists who have employed this perspective are Paul and Patricia Brantingham (1981; 1984), Rodney Stark (1987), Robert Sampson (1987), Robert Bursik (1984; 1989), and Bryan Vila (1994). In terms of testing the theory of social disorganization and its relationship to crime, Sampson and Groves (1989) measured the usual external factors such as social class, residential mobility, and family disruption as well as the more unusual indicators of community supervision of teenage gangs, informal friendship networks, and participation in formal organizations. Using data from British communities, Sampson and Groves concluded that the model was supported and that measures of social disorganization were good predictors of rates of crime victimization, if not good predictors of the rates of criminal offenses.

Putting aside the myriad of criticisms of social ecology and social disorganization, from the plant metaphor to explain the formation and change of human communities to the tautological nature of social disorganization as both description and cause of the condition to the fallacy of stable ecological patterns, the social ecological approaches have enjoyed considerable influence (Einstadter and Henry, 1995). Among the modern and extended contemporary versions of the influence of environmental factors on crime has been Oscar Newman's (1972) "defensible space," which argues that the actual physical forms of the urban environment affect crime, and the "routine activity approach" of Lawrence Cohen and Marcus Felson (1979), which argues that the structural changes in everyday life activities, such as the amount of time invested in recreation and work or the style of postmodern urban planning and city architecture, affect crimes against both persons and property.

Like social ecology and social disorganization theorists, *anomie/strain* theorists are functionalist theorists who use both a systems model and an organic metaphor to describe society. In other words, communities, societies, and the world consist of systems of interrelated parts, with each part making a necessary contribution to the viability of the whole. These groups of theorists also share a strong belief in the necessity of conformity through consensus. Finally, each of these groups subscribes to the notion that there are typically both functional and dysfunctional phenomena in society.

Where these theorists differ, however, is in their conceptions of criminal adaptation. In the ecological scheme of things, crime is seen as a problem of adapting to environmental changes as communities are organized and disorganized. In the anomic scheme of things, crime is seen as a problem of adapting to the organization of society, and criminals are viewed as people trying to fit in. Stated differently, anomie and strain theorists argue that deviant behaviors are normal responses to the abnormal circumstances or structural contradictions that a society has organized itself around.

The anomie traditions can be traced to the works of the French sociologist Emile Durkheim in the late nineteenth century, and in the middle of the twentieth century to Robert Merton, former president of the American Sociological Association. According to Durkheim, crime is susceptible to such changing conditions as population growth, industrialization, urbanization, and so on. During periods of rapid social

Emile Durkheim

change, it is argued, there are inadequate or inappropriate means of social control. Without advance notice, societies are unable to develop appropriate modes quickly enough to regulate or govern social interaction. When such social conditions exist, Durkheim refers to them as "anomic conditions." Not so much that these conditions are free of norms or that they are experiencing a condition of normlessness, but rather that a period of time exists where the traditional norms are no longer applicable, and the new norms have not yet fully evolved (Curran and Renzetti, 1994). Holding the view that in order for humans to be content they must be able to satisfy innate needs and desires, Durkheim ([1893] 1947; [1897] 1951) generally maintained that when there were disruptions of the collective order, individual expectations and desires were raised too high for societal satisfaction. In turn, these anomic and contradictory conditions accounted for the rises in both the suicide and crime rates.

Merton (1938; 1957) revived and reformulated Durkheim's concept of anomie. Whereas Durkheim used the term to refer to the lack of social regulation (normlessness) during periods of rapid change, Merton used the term to refer to the everyday operations of certain societies. Merton moved the discussion of strain away from the individualistic orientation of Durkheim and toward the societal malintegration of cultural ends and structural means when he introduced the concept of *blocked opportunity* theory. In short, Merton argues that crime or deviant adaptations emerge especially in those societies where material wealth is idealized and where the available or legitimate means for obtaining the valued ends are systematically denied to groups of people. In response to this social problem of anomie/strain, people adapt in one or more of several ways, including acceptance of innovation or the pursuing of the cultural goals of success through illegitimate or criminal means.

Recently, Robert Agnew (1985; 1992) has developed a revised strain theory that is perhaps closer to the older Durkheimian version of anomie. Agnew reintroduced the more individualistic-psychological dimensions of anomie with his emphases on personal stress, frustration-aggression, pain-pleasure, and behavioral learning. He also "acknowledges that societal-level forces that cause strain may not universally apply because they can be modified by individual and interpersonal assessments" (Einstadter and Henry, 1995: 150). In short, although Agnew recognizes the importance of social structure, he recognizes human agency and choice as well.

Once again, setting aside the problems associated with strain analyses of class, consensus, and determinism, strain/anomie theory remains popular as delinquent and gang research (Short, 1964; Brennan and Huizinga, 1975; Segrave and Hastad, 1985) has "consistently found delinquents to perceive their opportunities as more limited compared to non-delinquents" (Braithwaite, 1989: 32). Moreover, it is in the entangled relations between anomie/strain theory and subcultural theories as articulated by "opportunity theory" that one finds the material grounding for both.

The third branch or approach to the related perspectives of CSO are the *subcultural* theories that emphasize the importance of the social values of informal groups. These include theories that are more Durkheimian based, such as Albert Cohen's (1955) delinquency as a psychological form of "reaction-formation," Walter Miller's (1958) "focal concerns," and Marvin Wolfgang and Franco Ferracuti's (1967) "subculture of violence," and those that are more Mertonian based, such as Richard Cloward and Lloyd Ohlin's (1960) "differential opportunity" and Freda Adler's (1975) and Rita Simon's (1975) theories of female "emancipation," as they came to be called.

Although uninfluenced about the utility or rationality of delinquency, Cohen, nevertheless, substitutes the blocked goal of status among peers for Merton's blocked goal of achieving wealth. Failing to achieve middle-class status by family or academic success, delinquents experience strain. Their collective solution is to resign themselves to their subordinate position among their peers where they form subcultural groups whose values of non-utility, maliciousness, and negativity are antithetical to middle-class values (Cohen, 1955).

By contrast, Miller's delinquent subculture was a part of lower-class tradition. He rejected Cohen's idea that a delinquent subculture arose through a conflict with middle-class values. Miller argued, instead, that delinquency was the natural product of the values (*focal concerns*) of lower-class culture. His central thesis is that illegal behavior is motivated by an attempt to achieve ends, states, or conditions that are valued in the lower class such as trouble, toughness, smartness, excitement, fate, and autonomy (Miller, 1958).

In response to the criticisms of Cohen and Miller that their subcultural theories may be a better reflection of middle-class stereotypes about the poor than of the latter's lifestyle, Cloward and Ohlin (1960) established a theory that, in effect, combined some of the insights of anomie/strain approaches and some of the insights of the subcultural approaches. For them, the key to understanding crime and delinquency is to recognize that there exists differential access to both legitimate and illegitimate opportunities. Their point is that different types of lower-class neighborhoods exist and that each gives rise to different types of delinquent subcultures: criminal, conflict, and retreatist. The empirical evidence as to Cloward and Ohlin's delinquent subcultures is mixed at best, with retreatist subcultures appearing not to exist, and the others tending to be less specialized.

Using a framework of focal concerns similar to Miller's thesis, Wolfgang and Ferracuti analyzed adult homicides, involving crimes of passion rather than of premeditation or mental illness. They claimed to have found a relatively homogeneous group of young, nonwhite, and lower-class males whose value system constitutes a subculture of violence. These values not only favor the use of violence in a variety of situations, but they confirm the expectation of violence and the need and the willingness to participate in violent activity (Wolfgang and Ferracuti, 1967).

Although the above theories of lower-class values and behavior are seductive for those looking for kinds-of-people explanations of crime, they have all been subjected to a number of criticisms, the most serious of which questions the very existence of a lower-class culture of any kind (Leacock, 1971; Piven and Cloward, 1971; Ryan, 1971). Moreover, there is research that shows that lower-class gang members subscribe to conservative middle-class values (Campbell, 1984). Other research indicates that lower-class parents report a greater disapproval of interpersonal violence than higher-income parents (Erlanger, 1974). Of course, the very notion of a "lower-class lifestyle" confuses values and actions in the first place, and plays down the relative homogeneity of culture in mass society.

Finally, another variation of CSO were the prefeminist statements on women's crime that occurred in the middle 1970s. In the work of both Freda Adler (1975) and Rita Simon (1975), the relationships of gender, crime, and opportunity were explored. Each argued that the women's liberation movement affected both access to legitimate and illegitimate opportunities for women. Where Adler argues that new opportunities provide parallels in the behavior of female and male criminality so that both will rise during emancipation, Simon argues that violent crimes will decrease while property crimes will increase. For the most part, the claims of the emancipation theorists were overstated, although in the area of petty property offenses, women have made some gains on men. However, as the discussion on feminist criminology later in this chapter reveals, increases in petty property crimes have had more to do with some groups of women's increasing economic marginality and vulnerability than with their social, political, and economic liberation.

## Crime and Social Process (CSP)

Although CSP naturally involves learning and cognitive development, unlike positive and negative reinforced learning, interactionism, differential association, labeling, and the social construction of autobiographies assume that people are active rather than passive agents in their lives. CSP views human action as part of a social process that develops over time as people interact with others. In short, these interpretive social process theories, as Einstadter and Henry (1995) refer to them, attempt to explain the meaning of crime and deviance as people learn information, acquire values, and participate in behavioral patterns with others. Moreover, in seeing criminals and noncriminals alike as co-producers of a dynamic interactive process that forms their social world, this hermeneutic criminological approach assumes that there are not necessarily underlying causes for every criminal act. Or as Michael Phillipson (1971: 24) has stated, "crime can only be understood by showing how intimately it is bound up with the non-criminal features of society," referring to the fact that deviance (or crime) is ultimately a product of the interaction between deviants/criminals, potential deviants/criminals, and the various modes of deviance/crime control.

The first twentieth-century criminologist to forcefully argue that criminal behavior must be understood in the context of how individuals construct their social reality through communication with one another was Edwin Sutherland. His theory of *differential association*, which first appeared in 1939 and which was later revised in 1947, remains to this day among the most influential interpersonal theories of crime. It should be further underscored that differential association theory had special meaning within the context of Thorsten Sellin's (1938) *culture conflict*, which argued that in heterogeneous societies there are many diverse subcultures and conduct norms in conflict with one another. Members of one subculture may violate the dominant cultural norms (or laws) by following the indigenous conduct of their groups' norms. What Sutherland desired to reveal about crime as a learned rather than an inherited phenomenon was that the crucial element in becoming a delinquent or a criminal was a matter of learning specific situational meanings or definitions of the behavior in question. For Sutherland, differential association referred to the process of social interaction by which such definitions were acquired.

Sutherland explained that crime is learned essentially the same way as any other behavior is learned—through interpersonal communication and social interaction, mostly in primary but also in secondary and mass groupings. What is learned, he argued, was not merely the techniques of criminality, but, more important, the attitudes and motivations for crime. In this way, Sutherland's theory addresses questions that the social ecologists, anomie/strain, and subcultural theorists leave unanswered, namely, what accounts for the fact that the majority of people living in socially disorganized communities and experiencing anomie/strain fail to join illegitimate subcultures or fail to become delinquents or criminals. Differential association could also explain why members of the corporate classes may defraud consumers or participate in price-fixing conspiracies. Like the other sociological theories of crime and delinquency, differential association has been subjected to a number of criticisms. Overall, however, various measures of Sutherland's postulated "frequency, duration, priority, and intensity" of peer associations demonstrate a strong correlation between peer association and criminality (Short, 1957; 1958; Johnson, Marcos, and Bahr, 1987). Although this neither proves causality nor explains how learning actually takes place, differential association is certainly an indispensable process in becoming criminal.

Unlike the instrumental conditioning approach of "differential reinforcement theory" (Burgess and Akers, 1966; Akers, 1985), which maintains that learning criminal behavior is through operant conditioning, Sutherland's differential association claims that crime is learned in interaction with other persons in a process of communication. From an integrative perspective, one of the more interesting theoretical offshoots of differential association is the work of Daniel Glaser (1956; 1973; 1978). Glaser introduces the concepts of *differential identification* and *differential anticipation.*

Glaser wanted to answer the question, "Why is it that there are those who are exposed to an overabundance of definitions favorable to crime but who, nevertheless, obey the law?" His first answer to that question was "differential identification." Subsequently, he developed his own theory of "differential anticipation."

Differential identification according to Glaser relies on the *principles of modeling* as *well as on reference group theory.* According to this view of social learning, one does not need intimacy let alone personal interaction for communication to occur. People can use their imaginations, their aspirations, and their desires to identify with other groups or classes as their images are portrayed, for example, through the mass media. From this perspective, criminality results when a person identifies more with members of criminal groups than with members of conformist groups.

Differential anticipation moves considerably beyond the position of differential identification in that it attempts to integrate aspects of strain, operant conditioning, rational choice, and control (bond) into one general theory of crime. In the classical scheme of things, individuals avoid pain and seek pleasure. Hence, they will engage in behaviors in which they expect to receive the greatest rewards and the least punishment. Glaser argues that these expectations are derived from three sources: differential learning (i.e., tastes, skills, rationalizations); perceived opportunities (i.e., evaluation of circumstances, advantages, risks); and social bonds (i.e., stakes in conformity versus nonconformity). He maintains accordingly that crime results where and when the expectations of gratification from it exceed the unfavorable anticipations of differential learning, perceived opportunities, and social bonds.

Although differential anticipation theory has been critiqued for its difficulty of testing and for its tautological nature (Curran and Renzetti, 1994), it does provide a useful framework for incorporating a number of the constitutive elements involved in the interrelated processes of crime, stigma, punishment, and communitarianism (Braithwaite, 1989).

*Labeling* theory, sometimes referred to as *social reaction* theory, *symbolic interactionism*, or *phenomenology*, was popularized in the 1960s but has a long tradition dating back to the ideas of George Herbert Mead (1934) and Frank Tannenbaum (1938). When introduced in the 1960s, labeling constituted a new approach to explaining crime, one which departed significantly from both the positivist and classical paradigms. Labeling theorists (Becker, 1963; Goffman, 1963; Kitsuse, 1962; Lemert, 1967; Schur, 1973), including those who maintained that their approach was more about injecting sensitivity than about theorizing per se, shifted attention away from the positivistic concern with the peculiarities of the criminal actor and toward the *criminalization processes* or to the ways in which emphases on certain behaviors came to be defined as criminal. In this sense, the labeling approach introduced an appreciation for the relativity of crime and the importance of context, both situational and historical.

Labeling theorists were also concerned with the consequences of these definitions as they were applied to individuals who had engaged in such activities. "The key principle of the interactionist/labeling perspective is that people can adopt deviant or criminal identities as a result of cumulative negative social reaction in the course of official institutional processing by social control agencies" (Einstadter and Henry, 1995: 201). In short, deviance and criminality are not absolute categories of moral wrongdoing nor are they qualities of the act the person commits. Instead, in relativistic terms, deviance and crime refer to the aftermaths of the application by others of rules or sanctions to those who offend.

Rooted in the "looking-glass" concept of self and as a part of the "symbolic interactionist" tradition more generally (Blumer, 1969), the labeling perspective maintains that people act in this world based on their interpretive meanings of things as these arise in the context of social interaction. Meaning, in other words, is a two-way communication process that is both created and received at the same time. Individuals in such a dialectical relationship are both determined and determining. As for meaning and personal identification, a person's self-image or conception is constructed by the way he or she interprets how others view him or her. Finally, people construct their meanings of self, situation, and society in negotiation with other people.

Labeling theorists were specifically concerned with the negativized or stigmatized statuses or identities that were formed in response to the official or formal designation of the terms *delinquent* or *criminal*. Edwin Lemert distinguishes between primary deviance and secondary deviance. The former refers simply to rule breaking or to the initial illegitimate act/s before a person has yet to identify with the deviant label. The reasons for this transgression could be social, economic, or political; a person could be acting out of hedonistic impulse or out of the need for food. The latter refers to illegitimate act/s that follow the successful application of the negative label to the neophyte offender. It also refers to deviations that result from strong public or societal reactions. Secondary deviance, or criminality, is that behavior which occurs after a person comes to accept, internalize, or identify with the label "delinquent" or "criminal." The implications are that by negatively labeling primary delinquents/criminals the production of secondary delinquents/criminals occurs as legitimate opportunities and interactions are closed off. As Goffman (1963) argued, the official processing produces stigma, a "spoiled identity" or "master status," that results in a deviant or negative self-image.

The empirical verification of secondary deviation and of labeling more generally has not occurred. Nevertheless, as Braithwaite's (1989) theory and analysis of crime, shame, and reintegration argues, the degree or kind of negative label used is important in "tipping" one away from or toward crime. Finally, as Cohen has maintained, the label itself can totally reorient one's self-perceptions. The point is that the negative label does more than merely signify that a person had engaged in such-and-such deviant behavior:

> *Each label evokes a characteristic imagery. It suggests someone who is normally or habitually given to certain kinds of deviance; who may be expected to behave in this way; who is literally a bundle of odious or sinister qualities. It activates sentiments and calls out responses in others: rejection, contempt, suspicion, withdrawal, fear, hatred (Cohen, 1966: 24).*

*Social constructionism* is probably the most amorphous sociological grouping. Social constructionists include the works of such theorists as Schutz (1932, 1964), Garfinkel (1956, 1967), Sudnow (1965), Berger and Luckman (1967), Cicourel (1968), Quinney (1970), Douglas (1972), and Pfuhl (1980). Like the labeling and interactionist perspectives, constructionism assumes dissensus (conflict) unlike the consensus (order) assumed by anomie/stress and subcultural perspectives. Breaking from the positivist traditions of looking for causation and of hard determinism, constructionism focuses its criminological attention on the variable patterns of behavior even as these are applied to social groups within specific contexts. Again, humans have choices to make, but they are also subject to constraints (e.g., temporal social conditions). Therefore, their behavior, whether it is judged to be conforming or nonconforming, legal or illegal, is an outcome of interactive relationships.

The constructionists are less concerned with individual identity, process, and interaction and more concerned with how social relations and social arrangements come to be constructed. It is these larger relations, in other words, that provide the social space in which interpretation, identification, and labeling occur. Just as human behavior is not fixed in its meaning but subject to interpretation, negotiation, and reformulation, the same may be said of social organization. Hence, crime and criminals come to be viewed as socially and historically constructed phenomena. This does not deny the social reality of harm (crime) and offenders (criminals) independent of social group denunciation, but suggests the malleability not only in the variability in patterned behaviors but also in the ordering of deviant or legal categories in the first place.

Perhaps the best-known expression of the social constructionist perspective on crime is Richard Quinney's *the social reality of crime*, first articulated in 1970 in a book with the same title. The theory argues that the social reality of crime is constructed out of conflict in society. It further argues that crime is affected by the same dynamics that shape society's social, economic, and political structures. The theory is actually a system of interacting developmental propositions (Quinney, 1970; 1975). The five propositions are:

> *Crime as a legal definition of human conduct is created by agents of the dominant class in a politically organized society.*
>
> *Definitions of crime are composed of behaviors that conflict with the interests of the dominant class.*
>
> *Definitions of crime are applied by the class that has the power to share the enforcement and administration of criminal law.*
>
> *Behavior patterns are structured in relation to definitions of crime; within this context, people engage in actions that have relative probabilities of being defined as criminals.*
>
> *An ideology of crime is constructed and diffused by the dominant class to secure hegemony.*

The propositions do not constitute a theory about criminal behavior per se or about the predictability or causality of crime, but rather, as Quinney (1975: 41) says: "The phenomena denoted in the propositions and their relationships culminate in what is regarded as the amount and character of crime at any time." Quinney argues, in sum, that the social reality of crime is constructed by the interaction of the formulation and application of definitions of crime, the development of behavior patterns in relation to these definitions, and the construction of an ideology of crime.

## Crime and Social Structure (CSS)

Unlike the biological and psychological perspectives discussed in Chapters 5 and 6 and unlike the sociological perspectives discussed so far in this chapter, CSS is concerned with such things as "cross-cultural variations in crime rates, regional differences in forms of criminality, variations in crime rates across different socioeconomic groups, crime rate differences across urban communities, and kindred matters" (Gibbons, 1994: 96). The "kindred matters" that Gibbons refers to are the patterned variables of social-structural analysis associated with age, sex, race/ethnicity, and class differences as these relate to crime and crime control. In sum, the focus of CSS theories is not on the "Why do they do it?" question that primarily occupies the attentions of CSO and CSP theories, but rather it is on the "Why in the aggregate do we have the criminality that we do?"

Criminological answers to this question have varied over time. For example, in the 1930s, the works of Shaw and McKay, Sutherland, Sellin, Merton, and others provided a framework for what has been termed the "criminogenic culture" perspective on crime in American society (Gibbons, 1994). In the 1960s, Edwin Schur (1969) and others were writing about "our criminal society." By the 1990s, Steven Messner and Richard Rosenfeld in *Crime and the American Dream* (1994: v) maintained that "high levels of serious crime result from the normal functioning of the American social system." Shared in common, these perspectives argue essentially that various structural flaws encourage (or are responsible) for the criminality that society reaps. As has been the case since the publication of Willem Bonger's *Criminality and Economic Conditions* in 1916, the answers to the "Why do we have the crime we have?" question have differed and overlapped depending on one's view of society, human nature, and the origins and endurance of conflict, domination, inequality, alienation, and injustice. For Bonger, the first self-identified Marxist criminologist, crime, exploitation, and moral climate were inextricably caught up in the egoism and greed produced by capitalist relations. Both conflict and crime were reduced to products of economic conditions.

Non-Marxist *conflict* (pluralist) theories, by contrast, base their criminology on the notions of interest group conflict and differential power (Simmel, 1955; Coser, 1956; Mills, 1956; Dahrendorf, 1959). Therefore, conflict theorists

> *see society divided on several dimensions and depict its structure as made up of numerous groups, each defining its own interests and struggling for the power to define and control public issues. Conflict theorists recognize that crime may stem from differences in economic wealth, a clash of cultures, or from the outcome of symbolic and instrumental struggles over status, ideology, morality, religion, race, and ethnicity (Einstadter and Henry, 1995: 228).*

In particular, conflict criminologists (Sellin, 1938; Vold 1958; Turk, 1964; 1969) see specific groups of people becoming dominant through the acquisition or control of key resources—economic, social, political, and other means. In turn, these groups are able to criminalize the behavior of others, leaving themselves, for the most part, beyond incrimination (Kennedy, 1970). Crime, then, is located in a multidimensional, fragmented social order with ongoing struggles for control occurring at multiple sites of difference. Its roots are both instrumental and symbolic.

George Vold, for example, argued that conflict theory "is strictly to those kinds of situations in which the individual criminal acts flow from the collision of groups whose members are loyally upholding the in-group position" (Vold and Bernard, 1986: 276). Austin Turk and other conflict theorists wanted to know the processes by which certain behaviors became a crime and particular individuals became formally designated as criminals. Turk (1969: 14) argued further that "conflict processes through which definitions of deviance (criminality) are created and enforced are . . . generic to social life." Crime, then, is basically a product of inequality and conflict inherent in all societies.

*Marxist* theories view conflict in different terms as suggested by Bonger earlier. Rather than viewing power in terms of diffuse interest groups or segments, Marxists define power in terms of class affiliation. Marxists, moreover, place emphasis on structured inequalities as these relate to the distribution of wealth and power. In other words, although conflict and Marxist theories alike share a relativist perspective on law and crime as do subcultural, labeling, and constructionist theories, Marxist theories of crime are ultimately derivative of the political economy.

Marxist criminologists are not a unified group. They differ over the structure of the social order. They may be distinguished by how they view classes with respect to their nature and number, by the priority they give to powerful economic interests, and by the relationships they construct between class interests and the state. The most common divisions drawn are between the instrumental and structural Marxist criminologies (Bohm, 1982; Lynch and Groves, 1986).

Instrumental Marxism (Chambliss, 1975; Quinney, 1974; Krisberg, 1975) holds a power model in which capitalist societies are presented as a monolithic system of inequality. There are the dominant economic elites who use the state's law and criminal justice system to criminalize those challenging or threatening their position. Structural Marxism (Spitzer, 1975; Greenberg, 1981; Block and Chambliss, 1981) holds a dual power structure whereby the state in relation to specific economic interests plays a more dominant but semi-autonomous role. In this interdependent role, the state and law are viewed as attempts to resolve societal crises aroused by the inherent contradictions of capitalism.

According to the instrumentalists, crime can only be perpetrated and legitimated among the working and lower classes. Hence, the crime problem means the predatory street crime problem. According to the structuralists, not only can those acts threatening the interests or positions of the dominant classes become criminal, such as theft

Karl Marx

and kidnapping, but also any behavior that threatens the overall system of capitalism can be criminalized, such as corporate pollution and price-fixing. The structural and dialectical Marxist criminologies (Quinney, 1977; Michalowski, 1985) argue, moreover, that there can be crimes of the powerless and crimes of the powerful. More specifically, these structural–dialectical formulations include the "crimes of domination and repression" committed by economic elites, agents of criminal justice, and governmental workers as well as the "crimes of accommodation and resistance" committed by ordinary people (Quinney, 1977).

John Hagan's (1989) "*structural criminology*" focuses on power relations with the emphasis as much on relations as power. These relations may be instrumental as when white collar offenders manipulate ownership to engage in fraud and deception, or symbolic as in the labeling of victims and villains. Structural criminology involves a neo-Marxist conceptualization of stratification that stresses economic position rather than economic status:

> *For example, relational measures of class highlight positions of persons who are un-employed workers of the surplus population. It may be the fact of unemployment, more directly than low status, that leads to punitive sentencing decision. . . . it may be a po-sition of powerlessness, rather than a relative deprivation of status, that better ac-counts for punitive sentencing decisions. Indeed, what is potentially most interesting is that the law scarcely bothers to deny this (Hagan, 1989: 2).*

With the exception of the instrumental Marxist point of view that borders on "conspiracy theory," empirical evidence and research generally support most of the arguments about crime and social structure, namely that inequality rather than poverty per se promotes alienation and animosity, a breakdown in social cohesiveness, and the degrees of differential organization that generate crime in society (Blau and Blau, 1982; Hagan, 1989). Moreover, the different formulations of offenses and sanctions carried out by the various systems of crime control are biased against the poor and powerless in their day-to-day processes of law enforcement and adjudication (Barak, 1980; Reiman, 1979; 1990).

In sum, so long as there are substantial portions of powerless people in society, marginalized from the economic, political, and social means of production, there will be a relationship between the kinds or degrees of inequality and the crime committed by both the powerless and powerful (Braithwaite, 1979; 1989).

*Feminist* approaches to criminology are not any more monolithic than the approaches of other criminologies, mainstream or critical. Like other theoretical perspectives that take society and the social order seriously, feminist criminologists do not have a unitary view of human order, the state, law, and crime (Einstadter and Henry, 1995). Some authors point to the major division between radical feminists like Brownmiller (1975), Dworkin (1981), and MacKinnon (1989), who take an instrumental view of the state as a neutral resource to be captured, and Marxist/socialist feminists like Messerschmidt (1986), Currie (1989), or Smart (1989), who take a structural view of the state as a relatively autonomous entity or set of relations that operate in the broad interests of capitalism and patriarchy.

Other authors point to the fact that there are and have been several strands or varieties of feminism and feminist theory, including but not limited to liberal feminism, radical feminism, Marxist feminism, socialist feminism, black feminism, lesbian feminism, and third-world feminism. Generally, however, as feminist thought has matured there has been a tendency, on the one hand, to be inclusive of the differences in feminisms and, on the other hand, to be cognizant of the commonalities of gender, power, and context (Caulfield and Wonders, 1994). As Sally Simpson (1989: 606) has noted, as feminist criminology became more encompassing of the life experiences that pertain to *both* girls and boys, women and men, it took "into account the gendered understanding of all aspects of human culture and relationships."

The shared contentions of feminist criminologies argue that social science and criminology have traditionally been shaped by a male point of view and experience. Androcentric, or male-dominated, criminologies, have been, for the most part, blind to the relationship between crime/crime control and the differences in gender experience and social construction (Smart, 1976; Leonard, 1982; Carlen, 1985; Barak, 1986; Messerschmidt, 1986, 1993; Carlen and Worrall, 1987; Daly and Chesney-Lind, 1988; Gelsthrope and Morris, 1990; Simpson, 1989; Stanko, 1985, 1990; Cain, 1989; Rafter and Heidensohn, 1995). In response, early feminist criminologies (Klein, 1973) critiqued the late-nineteenth to mid-twentieth-century studies that attempted to explain female criminality based on moralisms, physical differences, male conjecture, social and biological influences, or some combination of these factors as found in the works of Lombroso and Ferrero (1900) and Pollak (1950). Subsequent feminist critiques (Messerschmidt, 1986; Simpson, 1989) were directed at the prefeminist claims of "the new female criminal" or of the Women's Liberation Movement thesis of crime as a result of the breaking down of gender distinctions and the "rising tide of female assertiveness" (Adler, 1975; Simon, 1975).

Put succinctly, feminist criminologies are about the business of engendering a discipline that has focused almost exclusively on male behavior, and whose theories of delinquency and criminality subsume that what applies to males and male criminality also applies to females and female criminality (Morris, 1987; Daly, 1989, 1994; Gelsthorpe, 1989; Chesney-Lind, 1989; Currie, 1989; Chesney-Lind and Sheldon, 1992). As Eileen Leonard (1982: 182) wrote during the transition period between prefeminist and feminist criminology, "given their vastly historical, social, and economic experiences, women should not be expected to behave like men." The point was that the experiences of girls and women in relationship to conformity and nonconformity had to be studied.

Initially, feminist criminology aspired to develop a gendered theory of crime. A gendered theory of crime takes into account both the effects of gender and gender stratification on women's lives and development. A gendered theory of crime recognizes that "people's perceptions, opportunities, and experiences are shaped not only by the mode of production under which they live, but also by the form of *gender relations* dominant in their society" (Curran and Renzetti, 1994: 272). As James Messerschmidt (1986) argues, the modern system of corporate capitalism requires both the "relations of production" and the "relations of reproduction," the former referring to the economic system that gives rise to class relations and exploitation of workers by owners;

the latter referring to the ways in which people organize their activities so as to reproduce, socialize, and maintain their communities. Taken together, it is argued that these two systems of relations have yielded social arrangements in which males appropriate the labor power of females and control their sexuality. It is also argued that these two systems produce the kind of legal conformity and nonconformity experienced by the gendered roles of male and female.

For feminists, then, the first order of criminological exchange was coming to grips not only with capitalism but with patriarchy or sex/gender systems in which men dominate women and in which masculinity is more highly valued than femininity. The question asked was, "How is gender inequality implicated in the crimes of both males and females and in the different formal and informal responses to control their behavior?" Gradually, however, the question became more complex for feminist criminologists as issues of commonality, difference, and human agency entered into the discussion.

For example, Kathleen Daly and Meda Chesney-Lind (1988: 498) are concerned with how crime or the behavior and identities associated with masculinity and femininity are "socially constructed from relations of dominance and inequality between men and women." They point out the "different natures, different talents, and interests that define Western notions of manhood and womanhood" as these "rest on a string of male-centered oppositions to and negations of woman and femininity" (Daly and Chesney-Lind, 1988: 498). Messerschmidt (1993) adds significantly to the discussion by pointing out that there are many different types of masculinities and femininities, not just the patriarchally constructed ones. Daly (1991; 1992) calls for abandoning the implied gender-based overlay of victimization and criminalization with women as victims and men as perpetrators, bringing back in the passive and active roles of men and women. Finally, contemporary gendered or feminist analyses of crime and delinquency (Campbell, 1984; Chesney-Lind, 1989; Cain, 1989; Chesney-Lind and Sheldon, 1992; Mann, 1993) take into criminological account the inextricable linkages between inequalities of gender, class, and race. These connections between race, gender, and class will be taken up in more detail in Chapter 11.

In sum, most feminist criminologists argue that male dominance and female restriction, in a capitalist and patriarchal society like ours, in part reflect the sex-role expectations that are enforced by both the informal and formal control systems. Moreover, as societal expectations for women's roles expanded to include both wage and domestic labor, both vulnerability and opportunity increased. Freed from domestic captivity, women were now vulnerable to the marketplace and subject to more public interaction and, hence, more criminal victimization. On the other hand, women were also subject to new opportunities to engage in alternative forms (i.e., crime) of meeting their needs of femininity (and masculinity). Similarly, gender disparities in the criminal justice system have been reflective of restrictive female sex roles and of a patriarchal system of social control. The evidence also generally supports the idea that female status, or criminal, offenders are treated with more penal severity than are their male counterparts for comparable offenses. Finally, during the past decade or two, the relationships between poverty, victimization, and female crime that were experienced by many offenders were particularly hard on young, single minority women. All of these conditions necessitate the importance of attending to the material and structural forces that shape women's lives and experiences.

## Summary and Conclusions: Why We Have Crime

As this chapter portrays, sociological theories of criminal behavior and of crime encompass a lot of territory, ranging from the positivist-oriented theories of social ecology, anomie/strain, and subculture, to the interactionist-oriented theories of differential association, labeling, and social constructionism, to the structurally oriented theories of power, conflict, class, gender, and race. These theories have been classified according to whether or not their emphasis is on social organization, social process, or social structure. The first two groups of classification pay more attention to personal differences while the last group pays more attention to structural differences. Yet, again from an integrative perspective, this is really a matter of degree or emphasis, as both the theories and theorists from these groups overlap in the everyday realities of crime and justice.

Taken together, the three classifications of sociological explanations of crime yielded three varieties of criminological exploration each, for a total of nine sociological perspectives on crime and delinquency. In turn, each of these perspectives was further broken down into suborientations. All of the categories and their ideas about criminals, crime, and criminalization have, to varying degrees, made valuable contributions to the study of crime and delinquency. In the aggregate, these sociological theories provide numerous insights into the multiple dimensions of social organization, social process, and social structure as these interact with crime and social control.

Compared to the biological and psychological approaches with their kinds-of-people theories of criminal behavior, the sociological approaches are broader in that they conceptualize kinds-of-environment as well as kinds-of-people theories of criminality. Hence, unlike the biological and psychological explanations that attempt to answer only one of the two fundamental questions of criminology, "Why do they do it?" the sociological explanations also attempt to answer the question "Why do we have the crime we have?" In this sense, although the psychological approaches are central to integration from the perspective that they are directly linked to both biology and sociology, the sociological approaches are integral to integration because they connect the individual, the group, and the society.

## Discussion Questions

1. Using various sociological theories as examples, compare and contrast the "crime and social organization" perspective with the "crime and social process" perspective.

2. What are the primary differences between the subcultural theories described within the "crime and social organization" framework?

3. Both Marxist and feminist analyses of crime and social control have changed over time. What are some of the similarities and differences between these two criminologies?

4. How does this theory of differential association explain both juvenile delinquency and white collar crime?

5. Compare and contrast Durkheim's concept of anomie with Merton's and Agnew's theories of anomie/stress.

# References

Adler, Freda. 1975. *Sisters in Crime: The Rise of the New Female Criminal*. New York: McGraw-Hill.

Agnew, Robert S. 1985. "A Revised Strain Theory of Delinquency." *Social Forces* 64:151–167.

———. 1992. "Foundation for a General Strain Theory of Crime and Delinquency." *Criminology* 30:47–87.

Akers, Ronald L. 1985. *Deviant Behavior: A Social Learning Approach*. 3rd ed. Belmont, CA: Wadsworth.

———. 1994. *Criminological Theories: Introduction and Evaluation*. Los Angeles: Roxbury Publishing Company.

Barak, Gregg. 1980. *In Defense of Whom? A Critique of Criminal Justice Reform*. Cincinnati: Anderson Publishing Company.

———. 1986. "Feminist Connections and the Movement against Domestic Violence: Beyond Criminal Justice Reform." *Journal of Crime and Justice* 9:139–162.

Becker, Howard. 1963. *Outsiders: Studies in the Sociology of Deviance*. New York: Free Press.

Berger, Peter, and Thomas Luckman. 1966. *The Social Construction of Reality*. Garden City, NY: Doubleday.

Blau, Judith, and Peter Blau. 1982. "The Cost of Inequality: Metropolitan Structure and Violent Crime." *American Sociological Review* 47:114–129.

Block, Alan, and William J. Chambliss. 1981. *Organizing Crime*. New York: Elsevier.

Blumer, Herbert. 1969. *Symbolic Interactionism: Perspective and Method*. Englewood Cliffs, NJ: Prentice-Hall.

Bohm, Robert. 1982. "Radical Criminology: An Explication." *Criminology* 19:565–589.

Bonger, Willem. 1916. *Criminality and Economic Conditions*. Boston: Little, Brown and Company.

Braithwaite, John. 1979. *Inequality, Crime and Public Policy*. London: Routledge and Kegan Paul.

———. 1989. *Crime, Shame, and Reintegration*. Cambridge: Cambridge University Press.

Brantingham, Paul J., and Patricia L. Brantingham. 1981. "Introduction: The Dimension of Crime." In P. J. Brantingham and P. L. Brantingham, eds., *Environmental Criminology*. Beverly Hills, CA: Sage.

———. 1984. *Patterns of Crime*. New York: Macmillan.

Brennan, T., and D. Huizinga. 1975. *Theory Validation and Aggregate National Data*. Integration Report of the Office of Youth Opportunity Research FY 1975. Boulder, CO: Behavioral Research Institute.

Brownmiller, Susan. 1975. *Against Our Will: Men, Women and Rape*. New York: Simon and Schuster.

Burgess, Robert, and Ronald Akers. 1966. "A Differential Association-Reinforcement Theory of Criminal Behavior." *Social Problems* 14:128–147.

Bursik, Robert. 1984. "Urban Dynamics and Ecological Studies of Delinquency." *Social Forces* 63:393–413.

———. 1989. "Political Decision-making and Ecological Models of Delinquency: Conflict and Consensus." In S. F. Messner, M. D. Krohn, and A. E. Liska, eds., *Theoretical Integration in the Study of Deviance and Crime*. Albany: SUNY Press.

Cain, Maureen. 1989. *Growing Up Good: Policing the Behavior of Girls in Europe*. London. Sage.

Campbell, Anne. 1984. *The Girls in the Gang: A Report from New York City*. London: Basil Blackwell.

Carlen, Pat. 1985. *Criminal Women: Autobiographical Accounts*. Cambridge: Polity Press.

Carlen, Pat, and Ann Worrall, eds. 1987. *Gender, Crime and Justice*. Milton Keynes, England: Open University Press.

Caulfield, Susan, and Nancy Wonders. 1994. "Gender and Justice: Feminist Contributions to Criminology." In Gregg Barak, ed., *Varieties of Criminology: Readings from a Dynamic Discipline*. Westport, CT: Praeger.

Chambliss, William. 1975. "Toward a Political Economy of Crime." *Theory and Society* 2:149–170.

Chesney-Lind, Meda. 1989. "Girl's Crime and Woman's Place: Toward a Feminist Model of Female Delinquency." *Crime and Delinquency* 35:5–29.

Chesney-Lind, Meda, and Randall Sheldon. 1992. *Girls, Delinquency and Juvenile Justice*. Pacific Grove, CA: Brooks/Cole.

Cicourel, Aaron. 1968. *The Social Organization of Juvenile Justice*. New York: Wiley.

Cloward, Richard A., and Lloyd E. Ohlin. 1960. *Delinquency and Opportunity—A Theory of Delinquent Gangs*. New York: Free Press.

Cohen, Albert. 1955. *Delinquent Boys: The Culture of the Gang.* Glencoe, IL: Free Press.

———. 1966. *Deviance and Control.* Englewood, Cliffs, NJ: Prentice-Hall.

Cohen, Lawrence, and Marcus Felson. 1979. "Social Change and Crime Rate Trends: A Routine Activities Approach." *American Sociological Review* 44:588–608.

Coser, Lewis. 1956. *The Functions of Social Conflict.* New York: Macmillan.

Curran, Daniel, and Claire Renzetti. 1994. *Theories of Crime.* Boston: Allyn and Bacon.

Currie, Dawn. 1989. "Women and the State: A Statement on Feminist Theory." *The Critical Criminologist* 1(2): 4–5.

Dahrendorf, Ralf. 1959. *Class and Class Conflict in an Industrial Society.* London: Routledge and Kegan Paul.

Daly, Kathleen. 1989. "Gender and Varieties of White-Collar Crime." *Criminology* 27:769–793.

———. 1991. "Feminists Working Within and Against Criminology." *The Critical Criminologist* 3(1): 5–6, 11.

———. 1992. "Women's Pathways to Felony Court: Feminist Theories of Lawbreaking and Problems of Representation." *Review of Law and Women's Studies* 2:1–42.

———. 1994. *Gender, Crime and Punishment.* New Haven, CT: Yale University Press.

Daly, Kathleen, and Meda Chesney-Lind. 1988. "Feminism and Criminology." *Justice Quarterly* 5:497–538.

Douglas, Jack, ed. 1972. *Research on Deviance.* New York: Random House.

Durkheim, Emile. [1893] 1947. *The Division of Labor in Society.* New York: Free Press.

———. [1897] 1950. *The Rules of Sociological Method.* Glencoe, IL: Free Press.

Dworkin, Andrea. 1981. *Men Possessing Women.* London: Women's Press.

Einstadter, Werner, and Stuart Henry. 1995. *Criminological Theory: An Analysis of Its Underlying Assumptions.* Fort Worth: Harcourt Brace.

Erlanger, Howard S. 1974. "The Empirical Status of the Subculture of Violence Thesis." *Social Problems* 22:282–292.

Garfinkel, Harold. 1956. "Conditions of Successful Degradation Ceremonies." *American Journal of Sociology* 61:420–424.

———. 1967. *Studies in Ethnomethodology.* New York: Basic Books.

Gelsthrope, Loraine. 1989. *Sexism and the Female Offender.* Aldershot: Gower Press.

Gelsthrope, Loraine, and Allison Morris, eds. 1990. *Feminist Perspectives in Criminology.* Philadelphia: Open University Press.

Gibbons, Don. 1994. *Talking About Crime and Criminals: Problems and Issues in Theory Development in Criminology.* Englewood Cliffs, NJ: Prentice-Hall.

Glaser, Daniel. 1956. "Criminality Theory and Behavioral Images." *American Journal of Sociology* 61:433–444.

———. 1973. "Role Models and Differential Association." In E. Rubington and M. S. Weinberg, eds., *Deviance: The Interactionist Perspective.* New York: Macmillan.

———. 1978. *Crime in Our Changing Society.* New York: Holt, Rinehart and Winston.

Goffman, Erving. 1963. *Stigma: Notes on the Management of Spoiled Identity.* Englewood Cliffs, NJ: Prentice-Hall.

Greenberg, David, ed. 1981. *Crime and Capitalism: Readings in Marxist Criminology.* Palo Alto, CA: Mayfield.

Hagan, John. 1989. *Structural Criminology.* New Brunswick, NJ: Rutgers University Press.

Johnson, Richard, A. C. Marcos, and S. J. Bahr. 1997. "The Role of Peers in the Complex Etiology of Adolescent Drug Use." *Criminology* 25:323–345.

Kennedy, Mark. 1970. "Beyond Incrimination: Some Neglected Facts of the History of Punishment." *Catalyst* 5:1–16.

Kitsuse, John. 1962. "Social Reaction to Deviant Behavior." *Social Problems* 9:253–271.

Klein, Dorie. 1973. "The Etiology of Female Crime: A Review of the Literature." *Issues in Criminology* 8:3–30.

Krisberg, Barry. 1975. *Crime and Privilege: Towards a New Criminology.* Englewood Cliffs, NJ: Prentice-Hall.

Leacock, L. 1971. *The Culture of Poverty: A Critique.* New York: Simon and Schuster.

Lemert, Edwin. 1967. *Human Deviance, Social Problems and Social Control.* Englewood Cliffs, NJ: Prentice-Hall.

Leonard, Eileen. 1982. *Women, Crime and Society: A Critique of Criminological Theory.* New York: Longman.

Lombroso, Cesare, and William Ferrero. 1900. *The Female Criminal.* New York: Appleton.

Lynch, Michael, and W. Byron Groves. 1986. *A Primer in Radical Criminology.* Albany, NY: Harrow and Heston.

MacKinnon, Catherine. 1989. *Toward a Feminist Theory of the State.* Cambridge, MA: Harvard University Press.

Mann, Coramae Richey. 1993. *Unequal Justice: A Question of Color.* Bloomington, IN: Indiana University Press.

Mead, George Herbert. 1934. *Mind, Self and Society,* ed. C. W. Morris. Chicago: Chicago University Press.

Merton, Robert. 1938. "Social Structure and Anomie." *American Sociological Review* 3:672–682.

———. 1957. *Social Theory and Social Structure.* New York: Free Press.

Messerschmidt, James. 1986. *Capitalism, Patriarchy, and Crime: Toward a Socialist Feminist Criminology.* Totowa, NJ: Rowman and Littlefield.

———. 1993. *Masculinities and Crime: Critique and Reconceptualization of Theory.* Boston: Rowman and Littlefield.

Messner, Steven, and Richard Rosenfeld. 1994. *Crime and the American Dream.* Belmont, CA: Wadsworth.

Michalowski, Ray. 1985. *Order, Law and Crime: An Introduction to Criminology.* New York: Random House.

Miller, Walter. 1958. "Lower Class Culture as a Generating Milieu of Gang Delinquency." *Journal of Social Issues* 14:5–19.

Mills, C. Wright. 1956. *The Power Elite.* New York: Oxford University Press.

Morris, Allison. 1987. *Women, Crime and Criminal Justice.* Oxford: Blackwell.

Newman, Oscar. 1972. *Defensible Space.* New York: Macmillan.

Park, Robert, and Ernest Burgess. 1925. *The City.* Chicago: Chicago University Press.

Pfuhl, Edwin. 1980. *The Deviance Process.* New York: Aldine.

Phillipson, Michael. 1971. *Sociological Aspects of Crime and Delinquency.* London: Routledge and Kegan Paul.

Piven, Francis Fox, and Richard Cloward. 1971. *Regulating the Poor.* New York: Pantheon.

Pollak, Otto. 1950. *The Criminality of Women.* Philadelphia: University of Pennsylvania Press.

Quinney, Richard. 1970. *The Social Reality of Crime.* Boston: Little, Brown and Company.

———. 1974. *Critique of Legal Order.* Boston: Little, Brown and Company.

———. 1975. *Criminology.* Boston: Little, Brown and Company.

———. 1977. *Class, State, and Crime.* New York: David McKay.

Rafter, Nicole Hahn, and Frances Heidensohn, eds. 1995. *International Feminist Perspectives in Criminology.* Philadelphia: Open University Press.

Reiman, Jeffrey. [1979] 1990. *The Rich Get Richer and the Poor Get Prison.* New York: John Wiley.

Ryan, William. 1971. *Blaming the Victim.* New York: Random House.

Sampson, Robert. 1987. "Communities and Crime." In M. Goffredson and T. Hirschi, eds., *Positive Criminology.* Newbury Park, CA: Sage.

Sampson, Robert, and W. Byron Groves. 1989. "Community Structures and Crime: Testing Social Disorganization Theory." *American Journal of Sociology* 94:774–802.

Schur, Edwin. 1969. *Our Criminal Society.* Englewood Cliffs, NJ: Prentice-Hall.

———. 1973. *Radical Non-Intervention: Rethinking the Delinquency Problem.* Englewood Cliffs, NJ: Prentice-Hall.

Schutz, Alfred. [1932] 1967. *The Phenomenology of the Social World.* Evanston, IL: Northwestern University Press.

———. 1964. *Collected Papers,* 3 vols. Ed. Maurice Natanson. The Hague, Netherlands: Martinus Nijhoff.

Segrave, J. O., and D. N. Hastad. 1985. "Evaluating Three Models of Delinquency Causation for Males and Females: Strain Theory, Subculture Theory, and Control Theory." *Sociological Focus* 18:1–17.

Sellin, Thorsten. 1938. *Culture Conflict and Crime.* New York: Social Science Research Council.

Shaw, Clifford, and Henry McKay. 1931. *Social Factors in Juvenile Delinquency: Report of the Causes of Crime.* National Commission on Law Observance and Enforcement, Report No. 13. Washington, DC: U.S. Government Printing Office.

———. 1942. *Juvenile Delinquency and Urban Areas: A Study of Delinquents in Relation to Differential*

*Characteristics of Local Communities in American Cities.* Chicago: Chicago University Press.

Short, James. 1957. "Differential Association and Delinquency." *Social Problems* 4:233–239.

———. 1958. "Differential Association with Delinquent Friends and Delinquent Behavior." *Pacific Sociological Review* 1:20–25.

———. 1964. "Gang Behavior and Anomie." In M. B. Clinard, ed., *Anomie and Deviant Behavior.* New York: Free Press.

Simmel, Georg. [1908] 1955. *The Sociology of Conflict.* Trans. K. H. Wolff. Glencoe, IL: Free Press.

Simon, Rita. 1975. *Women and Crime.* Lexington, MA: D. C. Heath.

Simpson, Sally. 1989. "Feminist Theory, Crime, and Justice." *Criminology* 27:605–631.

Smart, Carol. 1976. *Women, Crime and Criminology: A Feminist Critique.* London: Routledge and Kegan Paul.

———. 1989. *Feminism and the Power of Law.* London: Routledge.

Spitzer, Steven. 1975. "Towards a Marxian Theory of Deviance." *Social Problems* 22:638–651.

Stanko, Elizabeth. 1985. *Intimate Intrusions: Women's Experience of Male Violence.* London: Virago.

———. 1990. *Danger Signals.* London: Pandora.

Stark, Rodney. 1987. "Deviant Places: A Theory of the Ecology of Crime." *Criminology* 25: 893–909.

Sudnow, David. 1965. "Normal Crimes: Sociological Features of the Penal Code in a Public Defender Office." *Social Problems* 12:255–270.

Sutherland, Edwin. [1939] 1947. *Principles of Criminology.* 3rd and 4th editions. Philadelphia: Lippincott.

Tannenbaum, Frank. 1938. *Crime and the Community.* Boston: Ginn.

Thrasher, Frederick. 1927. *The Gang: A Study of 1,313 Gangs in Chicago.* Chicago: University of Chicago Press.

Turk, Austin. 1964. "Prospects for Theories of Criminal Behavior." *Journal of Criminal Law, Criminology, and Police Science* 55:454–461.

———. 1969. *Criminality and the Legal Order.* Chicago: Rand McNally.

Vila, Bryan. 1994. "A General Paradigm for Understanding Criminal Behavior: Extending Evolutionary Ecological Theory." *Criminology* 32:311–359.

Vold, George. 1958. *Theoretical Criminology.* New York: Oxford University Press.

Vold, George, and Thomas Bernard. 1986. *Theoretical Criminology.* 3rd ed. New York: Oxford University Press.

Wolfgang, Marvin, and Franco Ferracuti. 1967. *The Subculture of Violence.* London: Tavistock.

### Chapter 8

# Contributions from Law and Economics: "Reason and Rationality"

Although most of the explanations in the three previous chapters have had a tendency to embrace determinist models of criminal behavior, in this chapter the attention turns to classical explanations of crime, where the focus is on law, liberty, and reason. From the classical perspectives of law and economics, crime is the result of the rational calculation of human beings exercising their free will. Accordingly,

> *All individuals choose to obey or violate the law by a rational calculation of the risk of pain versus potential pleasure derived from an act. In contemplating a criminal act, they take into account the probable legal penalties and the likelihood that they will be caught. If they believe that the legal penalty threatens more pain than the probable gain produced by the crime, then they will not commit the crime. Their calculation is based on their own experience with criminal punishment, their knowledge of what punishment is imposed by law, and their awareness of what punishment has been given to apprehended offenders in the past (Akers, 1994: 50).*

Nevertheless, even Beccaria, for example, "subscribed to a notion of human agency simultaneously involving 'free' rational calculation *and* 'determined' action" (Beirne, 1991: 812). Similarly, the classical idea of pure rationality was also subject to pre- and subrationality as well as to the variability of human rationality, both individually and historically. Finally, the utility of the law and its enforcement was not primarily in avenging wrongs done to the state or the victim, but rather in reasonable penalties applied in a reasonable fashion so that they encouraged people to obey the law.

Here I will explore not only those legal and economic contributions that provide insights into making sense out of patterns of crime and crime control, but also a wider critique and deconstruction of criminal law and social justice. According to the classical perspective, with the exception of the lawbreaking behavior itself, there are no fundamental differences between criminals and noncriminals. Crime is viewed, in part, as a response to the predictability of punishment or the extent to which the criminal justice system is fair, expedient, and efficient in its distribution of penalties. Crime, in the classical framework, refers only to that behavior defined by the legal code. Without law, there is no crime. And the law is a response to the injury or harm done to society. Hence, the punishment has had to "fit the crime" (not the offender) so that sufficient grounds (or general deterrence) were provided to citizens for making rational decisions not to engage in illegal activities.

The classicists hold to beliefs about the necessity of certainty and celerity, if not severity, in punishment. They also believe that the law "should not be involved in the control of any activities which do not harm others, do not contradict their self-interest or threaten the Social Contract" (Young, 1981: 259). Both Beccaria and Bentham, for example, were firm in their agreement about acts becoming offenses only when they were detrimental to the community or society. They also both believed in equal protection and treatment through a *due process of law* regardless of a person's class, race, or gender. For Beccaria, laws were the basis on which independent and isolated people united to form a society. In the process, they agreed to support and defend one another. Compared with Bentham, Beccaria's primary concerns with harms were confined to the economic marketplace and referred to those behaviors that restricted the accumulation of wealth (Beirne, 1991). Lawbreakers were those who chose to limit other peoples' acts to acquire wealth as defined by law.

Bentham had a broader view of social rights (pleasure) and obligations (pain) than Beccaria. He was less concerned about protecting the formal rights of individuals or social interest groups than he was about protecting "the collective human rights of society" as a whole (Galliher, 1989). Moreover, Bentham elaborated a whole list of behavioral harms that caused a variety of pains. In order of seriousness these were: crimes against the state; crimes that injure the security and property of individuals; and crimes disruptive to the public peace. And criminal punishment was to be reserved for those who harmed others.

Classical criminology spans a period of some two and one-half centuries, dating back to the emergent period (1750–1800) of the Enlightenment and such classical thinkers as Montesquieu, Voltaire, Beccaria, and Bentham. Predating the emergence and development of positivist criminology, classical criminology and its various expressions are usually addressed in most textbooks before, rather than after, a discussion of the positivist criminologies. I have elected to reverse this order for three reasons. First, because classical criminologies are less explanations of criminal behavior than they are explanations of crime, it is very well the case that the former has as much, if not more, in common with environmental or structural explanations than with naturalistic or individual explanations of crime. Second, implications of the traditional and postclassical formulations of legal and economic models of crime recognize the contradictory needs for law and order and for reform and change. Third, as was discussed in Chapter 1, the rigid dichotomization between classical and positivist criminologies may, in fact, be an exaggeration of the alleged separation of behavior grounded in free choice versus determinism.

Taken as a whole, diverse and often contradictory explanations of crime and punishment are traditionally referred to as classical criminologies. In reality, however, these theories may actually refer to classical, neoclassical, or postclassical rational choice theories. Although a myriad of related theories, including but not limited to humanitarian rational, administrative-managerial, due process, just deserts, economic, time allocation, situational choice, and routine conflict theories have been identified as falling within the classical school of criminology, Einstadter and Henry (1995) have provided a useful classification of theories and theorists that employ rational choice explanations of crime. These include contemporary neoclassicists, such as the American Friends Service Committee (1971), Fogel (1975), and Von Hirsch (1976); economists of crime, such as Becker (1968), Reynolds (1973), Sullivan (1973), Ehrlich (1973; 1982), and Schmidt and Witte (1984); and postclassical rational choice and routine activity theorists, such as Cornish and Clarke (1986; 1987), Cohen and Felson (1979), Roshier (1989), and Kennedy and Forde (1995).

Although these classicists sometimes differ remarkably in kind and degree, what they fundamentally share in common, whether framed in the context of jurisprudence or laissez-faire, is a belief in an economic theory of crime that emphasizes the criminal act as defined by law. "The key idea is that people are more or less free to choose crime as one of a range of behavioral options. The relative attractiveness of any choice is affected by the costs associated with criminal actions" (Einstadter and Henry, 1995: 44).

The costs are essentially of two kinds. One refers to the cost-benefit calculation that is regarded as governing both the individual (criminal) behavior and society's response to the same vis-a-vis the application of laws, justice, and punishment. The other refers to the costs associated with situational and contextual constraints that may be manipulated as a means of influencing the opportunities for or against crime. Herein lies the possibility of bringing the social experiences of class, race, and gender back into human agency and choice.

In the classical schemes of criminology, "humans are seen as independent, free-thinking, and rational decision makers who can control their own destiny by defining their self-interests" (Einstadter and Henry, 1995: 47). As pleasure-seeking and self-seeking animals, humans base their individual choices on their desire to maximize pleasure and minimize pain. According to Bentham (1765), pleasure and pain mean more than simple sensual experience. In addition to the physical dimensions, there are also the political, moral, and religious dimensions of pleasure and pain. In other words, crime is not merely a matter of free choice and rational calculation. Crime also involves situational constraints and determinable available options.

Classicists have also shared a consensus view of society expressed in the concept of *social contract* as articulated in the works of Hobbes (1651), Locke (1690), and Rousseau (1762). According to the social contract theory, individuals give up a part of their liberty (freedom) to the state so that they will enjoy peace and security, free from the chaos, anarchy, and disorder that was presumed to exist prior to the contract. It is also noteworthy that Beccaria (1764) did not believe that people entered into such contracts voluntarily, but rather that they did so out of necessity. Nevertheless, classicists, early or late, generally agree that a consensus prevails in society about the desirability of "protecting private property and personal welfare" (Taylor, Walton, and Young, 1973: 2).

Before turning to a general overview of the varieties of classical criminology, I will provide a brief discussion of the functions and development of criminal law and its relationship to a developing political economy. After that follows a more particularized discussion of the law in relationship to the recent deconstructionist, postmodernist, and state-relational analyses of crime and the administration of justice.

## From Torts to Felonies

In the most generic sense, laws involve the security of peace and the maintenance of order. Laws allow societies to conduct their commerce in an orderly fashion. Laws provide a minimal amount of social cohesion or solidarity among people living in communities or nation-states where a collective ethic of shared responsibility for nonconformity or deviant behavior has been transformed into a political territorial community based on the fiction of individual responsibility, and where the power of the pardon has been transferred from the people to the state. At this level of development, laws function to facilitate social control in two ways: First, social control is enhanced through the law's establishment of rules of conduct for both governmental authorities and the general citizenry. Second, it is enhanced through the law's allocation of authority or distribution of power throughout a stratified society.

In the context of social change, laws become vehicles of authority and ideology as well as breeders of values and of social conformity. Laws also provide the important standards and rationales for the way things are done. However, as the legal deconstructionists (Tushnet and Jaff, 1986; Milovanovic, 1988; Russell, 1994) have shown recently, and as legal realism and sociological jurisprudence had similarly revealed thirty and sixty years earlier, laws are arbitrary. Laws represent negotiated compromises of disputes and conflicts. Laws establish guidelines, or legal norms, which may transcend the needs or interests of particular parties or which may, indeed, reflect the needs of powerful interests. Either way, out of these particular conflicts emerge boundaries of behavior where individuals, groups, organizations, and so forth can calculate or predict the consequences of personal, social, or business actions. The legal order, ultimately, functions to maintain social order by its monopoly and exercise of the power to punish illegal behavior.

Over the past millennium, in response to the complexity of political, economic, and social relationships, there has evolved a variety of law types. The distinction between "public" and "private" law is one based on whether the state has been injured. Public laws include the areas of constitutional law, administrative law, and criminal law. Private laws, in contrast, involve the rules governing the exclusive relationships between individuals only. Private laws include laws of property, contracts, and torts. These grievances are of a personal nature and do not involve the interests of the state.

Historically, the criminal law or felonious prosecution evolved out of the civil law or out of torts. Disputes in premodern and pre-nation states were not resolved by central authorities but rather through local interaction of members of the community. In other words, originally all crimes were torts and all injuries were considered to be private matters. In the early history of the law, the state (in those days represented by the king) did not concern itself with punishing wrongs except the ones directed against the state, such as treason. Custom still prevailed, in as far as injuries to wronged people were handled by the family and the community. Therefore, justice was still a private matter. Eventually, the custom of private or community wrong would be replaced by the principle that the state is harmed when one of its subjects is harmed (Quinney, 1975).

Among social theorists—anthropologists, sociologists, political scientists, legal and economic scholars, and criminologists—the criminal law is viewed as a formal mechanism for maintaining social order. Most would agree that the law emerges "when the social structure of a society becomes complex enough that social control and dispute settlement cannot be based entirely on the informal mechanisms of custom and private settlement" (Akers and Hawkins, 1975: 42). Consensus theorists of the law, including Durkheim (1893), Ross (1901), Sumner (1906), Ehrlich (1936), and Davis (1966), emphasize law as growing out of the folkways and mores or deeply held societal norms. Law is said to express the unformed intuitive standards of right and wrong that crescively develop over time. Conflict theorists of the law, including Bonger (1916), Vold (1958), and Turk (1969), deemphasize the norms and values of agreement and instead focus attention on value-antagonisms or conflicts. Law is said to reflect the political, economic, and social expression of particular interests. Specifically, criminal law emerged during the fourteenth, fifteenth, and sixteenth centuries for the purposes of protecting and rationalizing the early origins of laissez-faire and monopoly capitalism (Tigar and Levy, 1977).

As early capitalism developed in England and Europe, as the system of commercialism started to blossom, and as an economy based on market exchange of land and property emerged and displaced peasant workers (serfs) to the highways, more and more behavior came to be viewed as threatening or disruptive to the newly evolving order of mercantilism. The first set of laws to reflect the class conflict brought about by capitalization was the British vagrancy statutes of 1349. These statutes made it a crime to give food or lodging to any person who was unemployed and of sound mind and body. These laws served both religious and economic interests. First, these statutes helped to remove the financial burden from religious houses to assist the poor with alms. Second, these statutes acted to discourage the movement of serfs from the rural communities into the cities, where the rapid growth and development of industry promised a new and better style of life for the underprivileged working classes.

As a substitute for their freedom from serfdom, the lower classes were forced to accept the wages that landowners and merchants could afford to pay. In his classic study of the law of vagrancy, Chambliss argues that various changes in the social setting and social structure, located primarily in the economic institution of society, resulted in the conscious attempt by lawmakers to alleviate conditions that favored the propertyless classes over the property-owning classes.

> *The prime-mover for this legislative innovation was the Black Death, which struck England about 1348. Among the many disastrous consequences this had upon the social structure was the fact that it decimated the labor force. It is estimated that by the time the pestilence had run its course at least fifty per cent of the population of England had died from the plague. This decimation of the labor force would necessitate rather drastic innovations in any society but its impact was heightened in England where, at the time, the economy was highly dependent upon a ready supply of cheap labor (Chambliss, 1969: 53).*

Similarly, the laws of theft resulting from the judicial decision of the *Carrier Case* in 1473 (which charged an employee, who had been hired to transport bales of wool but took them instead, with a felony) reflected the growth of industry, manufacturing, and trade generally, as well as the influential interests of the middle-class merchants and entrepreneurs in fifteenth-century England. In his classic study of theft, law, and society, Jerome Hall (1952) revealed the growing political and economic interdependence between crown and state and the early interests of commercial capitalism under the rule of Edward IV. By the sixteenth century, the various laws reflecting commercial interests had expanded outward, first engulfing laborers and idle persons and eventually the newly emerging criminal or dangerous classes. By the eighteenth century, the interests of the church and crown had been pretty much swallowed up by the interests of the propertied classes and the state.

Eventually, as changes in internal and external trade relations took place between Europe and its colonies, and as developments in commerce and manufacturing occurred, the conflicts of interests between the propertied and unpropertied classes intensified as did the opportunities for the theft of surplus commodities. Accordingly, both the civil and criminal sides of English common law, including the Anglo-American colonial law, became increasingly dependent on the class interests of property. For example, between 1688 and 1820, the number of capital statutes grew from approximately fifty to over two-hundred (Radzinowicz, 1948).

## Postmodernism and the Critique of Rational Law

The *law* has been one of the metanarratives or "grand schema for maintaining control over disparate meanings, fragmented values and perceptions, and a multiplicity of interpretations" (Manning, 1995: 9). From a postmodern perspective, inclusive of the philosophic threads of poststructuralism, semiotics, and deconstructionism, classical and positivist criminologies alike have depended on a rational view of crime and crime control. One part of the critique originates from criminology's failure to adequately develop a theory of state or law. Another part of the critique hinges on criminology's failure to acknowledge its "soft" consensus perspective on law and order. Most criminologists, it is argued, have assumed too much knowledge about the workings of the origins, development, and application of law (Barak, 1980). As a consequence, most of the contemporary literature on crime and social control

> *begins by taking the existence of political power and state law for granted. Often these things are simply treated as inevitable facts of life, and little information about political power and how state law developed is presented. Overlooking these things does not mean that we have simply avoided being overburdened with unimportant historical facts. It means that we have seriously limited our ability to understand how changes in basic elements of social order in a society will produce changes in how it defines and deals with disruptions of that order (Michalowski, 1985: 69).*

Dragan Milovanovic (1988: 102) has argued that the movement in critical legal studies (CLS), with its diversity in theoretical perspectives, still remains a field "currently in search of [a] theory." Before introducing one attempt to develop an understanding of law and public policy in terms of a theory of structural contradictions and a dialectical model of legal order, a postmodern critique of the case-law method is presented.

Peter Manning (1995) has characterized the individualistic-case approach to law as omitting several relevant matters. First, Manning argues, these decisions gloss over the *field* of both objective and subjective social forces that shape the decision. Second, he continues, such decisions ignore the *framing* of the facts of the case as well as the associative paradigms and cognitive domains underlying legal reasoning. Finally, Manning contends, legal doctrine, legal rules, and prior decisions cannot account for the larger *surroundings* or cultural dimensions of legal decision making. Because of its focus on the "rational case deciders" of legal decision makers, who are assumed to be neutral and objective, who are expected to weight and compare all the known set of options, and

Ted Bundy representing himself and cross-examining Utah state trooper Robert Haywood in Miami trial, 1979.

whose outcomes and decisions are presumed to be consistent with precedent-setting or analogous decisions of the past as well as with clear and unambiguous organizational goals and objectives for the future, Manning (1995: 5) contends that "a rather narrow 'individualistic' perspective dominates socio-legal approaches to decision making."

The critique of *legal formalism* has found expression in deconstructionism and in the application of critical legal studies. "Deconstruction questions the ontology of being and the philosophic means by which reality is constituted" (Manning, 1995: 9–10). Deconstruction rejects the notion that communication works solely by means of patterns of binary oppositions. In other words, deconstruction denies that such dualities as " 'arrest' or 'non-arrest,' 'guilty' or 'innocent,' 'prison sentence' or 'parole' can be correlated with selected 'variables' to characterize or 'predict' patterns of decisions made by courts, juries, prosecutors, or police officers" (Manning, 1995: 6). Deconstructionism also rejects *logocentrism*, or the modern philosophy that a person, the intentional speaking subject, is also the determinant of meaning. Lastly, deconstructionism rejects finality, or the belief that complete analysis and total understanding are ever possible, because "the great forms of reasoning, law, literature, and philosophy, and even the social sciences, are dependent upon the communicative constraints of language" (Manning, 1995: 11).

More specifically, Mark Tushnet and Jennifer Jaff (1986) have examined legal formalisms in relationship to an important plea-bargaining case, *Bordenkircher v. Hayes*

(434 U.S. 357 [1978]), to reveal how four formalisms could or could not have applied to the case and the administration of criminal justice. In their critique of legal formalism as falsely ascribing to a "position which claims that results in any particular case are in some non-trivial sense determined by a set of general principles," they identified the following types of formalism: classical doctrinal formalism; moral philosophy; law and economics; and sociology of professions (Tuslinct and Jaff, 1986: 361). The first two formalisms rely, respectively, on principles of law drawn from controlling legal documents or on principles of morality. The latter two formalisms rely, respectively, on legal principles derived from what are presumed to be logical consequences of human rationality and strategic behavior in situations with limited resources, or on principles derived from the systemic observation of the actions of legal participants.

In a subsequent analysis of *McCleskey v. Kemp* (481 U.S. 279 [1987]), legal formalism, and the application of the death penalty, Katheryn Russell (1994) introduces yet another legal formalism: the "sociology of race relations," which exposes the notion that legal cases are decided in a race-neutral manner. One could certainly discern a legal formalism that addresses the "sociology of gender relations" as well. These critical legal analyses of the criminal law raise questions about the absolute nature of legal decision making. In fact, they support the CLS principles of indeterminacy and anti formalism in the law, despite superficial appearances to the contrary. The point is, despite formal arguments to the contrary, legal decision making is fraught with all kinds of contradictions, not the least of which have more in common with interests of class, race, and gender than they do with the principles of substantive or procedural due process.

The rise of legal formalism and rationalism was a product of the rise of modernism and the Enlightenment, as we have already discussed. Since the eighteenth century, the object of law was "to define and refine measures which would provide an objective basis of assessing causation, the nature of wrongdoing and the method of assessment of harm" (Laster and O'Malley, 1995: 3). In both civil and criminal law, the focus had been on physical harm and pecuniary loss. However, beginning in the period of late modernity (after World War II), the law has "witnessed a reassertion of the significance of emotional states" (Laster and O'Malley, 1995: 3). Laster and O'Malley argue that the postmodern or post-Enlightenment assumptions about rationality, objective truth, and formal legal equality are bringing back into focus the interplay of reason and emotionality that the Enlightenment had sought to dichotomize.

Laster and O'Malley (1995: 2) argue that during the Enlightenment, "emotionality was discursively assigned to the weak and marginalized, and constructs of Being developed which associated morality, strength and progress with the taming of feelings." During the present postmodern period, they argue, the reassertion of emotional harm in criminal and civil law is connected to a rise in consumer culture and to an increased sensitivity to human dignity. "The rationale for such law has less to do with tangible or immediate likelihood of harm than with the affront to dignity, emotional harm and the possibility of a link between attitudes and future behavior" (Laster and O'Malley, 1995: 5). Turning this postmodern twist in rationality/emotionality, Laster and O'Malley share an affirmative view like the one held by CLS that the law can be reconstituted or transformed.

Building on the work of structural contradictions and a dialectical theory of law creation (Block and Chambliss, 1981; Chambliss, 1988), Nancy Wonders and Frederic Solop (1994) provide an outline for a *relational* theory of the state (and law). They contend that the "state is not one concrete entity that can be explained in its totality by a single theory" (Wonders and Solop, 1994: 205). It makes better sense, they argue, to think of the state as a relational construct involving intersections of the political economy, apparatuses of administration and legislation, people, culture, and ideologies. Like molecular structures that are not determined by any one component, the character of state structures is not determined by any of its particular components. Both structures are constructed as fluid and dynamic, each capable of becoming different and unique structures as their components, in time and space, combine in various ways.

A relational model of the state and law is a useful framework for developing an integrative criminology because it incorporates mid-level analyses of organizational behavior with macro-level analyses of the historical and structural forces that act to shape policy, law, and social behavior. Such a model allows us to understand how people come together as citizens, police, criminals, and victims to make history. Within this model of legal change, there can be an emphasis on "the importance of power, legitimacy, and accumulation" as well as on "the importance of ideology and culture and the ability of people to shape society through social movements, protest, or the legislative process" (Wonders and Solop, 1994: 221).

## Economic Models and Rational Choice Theories of Crime

Although thinkers such as Adam Smith, Jeremy Bentham, and Karl Marx, from the early Enlightenment to the nineteenth century, wrote about economics and crime, most contemporary economic models of crime do not refer to their ideas. In Chapter 7, sociological reference to these ideas was expressed in the conflict and Marxist models of crime. In particular, the works of Bonger, Quinney, and Chambliss were discussed in terms of the relations of production or of a political economy of crime. Bonger (1916) argued, for example, that all crimes, whether committed by the powerless or the powerful, were the result of an egoism engendered by a capitalist economic system. Quinney (1975) contended that crime was that which threatened the well-being of the capitalist economy, whereas Chambliss (1986) contended that crimes of the rich and poor alike were a product of the structural contradictions of an evolving political economy. In each of these economic models, crime is not viewed as a rational phenomenon but is regarded as some kind of social pathology brought about by the arrangements of the political economy.

By contrast, most orthodox (classical) economic analyses of crime assume that criminal behavior, like any economic activity, is rational.

*A person commits an offense if the expected utility to him exceeds the utility he could get by using his time and other resources at other activities. Some persons become "criminals," therefore, not because their basic motivation differs from that of other persons, but because their benefits and costs differ (Becker, 1968: 176).*

Gary Becker and others such as Sullivan (1973) and Reynolds (1973) are simply saying that criminals are normal or no different than you and I. They are not sick, abnormal, deviant, or deprived and are, therefore, not in need of rehabilitation or treatment. Criminals, in other words, are relatively simple people who engage in rational and normal calculations in order to maximize their preferences subject to given constraints. Crime is a matter of expected rewards and punishments for engaging in law-abiding versus law-violating behavior. These kinds of rational–choice economic models suggest that "participation in crime varies directly with its net benefits and inversely with the attractiveness of legitimate activity" (Quinney, 1975: 280).

In the classical economic–rational choice models of crime, the solution to crime is to simply increase the costs (i.e., punishment) of doing crime. Neither the criminal nor the criminal justice system is in need of reform. By contrast, neoclassical approaches focus attention on the arbitrariness of decision making and the wide-scale discretionary powers of the administration of justice (Fogel, 1975; Von Hirsch, 1976). Neoclassical researchers, for example, question the disparities involved in rehabilitation and in the administration of the death penalty. They also favor determinate sentencing, while suggesting that an unfair or discriminatory use of penal sanctions contributes to the retributive sentiments of ex-convicts. The neoclassicists, then, return to a concern with the process and the incentives and disincentives of the criminal justice system.

Similarly, the most recent approaches are characterized as "postclassical" because their concerns have less to do with the opportunities of law enforcement and more with "the wider environment as a smorgasbord of choice opportunities available to the potential offender" (Einstadter and Henry, 1995: 47). These choice opportunities approaches (Heineke, 1978; Schmidt and Witte, 1984) have recently been expanded by the developments of "routine activities theory" (Cohen and Felson, 1979; Felson, 1987), "situational choice theory" (Clarke and Cornish, 1983; Cornish and Clarke, 1987), "routine conflict theory" (Kennedy and Forde, 1995), and "evolutionary ecological theory" (Cohen and Machalek, 1988; Vila, 1994).

What all of these theories have in common, besides their roots in the ecological and control schools of criminology, is the shared view of humans as the "rational man" of classical theory. The evolutionary models, however, add the integrative dimensions in which biological and psychological differences shape the choice of behavioral strategies for needs fulfillment. The rest of this section will highlight the recent developments in postclassical or rational choice models of crime.

*Routine activities* theory combines elements of deterrence, utility, and rational choice. Lawrence Cohen and Marcus Felson's routine activities theory takes the basic elements of time, place, objects, and persons and develops a theory of crime events. "In order for a personal or property crime to occur, there must be at the same time and place a perpetrator, a victim, and/or an object of property" (Akers, 1994: 60). Cohen and Felson identify three categories of variables: motivated offenders, suitable targets or victims, and the lack of capable guardians or protectors of property. They argue that criminalization/victimization is more likely to occur as these three elements converge. Their theory assumes that the conjunction of these elements of crime is related to the normal (rational) or routine activities of potential victims, guardians, and perpetrators. Accordingly, "rather than a discretionary and inconsistent criminal justice system reducing effective controls and lowering costs, these theorists see environmental situations providing or denying opportunities or facilitating or suppressing the criminal event" (Einstadter and Henry, 1995: 55). Empirical evidence (Messner and Tardiff, 1985; Sherman, Gartin, and Buerger, 1989; Kennedy and Forde, 1990) supporting routine activities theory has been reported.

Two other related rational choice approaches include Ronald Clarke and Derek Cornish's *situational choice* model and Leslie Kennedy and David Forde's *routine conflict* theory. Clarke and Cornish regard criminal behavior "as a function of choices and decisions made within a context of situational constraints and opportunities" so that each offender's skills in interaction with each offense's risks and payoffs structure the offender's choice of behavior.

Kennedy and Forde's model, in turn, incorporates the routine activities emphasis on the lifestyle of victims with the rational choice emphasis on the situational choices of potential offenders and calls for the development of a theory of routine conflict. Borrowing from Erving Goffman's "presentation of self in everyday life," (1959) this approach emphasizes the "situated transactions" where individual meaning is derived from the ways in which others act toward you. In other words, people come to situations with their learned repertoires for managing conflict in their daily lives. These repertoires also reflect on the relative structural position or location of individuals in a social system, which may be examined along a number of dimensions of social status, including age, income, gender, race, and class.

Rounding out these variable rationality approaches is Cohen and Machalek's *evolutionary ecological* model, which argues essentially that crime is the "use of accumulated and available alternative behavior strategies to satisfy needs by expropriating others of valuables, whether these be property, power, sex, or prestige" (Einstadter and Henry, 1995: 56). In what becomes an integrated model, they combine assumptions about rational-economic calculation with ideas from biology, psychology, and structural theory to argue that crime is the outcome of limited behavioral choice based on the set of behavioral strategies that people develop over the course of their life cycles.

In sum, to varying degrees, each of these rational choice explanations take social perceptions into account. Moreover, they all recognize partial rationality as incorporated in the limitations and constraints on choices through lack of information, moral values, and other influences on criminal behavior. In other words, when rational choice theorists assume that criminals reason and that crime is rational, they go to great lengths to qualify or circumscribe reasoning and rationality. In fact, Akers (1994: 60) makes an interesting observation when he states that "except for psychoanalytic theory and some versions of biological theory, all other criminological theories assume no more or less rationality in crime than do most rational choice models."

Hence, the alleged polarity between the positivist-determinist criminologies versus the classical free-choice criminologies is, once again, revealed as an exaggeration because the ideals of each of these criminologies have, in fact, to varying degrees accommodated the realities of the other. Less explicitly, the social relations similarly reveal the extent to which the rationality/nonrationality distinctions between positivist, classical, and critical criminologies are false ones. In the constitutive reality of crime articulated in Chapter 10, crime is viewed as both rational and pathological, whereas criminals are viewed, for the most part, as rational and emotional beings who engage in behavior that may be reasonable or unreasonable.

## Summary and Conclusions: Why People Commit Crimes

The value of legal and economic models of rational crime is a debatable one. After more than two centuries, classical perspectives remain both controversial and provocative. Traditionally, as Taylor, Walton, and Young (1973: 9–10) pointed out some time ago, the modified neoclassical position is "the major model of human behavior held by agencies of social control in all advanced industrial societies." Today, even as the postmodern emotional harms have reasserted themselves, this is no less true as "the doctrine of the limited state" still provides the dominant legal and constitutional perspectives in both civil and criminal matters. Moreover, as an explanatory framework for making common sense out of the pecuniary, if not personal, crimes committed in the suites or in the streets, the classical perspectives still have much currency, especially among politicians and the body politic.

Where classical criminologies have always failed, however, is in their inability to square the ideals and the realities of law and order. There have been and still are significant divergences between formal and informal realities and between procedural and substantive equality (Reiman, 1979; Barak, 1980; Young, 1981). In other words, it is one thing to assume formal equality between people, ignoring the structural differences brought about by race, class, and gender, but another thing to assume that an informal level playing field of justice exists. Consequently, rational choice theory and its variants often tend to exclusively blame criminals for their criminalization and victims for their victimization. In turn, solutions to the crime problem tend to focus on issues of security and target hardening. Such high-tech approaches to crime control are politically potent because they do not challenge the status quo nor do they call for a change in the prevailing social arrangements.

John Galliher (1989) has also pointed out that classicism fails because, on the one hand, it dismisses the differential satisfactions people obtain from the same criminal act and, on the other hand, it dismisses the differential pains experienced by the same sanctions applied to people of varying social class positions. Moreover, as the neoclassicists, early or late, have continuously maintained, classical rational choice models fail because they do not account "for the differences in people's ability to reason, to calculate their interests, and to set goals and objectives" (Einstadter and Henry, 1995: 69). In addition, these models have failed because they do not consider spontaneous crimes or "the role of peer groups and their different effects on the rational calculus" (Einstadter and Henry, 1995: 69). These criticisms (and others) of rational models of criminality also recognize that criminals and noncriminals alike are also driven toward the acquisition of pleasure and the avoidance of pain, independent of free will. Interestingly, Beirne (1993) has shown how both Bentham and Beccaria, on a closer revisionist reading, shared an appreciation for the interaction between innate desires and rational calculations.

Despite these criticisms and those raised by postmodernists, critical legal theorists, and others, reason and rationality should not be set aside when it comes to understanding and explaining crime or criminal behavior. On the contrary, following the critique of the postclassical perspective and the emergence and rise of the economic rational and situational choice theorists, I believe that it makes more sense to expand some aspects of these models and to apply them in a more socially oriented ecological way. For example, Cohen and Felson stressed the spatial and temporal structure of routine legal activities. However, these relations could also include the structure of routine political and economic activities because these routine activities refer to the "recurrent and prevalent activities which provide for basic population and individual needs," including "formalized work, as well as the provision of standard food, shelter, sexual outlet, leisure, social interaction, learning, and childbearing" (Cohen and Felson, 1979: 593).

In the end, crime may, indeed, be rational. Human beings, however, act and react both emotionally and rationally to a lot of things at the same time, including incentives and disincentives. Classicists, past and present, unfortunately, have confined their analyses of incentives and disincentives to the legal machinery as if this was the only means of social control. Of course, social control has never been limited to the operations of the formal systems of law and criminal justice administration. On the contrary, most of the incentives and disincentives for conforming and nonconforming behavior are to be found within the informal arenas of control, involving the family, school, and the work place.

Beginning in the next chapter with a critique of the modernist attempts to integrate criminological theory, Part III incorporates the contributions found in Part II as it attempts to provide a post-postmodern integrative framework for making sense out of crime and crime control. In the process, the various linkages between modern and postmodern criminologies, between media and cultural studies, and between the theories of crime and the practices of crime control are developed. All of this is done with the belief that a truly comprehensive model, capable of altering the existing practices of crime and crime control, requires nothing

## Discussion Questions

1. Compare and contrast Beccaria's definition of harm with Bentham's idea of pleasure and pain.

2. What are the primary differences between classical and neoclassical criminology? Which of these perspectives do you believe is more dominant today? Why?

3. Throughout modern history (the last 500 years), how have the changes in the political economy been connected to the changes in the penal law?

4. Explain Akers's idea of how other criminological theories assume no more or less rationality in crime than do most rational choice theories.

# References

Akers, Ronald L. 1994. *Criminological Theories: Introduction and Evaluation.* Los Angeles: Roxbury Publishing Company.

Akers, Ronald L., and Richard Hawkins. 1975. *Law and Control in Society.* Englewood Cliffs, NJ: Prentice-Hall.

American Friends Service Committee. 1971. *Struggle for Justice.* New York: Hill and Wang.

Barak, Gregg. 1980. *In Defense of Whom? A Critique of Criminal Justice Reform.* Cincinnati: Anderson Publishing Company.

Beccaria, Cesare. [1764] 1964. *On Crimes and Punishment.* Trans. Henry Paolucci. Indianapolis, IN: Bobbs-Merrill.

Becker, Gary S. 1968. "Crime and Punishment: An Economic Approach." *Journal of Political Economy* 76(2): 169–217.

Beirne, Piers. 1991. "Inventing Criminology: The 'Science of Man' in Cesare Beccaria's Dei Delitti E Delle Pene (1764)." *Criminology* 29(4): 777–820.

———. 1993. *Inventing Criminology: Essays on the Rise of 'Homo Criminalis.'* Albany, NY: SUNY Press.

Bentham, Jeremy. [1765] 1970. *The Limits of Jurisprudence Defined, Being Part Two of An Introduction to the Principles of Morals and Legislation.* Westport, CT: Greenwood Press.

Block, Alan, and William J. Chambliss. 1981. *Organizing Crime.* New York: Elsevier.

Bonger, Willem. 1916. *Criminality and Economic Conditions.* Boston: Little, Brown and Company.

Chambliss, William J., ed. 1969. *Crime and the Legal Process.* New York: McGraw-Hill.

———. 1988. *Exploring Criminology.* New York: Macmillan.

Clarke, Ronald V., and Ronald V. Cornish, eds. 1983. *Crime Control in Britain: A Review of Policy and Research.* Albany, NY: SUNY Press.

Cohen, Lawrence, and Marcus Felson. 1979. "Social Change and Crime Rate Trends: A Routine Activities Approach." *American Sociological Review* 44:588–608.

Cohen, Lawrence, and Richard Machalek. 1988. "A General Theory of Expropriative Crime: An Evolutionary Ecological Approach." *American Journal of Sociology* 94:465–501.

Cornish, Derek B., and Ronald V. Clarke, eds. 1986. *The Reasoning Criminal.* New York: Springer Verlag.

———. 1987. "Understanding Crime Displacement: An Application of Rational Choice Theory." *Criminology* 25(4): 933–947.

Davis, Kingsley. 1966. "Sexual Behavior." In Robert K. Merton and Robert A. Nisbet, eds., *Contemporary Social Problems.* New York: Harcourt Brace Jovanovich.

Durkheim, Emile. [1893] 1933. *The Division of Labor in Society.* New York: Free Press.

Ehrlich, Eugen. 1913. Fundamental Principles of the Sociology of Law. Cambridge, MA: Harvard University Press.

Ehrlich, Isaac. 1973. "Participation in Illegitimate Activities: An Economic Analysis." *Journal of Political Economy* 81:521–567.

———. 1982. "The Market for Offences and the Public Enforcement of Laws: An Equilibrium Analysis." *British Journal of Social Psychology* 21(2): 107–120.

Einstadter, Werner, and Stuart Henry. 1995. *Criminological Theory: An Analysis of Its Underlying Assumptions.* Fort Worth: Harcourt Brace.

Felson, Marcus. 1987. "Routine Activities, Social Controls, Rational Decisions and Criminal Outcomes." *Criminology* 25(4): 911–931.

Felson, Marcus, and Lawrence Cohen. 1980. "Human Ecology and Crime: A Routine Activities Approach." *Human Ecology* 8(4): 389–406.

Fogel, David. 1975. *We Are the Living Proof: The Justice Model for Corrections.* Cincinnati: Anderson Publishing Company.

Galliher, John F. 1989. *Criminology: Human Rights, Criminal Law and Crime.* Englewood Cliffs, NJ: Prentice-Hall.

Goffman, Erving. 1959. *The Presentation of Self in Everyday Life.* Harmondworth, England: Penguin.

Hall, Jerome. 1952. *Theft, Law and Society.* 2nd ed. Indianapolis, IN: Bobbs-Merrill.

Heineke, John M., ed. 1978. *Economic Models of Criminal Behavior.* New York: North-Holland.

Hobbes, Thomas. [1651] 1950. *Leviathan.* New York: Dutton.

Kennedy, Leslie W., and David R. Forde. 1990. "Routine Activities and Crime: An Analysis of Victimization in Canada." *Criminology* 28:137–152.

———. 1995. "Pathways to Aggression: Towards a Theory of 'Routine Conflict.'" Conflict Series

Paper No. 1. Centre for Criminological Research, University of Alberta, Edmonton, Canada.

Kennedy, Mark. 1970. "Beyond Incrimination: Some Neglected Facts of the History of Punishment." *Catalyst* 5:1–16.

Laster, Kathy, and Pat O'Malley. 1994. "Sensitive New-Age Laws: The Reassertion." Paper presented at the American Society of Criminology Meetings, Miami.

Locke, John. [1690] 1964. *Two Treatises of Government.* Cambridge: Cambridge University Press.

Manning, Peter. 1995. "Postmodernism and the Law." In W. R. Janikowski and D. Milovanovic, eds., *Legality and Illegality: Semiotics, Postmodernism and the Law.* New York: Peter Lang.

Messner, Steven F., and Kenneth Tardiff. 1985. "The Social Ecology of Urban Homicide: An Application of the 'Routine Activities Approach.'" *Criminology* 23:241–267.

Michalowski, Ray. 1985. *Order, Law and Crime: An Introduction to Criminology.* New York: Random House.

Milovanovic, Dragan. 1988. *A Primer in the Sociology of Law.* Albany, NY: Harrow and Heston.

Quinney, Richard. 1975. *Criminology.* Boston: Little, Brown and Company.

Radzinowicz, Leon. 1948. "International Collaboration in Criminal Science." In L. Radzinowicz, ed., *Modern Approach to Criminal Law.* Vol. IV of the English Studies in Criminal Science. Cambridge, England.

Reynolds, Morgan. 1973. *The Economics of Criminal Activity.* Introductory Economics Series, Module 12. Andover, MA: Warner.

Roshier, Bob. 1989. *Controlling Crime: The Classical Perspective in Criminology.* Philadelphia: Open University Press.

Ross, E. A. [1901] 1922. *Social Control.* New York: Macmillan.

Rousseau, Jean. [1762] 1962. *The Social Contract.* New York: Oxford University Press.

Russell, Katheryn K. 1994. "A Critical View from the Inside: An Application of Critical Legal Studies to Criminal Law." *Journal of Law and Human Behavior* 85(1): 222–240.

Schmidt, Peter, and Ann D. Witte. 1984. *An Economic Analysis of Crime and Justice: Theory, Methods, and Applications.* Orlando, FL: Academic Press.

Sherman, Lawrence, Patrick Gartin, and Michael Buerger. 1989. "Hot Spots of Predatory Crime: Routine Activities and the Criminology of Place." *Criminology* 27:27–56.

Sullivan, Richard F. 1973. "The Economics of Crime: An Introduction to the Literature." *Crime and Delinquency* 19(2): 138–149.

Sumner, William Graham. 1906. *Folkways: A Study of the Sociological Importance of Usages, Manners, Customs, Mores and Morals.* Boston: Ginn.

Taylor, Ian, Paul Walton, and Jock Young. 1973. *The New Criminology: For a Social Theory of Deviance.* London: Routledge and Kegan Paul.

Tigar, Michael E., and Madeleine R. Levy. 1977. *Law and the Rise of Capitalism.* New York: Monthly Review Press.

Turk, Austin T. 1969. *Criminality and Legal Order.* Chicago: Rand McNally.

Tushnet, Mark, and Jennifer Jaff. 1986. "Critical Legal Studies and Criminal Procedure." *Catholic University Law Review* 35:361–379.

Vila, Bryan. 1994. "A General Paradigm for Understanding Criminal Behavior: Extending Evolutionary Ecological Theory." *Criminology* 32:311–359.

Vold, George B. 1958. *Theoretical Criminology.* New York: Oxford University Press.

Von Hirsch, Andrew. 1976. *Doing Justice: The Choice of Punishments.* New York: Hill and Wang.

Wonders, Nancy A., and Frederic I. Solop. 1994. "Understanding the Emergence of Law and Public Policy: Toward a Relational Model of the State." In W. Chambliss and M. Zatz, eds., *Making Law: The State, the Law and Structural Contradictions.* Bloomington, IN: Indiana University Press.

Young, Jock. 1981. "Thinking Seriously About Crime: Some Models of Criminology." In M. Fitzgerald, G. McLennan, and J. Pawson, eds., *Crime and Society: Readings in History and Society.* London: Routledge and Kegan Paul.

# *Integrating Criminological Theories: A Critique*

Integrating criminological theories is not a particularly new endeavor (Merton, 1938; Sutherland, 1947; Cohen, 1955; Cloward and Ohlin, 1960; Reckless, 1973; and Quinney, 1977). However, recently it has become more explicit in its conceptions, discourses, and propositions (Schur, 1984; Schwendinger and Schwendinger, 1985; Messerschmidt, 1986; Coleman, 1994; Thornberry, 1987; Cohen and Machalek, 1988; Hagan, 1989; 1990; Messner, Krohn, and Liska, 1989; Matsueda, 1992; Kaplan, 1993; Markowitz, 1994; Marenin, 1994; Menard and Elliott, 1994; Miethe and Meier, 1994; Roundtree, Land, and Miethe, 1994; Vila, 1994; Unnithan et al., 1994; and Bernard and Snipes, 1996). The interest in theoretical integration, general or specific, stems from the fact that there is "a large and bewildering collection, rather than a shortage, of criminological materials." As Gibbons (1992: 2) has argued, "our stockpile of theoretical claims and research evidence has grown markedly since the 1950s [when] we had no routine activities theorizing or research, no evidence on income inequality and crime, no substantial body of data on unemployment and crime, no sophisticated theories to account for state-by-state variations in rates of forcible rape, very few detailed analyses of white collar crime, and no large literature on homicide."

The current interest in integration also stems from the fact that criminologists share a desire, conscious or unconscious, to develop (if possible) "central notions" capable of providing coherence to otherwise fragmented theories of crime and crime control. For example, Jack Gibbs (1989) has identified "control" and Steven Messner and Richard Rosenfeld (1994) have identified "culture" as centralizing notions. Similarly, integrated causal theories suggest the possibility of a comprehensive explanation in the variance in lawbreaking and conforming conduct. Integrated theory also holds out the prospect of synthesizing the etiology of crime with the practices of social control (e.g., parenting, criminal justice). To date, however, "criminologists have not managed to articulate a large collection of relatively formalized arguments in a general or integrated form" (Gibbons, 1992: 2).

Herein lies the modernist debate about whether integrative explanations of crime can move from conceptual to propositional theory. By contrast, postmodernists are more concerned with the conceptual than the propositional. Their debate revolves around whether integrative explanations can articulate an interpretive rather than a predictive model of crime and crime control. Similarly, as two proponents of modernist integration, Thomas Bernard and Jeffrey Snipes (1996: 322), have opined, "There has been too much emphasis in the integration debate on theories themselves and not enough emphasis on the observable variables and the observable relations among them." In my post-postmodernist view, there has also been too much accent in the integration debate on linear causality and not enough accent on reciprocal causality.

Each of the chapters in Part III of this book addresses questions related to various kinds of integration. In effect, the integrative models reviewed in these chapters cover both modernist and postmodernist theories, perspectives, and approaches to crime and crime control. Not unlike criminological theory building more generally, integrated theory building also finds itself consumed more by theory competition than by theory integration (Akers, 1994). Historically, although it is argued that theories of integration have become more formal, explicit, and propositional over time (Gibbons, 1994;

Einstadter and Henry, 1995), theoretical integration still exists, mostly at the discursive and conceptual levels of development. This may turn out to be a blessing in disguise as these informal formulations prove to be of more value or use for addressing the practical problems of crime and crime control than the more propositional or formal formulations.

Chapter 9 provides an introduction to criminological integration. It also generates a friendly critique of modernist theoretical integration aimed at the questionable objective of delivering some kind of positivist prediction of "what causes criminal behavior." Although not rejecting efforts at theoretical integration per se, the weaknesses and biases of modernist models are linked to a critical and pluralistic discussion of knowledges and the inadequacies of causative-predictive criminology.

As this review and critique of theoretical integration unfolds, the stage is set for Chapter 10 and its preference for a postmodernist integration of criminological knowledges where everything, at both the micro and macro levels, affects everything else, and where these effects are continuously changing over time (Thornberry, 1987; Vila, 1994; Henry and Milovanovic, 1996). In my view, it is these holistic integrative models (e.g., interactional, ecological, constitutive) of crime and crime control that hold out the most promise for developing the fields of criminology. I profess this for essentially two reasons: First, it is these models that bring together modernist and postmodernist sensibilities of crime and punishment, thus capturing the whole picture of the social reality of crime. Second, it is these models that stress the all-important reciprocal relations between individual and social development as these intersect with crime and crime control.

Following the explication of a post-postmodern integrative constitutive criminology are two chapters that further elaborate and develop applications of criminological knowledges across the disciplines. Chapter 11 articulates a cultural studies approach to crime and criminals, drawing on the interrelated knowledges of racial/ethnic studies, gender studies, and media studies. Chapter 12 expounds on an interdisciplinary approach to crime and crime control that also incorporates a diversity of bodies of knowledge.

## Integrating Criminology: Meanings and Approaches

Most people, when they think about theoretical integration, think about the combination of single theories, or elements of those theories, into a more comprehensive statement. However, such a limited view of integration misses the different kinds and degrees of integration that exist. For example, a review of the criminological literature on theoretical integration reveals a strong reliance on learning and control theories, a weaker reliance on strain, followed closely by subcultural, conflict, and Marxist theories. Rarely included are theories of biology, personality, gender, economics, or law (Einstadter and Henry, 1995). Hence, the focus and centralizing constructs of criminological integration have been primarily sociological and conventional in kind and degree.

Integrated theories may be specific or general. Whereas the specific integrated theories have focused on a single form of criminality, such as domestic violence, for example, the general integrated theories best apply to a relatively broader range of crime forms or patterns of criminality. As for those who have ever entertained the ideas of a general integrative framework, there does not seem to be agreement about what is meant by either general theory or by integration. For example, Braithwaite's (1989) integrative model of *crime, shame, and reintegration* is both general and integrative, whereas Michael Gottfredson and Travis Hirschi's (1990) *general theory of crime* is not an integrated argument because it emphasizes lack of self-control to the exclusion of other variables.

More specifically, Braithwaite's general theory of crime assumes generality because it applies to a significant portion of the lawbreaking population. It assumes integration because it incorporates elements from a number of existing theoretical traditions with his own ideas about the role of shaming and reintegration in shaping criminal pathways. By contrast, Gottfredson and Hirschi's theory is general, but not integrative, because it argues that there are commonalities among various forms of deviant behavior. However, the causal glue holding these expressions of crime or deviance together are reduced to persons who lack self-control, excluding the possibility of other causal factors. Similarly, Akers's (1994) *social learning theory of crime* is not integrative because it, for example, absorbs and reduces rather than interacts with social bonding and commitment. By contrast, Larry Baron and Murray Straus's (1990) theory of *variations in forcible rape* exemplifies a specific, integrated argument, combining elements of social disorganization, gender inequality, pornography readership, and "cultural spillover" arguments.

Integrated theories, whether general or specific, have tended to explore the relationship between two kinds of causal questions; that is, most integrative efforts have recognized the social structure and its relationship to rates of crime in the aggregate as well as the individual and his or her role in becoming a delinquent or a criminal. Traditionally, modernist theories of criminological integration have been divided into "conceptual" and "propositional" accounts (Liska, Krohn, and Messner, 1989): The former types of integration reveal how concepts from one theory are shown to overlap in meaning with concepts from another theory; the latter types of integration relate propositions from different theories. Thus, conceptual integration "likens a concept from one theory to a concept from another, concluding that the theories themselves are similar" (Bernard and Snipes, 1996: 308). Propositional integration, by contrast, is a formalistic exercise that involves linking separate theories by a given principle.

Hirschi (1979) has identified three principles of propositional integration: (1) end to end, (2) side by side, and (3) up and down. End-to-end integration is developmental in that it advances the notion that a causal order across propositions of the various theories to be integrated is possible. Simply put, the dependent variable in theory A becomes the independent variable in theory B. Side-by-side integration is more confusing because it recognizes that different theories may have their own as well as overlapping areas of influence. For example, although theory A may explain violent behavior in general and theory B may explain the behavior of serial killers in particular, both theories may also explain some common aspects of the abusive treatment of small animals, such as birds and cats, by preadolescents. Up-and-down integration "involves raising the level of abstraction of one theory, such that its propositions merely follow from the conceptually broader theory" (Bernard and Snipes, 1996: 308). In other words, the principles or assumptions of one theory are broad enough to subsume those of another theory so that the propositions or hypotheses of B are deduced from A.

Finally, modernist theories of integration can be divided up by whether they assume a static (consensus) or dynamic (conflict) state of affairs.

> *The "static state" theories would include those emphasizing organized structures and objectively measurable social roles, containing individuals with limited internal attributes and a limited capacity for spontaneity, as in biological, early personality theories or theories based on rational choice. The "dynamic state" theories would include those giving more weight to subjective interpretation, negotiated and spontaneous interaction, informal and creative process, and conflicts between differences, such as labeling theory, social constructionism, and anarchist criminology (Einstadter and Henry, 1995: 308).*

## A Discussion of Modernist Integration and Causation

In their final chapter of *Criminological Theory*, Einstadter and Henry (1995) wanted to know whether it made more sense to invoke criminological theory as a "fission" of multidisciplinarity or a "fusion" of interdisciplinarity. In other words, should sociological, psychological, and biological contributions, for example, be brought to the table and kept on separate (fission) plates or should they be mixed up and distributed on the same (fusion) plates? They contended that the "key to demystifying these new integration attempts is to recognize that the *emphasis* of different perspectives gives greater weight to some features than to others in the attempt to understand, explain, and respond to harmful behavior" (emphasis in the original; Einstadter and Henry, 1995: 302). So they concluded that rather than merge the different emphases, it was preferable to respect their differences, to retain their integrity as part of the array of criminological approaches. Einstadter and Henry's concern was that, by meshing the theoretical approaches, there would be a loss of value in the uniqueness of different contributions to criminological understanding.

I am both in agreement and disagreement with their position depending on the different ways in which integration is interpreted and operationalized. When it comes to modernist theoretical integration as discussed earlier, I agree with Einstadter and Henry. When it comes to postmodern criminological integration, as will be discussed, I disagree. In short, I believe that criminology should accommodate both a fission of theories and a fusion of knowledges. In order to explain what I mean by these two kinds of integrative practices, it is first necessary to discuss causality as the centralizing concept of the modernist criminological enterprise.

In general, "the basic notion of causality is expressed by the idea of independent cause in which an event A produced an event B, such that either B cannot occur without A (in which case A is a necessary cause) or B will be produced by A but can also occur without it (in which case A is a sufficient cause)" (Henry and Milovanovic, 1996:

125.) Stated differently, criminologists and other social theorists are concerned with how the events they define as crime are produced by antecedent events. When it comes to criminality, of course, causes become much more complex because there are a number of relevant variables interacting in the production of crime and criminals.

Typically, therefore, criminologists speculate or hypothesize about the causal relationship between more than two events or states of affairs. Einstadter and Henry (1995) have identified four types of causality relationships: linear, multiple, interactive, and dialectical. A review of the types of causal relationships that are involved in criminological theory helps to differentiate between what I refer to as the "modern" emphasis on an integration of theory and the "postmodern" emphasis on an integration of knowledge.

*Linear causality*, also referred to as *interdependent causality*, consists of a "sequential chain in which each subsequent occurrence of an event produces the conditions for the next event, until the final criminal event occurs" (Henry and Milovanovic, 1996: 125). This type of causality may also be thought of as a "conditional" causal relationship because no one event in the sequence can produce, for our purposes, crime or delinquency. In the case of Hirschi's control theory of delinquent behavior, for example, the outcome of delinquency is derived as follows: weak attachment to parents ⟶ weak attachment to school ⟶ weak commitment to conventional means ⟶ identification with delinquent peers ⟶ causes delinquent behavior.

*Multiple causality* consists of two versions: many causes and combined causes. In the former version, any of the events is capable of producing crime. Each of the events (e.g., weak attachment to parents, weak attachment to school, identification with delinquent peers) is sufficient but not necessary for crime or delinquency to occur. In the latter version, it is the combination of multiple events (causes) that together coproduce the deviant outcome. On the one hand, unlike linear causality, a temporal order of events is not required, only that it occurs. On the other hand, like linear causality, no one event can produce the crime. With respect to delinquency, LaMar Empey and Mark Stafford (1991) have suggested that this behavior may be the outcome of both independent multiple causality and interdependent linear causality.

*Interactive causality*, or *reciprocal causality*, makes the whole concept of causality even more complicated. In these situations, events are cyclical and move forward and backward. In other words, cause and effect influence each other and often assume a sequence of events over time that can form a spiral process leading to ever-increasing delinquency or criminality. Thus, weak attachments with parents may be further weakened by failing at school or getting into trouble with delinquent peers, which, in effect, may cause a weakening of commitment to conventional means, and so on (Empey and Stafford, 1991).

*Dialectical causality*, or *codetermination causality*, may be thought of as a case of multiple interactive causality. The dialectical codeterminacy model of causality involves reciprocity between several causes and outcomes. Moreover, such models of delinquent causality recognize that there is a whole lot less black and white and a lot more gray when it comes to commitment to delinquent peers. That is to say, delinquent and nondelinquent values can overlap. For instance, values of material success, consumerism, and property may be the outcome of both conventional and delinquent constructs. Adolescents, in short, may identify with both conventional and nonconventional means of behavior.

Dialectical causality is different from the other types of causalities in three fundamental ways. As Henry and Milovanovic (1996: 126) explain,

> *First, the cause and outcome are not conceived as discrete entities but are interrelated and overlapping, such that some part of cause is constituted by some part of the event produced in part by it and vice versa; but all of the event is not all of the cause (and vice versa). Second, and related to this, neither "cause" nor "event" has causal priority since each has simultaneous transformative powers over the other, regardless of the extent. Third, changes in either the "cause" or the "event" are not temporarily separated because their interrelatedness means that as one changes, the other must change, and with it the first must change also. Reciprocity of influence then is instantaneous, although cumulative mutual transformation may extend over time.*

Dialectical causality, then, not only raises questions about whether theorists have correctly ordered their causal variables, but, more fundamentally, it questions whether there is a correct ordering of causal variables to order in the first place. In turn, dialectical causality questions both the legitimacy and accuracy (or predictive value) of the other types of causality as each of these to varying degrees relies on the mathematical techniques of *path analysis*—an estimate of the relative effects of a set of independent variables on a dependent variable, based on the observed correlations among the hypothesized causal relations among variables—"in order to establish a path coefficient for each of the indicated causal connections, building up a complete picture (i.e, variance explained) of the independent effects of each variable relative to the rest" (Henry and Milovanovic, 1996: 122). But, again, this type of formal and propositional theoretical model building of crime assumes that a correct ordering among variables is not only possible, but that it even exists in the first place. It is the view of constitutive criminology, however, that no such causative-predictive relationship of crime, in fact, endures. Hence, theory is better at explaining crime than at predicting criminal behavior.

In other words, most of the theoretical model building in criminology is of a less formal, semiformal, and discursive nature that can help to organize and explain the data about crime and criminals that have been collected. And although theory building, integrative or nonintegrative, may not ever be able to locate a correct ordering of causal variables, it can help to move the policies and practices of social control toward a more complex and multidimensional response to crime. In the process of attempting to integrate various models or theories of crime and delinquency, there comes an appreciation of the connections between different perspectives and approaches, even if ultimately this does not result in predictive integrative models of crime and crime control.

With the perspective of dialectical causality firmly in mind, I now turn to an overview of modernist attempts at theoretical integration. Although not exhaustive of the growing integrative literature on crime, criminals, crime fighters, and victims, this review is representative of the broad range of integrative efforts that have emerged during the past two decades. As the various examples of theoretical integration are discussed in the next section, think about the theoretical biases that circumscribe the approaches to integration.

## Modernist Constructions of Integrated Theory

As noted earlier in the chapter, an important distinction between the various models of integration hinges on the scope or range of deviance or criminality addressed by a specific causative model. Integrative models can be general, pertaining to all forms of criminality, for example, inclusive of street, white collar, organized, corporate, and governmental offenders. Or models can be specific, referring to a particular crime, such as rape or murder, or to a grouping of crimes, such as those integrated explanations directed at the "crimes of the powerful." Although most discussions of integrative approaches have directed their attention to the "crimes of the powerless," notable exceptions are Box (1983) and Henry and Milovanovic's (1996) discussions of the crimes of the powerful. In the discussion that follows, the emphasis is on the full range of integrative models inclusive of all forms of criminality (see Table 9.1).

**TABLE 9.1  Modernist Constructions of Integrated Theory**

| Theorists | Work | Date |
|---|---|---|
| Howard Kaplan | *Self Attitudes and Deviant Behavior* (self-esteem/self-derogation of adolescent deviance) | 1975 |
| Richard Quinney | *Class, State, and Crime* | 1977 |
| Delbert Elliott et al. | "An Integrated Theoretical Perspective on Delinquent Behavior" | 1979 |
| Richard Johnson | *Delinquency and Its Origins* | 1979 |
| Mark Colvin and John Pauly | "A Critique of Criminology: Toward an Integrated Structural-Marxist Theory of Delinquency Production" | 1983 |
| Steven Box | *Power, Crime, and Mystification* | 1983 |
| James Q. Wilson and Richard Herrnstein | *Crime and Human Nature* | 1985 |
| Frank Pearson and Neal Weiner | "Toward an Integration of Criminological Theory" | 1985 |
| Marvin D. Krohn | "The Web of Conformity: A Network Approach to the Explanation of Delinquent Behavior" | 1986 |
| Thomas Bernard | *Theoretical Criminology* (unified conflict theory of crime) | 1986 |
| Rodney Stark | "Deviant Places: A Theory of the Ecology of Crime" | 1987 |
| James W. Coleman | "Toward an Integrated Theory of White-Collar Crime" | 1987 |
| John Hagan | *Structural Criminology* (power-control theory of crime) | 1988 |
| John Braithwaite | *Crime, Shame, and Reintegration* | 1989 |
| Terance Miethe and Robert Meier | *Crime and Its Social Context: Toward an Integrated Theory of Offenders, Victims, and Situations* | 1994 |
| Becky Tatum | "Race, Class, Alienation and Delinquency: Assessing Motivational Factors Through the Application of Structural Models" | 1995 |

Usually, the causal logic of integrative theorization tends to be a composite of causal relationships taken from the other theories. For example, Elliott, Ageton, and Cantor's (1979) integrated theory of delinquency and Elliott, Huizinga, and Ageton's (1985) integrated theory of delinquency and drug use both combine elements of social ecology theory, social learning theory, social control theory, and subcultural theory. Their models contend that social disorganization, strain, and inadequate socialization result in a weakening of conventional bonding and a strengthening of delinquent bonding, which results in delinquent behavior.

In the end-to-end integrated model of delinquency, as revealed in Figure 9.1,

> *weak conventional bonding (low social control) is seen as causally prior to strong delinquent bonding (social learning). Individual interactions with the family, for example, generally occur before the individual can establish a peer group. Also, strain, inadequate socialization, and social disorganization are treated as the most exogenous variables in the model. These three concepts involve social structural conditions, as well as preadolescent developmental characteristics, and would be expected to occur before bonding to conventional and delinquent groups occurs (Bernard and Snipes, 1996: 311).*

This is also an example of a macro–micro form of integrative theorizing. At the same time, Elliott et al. recognize the contradictory assumptions between control theory and the disposition of everyone to deviate, on the one hand, and the paradoxical nature between strain theory without any inherent disposition to deviate and learning theory with its variation in motivation to commit and refrain from deviation, on the other hand. Ultimately, these positions are reconciled by Elliott and colleagues, taking essentially the side of strain and learning theory. Testing of their models has generally supported their integrated versions, with support for the influence of social learning and delinquent bonding being strongest (Elliott, Huizinga, and Menard, 1989; Menard and Elliott, 1994).

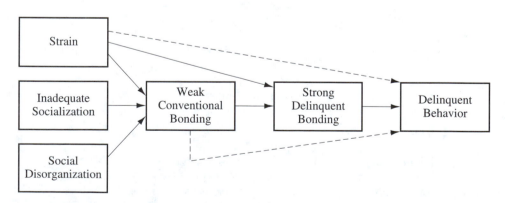

**FIGURE 9.1    Elliott's Integratred Theory of Delinquency**

*From:* Delbert Elliott et al., *Explaining Delinquency and Drug Use* (Beverly Hills, CA: Sage, 1985), page 66. Reprinted with permission.

Although Elliott's model, in general, is typical of those integrative theories that reveal some kind of linear and sequential progression, there are essentially three models for grouping integrative criminological theories: (1) social process-micro; (2) social structure-macro; and (3) agency-context or micro–macro. As revealed later, there appears to be a proclivity among integrationists to combine both micro and macro factors in their explanations. That is to say, most integrative efforts attempt to link theories that emphasize both individual and structural variables. Most of these integrative attempts focus almost exclusively on factors that cause crime. On the other hand, some of these efforts make connections between crime, victims, and crime control. A minority focuses on either micro individual processing or macro social relations, with the edge favoring the latter models.

Some may disagree with my categorization of the integrative attempts below and it may, in fact, be that all of these integrative approaches should be characterized as striving to accommodate both micro and macro elements of causation. Nevertheless, I have divided the following theoretical examples of modernist integration into whether the emphasis is on kinds-of-people (micro), kinds-of-organization (macro), or kinds-of-culture explanations that bring together in some fashion the individual and structural dimensions of criminality.

## Social Process–Micro Models

Social process-micro models tend to emphasize the integration of kinds-of-people explanations of criminal behavior. James Q. Wilson and Richard Herrnstein (1985), in *Crime and Human Nature*, presented what they regarded as a comprehensive or general theory of crime. Their theory is an eclectic, social learning–behavioral choice formulation that relies on both positivist determinism and rational free will. It combines factors involving human agency, individual action, and social process. Issues of organization and culture are not explored. Wilson and Herrnstein's discursive theory claims various linkages between criminality and hereditary factors, impulsivity, low intelligence, family practices, school experiences, and the effects of mass media on the individual. However, they attempt to make it look more formalistic by using pseudo-mathematical formulas without any values assigned to their symbols.

In the final analysis, Wilson and Herrnstein have provided a micro-social process theory of specific rather than general crime. That is to say, their so-called general theory of crime pertains only to "aggressive, violent, or larcenous behavior" or to those individuals who hit, rape, murder, steal and threaten (Wilson and Herrnstein, 1985: 22). Omitted from their general analysis is any consideration of white collar, corporate, or governmental criminals. Immune from their examination are the Wall Street inside traders, the violators or nonenforcers of occupational safety regulations, or the perpetrators of Iran–Contragate, for example. At the same time, interactions between individuals and the social structure are unrelated to legitimate and illegitimate opportunities. Not only did they restrict themselves to certain crimes and criminals, but they also selectively reviewed the evidence bearing on their arguments. A decade after its publication, most criminologists had (because of all its flaws) dismissed this "best seller" as a theory for advancing the field's understanding of criminality.

In an article in *Social Problems*, Marvin D. Krohn (1986) proposed an explanation of delinquency derived from social learning, social bonding, and social control theories. It was not an integrated theory per se, but rather a bridging of theoretical propositions from the delinquency-enhancing effects of differential association and the delinquency-constraining effects of social bonds. On the other hand, Krohn's *network theory* is integrative to the extent that it connects individuals and groups in a process of social interaction.

Krohn specifically identifies structural characteristics of social networks. He argues that the two most important characteristics are "multiplexity" and "density." The former refers to the number of different relationships or contexts that two or more people share in common; the latter refers to the ratio of existing social relationships to the maximum number of total possible relationships in a network. The theory assumes that network density is inversely related to population density: the higher the population density (the number of persons within a given geographical area), the lower the network density. Consequently, the argument maintains: the lower the network density, the weaker the constraints against nonconformity, and the higher the delinquency rate. Generally, this micro-social process theory as another expression of the social learning integration of principles of differential association and reinforcement has been empirically sustained (Akers, 1994: 195)

## Social Structure–Macro Models

In *Class, State, and Crime*, Richard Quinney (1977) articulated a class-structural analysis and integrative general theory of crime. The central relations of this theory are the contradictions of capitalism and the developing political economy. The product of the relations of production, explains Quinney, results in two interconnected sets of crime: The *crimes of domination and repression* are committed by capitalists and agents of control; the *crimes of accommodation and resistance* are committed by workers and ordinary people.

Quinney's up-and-down integrative argument is that all criminal activities are class specific. Where people are located in the socioeconomic structure of society determines the types of crimes that they rationally engage in. These crimes are driven by the contradictions of survival for individuals and organizations alike in a capitalist system. For capitalists, who are about the business of accumulating profits, avoiding bankruptcy, resisting hostile corporate takeovers, assuring survival in a competitive marketplace, and subduing counterforces of regulation, they or their agents engage in crimes of economic domination, governmental control, and social injury. For everybody else, who are about the business of struggling to make ends meet and to resist alienation, crimes become economic, predatory, and political means for survival and social change.

Not only are the differential crime opportunities class specific, but so too are the accompanying motivations for crime and crime enforcement and nonenforcement. In other words, the inequity in both the definition of crime and the application of the criminal law is reflected in the reproduction of the contradictions of class relationships. Quinney's integrated theory of crime and criminal justice is empirically supported, but the problem with such kinds of organizational explanations is that they fail to take agency or individualization into account. Not all people or corporations in the same class-specific relationships engage in criminal activities. Explaining why some do and others do not requires an integration of the macro-social structure with the micro-social process models.

Mark Colvin and John Pauly (1983), in the *American Journal of Sociology*, contributed an integrative theoretical approach for explaining serious patterned delinquent behavior. Their structural-Marxist theory argues that the entire process of delinquency production is a "latent outcome of the reproduction of capitalist relations of production and the class structure" (Colvin and Pauly, 1983: 515; see also, Schwendinger and Schwendinger, 1985). Their discursive semiformalistic theory holds essentially that most lower-class workers are subject to coercive power relations outside the home. As a result, these workers' capacity to relate to their children as parents is reduced to harsh and punitive repression. This, in turn, weakens both the bond between children and parents and the identification with the values of conformity. The argument continues that as the parental and social bonds generally weaken, delinquent behavior becomes an increasingly likely outcome. Empirical testing of their kinds-of-organization explanation of crime found mixed results (Messner and Krohn, 1990). The weakness of this theory, like most macro-social structural explanations, however, is its failure to come to terms with personal motivation or the agency (volition) of the individual offender.

In a special theory issue of *Criminology*, Rodney Stark (1987) introduced an integrated set of thirty propositions as a first approximation of a theory of *deviant places*. Rather than kinds-of-people theories, Stark was calling for kinds-of-places explanations. He hoped to revive "a sociology of deviance as an alternative to the social psychological approaches that have dominated for 30 years" (Stark, 1987: 894). His integrated macro-social structure kinds-of-organization approach was specifically related to understanding the relations between poverty and delinquency.

Stark was concerned with the ecology of crime. He wanted to account for the ecological concentration of deviance. "What an ecological theory of crime is meant to achieve is an explanation of why crime and deviance are so heavily concentrated in certain areas, and to pose this explanation in terms that do not depend entirely (or evenly primarily) on *compositional* effects—that is, on answers in terms of 'kinds of people' " (Stark, 1987: 904). Simply put, this ecological theory predicts that the deviant behavior of the poor will vary as the ecology varies.

Moving to an integrated analysis on the "traits of places and groups rather than on traits of individuals," Stark (1987: 894) seeks to rediscover the "poor neighborhoods [that had] disappeared to be replaced by individual kids with various levels of family income, but no detectable environment at all." Advocating a human ecology approach to deviance, Stark identifies what he considers to be the five most salient aspects or factors of urban neighborhoods that characterize high-deviance areas: density, poverty, mixed use, transience, and dilapidation. Depending on a neighborhood's combination of factors and its responses to these, the problem of crime will vary. In brief, as neighborhoods provide differential opportunity structures and differential motivations for crime and deviance, they simultaneously attract deviant and crime-prone people while they repel the least deviant as mechanisms of social control are diminished in presence and impact.

Stark provides empirical support for this theory by comparatively examining racial patterns in arrest and imprisonment. He demonstrates that these patterns are far more equitable in the South than in the North and West:

> *The ratio of black prison inmates per 100,000 to white prison inmates per 100,000 reveals that South Carolina is the most equitable state (with a ratio of 3.2 blacks to 1 white), closely followed by Tennessee, Georgia, North Carolina, Mississippi, and Alabama, while Minnesota (22 blacks to 1 white) is the least equitable, followed by Nebraska, Wisconsin, and Iowa. Black/white arrest ratios, calculated the same way, also show greater equity in the South, while Minnesota, Utah, Missouri, Illinois, and Nebraska appear to be least equitable (Stark, 1987: 905).*

Stark concludes that high crime rates among blacks are, in large measure, the result of *where* they live, rather than a result of race or racism per se. He continues that "what *is* true about the circumstance of southern blacks is that they have a much more normal ecological distribution than do blacks outside the South" (Stark, 1987: 905). What he means by "normal" is that a larger proportion of southern than northern blacks live in suburbs, small towns, and rural areas where they benefit from factors conducive to low crime rates. Conversely, blacks outside the South are heavily concentrated in places (cities larger than 100,000 population) where the probabilities of committing a crime are high.

## Micro–Macro Models

As noted previously, the micro–macro theories of integration focus on both the individual and the structure plus on some kind of interaction between the two. The variations in these integrative approaches are wide and diverse. For example, integrative formulations include but are not limited to those that range from self-esteem/self-derogation theories to social–psychological theories, from path analysis sequential theories to unified conflict theories, from theories focusing on a specific crime to theories focusing on crime in general, or from theories that exclusively address crime and criminals to those that address the contextual relations of criminals and victims.

In *Delinquency and Its Origins*, Richard Johnson (1979) presented an integrative-path analytic model of delinquency. He identified a number of independent paths or causal sequences involving different combinations of influences. These influences or factors included social class, family experiences, perceptions of future opportunities, delinquent associates, delinquent values, and perceptions of risks of being apprehended for deviant acts. Johnson's own research provided mixed empirical results.

Some would argue, as Hirschi (1987) has done with respect to Elliott, Ageton, and Cantor (1979), that Johnson's integrative approach is too eclectic. Hence, it muddies the empirical waters as it becomes more rather than less difficult to disentangle causal influences, and to weight or identify the differential contribution that each of the factors makes to the behavioral outcome of delinquency. Moreover, how does one determine whether integrative theories should be lined up end-to-end, side-by-side, or up-and-down? On the other hand, from a discursive or conceptual rather than a propositional or formalistic perspective, integrative theorizing that is not restricted to predictive causality is not necessarily concerned with the disentanglement and precise weighting of the differential factors involved in the production of crime.

One of the earliest conceptual integrative approaches seeking to explain corporate crime appeared in Steven Box's (1983) *Power, Crime, and Mystification* (1983). This side-by-side conceptual model makes use of the conventional modernist theories: anomie/strain, bonding/control, social learning, neutralization, subcultural, opportunity structure, and social control. For Box, corporate crime is the result of corporations striving to achieve their particular goals in an otherwise uncertain environment. "Uncertainties are due to economic competition, the government, workers, the public consumers, and so on. The corporation attempts to overcome uncertainties by illegally eliminating or otherwise reducing them through fraud, bribery, manipulation, price-fixing, and other devious practices" (Henry and Milovanovic, 1996: 145).

Box employs anomie and strain as the motivational source of corporate crime. "Motivational strain" is translated into illegal acts through differential associations and corporate subcultures where elites learn to rationalize and neutralize their infractions with the social and moral contracts. At the same time, lack of rule enforcement of corporate misbehavior and the low risk of punishment serves to reinforce rather than deter corporate crime. In Box's discursive integrative scheme of things (see Figure 9.2), elites come to view themselves as above the law or their behavior as not serious or threatening. Ideologically and practically speaking, Box argues that corporations are relatively free to commit violations that both the public and control agencies view first and foremost as regulatory rather than criminal matters. Due to its discursive nature and side-by-side integrative approach, this model of integration has not been the subject of empirical tests and probably will not be.

Another conceptual attempt to integrate into one framework all of the major macro and micro theories of criminal behavior appeared in the *Journal of Criminal Law and Criminology*. Frank Pearson and Neil Weiner's (1985) model of integration is derived from identifying concepts that are common to particular theories and, in turn, framing these concepts within a general framework. This model searches for common vocabulary in which terms from one theory have analogs in other theoretical formulations; it does not attempt to develop formal propositions for the purposes of testing.

The Pearson–Weiner model employs a social learning theory of crime as its central organizing concept. The framework employs micro-social process factors, macro-social structure factors, and feedback or behavioral consequence factors. Their integrative social learning framework accommodates factors that reside both inside and outside the individual offenders, and it is broken down into eight general concepts involving six antecedent constructs that occur causally prior to criminal behavior and two feedback mechanisms that occur after criminality. The antecedent factors include *utility* (reward/punishment), *behavioral skill* (techniques for committing crime learned through imitation and reinforcement), *signs of favorable opportunities, behavioral resources, rules of expedience* (learned guidelines for maximizing rewards, avoiding

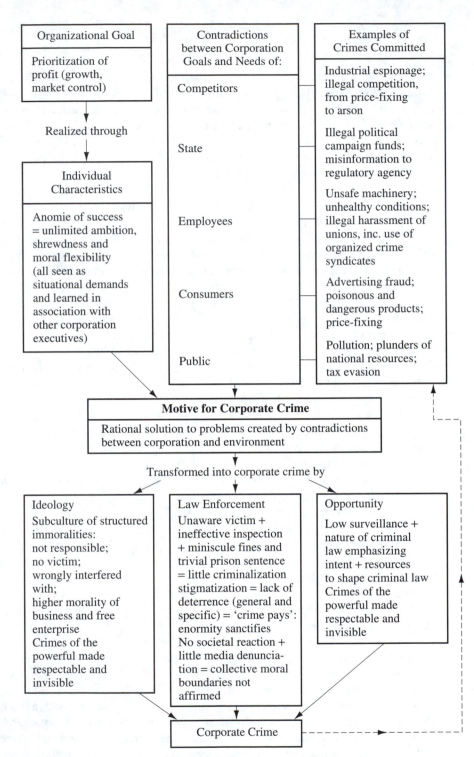

**FIGURE 9.2    Box's Integrated Theory of the Crimes of the Powerful**

*From:* Stephen Box, *Power, Crime, and Mystification* (London: Tavistock, 1983), page 64. Reprinted with permission.

negative sanctions, and imitating successful role models), and *rules of morality*. The feedback mechanisms (social control) include *utility receptions* (acquisitions of rewards and punishments by the behavior) and *information acquisition* (knowledge received about the behavior that may be used in a future decision).

Next, they argue that all of the most significant theories of criminology, including social learning, differential association, negative labeling, social control, deterrence, economic, routine activities, neutralization, relative deprivation, strain, normative (culture) conflict, Marxist-critical/group conflict, and generalized strain and normative conflict, can be viewed as variations in, or subtypes of, their eight organizing concepts. Although their connections are perhaps tenuous, their conceptual integration of many different theories into a consistent, coherent, and dynamic framework is impressive. Of course, they did not produce any testable propositions because their incorporation of overlapping theories into their integrative framework does not allow for more than the discursive demonstration of definitional and operational similarities among different approaches to crime and delinquency.

Thomas Bernard's *unified conflict theory of crime* presented in the third edition of *Theoretical Criminology* (Vold and Bernard, 1986) is a conceptual model that integrates rates of crime, variations in individual criminal behavior, and criminal law and justice with propositions from conflict, social structure, and social learning theory. Hence, this integrative theory is not only macro–micro, focusing on process and structure, but it is also inclusive of both crime and crime control. Bernard's descriptive unification of criminal behavior and criminal law is expressed in five propositions:

   **I.** Schedules of Reinforcement in Complex Societies
  **II.** Behavior Patterns of Individuals
 **III.** The Enactment of Criminal Laws
 **IV.** The Enforcement of Criminal Laws
   **V.** The Distribution of Official Crime Rates

In sum, Bernard maintains that "criminal behavior is normally learned behavior responding to different reinforcement schedules operating in different social structure locations" (Vold and Bernard, 1986: 288). He also proposes that an integration of conflict and social learning theory accounts for criminal law as well as criminality. Such a unified model of criminal behavior and criminal law provides a framework that potentially could incorporate conventional theories of social structure and social learning with critical theories of race, gender, and class.

James Coleman (1989), in his book *The Criminal Elite*, articulates an integrated theory of white collar crime that explains both corporate and occupational crimes. On the one hand, his micro analysis consists of the motivations of "reckless" and "egocentric" offenders. On the other hand, his macro analysis consists of the "structure of opportunities" (legitimate and illegitimate). Coleman's discussion of motivation is not restricted to the psychological. He discusses, for example, the motivational existence of "cultures of competition" that can be checked by ethical standards, the media, and by the symbolic force of the law.

More specifically, Coleman underscores the presence of the "techniques of neutralization" in the corporate world that erode ethical standards of conduct through various rationalizations. These rationalizations, he argues, are the product of a corporate culture steeped in organizational conformity where the efficient bureaucracy breeds a kind of amoral pragmatism. He also argues that legitimate and illegitimate opportunities are differentially distributed according to the market and the responses of the legal systems. This means within large-scale organizational structures that white collar crimes are products of values established by the vagaries of the marketplace and law enforcement. In sum, Coleman maintains that the availability of rationalizations and subcultures is significant in the motivation of occupational crimes. Similarly, Coleman contends that with respect to corporate crimes, those firms with declining profitability are especially ripe for the commission of crime.

John Hagan (1988), in *Structural Criminology*, as well as earlier Hagan, Gillis, and Simpson (1985), Hagan and Palloni (1986), and later Hagan (1990), has developed a *power-control* theory of gender and delinquency. "Power-control theory is representative of an increasing trend toward qualifying relationships between concepts at one level of explanation by drawing on concepts at other levels of explanation" (Bernard and Snipes, 1996: 318). Not only does Hagan integrate the power relations between the parents relative to their position in the workplace with the relative freedom from parental control of boys and girls in a family, but he also explains the relationship between gender and delinquency with the interaction between a family's class position and control relations within the family.

In brief, the control of boys is less than that of girls. Therefore, the preference for risky behavior is also less for girls compared with boys. Hence, male adolescents engage in more delinquent behavior than females. Moreover, the interaction of gender and class is revealed in that the differences in gender treatment and preference are greater among patriarchal families than among egalitarian families. In other words, in those domestic households where mothers have relative power compared to fathers, girls are no more likely to be controlled than boys. Hence, the differences in delinquency between boys and girls are less in egalitarian than in patriarchal families.

In its most developed form, Hagan (1990: 137) joins Giddens's (1984) *structuration* theory (see Chapter 10) with his own power-control theory to "explain motivations and mechanisms by which gender is socially reproduced in relationship to various forms of deviance and control." His ultimate aim is to explain gender differences in vulnerability to crime and victimization. By joining macro theories of social/cultural structure, Hagan (1990: 137) not only combines elements of Marxist, conflict, gender analysis, and control theory with classical assumptions about human nature, but he also "focuses attention on a duality of structure in which mothers and daughters are both mediums and outcomes of domestic social control, and on an implicit patriarchal social construct in which the freeness of women to take risks in effect is exchanged for a reduced vulnerability to criminal law."

Although the first empirical tests of power-control theory generally supported the theory's tenets (Hagan, 1988), the research evidence is actually mixed, as have been the reactions from several sympathetic critics (Chesney-Lind, 1989; Chesney-Lind and Sheldon, 1992; Messerschmidt, 1993; Curran and Renzetti, 1994). All in all, Hagan has done a more satisfying job with operationalizing the intertwining structural forces involved with gender and delinquency than he has with integrating the micro-level assumptions about human agency. In sum, Hagan has short-changed the volition of both males and females, especially the latter, because they are uniformly portrayed as passive, compliant, and dependent.

John Braithwaite's (1989) original theory of *reintegrative shaming* in *Crime, Shame, and Reintegration* has been one of the most interesting expositions of both an integrative and a general theory of those crimes involving the victimization of individuals by other individuals. Braithwaite's unique contribution results from his proposal of a new theory within the context of a web of well-established theories. His micro–macro model of crime and crime control adds to the modernist mixture of traditional theories—such as labeling, subcultural, control, opportunity, and learning—the positive and negative reactions of lawbreakers. His theory, which is neither propositional nor conceptual per se, is better thought of as referring to a process by which several theoretical concepts of criminal behavior are linked together.

Braithwaite distinguished between the stigmatizing form of social disapproval of shaming, which frequently drives lawbreakers into further acts of misbehavior as they experience feelings of deviance, and reintegrative shaming or stigma, which maintains community bonds by emphasizing mild rebuking and degradation ceremonies, followed by gestures of reacceptance. His model revolves around these two forms of shaming in relationship to each other so that crime and deviance or law-abiding and conforming behavior becomes a matter of "tipping points" (see Figure 9.3). In other words, efforts at social control should be evaluated in terms of whether they tip contemporary offenders into the direction of compliance versus infraction.

Braithwaite's theory emphasizes the penal characteristics and social conditions that encourage or discourage reintegrative shaming. He also stresses the fact that some people are better bonded to society and more susceptible to shaming than others who may be more alienated. Organizationally, some societies, like Japan, tend to be more communitarian whereas others, like the United States, more individualistic. Accordingly, the former societies are viewed as having a more logical affinity with reintegrative shaming, the latter societies with stigmatizing shaming. Although there has been some limited empirical application with respect to the relationship between reintegrative shaming and nursing care compliance (Braithwaite, 1993), the relationship between shaming and the other theoretical frameworks is only beginning to be tested.

What is particularly integrative is the dualistic concept or symbiotic relationship of shaming in which the degrees and kinds of stigma and punishment are regarded as both the prevention and cause of future crime. Although Braithwaite's theory emphasizes the importance of degree in responding to crime, it tends to overemphasize the reactions to crime (secondary deviance). At the same time, it tends to downplay the reasons for the emergence of crime (primary deviance) in the first place. Nevertheless, the ultimate strength of Braithwaite's model of crime, shame, and reintegration lies within its reciprocal approach to causality.

Howard Kaplan (1975) has been engaged in the integrative project for more than two decades. One of his earliest formulations appears in his book *Self-Attitudes and*

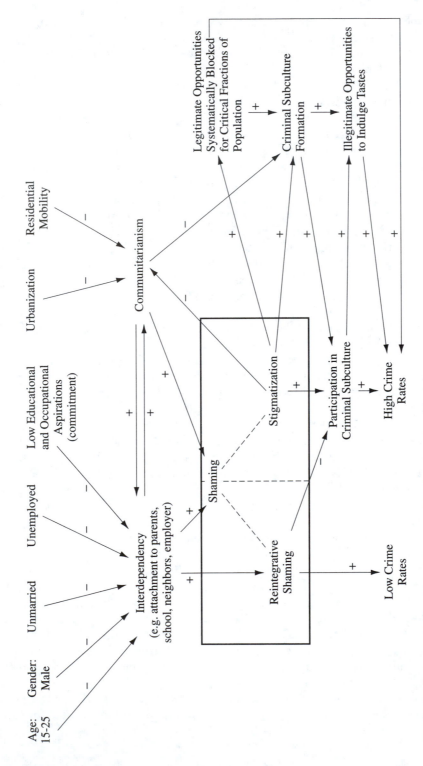

**FIGURE 9.3    Braithwaite's Theory of Reintegrative Shaming**

*From:* John Braithwaite, *Crime, Shame, and Reintegration* (Cambridge: Cambridge University Press, 1989), page 89. Reprinted with the permission of Cambridge University Press.

*Deviant Behavior.* Some have viewed Kaplan's *self-esteem/self-derogation* theory of adolescent deviance as "bringing together deviant peer influences (social learning theory), family and school factors (control theory), dealing with failure to live up to conventional expectations (strain theory), and self-concept (symbolic interactionism and labeling theory)" (Akers, 1994: 192). Others, such as Donald Shoemaker (1990), have treated Kaplan's approach as merely an elaboration of control theory, whereas Edward Wells (1978: 190) contended that the theory represented a rapprochement among the "dominant perspectives on the use of the self-concept in the study of deviance" during the 1960s, namely, structural interactionism and socialization-control analyses.

In its original formulation, delinquency (deviance) was viewed as a response to adolescent feelings of low self-esteem or self-derogation. Simply stated, according to Kaplan, all people are driven by a "self-esteem motive" to take actions that minimize negative self-attitudes and maximize positive perceptions of self. If people's experiences with conventional groups (i.e., family, schools) and with conforming to their expectations result in positive self-concepts, then deviance is not likely to occur. However, if this is not the case and people's experiences instead are negative, self-devaluing, and result in self-derogation, then the social control exercised by conventional groups becomes less effective as individuals turn to deviant groups and activities as a means of alleviating the feelings, attitudes, and stresses of self-derogation, on the one hand, and of developing feelings and attitudes of self-esteem, on the other hand. Kaplan and colleagues (1982; 1986) tested this early model, primarily involving adolescent substance abuse, and found mixed results.

In his latest formulation, Kaplan (1993: 1) has refined and elaborated his approach by providing an outline of a *general theory of motivated deviance* that elucidates in discursive fashion the integrative "contributions of several traditional perspectives on crime and deviance." This analysis' focus is on the ways various theoretical perspectives—strain, subculture, control, and labeling—on deviance "interdigitate" with his general theory. In other words, while incorporating a number of concepts other than those of self-attitudes and deviant behavior, all of these factors, more or less, still revolve around or intermingle with feelings of self-esteem as the centralizing concept.

> *In the course of the normal socialization process one experiences, the individual learns to value the possession of particular attributes, the performance of certain behaviors, and the particular experiences that are the outcome of the purposive or accidental responses of others toward the person. These attributes, behaviors, and experiences are the basis for the individual's feelings of self-worth. If the person is unable to evaluate himself or herself positively, then the person will be motivated to behave in ways that will gain the attributes, enable the performance of the behaviors, and increase the likelihood of the experiences that will increase feelings of self-worth and decrease the feelings of psychological distress that are associated with self-rejecting attitudes (Kaplan, 1993: 14).*

In his current articulation of a general and integrative theory of deviant behavior, Kaplan's complex and interactive approach takes the following into account: (1) the social definition of deviance/crime; (2) the motivation to commit deviant acts that violate group norms; (3) the motivation to commit deviant acts that conform to group norms; (4) the acting out of deviant dispositions; (5) the continuity of deviant behavior; and (6) the consequences of deviance.

Kaplan (1993: 13) begins with the recognition that social definitions of deviance or crime are "influenced by the co-existence of culturally diverse groups at a given point in time, the rapid and uneven social change that creates cultural diversity over time, and the differential political influence exercised by particular segments of the population." With this starting point in mind, he cannot separate criminal causation and criminal action: "The *causes* of social definitions of behavior as deviant (through their effects on social definition) indirectly influence motivation to perform deviant acts as well as the continuity of deviance" (Kaplan, 1993: 13).

Kaplan makes other important assumptions, such as "patterns of deviance provoke mutually influential consequences that, in turn, influence subsequent deviant behavior" (Kaplan, 1993: 42). He also argues that criminal patterns provoke and interact with public attitudes. These attitudinal responses are associated with formal and informal behavioral responses. The formal refers to the actions of the criminal justice system, the informal refers to social rejection and precautionary tactics of mass culture. Kaplan further assumes that the nature of crime control is a function of the characteristics of the offense, the offender, and the victim. Finally, he assumes that historical relativity and specificity in the responses to crime and deviance "under different conditions constrain the acting out of deviant impulses, increase the fixity of the early offender in a deviant career, and displace the deviant impulses on to alternate targets" (Kaplan, 1993: 13).

With the definitional aspects of the problem addressed, Kaplan turns his attention to questions of motivation, or "Why do they do it?" He argues that two sets of circumstances and two corresponding sets of satisfaction give rise to the motivation to commit deviant acts. According to Kaplan, the development of dispositions to perform deviant or criminal acts involves (1) the person's earlier commitment to the normative system that judges such acts as wrong and (2) the failure to achieve what was expected of the person according to the conventional standards. In short, the conventional failure to achieve specific values, such as parental acceptance or success in school, results in deviant acts aimed at alleviating or adjusting to the psychological distress associated with the failures.

At this point, Kaplan examines deviant dispositions in relation to both conventional failure and the social determinants of this failure. In discussing the social determinants of conventional failure, he also makes a useful distinction between what he refers to as *motivated* and *unmotivated* deviance. The former involves actions in which individuals do not wish to conform; the latter involves individuals who wish to conform but are unable to do so. Unmotivated deviance may take one of two forms: First, there is the failure to possess consensually valued traits as a result of the interaction between congenital and social circumstances. That is, independent of or contrary to one's wishes, a person finds himself or herself possessing physical or psychological impairments. These may include membership of undesirable racial, ethnic, religious, or socioeconomic categories. They may also include physical abnormalities or weaknesses in strength, intelligence, emotion, beauty, and other characteristics. Second, there are the unmotivated deviant acts that represent the failures to perform acts of consensus through the ignorance of normative expectations, the presence of conflicting expectations, or the absence of the instrumental resources to meet the expectation.

Kaplan's (1993: 21) model also addresses the issue of "counteracting motives" acknowledging that "whether or not a person acts out the disposition to commit deviant acts will depend upon (1) the strength of the motives to commit the act compared to the strength of the motives that dispose a person not to perform the act and (2) the situation context and other opportunities to perform the act." Kaplan's interactive and, I would suggest, dialectical and integrative framework holds the view that deviance or crime is interdependent on the satisfactions of "basic" and "other" needs. For example, certain basic (human) needs that cannot be satisfied by conformity will require or depend on the performance of deviance or crime. At the same time, the satisfaction of other (cultural) needs may depend on not performing deviant acts. Thus, "if the satisfaction of the needs that appear to be threatened by the performance of deviant behavior is more important to the person than the satisfaction of the needs that is expected to result from the deviant behavior, then the person is likely to refrain from the behavior" (Kaplan, 1993: 21).

Of course, whether one acts out the disposition to deviate will also depend on "opportunities." Kaplan's reference to opportunities is inclusive of the convergence of both the internal abilities and resources of potential transgressors and the external realities and situations favorable (or unfavorable) to deviant acts. Once again, dialectically, Kaplan (1993: 31–32) further recognizes that whether deviant or criminal actions continue or discontinue depends on the immediate positive or negative consequences that are experienced by the transgressors:

> *For example, the use of illicit drugs may cause the person to feel good about himself or to feel ill. The physical abuse of another person or the destruction of property may increase the person's sense of power. Engaging in gang fights may result in physical injury. These outcomes may positively reinforce or extinguish motivation to continue the behavior. Less directly, the factors that influence continuation or discontinuation of the deviant response (whether by reinforcing or extinguishing motives to behave in this way or by influencing opportunities for deviant behavior) are mediated by other consequences of the earlier deviant behavior. Such consequences include the approving responses of deviant associates, the disapproving responses of conventional groups, and the stigmatizing effects of formal sanctions.*

At this point, Kaplan proceeds to identify the "determinants of continuation" and the "determinants of discontinuation." Each of these sets of determinants involves three sets of factors. Briefly, the continuation, repetition, or escalation of deviant or criminal activity happens when there are circumstances that (1) provide positive reinforcement (satisfaction) for deviant behavior, (2) weaken the effects of motives that previously deterred the individual from transgressing, and (3) increase ongoing (or establish new) opportunities for the performances of crime and deviance. Conversely, the discontinuation or decreased involvement in deviance or criminality happens when there are circumstances surrounding the offending behavior that (1) fail to satisfy the personal needs of social beings, (2) provide adverse consequences such as arrest or imprisonment, that threaten the satisfaction of other needs, and (3) change the very nature of a person's needs or opportunities to meet those needs.

In summing up, Kaplan argues that his integrative framework of deviance is primarily a sociological phenomenon where the goal of a comprehensive explanation is to be found in the "web of simultaneously considered relationships that concern the onset, continuity, and consequences of deviant behavior" (Kaplan, 1993: 43). That is to say, for example, visible violations of the criminal law, depending on the formal and informal social responses evoked and "the degree of alienation of the population from the conventional order, may stimulate and provide models for deviant patterns among individuals who are disposed to so behave" (Kaplan, 1993: 43). In my mind, Kaplan's micro–macro model is more social-psychological than it is sociological because "identity preservation" seems central to its motivational dynamic. Finally, this theory remains primarily conceptual because its concern is more with the web of considered relationships than with the testing of particular relationships within the web itself.

Another macro–micro exploration still in its early stages of integrative development is Becky Tatum's (1995; 1996) *neocolonial model of adolescent crime and violence*. This model, like Kaplan's, is social-psychological. It is also consistent with his theory, but its focus is less general because it seeks to explain the crimes of marginally oppressed peoples and the relationship between their social context of experiences and their psychological states of alienation. "In particular, the theory examines the relationship between structural oppression, alienation, and three adaptive forms of behavior—assimilation, crime or deviance, and protest" (Tatum, 1996: 34).

Tatum's neocolonial model is also consistent with Vold and Bernard's (1986) general conflict approach. Like Darnell Hawkins's (1986) approach to examining homicide in relationship to the significance of race and its interconnections with other factors (e.g., social class, economic opportunities), the historical behavior of law, and the behavior of the agents of criminal justice in responding to the processing of offenders, Tatum's model attempts to link structural conditions, perceptions of African Americans, alienation, and crime and delinquency. Finally, this integrative model can lend itself to gendered analyses of crime and deviance as well.

Grounded in the models of colonialism (Fanon, 1963; 1967; Staples, 1975; 1989) and internal colonialism (Blauner, 1969; 1972; Staples, 1974), Tatum argues that the neocolonial model not only accounts for racial and class differences, but also that its historical orientation as well as its conceptualization of alienation separate it from other structural models. At the same time, this model shifts the study of crime "from the victims of oppression to exploitative structural systems" (Tatum, 1996: 48).

Specifically, the neocolonial model assesses behavioral adaptations to blocked structural opportunity from the perspective of race as the primary stratifier followed by class. Combining the perspectives of racial conflict and anomie, Tatum argues that African American and lower-class youth experience greater structural exclusion than white or middle-class youth. At the same time, the social psychology of bonding (control theory) interacts with perceptions of oppression and feelings as well as types of alienation, so that crime and violence are also viewed as subject to or dependent on the local environment. Ultimately, the neocolonial model asserts that structural exclusion, perceived oppression, and fewer community support systems available to lower-class youths, especially African Americans, result in higher levels of alienation and in higher inter- and intrapersonal levels of crime and violence.

Tatum concludes her discussion of the adequacy of the neocolonial model of explaining crime and delinquency this way: The model has not been subjected to rigorous examination; therefore, its full explanatory power has yet to be tested. Nevertheless, it does not seem like it will be too difficult to gather together the empirical evidence supporting the relationships between race and crime, structural oppression, and perceptions of alienation.

Terance Miethe and Robert Meier (1994: 171), in *Crime and Its Social Context: Toward an Integrated Theory of Offenders, Victims, and Situations*, argue that "contrary to the implicit claims of separate theories of criminality and victimization, it is impossible to explain the social ecology of crime, or variation across crime categories, without recognition of both aspects of offender motivation and criminal opportunities." It is their position that "the union of offender motivation and the availability of criminal opportunities are essential ingredients for a general theory of crime that explains both its etiology and epidemiology" (Miethe and Meier, 1994: 172). They also point out that the commission of crime and target selection are two separate processes in the etiology of crime. The former relies on deterministic components, whereas the later relies on rational-choice components. At the same time, they "recognize that criminal acts vary widely in terms of their social ecology and motivation" (Miethe and Meier, 1994: 171). Finally, after analyzing crime rates and individuals' risks of victimization, Miethe and Meier (1994: 179) conclude that crime cannot occur without a particular social context, and therefore:

> *Any adequate theory of crime must account for the convergence in time and space of motivated offenders and potential crime targets. The value of theories of victimization is in their recognition of how the routine activities of everyday life create the supply of criminal opportunities, whereas traditional theories of criminality identify the factors that trigger offender motivation. The particular situational context is where the union of motivated offenders and criminal opportunities takes place. From an integrated perspective, crime control may be obtained either by eliminating social conditions that foster criminal intentions, or by reducing the opportunity for its occurrence and the presence of "high risk" situations.*

Miethe and Meier's study in integration combines an examination of the predictive utility of both theories of criminality and theories of victimization in explaining aggregate rates and individuals' risks of predatory crime (e.g., robbery, burglary, rape, homicide, etc.) across different contexts. They perform statistical analyses "to indicate the correlates of predatory crime, the inadequacies of models which ignore either aspects of criminality or victim-selection factors, and the influence of socio-economic conditions in the wider geographical areas on individuals' risk of victimization" (Miethe and Meier, 1994: 7). What is perhaps most intriguing about their *"heuristic*

*model of criminal events"* (see Figure 9.4) is that, although it assumes a particular ordering between each component, the model incorporates or allows for both "path" (solid
arrows) and "residual path" (broken arrows) analyses.

In other words, their model permits the "occurrence of criminal events even when
the nexus of offender motivation, victim characteristics, and the social context are not
ideal or optimal" (Miethe and Meier, 1994: 64). For example, basic human behavior
and strong offender motivation (e.g., hunger, peer pressure, anger) may not need the
presence of rational targets. Conversely, attractive, accessible, and unprotected crime
targets may be too good too pass up, even for those without the offender motivations.
Ultimately, however, their heuristic model assumes that it is the social context that "determines the conditions under which crime occurs, and whether aspects of offender
motivation and target-selection factors enhance, impede, or have no impact on the
likelihood of victimization" (Miethe and Meier, 1994: 72).

Although Miethe and Meier's integrative model of offender motivation and
victim–criminal opportunities is inclusive, it primarily revolves around theories of social disorganization, routine activity (Cohen and Felson, 1979; Cornish and Clarke,
1986), and lifestyle exposure (Lofland, 1969). In fact, they focus their attention on four
major criminogenic factors that have been identified by a wide variety of theoretical
frameworks as accounting for the variation in crime rates, namely, low socioeconomic

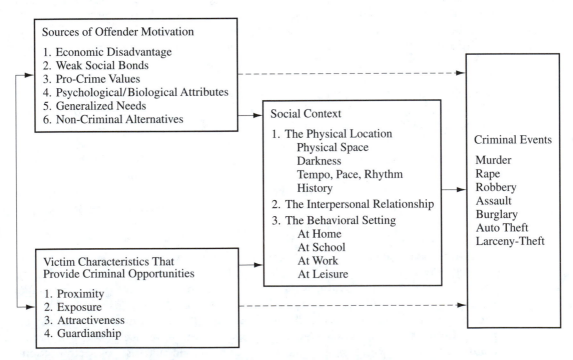

**FIGURE 9.4    Miethe and Meier's Heuristic Model of Criminal Events**

*From:* Terance D. Miethe and Robert F. Meier, *Crime and Its Social Context* (Albany, NY: SUNY Press, 1994), page 65.
Reprinted by permission of the State University of New York Press © 1994.

status, population mobility, ethnic heterogeneity, and single-parent families. After exhaustive testing of all sorts of data (e.g., census, National Crime Survey, city-wide telephone surveys), they conclude dialectically:

> *While general theories of criminality offer elegance and parsimony to our explanations of crime, the empirical results of our study do not readily support such a general perspective. Across various units of analysis, we find that many of the variables underlying theories of criminality and victimization have act-specific effects. Nonetheless, there is enough commonality in our results to suggest some virtue in a general theory of crime (Miethe and Meier, 1994: 170).*

## Summary and Conclusions: A Postmodern Criticism of Integration

It comes as no surprise that I come down on the side of integration. As an integrationist, my critique of modernist theoretical integration aims at the limited and reductionist versions that confine criminological integration to proving the value of one set of integrative variables over another set of integrative variables. In other words, I believe that there is much more to integration than the difficult tasks of integrating theories of crime, theories of victimization, theories of crime and victimization, or theories of crime and crime control. In the most general sense, these types of integration ignore other types of criminological knowledge that could be integrated separately or in relation to the various kinds of integrative theories discussed throughout this chapter. I am referring specifically, for example, to integrating the different kinds of criminologies (i.e., classical, positivist, feminist, cultural, newsmaking, peacemaking, and others) and the ways in which each of these interprets as well as operationalizes crime, criminals, victims, and crime control.

In the more limiting and particular sense, I am also supportive of those modernist attempts at theoretical integration reviewed in this chapter. However, although I believe that these integrative theories, whether formal and propositional or informal and conceptual, are both worth pursuing, I further believe that the current state of theoretical development, data measurement, and methodological sophistication is still too primitive, in most cases, to be able to discern the relative impact or weight of converging variables of crime and crime control. For the best exception to this lack-of-knowledge point of view that I can think of, see Roundtree, Land, and Miethe's (1994) "Macro–micro Integration in the Study of Victimization: A Hierarchical Logistic Model Analysis Across Seattle Neighborhoods."

It has been argued that the integrationist debate has preferredly targeted the abundance of theories that have not enriched the field of criminology, but that have instead impeded its scientific progress (Bernard, 1991). According to this argument, integration emerged as an "alternative to falsification as a way to reduce the number of theories in criminology, and it has arisen as a result of the perceived inability of falsification to accomplish this goal" (Bernard and Snipes, 1996: 302). Like Bernard and Snipes (1996: 303), I too believe "that integration and falsification are not incompatible," but I take issue with their view that "the purpose of integration is to enhance the falsification process."

Their argument may be technically correct in terms of theory advancement. Again, however, it does not address the other types of criminological integration. Bernard and Snipes (1996: 306) are also on the mark when they criticize the alleged incompatibility between integration and falsification as a product of the "distortions contained in the strain/control/cultural deviance interpretation." In brief, they claim that "those who oppose integration defend their position largely in reference" to Hirschi's (1979; 1989) distorted characterizations of strain and cultural deviance theories, "while those who favor integration typically deviate from it in one way or the another" (Bernard and Snipes, 1996: 324). Without going into their rather detailed critique of Hirschi and other analyses of strain and anomie, such as Kornhauser's (1978), and without referring to Cullen's (1983) elaborate reinterpretation of strain variables into structuring variables, suffice it to say, Bernard and Snipes have provided the best arguments I know for synthesizing theories rather than allowing them to remain in competitive isolation. Moreover, as Elliott (1985) claimed some time ago, as Bernard and Snipes (1996) recently maintained, and as I have implicitly, if not explicitly, argued throughout this book: Theoretical competition is generally pointless because most of the time different theories explain independent portions of the variance in crime. So why keep these variances in isolation? It makes far more sense to combine these partial explanations as a means of advancing criminological theory.

At the same time, however, I return to the point once again that, because of the various contradictions or tendencies and countertendencies involving both criminal motivation and the opportunities for crime, in all likelihood, criminologists will never be able to definitively ascertain the correct ordering of all the complex variables and how, over time, these influence each other. So, rather than confine integrative efforts to questions of theory alone and to particular theoretical frameworks, I argue that it makes more sense to think about and to engage in other forms of criminological integration. The rest of this book is dedicated to doing precisely that.

Finally, by elaborating the development of a post-postmodernist framework of integration in Chapter 10, I complete the rationale begun in this chapter for a broader approach to integration. In the process, I believe that I present a framework that represents an emerging paradigmatic shift in criminological thought. In the long run, I also believe that such an integrative model holds out the promise for developing a new criminology capable of transforming the practices of crime and crime control as we have known them for the past two hundred years or longer.

## Discussion Questions

1. Using various theories as examples, explain how integrated theories may be specific or general.

2. What are the primary differences between the four types of causality relationships: linear, multiple, interactive, and dialectical?

3. Why does Barak argue that criminology should accommodate both a fission of theories and a fusion of knowledges?

4. Compare and contrast Hagan's theory of power control to Giddens's theory of structuration.

5. Why does Miethe and Meier's heuristic model of criminal events ultimately assume that the social context determines crime?

# References

Akers, Ronald L. 1994. *Criminological Theories: Introduction and Evaluation.* Los Angeles: Roxbury Publishing Company.

Baron, Larry, and Murray A. Straus. 1990. *Four Theories of Rape.* New Haven: Yale University Press.

Bernard, Thomas J. 1991. "Twenty Years of Testing Theories." *Journal of Research in Crime and Delinquency* 27:325–347.

Bernard, Thomas J., and Jeffrey B. Snipes. 1996. "Theoretical Integration in Criminology." In Michael Tonry, ed., *Crime and Justice: A Review of Research* (Volume 20). Chicago: The University of Chicago Press.

Blauner, Robert. 1969. "Internal Colonialism and Ghetto Revolt." *Social Problems* 16:393–408.

———. 1972. *Racial Oppression in America.* New York: Harper and Row.

Box, Steven. 1983. *Power, Crime, and Mystification.* London: Tavistock.

Braithwaite, John. 1989. *Crime, Shame and Reintegration.* Cambridge: Cambridge University Press.

———. 1993. "Pride in Criminological Dissensus." *Law and Social Inquiry* 18:501–512.

Chesney-Lind, Meda. 1989. "Girl's Crime and Woman's Place: Toward a Feminist Model of Female Delinquency." *Crime and Delinquency* 35(1):5–29.

Chesney-Lind, Meda, and Randall G. Sheldon. 1992. *Girls, Delinquency and Juvenile Justice.* Pacific Grove, CA: Brooks/Cole.

Cloward, Richard A., and Lloyd E. Ohlin. 1960. *Delinquency and Opportunity—A Theory of Delinquent Gangs.* New York: Free Press.

Cohen, Albert K. 1955. *Delinquent Boys: The Culture of the Gang.* Glencoe, IL: Free Press.

Cohen, Lawrence E., and Marcus Felson. 1979. "Social Change and Crime Rate Trends: A Routine Activities Approach." *American Sociological Review* 44:588–608.

Cohen, Lawrence E., and Richard Machalek. 1988. "A General Theory of Expropriative Crime: An Evolutionary Ecological Approach." *American Journal of Sociology* 94:465–501.

Coleman, James W. 1987. "Toward an Integrated Theory of White-Collar Crime." *American Journal of Sociology* 93:406–439.

———. 1994. *The Criminal Elite.* New York: St. Martin's Press.

Colvin, Mark, and John Pauly. 1983. "A Critique of Criminology: Toward an Integrated Structural-Marxist Theory of Delinquency Production." *American Journal of Sociology* 89:513–551.

Cornish, Derek B., and Ronald V. Clarke, eds. 1986. *The Reasoning Criminal.* New York: Springer Verlag.

Cullen, Francis T. 1983. *Rethinking Crime and Deviance Theory: The Emergence of a Structuring Tradition.* Totowa, NJ: Rowman and Allenheld.

Curran, Daniel J., and Claire M. Renzetti. 1994. *Theories of Crime.* Boston: Allyn and Bacon.

Einstadter, Werner, and Stuart Henry. 1995. *Criminological Theory: An Analysis of Its Underlying Assumptions.* Fort Worth, TX: Harcourt Brace College Publishers.

Elliott, Delbert. 1985. "The Assumption That Theories Can Be Combined with Increased Explanatory Power." In R. F. Meier, ed. *Theoretical Methods in Criminology.* Beverly Hills, CA: Sage.

Elliott, Delbert, Susan Ageton, and Rachelle Cantor. 1979. "An Integrated Theoretical Perspective on Delinquent Behavior." *Journal of Research on Crime and Delinquency* 16:3–27.

Elliott, Delbert, David Huizinga, and Susan Ageton. 1985. *Explaining Delinquency and Drug Use.* Beverly Hills, CA: Sage.

Elliott, Delbert, David Huizinga, and Scott Menard. 1989. *Multiple Problem Youth.* New York: Springer Verlag.

Empey, LaMar T., and Mark C. Stafford. 1991. *American Delinquency, Its Meanings and Construction.* 3rd ed. Belmont: Wadsworth.

Fanon, Frantz. 1963. *The Wretched of the Earth.* New York: Prentice-Hall.

———. 1967. *A Dying Colonialism.* New York: Grove Press.

Gibbons, Don C. 1992. "Talking About Crime: Observations on the Prospects for Causal Theory in Criminology." *Criminal Justice Research Bulletin* 7(6): 1–10.

———. 1994. *Talking About Crime and Criminals: Problems and Issues in Theory Development in Criminology.* Englewood Cliffs, NJ: Prentice-Hall.

Gibbs, Jack P. 1989. *Control: Sociology's Central Notion.* Urbana, IL: University of Illinois Press.

Giddens, Anthony. 1984. *The Constitution of Society: Outline of the Theory of Structuration.* Oxford: Polity Press.

Gottfredson, Michael R., and Travis Hirschi. 1990. *A General Theory of Crime.* Stanford: Stanford University Press.

Hagan, John. 1988. "Feminist Scholarship, Relational and Instrumental Control, and a Power-Control Theory of Gender and Delinquency." *British Journal of Sociology* 39(3): 301–336.

———. 1989. *Structural Criminology.* New Brunswick, NJ: Rutgers University Press.

———. 1990. "The Structuration of Gender and Deviance: A Power-Control Theory of Vulnerability to Crime and the Search for Deviant Role Exits." *Canadian Review of Sociology and Anthropology* 27(2): 137–156.

Hagan, John, and A. Palloni. 1986. "Toward a Structural Criminology." *Annual Review of Sociology* 12:431–439.

Hagan, John, A. R. Gillis, and John Simpson. 1985. "The Class Structure and Delinquency: Toward a Power-Control Theory of Common Delinquent Behavior." *American Journal of Sociology* 90:1151–1178.

Hawkins, Darnell. 1986. *Black Homicide.* Lanham, Maryland: University of American Press.

Henry, Stuart, and Dragan Milovanovic. 1996. *Constitutive Criminology: Beyond Postmodernism.* London: Sage.

Hirschi, Travis. 1979. "Separate and Equal Is Better." *Journal of Research in Crime and Delinquency* 16:34–38.

———. 1987. "Review." *Criminology* 35: 193–201.

———. 1989. "Exploring Alternatives to Integrated Theory." In S. F. Messner, M. D. Krohn, and A. E. Liska, eds., *Theoretical Integration in the Study of Deviance and Crime: Problems and Prospects.* Albany, NY: SUNY Press.

Johnson, Richard E. 1979. *Juvenile Delinquency and Its Origins.* Cambridge: Cambridge University Press.

Kaplan, Howard B. 1975. *Self-Attitudes and Deviant Behavior.* Pacific Palisades, CA: Goodyear.

———. 1993. "Toward a General Theory of Deviance: Contributions from Perspectives on Delinquency and Criminality." Paper presented at the Annual Meeting of the American Society of Criminology, Phoenix, AZ.

Kornhauser, Ruth R. 1978. *Social Sources of Delinquency.* Chicago: University of Chicago Press.

Krohn, Marvin D. 1986. "The Web of Conformity: A Network Approach to the Explanation of Delinquent Behavior." *Social Problems* 33:81–93.

Liska, Allen E., Marvin D. Krohn, and Steven F. Messner. 1989. "Strategies and Requisites for Theoretical Integration in the Study of Crime and Deviance." In S. F. Messner, M. D. Krohn and A. E. Liska, eds. *Theoretical Integration in the Study of Deviance and Crime: Problems and Prospects.* Albany, NY: SUNY Press.

Lofland, John. 1969. *Deviance and Identity.* Englewood Cliffs, NJ: Prentice-Hall.

Marenin, Otwin. 1994. "The Coming Shift to Complexifying Theory (and Policy)." Paper presented at the Annual Meeting of the American Society of Criminology, Miami.

Markowitz, Michael W. 1994. "Toward the Progressive Development of Criminological Theory: An Application of the 'Articulation Project.'" Paper presented at the Annual Meeting of the American Society of Criminology, Miami.

Matsueda, Ross L. 1992. "Reflected Appraisals, Parental Labeling, and Delinquency: Specifying a Symbolic Interactionist Theory." *American Journal of Sociology* 97:1577–1611.

Menard, Scott, and Delbert Elliott. 1994. "Delinquent Bonding, Moral Beliefs, and Illegal Behavior: A Three-Wave Panel Model." *Justice Quarterly* 11:173–188.

Merton, Robert K. 1938. "Social Structure and Anomie." *American Sociological Review* 3:672–682.

Messerschmidt, James W. 1986. *Capitalism, Patriarchy, and Crime: Toward a Socialist Feminist Criminology.* Totowa, NJ: Rowman and Littlefield.

———. 1993. *Masculinities and Crime: Critique and Reconceptualization of Theory.* Boston: Rowman and Littlefield.

Messner, Steven F., and Richard Rosenfeld. 1994. *Crime and the American Dream.* Belmont, CA: Wadsworth Publishing Company.

Messner, Steven F. and Marvin D. Krohn. 1990. "Class, Compliance Structures, and Delinquency: Assessing Integrated Structural-Marxist Theory." *American Journal of Sociology* Sept (95):300–328.

Messner, Steven F., Marvin D. Krohn, and Allen E. Liska. 1989. *Theoretical Integration in the Study of Deviance and Crime: Problems and Prospects.* Albany, NY: SUNY Press.

Miethe, Terance D., and Robert F. Meier. 1994. *Crime and Its Social Context: Toward an Integrated Theory of Offenders, Victims, and Situations.* Albany, NY: SUNY Press.

Pearson, Frank S., and Neil A. Weiner. 1985. "Toward an Integration Criminological Theories." *Journal of Criminal Law and Criminology* 76:116–150.

Quinney, Richard. 1977. *Class, State, and Crime*. New York: David McKay.

Reckless, Walter. 1973. *The Crime Problem*. Englewood Cliffs, NY: Prentice-Hall.

Roundtree, Pamela W., Kenneth C. Land, and Terance D. Miethe. 1994. "Macro-Micro Integration in the Study of Victimization: A Hierarchical Logistic Model Analysis Across Seattle Neighborhoods." *Criminology* 32:387–414.

Schur, Edwin M. 1984. *Labelling Women Deviant: Gender, Stigma, and Social Control*. New York: Random House.

Schwendinger, Herman, and Julia Schwendinger. 1985. *Adolescent Subcultures and Delinquency*. New York: Praeger.

Shoemaker, Donald J. 1990. *Theories of Delinquency: An Examination of Explanations of Delinquent Behavior*. 2nd ed. New York: Oxford University.

Staples, Robert. 1974. "Internal Colonialism and Black Violence." *Black World* 23:16–34.

———. 1975. "White Racism, Black Crime and American Justice: An Application of the Colonial Model to Explain Race and Crime." *Phylon* 36:14–22.

———. 1989. *The Urban Plantation*. Oakland, CA: The Black Scholar Press.

Stark, Rodney. 1987. "Deviant Places: A Theory of the Ecology of Crime." *Criminology* 25:893–909.

Sutherland, Edwin H. 1947. *Criminology*. 4th ed. Philadelphia: Lippincott.

Tatum, Becky. 1995. Race, Class, Alienation and Delinquency: Assessing Motivational Factors Through the Application of Structural Models. Doctoral Dissertation. Albany, NY: State University of New York.

———. 1996. "The Colonial Model as a Theoretical Explanation of Crime and Delinquency." In Anne T. Sulton, ed., *African-American Perspectives on Crime Causation, Criminal Justice Administration, and Crime Prevention*. Boston: Butterworth-Heinemann.

Thornberry, Terence P. 1987. "Toward an Interactional Theory of Delinquency." *Criminology* 25:863–887.

Unnithan, N. Prabha, Jay Corzine, Lin Huff-Corzine, and Hugh P. Whitt. 1994. *The Currents of Lethal Violence: An Integrated Model of Suicide and Homicide*. Albany, NY: SUNY Press.

Vila, Bryan. 1994. "A General Paradigm for Understanding Criminal Behavior: Extending Evolutionary Ecological Theory." *Criminology* 32:311–360.

Vold, George B., and Thomas J. Bernard. 1986. *Theoretical Criminology*. 3rd ed. New York: Oxford University Press.

Wells, Edward L. 1978. "Theories of Deviance and the Self-Concept." *Social Psychology* 41:189–204.

Wilson, James Q., and Richard J. Herrnstein. 1985. *Crime and Human Nature*. New York: Simon and Schuster.

# Integrating Criminological Knowledges: A Post-Postmodern Synthesis

The Oklahoma bombed Federal Building, 1995.

In the age of ultramodern capitalism, Stephen Pfohl (1993: 125) argues that "the parasitism of capitalist power shifts to a New World Order of social domination based not simply upon the exploitation of human labor, but upon the technological invasion of human bodies by cybernetic feedback mechanisms, high-speed image processing, and self-liquifying social control." In today's innerconnected yet alienated and fragmented world of instantaneous telecommunications, the modernist preoccupation with making logical sense out of crime and social control has been joined by the postmodernist recognition of the need to make sensory sense, too. As Jeff Ferrell (1995: 1) states, "Situated pleasures, shared excitement, and 'adrenalin rushes' define the experience and meaning of crime for many of those who participate in it. . . . These moments of illicit pleasure and excitement . . . reproduce and resist the structures of social class, consumption, gender, and sexuality out of which criminality arises." Hence, explanations of crime, criminals, victims, and crime fighters should incorporate images that make sensory as well as logical sense.

It is not that sensory knowledge is something new. On the contrary, this type of knowledge predates modernist knowledge. However, during most of modernity, the body's senses were primarily struggling without intrusions from the social sciences. Over the past quarter of a century, with the emergence of what has ultimately become known as postmodernist knowledge, there has been a rediscovery of the senses.

For example, in *Seductions of Crime: Moral and Sensual Attractions in Doing Evil*, Jack Katz (1988) writes about the emotional logic and moral appeal involving murder, shoplifting, burglary, and vandalism in relation to censored desires rather than material deprivations. Similarly, the contributors to *Cultural Criminology* focus their examination of crime and culture on various collective behaviors (e.g., outlaw biker groups, skinhead violence, urban graffiti, youth gangs) organized around imagery, style, and symbolic meaning, and the pleasure derived from resisting authority and engaging in repressed areas of life (Ferrell and Sanders, 1995). A psychoanalytically informed perspective also views crime and punishment, criminality and noncriminality as dyads that share unconscious partnerships full of complex webs of repression, resistance, and reaction-formation (Duncan, 1996).

More generally, "the unspoken yearning for life to make aesthetic sense is a demand for existential integration of action and feeling, of deeds and consequences" (Broudy, 1991: 68). H. S. Broudy believes that the achievement of such unity by either science or art would be a milestone in the human enterprise of knowledge creation. Perhaps more realistically, I believe that such an integrated understanding calls for a synthesis of science and art, recognizing at the same time that the two are never fully separated anyway.

Zetetic studies, or the *science of research and artistic activity*, for example, has been one approach to the study of human knowledge as a whole, including its origins, growth, and transitions. One of its earliest founders was an electrical engineering professor, Joseph T. Tykociner, who as far back as the 1950s dreamed of integrating all research and knowledge in the sciences and humanities. Figure 10.1 depicts Tykociner's Zetetics and the Zetetic System of Knowledge, with its special terminology and a detailed mapping of systems of knowledge, including their functions and their interconnections.

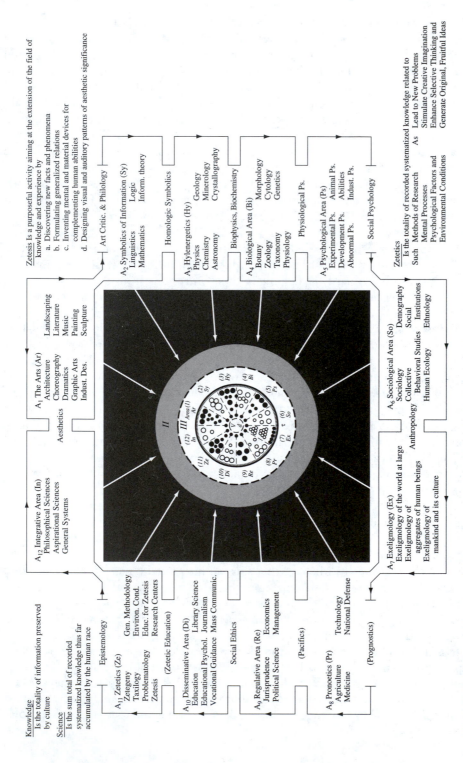

**FIGURE 10.1   Tykociner's Zetetics and the Zetetic System of Knowledge**

*From:* H. S. Broudy, "Integraton without Confusion," *Issues in Integrative Studies* (1991, No. 9), page 70. Reprinted with permission.

To appreciate the kind of synthesis accomplished by integrating criminologies, it is useful to briefly describe Zetetics and the philosophy of integration proposed by Tykociner (1959; 1966). Zetetics refers to the totality of culturally appropriated and recorded systematized knowledge related to methods of research, mental processes, psychological factors, and environmental conditions that are believed to establish new problems, to stimulate creative imaginations, to enhance selective thinking, and to generate original and fruitful ideas. Zetesis, or the practice of Zetetics, refers to purposeful activities aimed at the extension of the field of knowledge and experience by discovering new facts, formulating generalized relations, inventing mental and material devices for complementing human abilities, and designing visual and auditory patterns of aesthetic significance. A "zetetics of criminology" seems to be the culturally and globally "green" thing to do. Integrating our different criminologies, then, consistent with both a practice of Zetetics and the historical development of criminological inquiry, seems to me to represent at least one post-postmodern approach to crime and justice.

The integrative-constitutive framework developed in this chapter, although not as extensive as the zetetic system of knowledge, nevertheless represents an attempt to synthesize the specialized bodies of criminological and related knowledge. Always in a state of becoming, both of these frameworks are open ended and without closure. The very concept of *constitution* reflects the duality of "being built while building, of being made while making, of parts making wholes of which they are constituents" (Henry and Milovanovic, 1996: ix).

According to constitutive criminology, crime is the expression of energy to make a difference over others; it is the power to deny others, thus rendering the latter powerless to make their own differences—to create their own knowledge and action. Its theoretical contribution assumes, among other things, that humans are responsible for actively constructing their own world:

> *They do this by transforming their surroundings through interaction with others, not least via discourse. Through language and symbolic representation they identify differences, construct categories, and share a belief in the reality of that which is constructed that orders otherwise chaotic states. It is towards these social constructions of reality that humans act.*
>
> *In the process of investing energy in their socially constructed, discursively organized categories of order and reality, human subjects not only shape the world, but are shaped by it. They are co-producers and co-productions of their own and others' agency. They are channeled and changed, enabled and constrained, but all the time, building (Henry and Milovanovic, 1996: ix).*

In other words, crimes are recursive productions, routinized activities that have become part and parcel of historically and culturally specific discourses that have attained a relative stability over time and space. Materialistically rooted, these discourses of inequality "become coordinates of social action whereby 'criminals' are no less than 'excessive investors' in the accumulation and expression of power and control" (Henry and Milovanovic, 1996: x).

Constitutive criminology maintains that crime and crime control are indeterminable, interactional, interrelational, dynamic, and dialectical phenomena. As such, constitutive criminology presumes that causation in the positivist, predictive, determinist, and linear sense does not exist. That is, in the real, nonsocial scientific world neither criminals nor crimes are static, except when criminologists and others freeze the social reality of either for the purposes of trying to identify independent and dependent variables. Nevertheless, in terms of a soft determinist, neopositivist, and post-postmodern integration, "cause" may refer to the influences and variations that are possible in the context of the multiple interrelations of discourses, ideologies, imaginations, unconsciousnesses, histories, and political economies, all of which are never fully separated from each other (Henry and Milovanovic, 1996).

In this sense, crimes are coproduced outcomes of constitutive interrelational sets of motivations, routines, and resources. Each of these "subjects" of crime, in turn, may be viewed as "objects" for domination that represent coproduced reflections of all the other interrelated signifiers that are connected in continuous and noncontinuous ways that seek to reinforce mutually credible courses of action, ranging from illegal to legal behavior. Whether one is referring to those offenders experiencing ennui, rage, rationalization, seduction, or dehumanization, or one is referring to those victims experiencing harms of reduction or harms of repression, constitutive criminology assumes that both are the result of unequal power relations. At the same time, constitutive criminology recognizes as fundamental that overlapping spheres of particular "energies" coexist and that the intensity of these will vary over time. Thus, it makes more sense to speak about "indicators" or "influences" rather than "factors," "variables," and "causes" of crime. In terms of reducing the harms of reduction and the harms of repression (see Chapter 12), constitutive criminology talks in terms of "replacement discourses." These discourses of postmodernism allow back into discussion the aesthetic and sensual knowledges of crime and social control that were jettisoned by modernist sciences. In turn, these alternative discourses seek not only to socially transform the practices of crime and crime control, but also to change the associated practices of the prevailing political, social, and economic relations. The reasoning here is simple: Since crime is the outcome of its totality rather than a product of its parts (Henry and Milovanovic, 1996), the addressing of crime control and social change in terms of their dynamic totality can never be separated from the developing political economies.

From a constitutive perspective, by integrating criminologies we arrive at the synthesis of: (1) the material realities of harms of reduction and harms of repression; (2) the knowledges and discourses of criminology as represented by the social (and natural) sciences, the arts and humanities (including law), and popular culture; and (3) the dynamic interaction between social ecologies and the developing local, regional, and global political economies. This integrative-constitutive framework provides a model of crime and justice that incorporates the overlapping knowledges of classical, positivist, and critical criminology. It also establishes a "paradigm of modernity–postmodernity" capable of connecting what appears to be disparate or contradictory bodies of knowledge (Giddens, 1984). Finally, such a criminological stance appreciates that there are intervening processes that have mediating effects on the so-called "independent variables" of crime that modernist theories ignore (Agnew, 1995).

## *Modernist versus Postmodernist Thought: Dueling Paradigms and the Need for Synthesis*

Milovanovic (1995) has outlined the differences between modernist and postmodernist thought. In the Kuhnian sense that paradigms tend to crystallize around key validity claims, he has identified these modes of inquiry as "dueling paradigms" (see Table 10.1). Succinctly, the modernist mode represents the "normal science" of deductive logic, whereas the postmodernist mode represents the "revolutionary new science" of deconstruction and reconstruction. The perspective adopted here assumes that both these modes of science in combination and integrated with the knowledges of aesthetics associated with, for example, film theory are fuller ways to examine crime and social

### TABLE 10.1   Dueling Paradigms

|  | Modernist | Postmodernist |
|---|---|---|
| Society and Social Structure | Balanced, in equilibrium<br>Centered<br>Overencompassing, consensus-oriented<br>e.g., Freud, Hegel, Marx, Weber | Unbalanced, in flux<br>Decentered<br>Nonencompassing, conflict-oriented<br>Derrida, Foucault, Lacan, Lyotard |
| Social Roles | Individual as a member of a symphony orchestra. | Individual as a member of a jazz ensemble. |
| Subjectivity/ Agency | Humans are conscious, self-directed, and unified.<br>Desire to be checked. | Humans are unconscious too, determined, and nonunified.<br>Desire to be revered. |
| Discourse | Focuses more on the material and social. | Focuses more on the emotive and psychic. |
| Knowledge | Logics of science<br>Formal rationality<br>Universal, global | Logics of narration<br>Informal rationality<br>Situational, contingency |
| Space/Time | Unitary notions of space and whole dimensions.<br>Newtonian physics, Euclidian geometry | Multiple kinds of space and fractal dimensions.<br>Chaos theory, Twister Space |
| Causality | Empirical, deterministic, proportional<br>Focus is on measuring particles, points, and sequential events so as to prove the effect of input variables. | Hermeneutic, indeterministic, disproportional<br>Focus is on fields, moments, and flows of displaced energies that can not be precisely located or measured. |
| Social Change | Emphases are evolutionary, whether linear or dialectical.<br>Social planning is based on incremental adjustments. | Emphases are nonevolutionary, interactive, and historically specific.<br>Social planning is based on cultural adjustments. |

control than are the either/or approaches of modernism versus postmodernism commonly adopted by most criminologists, critical or conventional. To put it most directly, one mode without the other mode is simply incomplete and, at best, can generate only partial explanations of human interaction.

Before turning to a discussion of some of the fundamental differences between these two modes of thought, it must be acknowledged that the terms "modern" and "postmodern" occupy no fixed positions; their meanings are imprecise and highly contested. For example, some regard postmodernism as simply a perspective for understanding the conditions of late capitalism. Others view postmodernism as a new epoch, or a new historical era. In either case, the roots of postmodern analysis are located in French thought, particularly during the late 1960s and 1970s when the transition away from Hegelian to Nietzschean thought took place. At the same time, Lacanian notions of the subject, the framing effects of discourse, and the nature of the symbolic order began to challenge the modernist claims of the liberating potentials of the social sciences, of the materialistic gains of capitalism, and of the legal safeguards and abstract rights applicable to all individuals. Despite some ambiguity, these concepts usually refer to the critical reference points "that try to make sense of what appear to be disparate cultural, economic, political, and social changes taking place in architecture, art, philosophy, literary criticism, the social sciences, in every-day life, in popular culture, in industry, business, technology, and education" (Bloland, 1995: 523). Moreover, from an integrative-constitutive point of view, it makes little difference when this body of knowledge emerged because, as a method for investigating crime and social control, postmodernist knowledge can be used to examine any period or historical conditions.

For the purposes of this discussion, Harland G. Bloland's characterization of modernism and postmodernism in higher education is useful for understanding the criminological need to find common ground.

> *Modernism requires faith that there are universals that can be discovered through reason, that science and the scientific method are superior means for arriving at truth and reality, and that language describes and can be used as a credible and reliable means of access to that reality. With its privileging of reason, modernism has long been considered the basis for emancipation of men and women from the bonds of ignorance associated with stagnant tradition, narrow religions, and meager educations. Championing democracy, modernism promises freedom, equality, justice, the good life, and prosperity. Equating merit with high culture, modernism provides expectations of more rigorous standards for and greater enjoyment of the arts and architecture. Through science and scientific method, modernism promises health, the eradication of hunger, crime, and poverty. Modernist science claims to be progressing toward true knowledge of the universe and to be delivering ever higher standards of living with effectiveness and efficiency. Modernism promises stability, peace, and a graspable sense of the rational unfolding of history. Modernism equates change with progress, which is defined as increasing control over nature and society (Bloland, 1995: 524).*

By contrast, postmodernism problematizes the very notions of modernist order, control, and power. The point is that the major concepts and ideas of postmodernism provide a devastating attack on modernism.

> *Postmodernism interrogates the modern system, which is built on continuing, persistent efforts to totalize or unify, pointing out that totalization hides contradictions, ambiguities, and oppositions and is a means for generating power and control. . . . To see postmodernism as a way of understanding the limits of modernism is to view our world in the midst of profound change and to concentrate on the disillusionment we are experiencing with some of our deepest assumptions and cherished hopes relating to our most important institutions. We seek rational solutions in a world that increasingly distrusts reason as a legitimate approach to problem solving. We try to move forward in our lives and through our institutions in a milieu of declining faith in the possibility of progress (Bloland, 1995: 525–526).*

In short, according to postmodernist thought, neither the social sciences in general nor criminology in particular contain any grand narratives or universal laws of social behavior. Nor do postmodernist knowledges pretend to have a lock on any such narratives or laws, arguing, instead, that these are socially constructed illusions.

From my perspective, the major integrative question is to know whether it is possible to bring together these different modes of thought into some kind of holistic framework. Once again, for me, this is important because an integration of these two modes of thought would enable the most comprehensive understanding of crime and social control possible. Albeit many would argue that an integration involving modernist and postmodernist modes of social inquiry is an impossibility and, even if this were not the case, the integration of the two is to deny each mode of thought its distinctive integrity. By contrast, it is my contention that bringing the two modes together, without denying or dissolving their differences, invigorates the inquiry of both. At the beginning of his comparison of the modernist and postmodernist paradigms, for example, Milovanovic (1995: 1) acknowledges: "Although presented as dichotomies, the differences often fall along a continuum; some tending toward further polarization; others becoming discontinuities, such as the differences between the centered and de-centered subject, the privileging of disorder rather than order, the emphasis on Pathos rather than Logos, etc."

Specifically, in clarifying the more salient differences between modernist and postmodernist thought, Milovanovic (1995) selected eight dimensions to examine: (1) society and social structure, (2) social roles, (3) subjectivity/agency, (4) discourse, (5) knowledge, (6) space/time, (7) causality, and (8) social change. Although the key concepts of modernist and postmodernist can certainly be juxtaposed as Milovanovic has done, it is my contention that these different ways of posing and answering questions of social science, represent paradigmatically two necessary systems for organizing knowledge about crime and justice.

Despite the real and alleged differences between the modernist and postmodernist paradigms, it is these differences (and similarities) and the tensions or contradictions between them that, I believe, are constitutive of the fullest possible explanation of crime and crime control. Once again, I believe, taken together these two modes account for all the involved energies, even those that I would contend are really overlapping rather than opposing. Referring to Milovanovic's dichotomy of modernism and postmodernism, one can take issue with his classicist notion of agency to characterize the modern subject and with his notion of the postmodernist subject as a determining rather than a resisting subject. In modernist criminology, for example, positivist theories typically ascribe crime to determined rather than reasoning subjects. A post-postmodernist criminology, by contrast, ascribes crime to both the determining and determined subject. Instead of accentuating and, at times, confusing these differences, I believe it makes far more sense to celebrate their complementary points of view on human nature, social organization, and conforming and nonconforming patterns of behavior. In the spirit of postmodernism, neither paradigm has any special foundational credentials. It becomes possible that "dueling paradigms" could, with practical human intervention, produce a cross-fertilization of social science that bridges the different images of research on crime and justice. New methodologies, in short, that explore their mutually overlapping realities are called for.

One way of bridging or integrating knowledges is through the notion of texts. For example, the sociologist Richard Harvey Brown (1989: 1) maintains that "the conflict that exists in our culture between the vocabularies of scientific discourse and of narrative discourse, between positivism and romanticism, objectivism and subjectivism, and between system and lifeworld can be synthesized through a poetics of truth that views social science and society as texts." According to this view, "language is not a reflection either of the world or of the mind. Instead, it is a social historical *practice*" (Brown, 1989: 2). Moreover, the textual perspective claims that "the meanings of words are not taken from things or intentions, but arise from socially coordinated actions" (Brown, 1989: 2).

In order for such an integrative modernist–postmodernist paradigm to develop in criminology, we as criminologists will have to move well beyond our myopic worlds of competitive theories to a place for real and continuing dialogue. If criminology is to obtain the integrative objective of synthesizing these divergent modes of thinking, then it will have to reach a point wherein the postmodern stricture to listen and listen very hard and long to the other has strong currency. As Bloland (1995: 554) has noted in relationship to the academy more generally,

> Currently, we are precariously poised between a modern/postmodern incommensurable hostility and the conditions for tough authentic dialogue. In higher education our course is clear. We need to increase and sustain the dialogue, even as we acknowledge that the tension will not, and perhaps should not, be resolved.

## The Case for Knowledge Synthesis: Textuality and Society

A textualist understanding of social science and society, explicitly eschewed by the dominant positivist (modernist) epistemology, "stresses the constitutive rather than the causal or even the communicative dimensions of social practice. It thereby alerts us to the processes by which discourse becomes reified as a mirror of the very things, categories, and relations that it creates" (Brown, 1989: 15). Moreover, a textual analysis of knowledge argues ultimately that "both objectivist or positivist science, and subjectivist romantic hermeneutics, though apparently opposites, are in fact dialectically interdependent views of knowledge, self, and society" (Brown, 1989: 3). Although a vision of integrating criminologies includes multiple possibilities of synthesis, three different but related exercises of integration practiced by Robert Sampson and John Laub (1993), Bryan Vila (1994), and Bruce Arrigo (1995) are discussed briefly as useful integrations for criminologists to pursue.

In *Crime in the Making,* Sampson and Laub (1993) provide a model of "the pathways and turning points through life" characteristic of the social construction of crime. They argue that throughout the life course, the gaps or missing connections in criminological studies have resulted from the failures "to examine the processes of social control from childhood through adulthood" and "to account for major discontinuities, as well as continuities in development" (Sampson and Laub, 1993: 14). For a representation of their dynamic model of crime, deviance, and informal social control, see Figure 10.2.

The key to Sampson and Laub's developmental or "stepping stone" approach to delinquency and crime is located in the narrative data of life histories. Although their central organizing idea is that of social control in a broad sense, they, nevertheless, join structural and process variables in a theoretical model that makes the control theory assumption that "crime and deviance result when an individual's bonds to society is weak or broken" (Sampson and Laub, 1993: 18). Sampson and Laub's explanation of crime emphasizes "the role of *informal* social controls that emerge from the role of reciprocities and structure of interpersonal bonds linking members of society to one another and to wider social institutions such as work, family, and school" (Sampson and Laub, 1993: 18). A fuller integrative perspective would also incorporate the role of *formal* social controls as these interact with the informal social controls.

Supported by a quantitative and qualitative reanalysis of Sheldon and Eleanor Glueck's classic mid-century data set of 500 delinquents and nondelinquents from childhood to adulthood, Sampson and Laub maintain that informal social controls mediate the effects of both individual and structural background variables, thereby explaining the substantial overprediction of future criminality by delinquents, and, conversely, the occurrence of adult criminality by formerly adolescent nondelinquents.

> *Our strategy also included a new way of portraying life histories of individuals in context. Namely, our quantitative findings were systematically challenged through an intensive examination of qualitative data drawn from the Gluecks' original case files. Integrating divergent sources of information on life histories, the qualitative analysis supported the central idea of our theoretical model that there are both stability and change in behavior over the life course, and that these changes are systematically linked to the institutions of work and family relations in adulthood (Sampson and Laub, 1993: 248).*

Bryan Vila (1994) has presented "A General Paradigm for Understanding Criminal Behavior" that is certainly consistent with the spirit of integrating criminologies. Vila's evolutionary ecological theory avoids the common pitfalls of competitive theories as it moves toward the interactions between causal factors across disciplines. On one level, Vila is trying to reconcile or integrate such theories as strain, control, labeling, and learning primarily derived from the discipline of social psychology. On

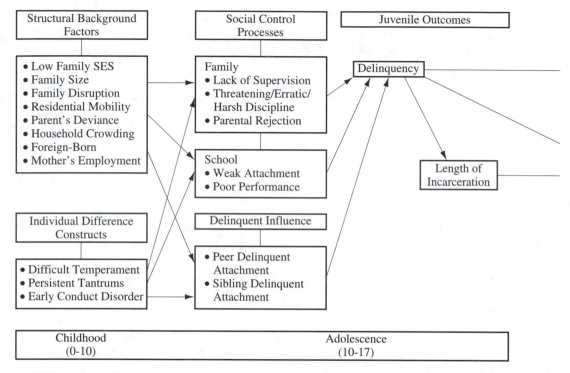

**FIGURE 10.2    Sampson and Laub's Dynamic Theoretical Model of Crime, Deviance, and Informal Social Control Over the Life Course**

Reprinted by permission of the publisher from *Crime in the Making: Pathways and Turning Points Through Life* by Robert J. Sampson and John J. Laub, Cambridge, Mass.: Harvard University Press. Copyright © 1993 by the President and Fellows of Harvard College.

another level, he is trying to understand changes over time and across disciplines that are derived in the "resource-acquisition" and "resource-retention" behaviors of social actors. Vila (1994: 315) pursues a model of synthesis, in short, that not only "has its roots in the 'interdiscipline' of evolutionary ecology, but [that] uses a problem-oriented, rather than a discipline-oriented, approach to understanding criminal behavior." For a representation of Vila's model of the "acquisition of behavior-influencing traits over the human life cycle," see Figure 10.3.

Finally, Arrigo (1995) has argued that the key to postmodernist integration is its nontotalizing analyses and nonglobalizing assessments. Postmodernist integrationists think of synthesis as referring to the "relational, positional, and provisional function to interpret, reinterpret, validate, and repudiate *multiple discourses* and their expressions of reality construction in divergent social arrangements" (Arrigo, 1995: 465). This form of integration does not "presume to understand the conditions or *the* causes of criminal or legal controversies by offering either a homeostatically based integrative model or a rigidly specialized theory" (Arrigo, 1995: 465). Postmodernist integration according to Arrigo (1995: 465) does, however, aspire to "understand the manifold and ever-

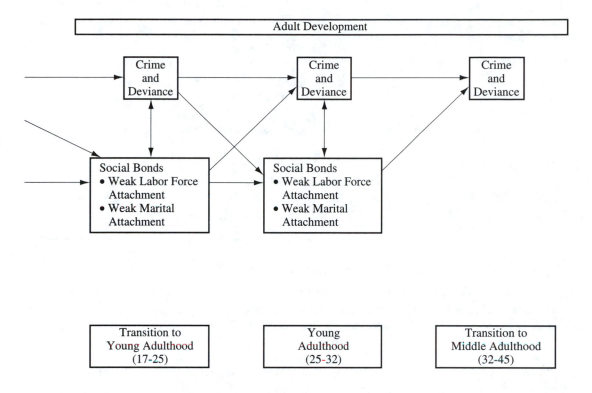

changing ways in which disparate groups communicate and give meaning to local sites of crime, justice, law, and community."

The contrastive and yet complementary analyses of Sampson and Laub, Vila, and Arrigo are not only consistent with Henry and Milovanovic's constitutive criminology, but they are also consonant with Anthony Giddens's (1984) "structuration theory" presented in his book *The Constitution of Society*. This theory, situated in the duality of objectivism and subjectivism, articulates a synthetic model for integrating criminologies.

## *Research Forms as Kinds of Knowledge: Integrating Methods*

Giddens (1984) examines both the tasks of social research and the traditional debate between quantitative and qualitative methods. He concludes that the research investigator can be inserted into the object of study at any one of four levels:

   **I.** Hermeneutic Elucidation of Frames of Meaning
  **II.** Investigation of Context and Form of Practical Consciousness (The Unconscious)
 **III.** Identification of Bounds of Knowledgeability
 **IV.** Specification of Institutional Orders

Giddens does not privilege any one of these levels of investigation, but simply views each as necessary parts in telling the full story of human behavior. To begin with,

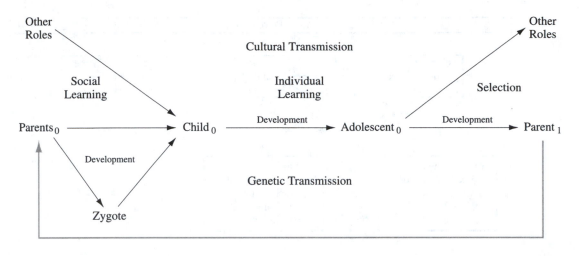

FIGURE 10.3    **Vila's Acquisition of Behavior-Influencing Traits over the Human Life Cycle**

*From:* Bryan Vila, "A General Paradigm for Understanding Criminal Behavior: Extending Evolutionary Ecological Theory," *Criminology* (1994, No. 3), page 332. Reprinted with permission.

all social science research, including criminological investigations, is hermeneutic (I). However, the presumption of interpretive (hermeneutic) moments frequently remains latent, especially "where research draws upon mutual knowledge that is unexplicated because researcher and research inhabit a common cultural *milieu*" (Giddens, 1984: 328). For instance, quantitative researchers often suppress the essential significance of interpretation in two ways. They either take level I–type analyses to be purely descriptive rather than explanatory, or they fail to see that the very formulation of research in the first place cannot be separated from various interpretations. Moreover, quantitative projects are often, but not always or necessarily, based on narrowly framed and taken-for-granted assumptions constructed in relatively limited rather than in expansive or ethnographic meanings.

In criminology, studies concerned with the meaning of crime and justice may be both explanatory and generalizing. Whether discussing ethnographic research on gangs or small-scale community research of informal and formal social control, these studies could, if replicated or carried out a number of times, become generalizable. As Giddens (1984: 328) emphasizes, "Research which is geared primarily to hermeneutic problems may be of generalized importance in so far as it serves to elucidate the nature of agents' knowledgeability and thereby their reasons for action, across a wide range of action-contexts." This is precisely the kind of information sought out by Sampson and Laub (1993) in *Crime in the Making* and in their "sociogenic" theory of informal social control played out through the pathways and turning points of life spans.

When it comes to level II analyses involving both the contexts and forms of practical consciousness/unconsciousness, only ethnomethodology circumscribes such an area or field for inquiry. Nevertheless, each of the other levels of research requires the interpretation of practical consciousness. Typically, however, whether implicitly understood or explicitly articulated, practical consciousness in theoretical criminology has relied on overdetermined models of rational or repressed criminals. In either case, the meaning of crime and the motivation of criminals have been viewed as part of the broader features of social conduct.

As Giddens argues, the study of unintended consequences and unacknowledged conditions of action can and should be carried on without using functionalist terminology. In other words, "no study of the structural properties of social systems [or crime] can be successfully carried on, or its results interpreted, without reference to the knowledgeability of the relevant agents" (Giddens, 1984: 329). Here it is also seen that identifying the boundaries of criminal and noncriminal knowledgeability in the sifting or developing contexts of time and space is fundamental to social science research on crime and its control. Once again, the investigation of level III presumes considerable knowledge of levels I, II, and IV. Without them, criminologists are confined to the untutored forms of structural sociology and overdetermination. The point is that "social data are never only an 'index' of an independently given phenomenon but always at the same time exemplify what it is they are 'about'—that is, processes of social life" (Giddens, 1984: 334).

Level IV refers to the specifying of institutional orders or to the largest units of analysis available to the social sciences. In the global political economy, institutional orders frequently cross-cut capitalist decisions or processes that are recognized between societies. This level of explanation involves analyzing the conditions of social and system integration via a description of the largest institutional (societal) components as these (re)produce everyday life in terms of designated structural principles, rather than in terms of social structures. According to Giddens's (1984: 374) duality of structure, "The structural properties of social systems do not exist outside of action but are chronically implicated in its production and reproduction."

Synergistically, all four levels of analysis are necessary to answer questions of social interaction and human development. Giddens (1984: 330) argues that the debate between the quantitative and qualitative social scientists, between those who favor so-called macrosociological analysis and those who favor so-called micro-interactive analysis, reflects the "methodological residue of the dualism of structure and action." His structuration theory contends that such a dualism is spurious and that social investigators need to be about the business of teasing out of "the empirical implications of the duality of structure" (Giddens, 1984: 330). Similarly, I am arguing that the dualism between modernism and postmodernism is spurious and that criminologists in particular need to be about the business of teasing out the empirical narratives of the duality of crime and criminal behavior.

Instead of focusing on either levels I and II because of a concern for the situated and meaningful character of social interaction as the qualitatively oriented do, or on levels III and IV because of a concern for the primacy of so-called macrosociological analysis and the application of quantitatively oriented methods, Giddens (1984: 334) argues that

> *I and II are thus as essential for understanding III and IV as vice versa, and qualitative and quantitative methods should be seen as complementary rather than antagonistic aspects of social research. Each is necessary to the other if the substantive nature of the duality of structure is to be "charted" in terms of the forms of institutional articulation whereby contexts of interaction are co-ordinated within more embracing social systems.*

This postmodern replacement of the modern dualism of structure, in other words, with a duality of structure recognizes *structure* to be both the medium and the outcome of the conduct it recursively organizes. Hence, crime and social control are coproductions of crime control because these are mediated in mass society.

Structuration analysis applies to both crime and crime control. In the case of the latter, Giddens shares a transcript of a strip of interaction in a courtroom involving a judge, a public defender (PD), and a district attorney (DA), who were discussing what the appropriate sentence should be for a detainee who had pleaded guilty to a second-degree burglary charge.

*PD:* Your honor, we request immediate sentencing and waive the probation report.

*Judge:* What's his record?

*PD:* He has a prior drunk and a GTO [grand theft, auto]. Nothing serious. This is just a shoplifting case. He did enter the K-mart with intent to steal. But really what we have here is a petty theft.

*Judge:* What do the people have?

*DA:* Nothing either way.

*Judge:* Any objections to immediate sentencing?

*DA:* No.

*Judge:* How long has he been in?

*PD:* Eighty-three days.

*Judge:* I make this a misdemeanour by PC article 17 and sentence you to ninety days in the County Jail, with credit for time served (quoted in Giddens, 1984: 330).

Finally, the ritualistic reproduction of the administration of criminal justice revealed in the above transcript is aptly captured by Giddens's analysis:

*Such a situated strip of interaction, like any other, can readily be pried open to indicate how what seems a trivial interchange is profoundly implicated in the reproduction of social institutions. Each turn in the talk exchanged between participants is grasped as meaningful by them (and by the reader) only by the tacit invocation of institutional features of the system of criminal justice. These are drawn upon by each speaker, who (rightly) assumes them to be mutual knowledge held also by the others. Note that the content of such mutual knowledge presumes vastly more than just awareness of the tactics of "proper procedure" in such cases, although that is also involved. Each participant knows a vast amount about what a "legal system" is, about normative procedures of law, about what prisoners, advocates, judges do, etc. In order to "bring off" the interaction, the participants make use of their knowledge of institutional order in which they are involved in such a way as to render their interchange "meaningful." However, by invoking the institutional order in this way—and there is no other way for participants in interaction to render what they do intelligible and coherent to one another—they thereby contribute to reproducing it. Moreover, it is essential to see that in reproducing it they also reproduce its "facticity" as a source of structural constraint (upon themselves and upon others). They treat the system of justice as a "real" order of relationships within which their own interaction is situated and which it expresses. And it is a "real" (i.e., structurally stable) order of relationships precisely because they, and others like them in connected and similar contexts, accept it as such—not necessarily in their discursive consciousness but in the practical consciousness incorporated in what they do (Giddens, 1984: 330–331).*

Simply stated, crime control is real precisely because these participants (and public spectators, media, and others) make it real. The same can be said of crime: It is real precisely because criminals, victims, crime fighters, the media, popular culture, and politics make it so.

## Integrating Knowledges: Toward a Post-Postmodern Synthesis

By integrating criminologies the researcher charts out the relations of the processes of social life that constitute the recursive pathways and tipping points in the integrative field of crime and crime control. In order to locate these social relations, it is argued, criminologists can best achieve this objective by unifying the visions and practices of both modernist and postmodernist criminology. By rejecting dualistic analyses in criminology that separate crime from criminals and noncriminals, that divide formal and informal systems of social control, and that disassociate crime and deviance from social ecology, and by favoring the duality of the structural relations of crime, criminals, and criminality, *Integrating Criminologies* attempts to bring to bear the available empirical and theoretical contributions from all those knowledge domains that impinge on the developmental aspects of crime, criminals, and crime control.

The message is that in order to understand human action and social interaction, involving both conforming and nonconforming behavior, it is necessary that the various knowledges from economics, philosophy, anthropology, biochemistry, psychology, law, sociology, cultural studies, ethnic studies, gender studies, media studies, political economy, and social history, which constitute the interdisciplinary field of criminology, be consulted and brought together as an integrative paradigm of modernity-postmodernity.

The goal of this kind of synthesis of interdisciplinary knowledges is to liberate the social relations or connections between all of the available knowledges that penetrate the worlds of crime and its control. To do anything else seems indefensible. It also seems foolish to continue to deny the wealth of criminological contributions from numerous cites. In terms of the duality of modernity and postmodernity, it also appears that interdisciplinary narratives of crime and crime control are the most sensible ways to facilitate the kind of integrative process envisioned here.

Theoretically, I am not talking about propositional equations but rather I am talking about discursive narratives and cultural production, including precisely the kinds of crime and justice a society makes. In order to fully comprehend or explain criminology as well as crime and crime control, a *post-postmodern integrative synthesis* incorporates the contributions from the classical, positivist, and critical criminologies. Beyond that, integrating criminologies requires the synthesis of these modernist knowledges with postmodernist thought. Finally, the interaction between these knowledges and popular knowledges (e.g., popular culture, mass communications) in the context of social ecologies and developing political economies accounts for the constitutive forms and practices of the harms of reduction and repression.

Before turning to Chapters 11 and 12 where narrative interdisciplinary approaches to crime and crime control are respectively presented, see Figure 10.4, which depicts an integrative system of classifying criminological thought, and Figure 10.5, which depicts a dynamic model of criminalization and social control. In Figure 10.4 a cultural "wheel" of criminological knowledges and discourses is represented as flowing and revolving in overlapping and interconnecting circles of disciplinarian fields. Moreover, this constitutive mapping is suggestive of the modernist and postmodernist dividing lines, recognizing, at the same time, how there are no real dividing lines in knowledge as the free flow of ideas keeps everything open and possible. In Figure 10.5 the world of crime and criminalization is represented as the intersection or point of convergence between the larger "environmental relations" of telecommunications, global political economy, culture, and so forth; the informal and formal "relations of social control"; and the "personal and community histories" of actual harms and injuries. Taken together, these two conceptualizations of knowledge and crime represent the interterritorial spaces where integrating criminologies can occur.

## Summary and Conclusions: Constituting Crime and Crime Reduction

When integrating criminologies we assume that many knowledges have a relationship with crime and its control. For example, both crime and crime control are reflective of age, sex, race, class, and other characteristics because these intersect with each other as well as with the personal sociohistorical experiences of individuals as members of distinct communities. Nonintegrationist criminologists, assuming otherwise, spend an inordinate amount of time arguing over and trying to prove the merits of one theory

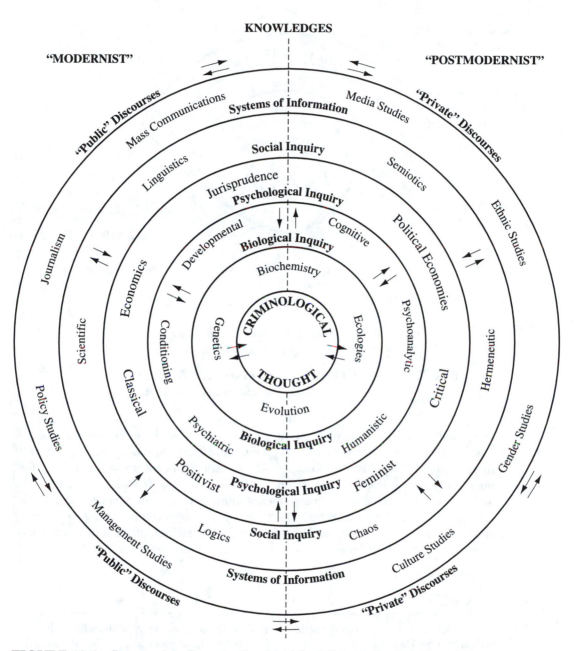

**FIGURE 10.4   Integrative-Constitutive Model of Criminological Knowledge**

over the other. More specifically, they seek to prove which of these theories of crime and crime control is more predictive than the other, and which of these may not be relevant at all. Integrationist or constitutive criminologists, by contrast, believing that it is more important to focus on all of the energies involved in the production of both

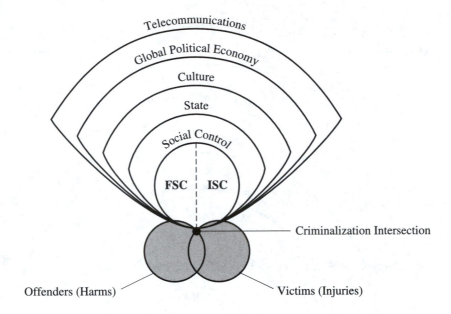

FSC = Formal Social Controls (police, courts, & corrections)
ISC = Informal Social Controls (family, school, community)

**FIGURE 10.5    An Integrative-Constitutive Model of
Criminalization and Social Control**

crime and crime control, play down the internecine warfare between competing theories that ultimately will not be able to predict individual criminality anyway. Short of turning to individual histories to explain the variations in conformity and nonconformity of persons, the tasks of integrating criminologies are to discuss and articulate the ways in which these constitutive elements interact to generally coproduce (1) the crimes committed by adolescents, adults, the public, corporations, and governments; and (2) the patterns, policies, and practices of the formal and informal means of social control. The rest of this book turns its attention to these two tasks.

## Discussion Questions

1. How does constitutive criminology explain both crime and criminal behavior?

2. Compare and contrast the modernist and postmodernist understandings of law, order, and criminality.

3. Why does Barak argue that explanations of crime and social control require the integration of both modernist and postmodernist approaches?

4. Explain the differences and the relationships between Giddens's four levels of investigating human experience.

5. What are the similarities and differences between Sampson and Laub's contemporary pathways and turning points through life analysis of crime and the Gluecks' analyses of delinquency before and after World War II?

# References

Agnew, Robert S. 1995. "Testing the Leading Crime Theories: An Alternative Strategy Focusing on Intervening Processes." Paper presented at the Annual Meetings of the Academy of Criminal Justice Sciences, March, Boston.

Arrigo, Bruce A. 1995. "The Peripheral Core of Law and Criminology: On Postmodern Social Theory and Conceptual Integration." *Justice Quarterly* 12(30): 447–472.

Bloland, Harland G. 1995. "Postmodernism and Higher Education." *Journal of Higher Education* 66(5): 521–559.

Broudy, H. S. 1991. "Integration Without Confusion." *Issues in Integrative Studies* 9:67–74.

Brown, Richard Harvey. 1989. "Textuality, Social Science, and Society." *Issues in Integrative Studies* 7:1–19.

Duncan, Martha Grace. 1996. *Romantic Outlaws, Beloved Prisms: The Unconscious Meanings of Crime and Punishment.* New York: New York University Press.

Ferrell, Jeff. 1995. "Adrenalin, Pleasure, and Criminological Verstehen." Paper presented at the Annual Meetings of the American Society of Criminology, November: Boston.

Ferrell, Jeff, and Clinton R. Sanders, eds. 1995. *Culture Criminology.* Boston: Northeastern University Press.

Giddens, Anthony. 1984. *The Constitution of Society.* Cambridge: Polity Press.

Henry, Stuart, and Dragan Milovanovic. 1996. *Constitutive Criminology: Beyond Postmodernism.* London: Sage Publications.

Katz, Jack. 1988. *Seductions of Crime: Moral and Sensual Attractions in Doing Evil.* New York: Basic Books.

Milovanovic, Dragan. 1995. "Dueling Paradigms: Modernist v. Postmodernist Thought." *Humanity and Society* 19(1): 1–22.

Pfohl, Stephen. 1993. "Twilight of the Parasites: Ultramodern Capital and the New World Order." *Social Problems* 40(2): 125–151.

Sampson, Robert J., and John H. Laub. 1993. *Crime in the Making: Pathways and Turning Points Through Life.* Cambridge: Harvard University Press.

Tykociner, Joseph T. 1959. *Zetetics.* Chicago: University of Illinois Press.

———. 1966. *The Outline of Zetetics.* Chicago: University of Illinois Press.

Vila, Bryan. 1994. "A General Paradigm for Understanding Criminal Behavior: Extending Evolutionary Ecological Theory." *Criminology* 32(3): 311–359.

# Integrating Cultural, Media, and Gender Studies: An Interdisciplinary Perspective on Crime Production

Juliette Lewis and Woody Harrelson in *Natural Born Killers*, 1994.

A cultural studies approach to the study of crime and crime control not only reflects a concern with the politics of difference and with identity politics, but it also overlaps with postcolonial studies and uses concepts and vocabularies "that attempt to reflect the diversity, the plurality, the diffuseness, and the blurring of boundaries of academic disciplines and between disciplines and the external world" (Bloland, 1995: 546). Some critique these approaches as being less than value free or objectively neutral, as they tend to side in terms of political action with the marginally downtrodden. In defense, contemporary cultural studies argues "that many dimensions of social stratification influence the unequal distribution of power and resources in our society. Racism, sexism, classism, heterosexism, ageism, ableism, and others—each system of social domination has its own separate history, dynamic, conditions of existence and material and ideological components" (Dines and Humez, 1995: xviii). Hence, in the multicultural world of late modernism each of the "isms" produces its own unique social experiences, movements, and consciousnesses that need to be expressed and accounted for.

Steeped in postmodernism and poststructuralism, cultural studies are also joined by gender/feminist studies, racial/ethnic studies, and media/communications studies, where there is a convergence of interest in popular discourse and the social construction of reality. More specifically, a cultural studies approach to crime and crime control attempts to bring the intersection of class, race, and gender together with the dynamics of mass communications and identity formations. Hence, to fully understand criminal behavior (i.e., to peer into people's souls) and to be able to explain crime trends beyond the statistics and the predictions, criminologists need to tell the story of crime and crime control in probabilistic terms as it is derived from the everyday interaction of individual life and social history. In part, this story is about the dominant ritual forms involved in the reproduction of capitalist crime and punishment. In part, the story of crime production is about the development and contextualization of life histories as these intersect with various social ecologies and political economies.

Methodologically, a cultural studies approach to crime and its control in massmediated society incorporates studies in political economy, in textual readings, and in audience receptions (experiences). Like Giddens's structuration theory discussed in Chapter 10, Douglas Kellner (1995) has argued that in order to know a media cultural product, such as a television show or advertising image or romance novel, for example, one needs to be able to: (1) comprehend the socioeconomic context in which it is created (political economy, production); (2) examine its constructed meaning(s) through careful attention to its particular visual, verbal, and auditory codes or languages (textual analysis); and (3) ascertain through ethnographic research what its real-world audiences contribute to the meaning-making processes (audience reception). In a more general sense, Bennett Berger (1995: 12) picking up on Max Weber's emphasis on the importance of both the "ideal" and the "material," writes: "Cultural understanding requires attention not only to image, sound, word, gesture, and the symbolic character of human things but . . . to the material as well as the ideal interests of persons and groups in those symbolic realms." The understanding of crime and crime control requires no less. Thus, from a cultural studies perspective, it is argued that crime in the United States is expressive of an anomically based market economy with an emphasis on radical individualism and a high degree of dependence on consumptive capital and symbolic self-esteem.

In late modernism and advanced capitalism, for example, " 'consumer freedom' requires that one's identity, and related consumer needs, evolve along the lines of market expansion. If increased consumption is only guaranteed by the recurrent 'reinvention' of oneself, then the recurrent reinvention of oneself becomes a core democratic 'right' " (Cerroni-Long, 1996: 147). Others have argued that in the postmodern world, identities are a matter of choice, considered to be self-selected and even modifiable at will (Hollinger, 1995; Walters, 1990). In the context of constantly reinventing one's identity in consumptive society, you are not only what you eat, drink, smoke, wear, drive, habituate, and so forth, but you are also the image you provoke, the style you express, and the politics you reflect. Finally, in terms of radical individualism and postmodern capitalism, the production of desire is consumed (satisfied), whether we are talking about a personal computer, an Armani suit, or a pair of Nike shoes, by that clarion refrain of the marketplace—*Just Do It!* Just doing it, of course, often involves criminal behavior.

Although this chapter does not represent an exhaustive expression of the plurality of voices on crime and punishment, it does attempt to capture the narrative themes or representations of the newer racial, sexual, cultural, and transnational perspectives in relationship to each other and to the older class stratification systems of inequality. There is also an appreciation for the ethnographic voices of convicted offenders (if not "criminals") on "crime" (Cromwell, 1996). These contextual realities are portrayed not for the purposes of developing racially, sexually, or culturally specific theories of crime and social control, but for the purposes of understanding the continuities and discontinuities in the social experiences of different groupings of peoples as these intersect *ideologically* across the horizons of individual and environmental development.

From an integrative-constitutive perspective, such contextual realities of crime production are presented in order to provide a background or framework for incorporating inclusive explanations of crime and justice. For example, Dorothy E. Roberts (1993: 1945) examined what she termed "the terrible intersection of crime, race, and reproduction" and "the convergence of two tools of oppression—the racial construction of crime and the use of reproduction as an instrument of punishment." Roberts argues that the technology of power that links crime, race, and reproduction exemplifies how racism and patriarchy function as mutually supporting systems of domination and how criminologists need to incorporate such awareness into their criminological analyses.

> *It is most likely that this tactic of domination will be meted out through the control of black women's bodies. Discouraging black procreation is a means of subordinating the entire race; under patriarchy, it is accomplished through the regulation of black women's fertility. In our effort to dismantle hierarchies of gender, race, and class, a critical initial task is to explore how each of these hierarchies sustains the others (Roberts, 1993: 1977).*

"Race matters," so much so that Roberts (1993: 1945) contends it identifies criminals. She further argues that race is not only embedded in the very foundation of the criminal law, but that it helps to determine "who the criminals are, what constitutes a crime, and which crimes society treats most seriously."

In a different but parallel manner, Robert Jensen (1995: 112) stresses that "gender matters." Jensen maintains that he comes to feminist theory with the realization that his "future as a fully moral and responsible human being depends on women's liberation" (Jensen, 1995: 112). He argues that men have to embrace feminism personally for their own sake as well as in the interests of justice.

> *When I began studying feminism six years ago, I did not immediately realize that feminism explained not only men's oppression of women, but my own isolation, alienation, and pain. Nor did I realize that I could understand myself through feminism without denying my participation in the oppression of women or falsely equating men's and women's problems. While I understood that the personal is political, I was slow to realize that the phrase applied not only to women but to me; it took time for me to understand that feminism required me to not only criticize patriarchal constructions of masculinity in the abstract, but to be unrelenting in my critique of my own behavior (Jensen, 1995: 111).*

Jensen's point, as my wife of more than twenty years has often reminded me, is: All men should never lose sight of our culturally produced maleness and associated privileges. With respect to the social relations of crime and punishment, their meanings have been both genderized and racialized (Daly, 1994).

Although it is impossible for people (or identities), regardless of their racial/ethnic, gender, and socioeconomic (class matters) backgrounds, to ever completely escape—for better or worse—from the social and ideological parameters of which they are a part of, the question of difference and sameness should not be simply reduced to one-dimensional portrayals of black/white, male/female, rich/poor, young/old, and other dichotomies. There are differences within sameness and sameness within differences, especially as one examines the combination of social and physical statuses involved in identity formations. For example, Regina Austin has commented about the black community and the dominant society. She claims that both are in a constant state of flux because of the challenges from without and within. In terms of the strains and multiple voices of the black community on crime, she writes:

> *There are tensions at the border with the dominant society, at the frontier between liberation and oppression. There is also internal dissension over indigenous threats to security and solidarity. "Difference" is as much a source of contention within the "community" as it is a factor marking the boundary between "the community" and everyone else.*
>
> *Nothing illustrates the multiple threats to the ideal of "the black community" better than black criminal behavior and the debates it engenders. There is no shortage of controversy about the causes, consequences, and cures of black criminality. To the extent there is consensus, black appraisals of questionable behavior are often in accord with those prevailing in the dominant society, but sometimes they are not. In any event, there is typically no unanimity within "the community" on these issues (Austin, 1992: 1769).*

Similarly, there is no unanimity when it comes to crime and crime control among women, men, rich, poor, middle class, straight, gay, old, and young. This does not mean that a consensus about crime and its control should not be consciously struggled for. However, typically, mandates to address crime are derived more from the unconscious motivations of ideological manipulation than from rational decision making (Alvarez, 1995). As for the individual production of crime, although it has a unique history of its own agency and making, it is also connected to the larger relations of the symbolic and social structures as these are expressed in the ideologically patterned practices of nonconformity and social control.

Following Stuart Hall (1995: 18), ideology refers to "those images, concepts and premises which provide the frameworks through which we represent, interpret, understand and 'make sense' of some aspect of social existence." Moreover, ideologies "do not consist of isolated and separate concepts, but in the articulation of different elements into a distinctive set or chain of meanings" (Hall, 1995: 18). In other words, although ideological statements about crime and punishment are made by individuals, they are not the product of individual consciousness or intention. The point is that criminals and noncriminals alike formulate their intentions or actions within ideologies. These ideologies "pre-date individuals and form part of the determinate social formations and conditions in which individuals are born. We have to 'speak [or act] through' the ideologies which are active in our society and which provide us with the means of 'making sense' of social relations and our place in them" (Hall, 1995: 19). This is not to imply that we must go along with accepted ideologies and policies nor that we necessarily arrive at our standpoints unconsciously.

Ideologies work by constructing for individual and collective subjects "positions of identification and knowledge which allow them to 'utter' ideological truths [about 'crime and crime control' in our case] as if they were their authentic authors. This is not because they emanate from our innermost, authentic, and unified experience, but because we find ourselves mirrored in the positions at the center of the discourses from which the statement we formulate 'make sense' " (Hall, 1995: 19). Politicians, criminal justice practitioners, offenders, victims, citizens, and media pundits alike all find, in short, that their perspectives or forms of social consciousness on crime and punishment are nothing less than the contemporary and prevalent viewpoints of ideologically constructed words and images. Often, the signs used to depict crime and criminals are rooted in stereotypic and mythic figures of good and evil connected with various ideologies of race, gender, and class inequality (Barak, 1994).

In simpler terms, ideologies of crime and crime control refer to the arguments promoting or defending the ideal values and material interests of advanced capitalism. In the reproduction of an advancing white-male, heterosexist, and transnational mode of capitalist domination, Pfohl (1993) argues that contemporary telecommunicative mediums of mass memory can serve to eclipse the traditional awarenesses of differential treatment of peoples by the agencies of social control. In referring to the long exclusion of women, peoples of color, the economically impoverished, and the sexually marginalized from participation in the social structuring of modernity, he argues further that "these persons are today doubly exiled by the violence of an ultramodern conjunction of power and knowledge: a fantastic, nihilistic, and cybernetically engineered will to will, a New World Order of CAPITAList power that is as terroristic as it is seductive, and as informational as it is forgetful of the sacrifices which constitute its materiality" (Pfohl, 1993: 125–126).

*Integrating Criminologies* views the culture of crime production as related to the culture of consumption, which varies from market society to market society, depending on the extent to which both economic institutions are embedded in noneconomic institutions, and consumer roles are circumscribed by relations of mutual obligation, dependence, and associated restraints (Colvin and Pauly, 1983; Granovetter, 1985; Sampson and Laub, 1993; Rosenfeld and Messner, 1994). At the same time, the reproduction of crime is viewed in relationship to the changing forms of social differentiation concerning gender, race, and class. These social relations interact in extremely complex ways to influence, if not the overall levels of crime, then at least the distribution of crime and offenders within late modernist Western cities as these vary by both the kind of society (i.e., corporatist, or social democratic) and the nature of the city (i.e., sunrise, rustbelt, tourist) within a particular society (Bottoms and Wiles, 1994). In short, crime varies from location to location within and between similarly populated areas, depending on its residents' marketable skills, in relation not only to the localization and globalization of an advancing political economy, but also to the commodification of consumption through the various venues of mass communications.

In general, the focuses of Chapters 11 and 12 are on the production, circulation, and consumption of crime and social control. Both chapters attempt to provide narrative accounts that revolve around the mass-mediated consumption of ever-increasing and enveloping electronic imagery of the lifestyle metaphysics of everyday crime and justice. In this chapter, the emphasis is on the insights of cultural, ethnic/racial, gender, and media-generated knowledges as these intersect with the phenomena of crime and its inquiry. In the next and final chapter, the emphasis is on linking the knowledges about the relationships between individuals and social control. Hence, this chapter focuses on the coproduction of offenders and crime. The final chapter focuses on the reproduction of offenders and offenses.

Finally, the nature of crime and its control as represented by the depictions of a constitutive-synthetic model of criminological discourses and knowledges (Figure 10.4) and a dynamic-integrative model of criminalization and social control (Figure 10.5) is inclusive of what could be classified as an exhaustive "inventory of criminological indicators" (ICI) including, but not limited to, the opportunities, routine activities, social ecologies, motivations, and other factors that are associated with patterns of criminality. Near the end of the chapter, I will outline an inventory of criminological indicators that are consistent with the integrative-constitutive model of crime developed in Chapter 10. Preceding this, however, I attempt to describe the connections between: (1) mass communications and New World cybernetics; (2) crime and the culture of consumption; (3) the variability of race, gender, and class; and (4) convicted offenders on crime.

## Mass Communications and New-World Cybernetics

Nearly a half century ago, C. Wright Mills (1951: 333) wrote, "Between consciousness and existence stand communications. . . . The forms of political consciousness may, in the end, be relative to the means of production, but, in the beginning, they are relative to the contents of the communication media." Mills (1951: 334) recognized, in short, that a "new society" was emerging, dominated by the electronic circulation of "mythic figures and fast moving stereotypes." In fact, Mills "viewed the expansion of forms of electronic information not simply as external forces, but as forms of social experience that blur the boundaries between 'first-hand contact' and prefabricated signs" (Pfohl, 1993: 126). In turn, he argued that the media seep into our images of self, are taken for granted, and to be altered would necessitate the modification of the modern experience and character as it is known. In mass-mediated society,

> *We are so submerged in the pictures created by mass media that we no longer really see them, much less the objects they supposedly represent. . . . They are a kind of common denominator, a kind of scheme for pre-scheduled, mass emotions . . . they expropriate our vision. . . . The attention absorbed by the images on the screen's rectangle dominates the darkened public; the sonorous, the erotic, the mysterious, the funny voice of the radio talks to you; the thrill of the easy murder relaxes you. In our life-situation, they simply fascinate. And their effects run deep: popular culture is not tagged as "propaganda" but as entertainment; people are often exposed to it when most relaxed of mind and tired of body; and its characters offer easy targets of identification, easy answers to stereotyped personal problems (Mills, 1951: 333, 336).*

Ultimately, Mills argued that the power of the electronic media posed a danger because increasingly it was impossible to tell the image from the source. Today, of course, the rapid fire deployment of media images is far more enveloping than in Mills's day. As part of the circulative production and consumption of enveloping electronic imagery, there is, perhaps, no other media content area that is more saturated with coverage than "crime and justice" (Surette, 1992; Barak, 1994). This is part and parcel of the ascendancy of a cultural preoccupation with a fear of crime and a "criminal metaphysics" of everyday life in the United States. In fact, it may very well be that there is little, if any, difference between the depths of contemporary political discourse on crime and its control other than the shimmering televisionary surfaces of *America's Most Wanted, NYPD Blue,* and *Homicide: Life on the Street.* Moreover, it does not help that the thematic depictions of women in mass-circulated stereotypes have been mostly as powerless victims of oppression in one form or another. Nor does it help that these portrayals of women as victims have also been echoed in the majority of criminology textbooks that were published between the early 1980s and the early 1990s (Wright, 1995).

In the ultramodern society, Pfohl (1993) contends that rituals of collective social representation, for example, crime and justice, are transformed into "cybernetic rites of sign-work" that blur the receivers' experiential boundaries between their internal and external worlds. Cybernetics, or the study of the control and communication systems in animals, peoples, and machines, also refers to the type of thinking that "carries one beyond (questions of) good and evil into a language of oscillating interface between command, control and communications" (Pfohl, 1993: 128). In the cybernetic world of selective crime images, Pfohl (1993: 135) asks, "How does 'one' live with a self secured by the virtually memoryless enactment of restrictive economic and military violence against others?" The unsatisfactory answer is that complicit in a global politics of exploitation, people get by through the ever-expanding consumptive domains of individualized pleasures.

> *So much so that when you read of stabbings rape gang violence child beatings drug abuse shootings PREMODELED IMAGES COME TO MIND. Without commas. RAPID FIRE IMAGES COME TO MIND. Images you've seen before. Maybe on television: moving electric pictures of dark young wild stereotypes rap addicted and inner city males. With baseball caps and badness. Stereotypical images of persons who white politicians say ought to be put away. With VIRTUALLY NO MEMORIES OF HOW THESE THOUGHTS (rather than others) HAVE COME TO OCCUPY YOUR MINDS. And VIRTUALLY NO COLLECTIVE RITUALS to put into play memories of an entirely different sort—memories of unprecedented white male CAPITAL initiatives; memories, for instance, of the near extermination of an entire continent of people with little taste for still life paintings, narcissistic mirrors of production and the self-defensive or DEATH DEFYING PLEASURES of PARASITIC OVERDEVELOPMENT; memories of the continuing material effects of enslaving, "freeing," and then transformatively redlining millions of Africans into a semipermanent U.S. underclass. What are the psychic body and cultural costs of such selective memories and forgettings? (Pfohl, 1993: 135–136).*

However, in the postmodern world this selective blurring of historical and contemporary social realities is augmented by Giddens's (1983) claim that modernization (technology, communications, and transportation) is a process by which time and space are "emptied out." That is to say, time ceases to be necessarily related to particular places. Instead, it becomes abstract clock time. Rather than events organizing time, events become organized and defined in relation to time. Moreover, at the same time, activities are free from the constraints of local contexts and particular moments, for example, video-recording an event so that it can be experienced independently of time. In short, the emptying out of "time/space distanciation" or "the stretching of social systems across time/space" where "social system" means "the patterning of social relationships across time/space, understood as reproduced practices" (Giddens, 1983: 377), has impacted greatly the human condition, affecting daily social life, and, inevitably, our institutions and our consciousness.

As Bottoms and Wiles (1994: 20) emphasize, "Abstract systems have allowed us to organise the social world across large space/time distances, and the organisational forms which we develop are no longer necessarily tied to either time or place. Social events are, as a result, much less dependent upon local traditions or cultures; events are just as likely to be influenced by what is happening far away in space and time as by that nearby." At the same time, during the postmodern period there has been an opening up of desire as the cybernetic ingenuity of market-sensitive and negative-feedback sensors appear increasingly able to capitalize on what had previously been repressed. As Pfohl (1993: 148) concludes, "in a parasitic kind of way U.S. CAPITAL has thus gotten 'funky,' stimulating the once *outlawed styles* of African-Americans and claiming them as (if) their own."

As the globalization of American culture escalated during the 1980s, for example, black music was given vast international importance (West, 1989). And Michael Jackson sang, *It really doesn't matter if you're black or white*, unless, of course, if you are neither white nor rich, but such distinctions are lost on the mass white-minded sectors of the U.S. economy. After all, rap music sells. So, "one marketing season after the next, white CAPITAL scans its borders and endeavors to appropriate and/or stimulate models that promise greater flexibility and adaptive expansion within its New World Order of cybernetic control" (Pfohl, 1993: 148). Thus, despite the mass-mediated message that race/ethnicity, gender, and class don't matter, they still do, especially as they are related to crime and crime control (Daly, 1994; Hawkins, 1995; Walker, Spohn, and Delone, 1996; Williams, 1991).

## Change in Late Modernity: Crime and the Culture of Consumption

Compared to the cities of the early twentieth century, there are a number of significant changes in motion in the nature of contemporary cities. These include: (a) the internationalization of capital and business; (b) globalization and localization; (c) changes in the production process; (d) time/space distanciation; (e) the relationship between the city and the hinterland; and (f) the search for peace and security (Bottoms and Wiles, 1994). Taken as a whole, these changes influence, or are at least not unrelated to, the changes in the contemporary practices of crime and social control.

In late modernity, the internationalization of business in the form of the emergent and then dominant multinational corporation parallels the development of the internationalization of capital from the beginning of the modern period around 1500. Today, both capital and labor are easily and rapidly moved around the world. In the international scheme of things, very weak links remain between local capital and major developments in a given city. In a sense, most cities cannot control their own destinies in late modernity because of their growing dependence on the globalization of capital. Cities and their development (or lack of development) and their distribution of types of crimes are increasingly tied to the internationalization of markets of goods and services, legal and illegal. These relations have implications not only for crime but also for social control (Barak, 1991a; Davis, 1992). At the same time, there is also a homogenization and internationalization of thinking.

> *Because major developments in cities now usually involve international capital, the networks which provide such capital also serve to internationalise the thinking behind developments. Shopping malls in Britain, for example, may often not only bear an uncanny resemblance to those in North America, but will literally be the product of an international learning and development process about how best to build and develop shopping malls. The result is the growth of the "international city" (already seen prototypically in airports) with a growing homogenisation of certain aspects of design, development, management, etc. (Bottoms and Wiles, 1994: 15).*

In late modernity, although there is an increasing role of the global political economy, there is also the need for localization to increase in importance. In the postindustrial, nonmanufacturing economic sectors, involving service industries that are consumed both locally and internationally, cities must compete with other cities and nations to attract economic activity that has become more a matter of corporate choice than geographical necessity.

> *International capital will seek to invest, and multi-national corporations to develop, where they believe profit can be maximised regardless of the needs or policies of regions or nation states. The state (either national or regional) may, of course, try to influence such decisions by affecting the profit calculations using devices such as tax breaks, favourable land and planning deals, attractive employment legislation, etc. (Bottoms and Wiles, 1994: 16).*

Of course, different cities as well as communities within cities are situated differently in terms of the advantages that they may offer, such as the availability of highly skilled labor or lifestyle amenities (e.g., attractive countryside, leisure and recreational facilities, international transportation) to potential investors. In short, there is a marked unevenness of local economic development in the cities of late modernity as evidenced by the so-called "sunrise" (service oriented) and "rustbelt" (industrial oriented) economies. The point is that, despite the effects of the general trends of later modernity on cities, there is still great variation within and between countries.

Some communities and cities, for example, with the downsizing of manufacturing and with the shifting of remaining manufacturing away from traditional locations, have experienced the conditions of urban blight and derelict areas. In other downtown areas all across the United States, the depression of the earlier abandoned inner cities of the late seventies and early eighties have disappeared. In their place has entered the redevelopment and major remodeling of the commercial geography of the inner city. Needless to say, these two very different urban experiences have produced different crime outcomes; the former yielding gentrification and a dispersal of crime, the latter ghettoization and an intensification of crime (Wilson, 1987).

Nevertheless,

> *All cities are now part of a metropolitan culture, embracing a kaleidoscope of images and styles with increasingly little connection with local conditions. Further, because there is local connection, then the cultural kaleidoscope is available for us to choose. We can choose the icons with which we wish to associate ourselves, with little constraint from the immediate conditions of our existence. The world sometimes appears as if it were a series of alternative fantasies which we can take up and discard at will. We can drive out of the city in our all-terrain vehicle, wear country clothes, and be part of a rural idyll and then return to the city shopping mall, buy baseball clothes, watch a film set in Australia and then eat an authentic Indian meal in the Taj Mahal. Of course, we have not all lost touch with reality that we do not recognise the fantasy element. Nevertheless, there is a sense in which we are increasingly free to choose and to*

*implement those choices in a concrete way, ranging from style of dress to style of home, and to have those choices recognized and responded to by others who are also making such choices. Self-identity in such a world is obviously, to some extent* elective. *Yet it must be emphasised that the cultural kaleidoscope we have just described is, largely, a* consumer market. *Without the money many of the choices in the new metropolitan culture are not available—or at least not available legally. To deny elective self iden-tity to those without money makes it almost inevitable that at least some of them will seek identities through other (and deviant) means (Bottoms and Wiles, 1994: 22).*

Later in the chapter, we will hear from some of those deviant identities.

In late modernity, the discussion of the city is even a bit obsolete. That is to say, although modern cultures still use the distinction between the urban and rural and suburban places, most contemporary writers recognize the erosion of urban/rural/suburban differences as a result of the urbanization or metropolitanization of larger and larger areas inclusive of all three. Moreover, in terms of time-space convergence, the reproduction of social life inside and outside the city depends increasingly on re-flexively acquired social knowledge rather than on traditions passed down from gen-eration to generation. As societies become more reliant on abstract systems and as reflexive knowledge becomes ever more specialized, people have to extend their trust in the expertise of others. In late modernity, however, with its expanded pluralities and diversities, trust becomes a scarcer commodity: "The result is that trust can only be given by taking risks and this inevitable risk-taking of modern life creates an ontolog-ical insecurity" (Bottoms and Wiles, 1994: 23), often referred to as "the fear of crime." It can be argued further that the city's problems of security, fragmentation, and trust in late modernity help to produce self-fulfilling prophesies of doom and destruction.

Finally, the internationalization and globalization of decontexualized choices available in the consumer market means that the social world becomes increasingly one of relativistic and individualized choices. In the process, the traditional normative val-ues that helped to maintain the particular nature of group solidarity and local commu-nity are undermined by a New World Order. In short, the normative relativity and the consumerization of culture make it "increasingly difficult for individual nation states clearly to define and reinforce (in Durkheim's sense) the outer boundaries they wish to maintain for their cultural and legal systems" (Bottoms and Wiles, 1994: 22).

The implications of these changes for market societies on crime appear to be sub-stantial. The pushes and pulls to crime seem to be everywhere in the late modernity of advanced capitalism. Braithwaite's (1989) integrative theory of crime argues, for ex-ample, that nations with high levels of inequality of wealth and power have high rates of both white collar and conventional crime. In part, this is because they produce a broad range of illegitimate opportunities that are more rewarding than legitimate op-portunities. Again, this is partly due to an erosion in the regulatory powers of the for-mal and informal means of social control as these respond to the growing divisions of inequality and privilege (Braithwaite, 1979).

As Anthony Harris (1991), Charles Derber (1992), David Friedrichs (1995), and others have argued, upper-class whites and underclass blacks may well have a rational and pronounced lack of fear about committing crime, in the former case because of a sense of immunity and in the latter case because of a relative indifference to the consequences. As Derber points out, "economic wilding," or the morally uninhibited pursuit of money by individuals or businesses at the expense of others, may have consequences far more damaging to society than the "street wilding" of inner-city, African American youths. During the Reagan-Bush years (1980–1992), for example, the real looters were not the urban, minority youths participating in the Los Angeles riot following the first Rodney King verdict which acquitted the police of mercilessly beating him on videotape for the world to see, but, instead, they were the high-level corporate executives in the savings-and-loan industries who reaped enormous rewards for themselves while causing much economic devastation for workers, consumers, and taxpayers (Rothstein, 1992).

In the contemporary age of insecurity, with wilding from above and below, U.S. citizens feel besieged and subject to attack, even during the period 1991 to 1996, when the rates for all categories of recorded crime were going consistently downward, especially in urban America. People feel vulnerable, whether they are or not, and they

believe that they have nobody to turn to in pursuit of trust and tranquility, certainly not to the federal government or the two-party system, considering the ubiquitous role of political organizations in major illegalities over the past fifty years, from the investigation and cover-up of the Kennedy assassination to Iraqgate. At the same time, political scandals, such as the Iran-Contra and the Savings and Loan episodes, interrelate not only to each other, but also to other types of crime and deviance as well. In fact, "there is an emerging body of evidence that much of what is mistakenly called the American 'street crime' problem is actually part of a complicated network of relationships among criminals and organizations at all strata of society" (Simon and Hagan, 1995: 20).

Although crimes by the state (Chambliss, 1989; Barak, 1991b) have a long history, until recently their episodes were fairly intermittent. During the Cold War period, however, state criminality experienced what David Simon and Frank Hagan (1995: 23) have referred to as the "institutionalization of deviant means (e.g., secrecy in the name of national security)." Moreover, as David Simon and D. Stanley Eitzen (1993: 291–306) have described, modern governmental scandals include a host of subcauses related to the structure of contemporary bureaucracy, including group think, the manufacture of guilt-neutralizing mechanisms, front activities and inauthenticity, dehumanization of enemies, and cooperation with organized crime and other outside organizations in the commission of their acts of fraud and deception. But, ultimately, "postmodern scandal results when culturally approved goals, in this case the enhancement of an administration or agency's power and/or prestige, cannot be accomplished by the usual legitimate means" (Simon and Hagan, 1995: 22).

What thematically relates all of the above forms of criminality is the "culture of consumption," or the expectations and obligations that motivate and shape acquisitive behavior in relation to dominant cultural values and goals. In addition, there is the ever-expanding role of the consumer personality. As Steven Messner and Richard Rosenfeld (1994) have argued, consumption plays a major role in explaining crime, not merely in terms of causal significance of poverty or economic inequality, but also in terms of the institutional significance of crime for the consumer role. Following strain and anomie theories, crime results from defective social conditions that interfere with the ability of persons or groups to consume at required or expected levels. However, as Rosenfeld and Messner (1995: 2) correctly point out, "Crime also reflects social arrangements widely viewed as normal and desirable—including equal and open access to the means of consumption, and fulfillment of the requirements of the consumer role." As they argued in their book, *Crime and the American Dream* (1994), the American Dream is fulfilled through consumption, and consumption is often not possible without crime. Let us look a bit closer at their *institutional-anomie* theory of crime.

Rosenfeld and Messner's (1995: 2) most recent articulation of their basic thesis is "that the consumer role is the principal structural locus of anomic cultural pressures in modern market societies." Whether the anomic tendencies of the consumer role lead to crime depends on "the embeddedness of consumption." That is to say, in countries such as Japan the "anomic pressures are subdued in market relations with strong noneconomic content and control, that is, in market relations that are embedded in noneconomic institutional domains" that foster trust and networks of interpersonal relations (Rosenfeld and Messner, 1995: 6). On the other hand, anomic pressures to engage in crime are stimulated by market societies where the economic bottom line pervades all institutional arenas and where social standing and personal worth are defined primarily in terms of individual material acquisition, such as in the United States.

Rosenfeld and Messner's argument about consumption and crime recognizes that acquisitive behavior is socially and culturally organized. In other words, the desire to own and possess things while appearing natural is actually a commodified desire produced by market societies. In such societies, the individual possesses essentially two roles or sets of expectations: work and consumption. Both of these roles embody "expectations and obligations that motivate certain behaviors, shape their expression, and convey cultural values and beliefs" (Rosenfeld and Messner, 1995: 3). In sum, market economies require that a large segment of the population be engaged in productive activity and that consumption continues to rise rather than drop or hold steady.

These two roles differ, however, in one fundamental aspect: The role of work exerts restraining power, whereas the role of consumption exerts liberating power. In the role of work, we behave as we do because we have to; in the role of consumer, we behave as we are able to, depending on our financial worth. Whereas Marx maintained that work defined the person, Thorsten Veblen ([1899] 1953) was quick to argue that in market societies, consumption also has great expressive significance for its members. In the ultramodern and postmodern world of today, where consumption often assumes priority over employment as a sign of social membership and status (Coleman and Rainwater, 1978), and where "the expectations of the consumer role are highly permissive by comparison [to the role of employee] and provide considerably more discretion with respect to how, when, where, and with whom the role is performed," then "consumption offers powerful gratifications not easily matched by the intrinsic satisfactions or extrinsic rewards of work" (Rosenfeld and Messner, 1995: 4–5).

A strong orientation to consume the American Dream, then, may serve as a means of overwhelming the restraints associated with employment and of undermining cooperative bonds of social control. This may be as true for criminals as noncriminals. It is also true for those crimes committed both against the state and by the state. But, it is not argued here that crime should be reduced to mere economics and self-determinism. On the contrary, it is not only the material-real expressions of the "freedom of consumption," but also the symbolic-ideal transference of one's social worth and self-esteem to an identification with a material measure driven by the processes of commodification.

Finally, in market societies, such as the United States where there is a highly developed "culture of narcissism" (Lasch, 1979), people are consciously and unconsciously motivated to seek out the psychic rewards of material success wherever and whenever they can. In the real world, of course, peoples' access to personal worth and social position is not at all equal and changes over time. For those folks who have derived material or psychic well-being from their work, there may be pressures for finding alternative (illegitimate) means to sustaining one's success should the legitimate means no longer prevail in doing so. For those without the opportunity to derive material or psychic gratification from their legitimate labor, the pressures to find alternative means for achieving success may intensify and spill over into deviant activities as well.

In the next section, we turn to a discussion of how these ideal and material realities of crime and social control are both connected with and affected by the intersection of race, gender, and class. Succinctly, the integrative perspective contends that race, gender, and class matter to all of us and that the unraveling of the intersections of the three is fundamental to explaining many of the puzzles associated with crime and its control.

## Variability and the Intersection of Race, Gender, and Class

Traditionally, variables of age, gender, ethnicity, class, and religion have been applied quite autonomously to such social problems as crime, violence, suicide, addiction, and others. For the past decade or so, however, social scientists in general and feminist criminologists, critical race theorists, and critical legal theorists in particular have begun to focus on the interactions of two or more of these variables and their combined impact for the behavior in question. A review of the empirical literature on violence, for example, revealed the confounding effects of gender, race, and class. Yet the articulation of the combined influences were difficult to tease out. As Sally Simpson (1991: 129) writes,

> *Extant research yields only a murky picture of essential differences between and among males and females of different classes and races. Until large-scale quantitative designs can readily and meaningfully sort out differences in crime rates and qualitative research can offer subjective accounts of how violence is interpreted and understood by different subpopulations of interest, criminological theory will continue to be only vaguely relevant to the real world.*

Nevertheless, knowledge of these interactive relationships and how they impact on each other is fundamental to the development of more inclusive and integrated theories of crime. In a different way, and in relation to the development of more inclusive and integrated theories of crime and social control, each of these variables has been viewed as a source of a particular form of oppression or experience. Depending on which particular triad of race-gender-class identity is involved, for example, these variables may be reciprocal and reinforcing of criminal behavior, or they may be contradictory and resistant to such behavior.

Although it is far too early in this line of inquiry to sort out the variations within these variables as they combine with each other, differences in patterns of criminal conduct relative to class, race, and gender have been addressed by criminologists. Generally, criminologists have provided four accounts for those differences in the patterns of criminality: (1) hereditary traits, (2) socialization practices, (3) structural opportunities, and (4) societal reactions. With the exception of the first point of view, there are various degrees of consensus about the others. The first view of inherent differences is pretty much rejected by most criminologists. This viewpoint suggests, for example, that lower-class individuals are members of the lower class because they are more likely to have pathological tendencies; that people of color are more likely to have innate attributes associated with predatory crime; that females are naturally less likely to be aggressive than males (Wilson and Herrnstein, 1985). The socialization viewpoint, epitomized in the tradition of Sutherland's differential association (1939) emphasizes subcultural influences and involvement with criminal conduct as a function of learned behavior in intimate relationships. The opportunity point of view, articulated in the classic work by Cloward and Ohlin (1960) and, more recently, in the work of Hagan (1994), stresses the differential access to criminal and noncriminal opportunities. The societal-reactions viewpoint emphasizes the biases found in both the informal and formal systems of crime control, from schools to employment to the criminal justice system (Anderson and Collins, 1992; Lynch and Patterson, 1991; Sulton, 1996; Walker, Spohn, and DeLone, 1996).

The integrative-constitutive perspective developed here incorporates an appreciation of differences in the patterns of crime attributed to socialization, opportunities, and bias in the context that everyone's life is framed by inequalities of race, class, and gender. As Margaret L. Anderson and Patricia Hill Collins (1992: 177) write,

> *African-Americans and other racial/ethnic groups are not the sole recipients of differential treatment by race; racial politics also encompass the experiences of whites. Women and men are both affected by gender, and the lives of the poor and their more affluent counterparts are intimately intertwined. By seeing that we are all part of one historically created system that finds structural form in interconnected social institutions, we gain greater insight about the actual and potential shape of our own lives.*

On the other hand, each of these categories must be taken on its own terms as well. For example, race theorist Clovis Semmes (1992) writes that cultural hegemony is the metaproblem out of which epistemological, conceptual, theoretical, and critical issues emerge in African American studies. Semmes contends that this cultural hegemony, or the systematic negation of one culture by another,

> *constitutes the major paradigmatic, historical, and structural phenomenon that has threatened African American institutional development and that has profoundly shaped this group's cultural strivings. Over time, the creation of institutions and culture among African Americans has been stimulated by the need to negotiate and respond to historical imperatives driven by the problem of systemic cultural negation (Semmes, 1992: xi).*

The integrative-constitutive perspective also, again, recognizes that categories such as gender, for example, encompass differences between women as victims and men as perpetrators. In other words, there are masculinities and femininities, not just male and female behaviors. In a variation on this theme, Katheryn Russell's (1994) insightful critique of the "racial inequality hypothesis" and how it may impact on crime, absent blocked opportunities, irrespective of class, and apart from economic inequality, sensitizes criminologists to the micro-level constructs of internal and external processes of racial inequality that individuals may have experienced during their life course. The external processes, for example, refer to "confrontations where individuals are derogated on the basis of racial/ethnic minority status"; internal processes, for example, refer to "individuals' perceptions that treatment they receive is based on their racial/ethnic minority status" (Russell, 1994: 312). Russell (1994: 312) also points out that

> there is no reason to presume that these processes (external or internal) are limited to interracial contacts. Arguably, micro-level perceptions of racial inequality can be expanded to include intraracial events. Poussant's (1983) discussion of the "self-hatred" thesis could be considered in this context.

The type of analysis suggested by Russell could potentially explain, for example, "The Differing Effects of Economic Inequality on Black and White Rates of Violence" found by Miles Harer and Darrell Steffensmeier (1992: 1049):

> In sum, our aggregate analysis reveals that the effects of economic inequality on arrest rates for violent crimes vary by race. For whites, high income inequality is a robust predictor of high violence rates, but for blacks it is a poor predictor.

Similarly, although poverty has been found to increase the level of suicide relative to homicide for whites, it does not for blacks (Huff-Corzine, Corzine, and Moore, 1991). As these findings point out, "subsequent studies . . . need to examine not just the direct effects of income inequality on black crime but also its indirect effects and, possibly, the reciprocal effects of crime on income inequality" (Harer and Steffensmeier, 1992: 1049). Like Russell, these other researchers also believe that we need fresh thinking about the way a highly unequal system of social stratification contributes to exceptionally high levels of violence in urban areas, whether we are talking about black-on-black crime or corporate-industrial pollution.

The message is that variations in patterned criminality in relationship to differences of gender, ethnicity, and class necessitate further examination by criminologists. For example, in studying the gender differences in criminality among heroin users, Jeanette Covington (1985: 329), among other things, found that

> Cultural deviance predictors were fairly effective in explaining male arrests but had no impact on female arrests. In fact, the most criminal females were those least attached to deviant subcultures. It [is] argued that these results reflect the absence of a subcultural image to reinforce female crime. Finally, the analysis of feminist predictors indicates that it is the most traditional females who report the most arrests. It is suggested that the limited criminal opportunities available to deviant females and the consequent need for many to attach themselves to males in passive, dependent relationships may select for such traditionalism in female criminals.

Taking into account the implications of these and all sorts of related findings, as I will argue in the final chapter, is essential for developing nonrepressive practices of social control and crime reduction.

Although the public stereotypes and mass-produced images of teenage ganging in America are predominated by males, African American males in particular, and even as the word "gang" has become a code word for race in the United States (Muwakkil, 1993), the social realities of gang composition are multicultural and involve the participation of both sexes. White, black, red, yellow, or brown, the diversity of gang activities also reflects the diversity of social and personal needs that gangs satisfy for their members. For example, in Hawaii, Karen Joe and Meda Chesney-Lind (1993) studied the interplay of gender and ethnicity, and the variation in youth gang membership and just what "membership" connoted, with respect both to the larger mass-produced images of gang activity and the more particular meanings that these social realities had for their participants. Their ethnographic research involved interviewing primarily Filipino and Samoan high-school-age gang members of both sexes. Joe and Chesney-Lind wanted to know the reasons why boys and girls joined gangs. What they found along the way was that gang members faced common problems, but they dealt with these in ways that were informed by gender and ethnicity.

*The interviews also confirm that extensive concern about violent, criminal activities in boys' gangs has distracted researchers from exploring the wide range of activities and experiences gangs provide their members. Girls and boys growing up in poor and violent neighborhoods turn to the gangs for many reasons, and the gangs themselves take on a variety of forms in response to the diverse challenges facing their members. Most importantly, the interviews reveal that girls and boys, even those in the same ethnic groups, inhabit worlds that are heavily influenced by gender. As a result, male and female gangs tend to provide different sets of experiences, skill, and opportunity to their members (Joe and Chesney-Lind, 1993: 2).*

Very briefly, the gang is a product of social forces; its members are girls and boys who have grown up in communities marked by poverty, racism, and rapid population growth. In the early nineties, more than 90 percent of the nation's largest cities reported youth gang problems, up from around 50 percent a decade earlier. Estimates by police, at the same time, put the number of gangs at about 5,000 and the number of gang members at about 250,000 (Curry et al., 1992). For both males and females, "the gang provides a needed social outlet and tonic for the boredom of low income life. The gang provides friends and activities in communities where such recreational outlets are pitifully slim" (Joe and Chesney-Lind, 1993: 29). In other words, there are many gang members who are not necessarily engaged in illegal activities while they pass the time of day. Nobody has any accurate figures on the relationship between licit and illicit gang membership. Nevertheless, most gang members, for example, do not fit the public image of consumers or sellers of drugs and weapons.

Gang activities and behaviors, however, are shaped through gender stereotypes and expectations. The list of prosocial activities is longer for the girls than the boys. By contrast, getting together with the guys quickly moves into cruising rather than hanging-out, and this, in turn, may often translate into fights and confrontations, especially with other groups of boys. Lastly, as Joe and Chesney-Lind (1993: 30) importantly point out, the gang is a sanctuary for its members.

> *The violence that characterizes their family lives and their communities is another prod into the gang for most of these youth. Gangs provide protection for both girls and boys. Many youth are drawn from families that are abusive, and particularly for girls, the gang provides the skills to fight back against the violence of their families.*
>
> *The marginalization of working and lower working class communities has specific meaning for young men as well. The displays of toughness and risk taking described by the boys . . . are a source for respect and status in an environment that is structurally unable to affirm their masculinity. Their acts of intimidation and fighting are rooted in the need for protection as well as the need to validate their manliness.*

The gang as refuge, then, helps to insulate its members from their very real insecurities and vulnerabilities. There is no reason not to believe that Joe and Chesney-Lind's findings and conclusions are not applicable to adolescent and gang behavior in most of North America. Yet seldom, if ever, are public policies of social and crime control designed according to this criminological understanding.

What about the relationship between class and crime? Once again, the theme is that a person's experiences by class or by socioeconomic status are also influenced by their intersecting experiences of gender and race/ethnicity. At the same time, there is a basic adage: Rich people don't hold up Quick Stops for $200 takes whereas poor people don't engage in price-fixing for millions of dollars.

Generally, the evidence of the last twenty-five years or so reveals that the gulf between the rich and the poor is widening. In fact, the middle class has been dwindling while the chances of becoming affluent or poor have been increasing. To put it simply, upward social mobility has diminished for many, particularly the poor and young, as income inequality grows and opportunities for unskilled work are reduced. At the same time, the costs of education are rising and the financial opportunities are decreasing, outside of government loans that create debts that take decades to pay off. Moreover, after adjusting for inflation, earnings have been going steadily downward for about two thirds of the population.

Holly Sklar (1995: 2) has described the situation this way:

> *Economic inequality is now so extreme that the richest 1 percent of American families have nearly as much wealth as the entire bottom 95 percent. More than a fifth of all children are living in poverty in this, the world's richest nation. That's according to the government, which undercounts both poverty and unemployment. Downward mobility has become the legacy for younger generations. Neither two incomes, nor college degrees assure that younger families will ever match their parents' living standards.*
>
> *For more and more people, a job is not a ticket out of poverty, but into the ranks of the working poor. Jobs and wages are being downsized in the "leaner, meaner" world of global corporate restructuring. Corporations are aggressively automating and shifting operations among cities, states, and nations in a continual search for greater public subsidies and lower-cost labor. Full-time jobs are becoming scarcer as corporations shape a cheaper, more disposable workforce of temporary workers, part-timers and other "contingent workers."*

Current economic trends are hospitable not only to the facilitation of increased deaths as health care costs spiral out of reach of more and more people, but to illegalities of all kinds, not just those involving street crime.

The cast of *Beverly Hills 90210*, 1995.

Elliott Currie (1996) argues, moreover, that in a market society in general (and in the United States in particular), as the pursuit of private gain increasingly becomes the organizing principle for all areas of social life, crime becomes a predictable accompaniment to the decline of the public and the rise of the private. In other words, market societies, according to Currie (1996: 38–41), are fertile ground for the growth of crime because they promote:

- an increased inequality and concentrated economic deprivation;
- a weakening of the capacity of local communities for informal support, mutual provision, and socialization and supervision of the young;
- a stressing and fragmenting of families;
- a withdrawing of public provision of basic services from those they have already stripped of livelihood, economic security, and informal community support;
- a magnifying of a culture of Darwinian competition for status and dwindling resources and by urging a level of consumption they cannot fulfill for everyone through legitimate channels.

In sum, the growing economic inequality in U.S. society does not suggest a future of stability and consensus. On the contrary, as Sklar, Currie, and others have argued, these trends and the prevailing economic policies seem more like a prescription for chaos than community.

## Criminals on Crime: Controlling Their Vulnerability

The convicted offenders quoted in this section are speaking more or less in their own words. With respect to five groups of criminals portrayed—working-class property offenders, white-collar offenders, sexual-homicide offenders, batterers, and gang-bangers—these predominantly male activities were selected because of their real, perceived, and imaginary threats to social order. In some cases, we hear directly from the perpetrators themselves. In other cases, we read from a montage of voices attributed to these offenders by authors who have conducted some kind of field work, whether as ethnographic researchers, magazine journalists, or clinical researchers. In combination, these portrayals provide a rich and accurate depiction of the views and worlds of convicted offenders. Although the social constructions of their participation in harmful behavior are representative of the offensive actions presented, the reader should keep in mind that even within specific offending categories, these offenders are not all alike. In battering cases, for example, variability presents itself in a continuum of batterers' profiles (i.e., psychopathic wife assaulters, overcontrolled wife assaulters, cyclical/emotionally volatile wife abusers); yet, there are common psychic characteristics among those individuals who batter women. Finally, students of crime should hold up the accounts presented here to various tested theories of criminal behavior (e.g., differential association, rational choice, and others) for the purposes of cross-validating the stories and the theories.

All people, criminals and noncriminals, defend their existence, fight for their integrity, and establish their ego identity. For most people, including some criminals, crimes do not provide the necessary venue for these kinds of individual self-actualizations. For other criminals, however, crime does provide at least a partial *raison d'etre* (Bing, 1991). In other words, crime allows one to say, "I am a criminal, I am a somebody." In its most fundamental form, the rationale can become: "I kill (or will be killed), therefore, I am." In short, the incidences and patterns of crime are primarily about gratifying emotional and material desires that have not been satisfied by the social realities in which individual (or groups of) offenders find themselves situated. This perspective on the production of crime fits squarely with the constitutive-integrative model of crime and social control, precisely because it relies on a contextualization of both.

The underlying themes that move across the accounts of property, white collar, sexual assault, and predatory offenders that follow have to do with the conscious and unconscious acts of people to save face from self, others, and society. To varying degrees, these offenders are consumed by their need to control real and symbolic threats to their psychic states of well-being. These individuals are going about the business of protecting themselves from vulnerabilities of all kinds (e.g., physical, emotional, material, psychological). These vulnerabilities are tied to their self-concept, sense of worth, and personal esteem, not only as they feel accepted or rejected by others and themselves, but as they feel connected to or disconnected from others, from the most intimate and personal relationships involving family to the most distant and impersonal relationships involving mass culture and global society.

## Working-Class Property Offenders

In one study of persistent property offenders, Neal Shover and David Honaker (1996: 11) examined the decision to steal in relation to rational choice theory. They found that contrary to deterrence theory, for example, the majority of these offenders "gave little or no thought to the possibility of arrest and confinement." As one offender stated, "I try to keep that [thought of arrest] the farthest thing from my mind that I can" (quoted in Shover and Honaker, 1996: 12). Another one said:

> Well, the only thing that I was worried about was . . . getting arrested didn't even cross my mind—just worrying about getting killed is the only thing, you know, getting shot. That's the only thing. . . . But, you know, you'd have to be really crazy not to think about that . . . you could possibly get in trouble. It crossed my mind, but I didn't worry about it all that much (Shover and Honaker, 1996: 12).

Shover and Honaker argue that to better understand the risk assessment of these offenders, one needs to investigate the personal and social contexts in which their decisions are made. For the most part, they found that thieves focused mostly on the money, the good times, and the other expected gains to be reaped. As one offender put it, "You're thinking about the big paycheck at the end of the thirty to forty-five minutes worth of work. . . . I didn't think about nothing but what I was going to do when I got that money, how I was going to spend it, what I was going to do with it, you know" (Shover and Honaker, 1996: 13). Being able to obtain or consume items and activities that blue collar work will ordinarily not provide becomes the object of desire.

> *It was all just a big money thing to me at the time, you know. Really, what it was was impressing everybody, you know. "Here Floyd is, and he's never had nothing in his life, and now look at him: he's driving new cars, wearing jewelry," you know (Shover and Honaker, 1996: 15).*

As another offender put it, "I just wanted to be doing something. Instead of being at home, or something like that. I wanted to be running, I wanted to be going to clubs, and picking up women and shooting pool." And, "I didn't want to [do any legitimate] work" (Shover and Honaker, 1996: 16).

## White Collar Offenders

Michael Benson (1996) interviewed a sample of thirty white collar offenders who had been convicted of economic offenses through the use of indirection, fraud, or collusion. One interesting finding was that typically these offenders denied criminal intent or that they were motivated by a desire to do wrong. Their crimes, in other words, were thought of as derivative of exceptional circumstances beyond their control (e.g., a failing business, a gambling habit). Although they did not necessarily deny culpability or that "their behavior probably could be construed as falling within the conduct proscribed by statute," they *felt* no guilt or shame as a result of conviction. On the contrary, indictment, prosecution, and conviction provoke[d] a variety of emotions among offenders" (Benson, 1996: 66), including embarrassment and rage.

For these offenders, a sense of their self-worth and their identities was not tied up with their criminal activities. Unlike the working-class offenders, the white collar offenders seem to distance themselves from assimilating criminal identities because their self-concepts are traditionally validated through conventional occupational roles. These offenders attempt to diminish the effect of legal status degradation ceremonies that transform them from law-abiding citizens to convicted felons. They do their best to resist the label "criminal" from becoming a permanently validated one. Often, they feel real resentment at the system, the media, and others for the high profile or public coverage of their crimes.

Finally, crimes such as antitrust violations or income tax violations are often viewed as common practices in the business world, which is—according to their perception—unfairly regulated, criminalized, and so forth. Not only do these white collar offenders not identify themselves as criminals, but, when they get caught, their "techniques of neutralization" may vary from arguments of exceptionality to arguments of delegitimation of the illegal behavior in question. The following excerpts all come from Benson (1996: 67–72):

> *What I could have done if I had truly had a devious criminal mind and perhaps if I had been a little smarter—and I am not saying that with any degree of pride or any degree of modesty whatever, [as] it's being smarter in a bad, and evil way—I could have pulled this off on a grander scale and I might still be doing it.*

> *You know (the plea's) what really hurt. I didn't even know I had feet. I felt numb. My head was just floating. There was no feeling, except a state of suspended anima-*

*tion. . . . For a brief moment, I almost hesitated, I almost said "not guilty." If I had been alone, I would have fought, but my family . . .*

*It was a way of doing business before we even got into the business. So it was like "why do you brush your teeth in the morning" or something. . . . It was a part of the every-day . . . It was a method of survival.*

*Everybody cheats on their income tax, 95% of the people. Even if it's for ten dollars, it's the same principle. I didn't cheat. I just didn't know how to report it.*

*First of all, no money was stolen or anything of that nature. The bank didn't lose any money. . . . What I did was a technical violation. I made a mistake. There's no ques-tion about that, but the bank lost no money.*

*I was faced with the choice of all of a sudden, and I mean now, closing the doors or do-ing something else to keep that business open. . . . I'm not going to tell you that this wouldn't have happened if I'd had time to think it over, because I think it probably would have. You're sitting there with a dying patient. You are going to try to keep him alive.*

## Sexual-Homicide Offenders

The excerpts in this section come from "An Interview With a Serial Murderer" by Eric Hickey (1996: 120–123). Hickey argues in the case of this particular serial sexual killer that "his crimes were adaptive strategies—at least to some extent, rationally conceived for the purpose of satisfying needs and/or desires" (Cromwell, 1996: 117). Although there may be commonalities among serial killers, especially serial sexual killers, there is also more than one profile of this kind of offender. What is perhaps most interesting about this offender's description and explanation of his behavior is the degree to which he has articulated the contradictions between the compulsive-determined behavior, on the one hand, and the rationally calculated and intentional behavior, on the other hand. Like most serial offenders (i.e., rapists, batterers, killers), his behavior reveals degrees of control and lack of control. His behavior also reveals the presence of vulnerability, rationality, and (mental) illness.

*Offender:* I was basically living a double life. I was one thing to this person and another thing to that person, all lies. And the reason for that is just a low self-image. You're not happy with who you are. You're not comfortable with who you are. You don't have any self-confidence. . . . One day I'd be fine, and the next time I'd be out, I'd have this compulsion to go out and kill somebody and so I started looking back at each instance, what was I thinking, and this is what I came up with, and it's kind of a higher stage process. The first stage is what I call distorted thinking. It's a distorted thought line, and I found that I was God's gift to earth. I'm the center of the universe. I'm perfect. I'm the smartest guy that ever lived. Nobody's as perceptive as I am. So long as nothing came against that self-image, I was fine. But the problem with that was that it, as I mentioned earlier, was all lies. . . . There was always going to be some challenge to this grandiose self-image. Sometimes it would be a lot of little things, sometimes it would just be the stress of having to live these little lies, having to always be looking over your back, and other times it would be a very definite event, a girl-friend leaves you or something like that. Whenever that happened, then there would be a fall . . . [a] psychological fall, and it's very debilitating, very disorienting, confusing, harrowing. It's a very scary feeling. I'm used to being perfect. I'm not about to put up with anything that tarnishes my own sense of perfection, so that would lead to internal negative response, and that's what I was saying to myself. I'm not gonna have this, and instead of being scared, frightened, knocked off balance, I wheeled into a retaliatory mode. I'm gonna fight this. I'm gonna stand up for my self-importance. The way to deal with that was simply to prove it. You're going to be a somebody, and my means of being a somebody was violence. To me violence had already been reinforced through time as a means of being the star, center stage in this drama. Up to this point I've had a fall, and I felt like I am not in control. I'm not top dog.

*Hickey:* The fall comes as a result of what?

*Offender:* Of any challenge to the feelings of superiority. If you live out in the real world, you're going to get them, at work, your relationships and so forth. That's why it's repetitive. That's why it continues, and violence to me had been reinforced as a means of taking control, as a means of getting even, getting even with the world. It's reaffirming that I was all those things, and the actual deed, the victimizing, the brutalizing, of another human being, was my proof, a seal, a seal of approval, self-approval, my evidence that I'm really a somebody, and the result of that would be a triumph, a restoration, I'm restored. I'm doing not what other people will, but what I will, and that would restore all those feelings of largeness, power, self-importance that strengthened the overloaded ego that I had in the first stage, and I'd be fine.

*Hickey:* There was a sexual component to most of the killings?

*Offender:* Yes. Sex was sort of a vehicle. So when that was done, climax was reached. You've already terrorized this person. You've already hurt them, beat them, whatever. But there would be a feeling of letdown. You're excited, and then all of a sudden you come down. Kind of like a ball game. All this had been acted out for years and in particular, it always involved stripping the victims, forcing them to strip themselves, cutting them, making them believe that they were going to be set free if they cooperated, tying them down and then the real viciousness started. The victim's terror and the fact that I could cause it at will . . . their pain didn't register. All I could relate to was the ritual and the sounds. All this was proof to me that, I'm in control, I am playing the star role here, this person is nothing but a prop. I'm growing and they're becoming smaller. Once both the violence and sexual aspect were completed, then that was it. That was the end of an episode.

## Battering

Donald Dutton, who has been a director of the Assaultive Husbands Program in Vancouver, British Columbia, and is author of two books on domestic violence, has done much to unravel the psyches of male batterers in particular. Although Dutton recognizes different battering types and is not reductionistic in his analysis, he has nevertheless come up with a psychological profile of *The Batterer* (1995) that relies, in part, on Lenore Walker's (1979; 1984) "cycle of violence" and, in part, on John Gunderson's (1984) "borderline personality," in combination with his own interviewing of and group work with male batterers.

> *All the case histories in this book have been drawn from my treatment groups. It was in these groups that I heard how powerless these men felt in their lives, especially in their intimate relationships. Most don't know how to even describe a feeling to themselves, let alone assert it to an intimate other. Some men, it seems, could listen to the blues every day for a decade before they could verbalize their own grief. They could brag of sexual conquest before they could talk of deep loneliness or their addiction to "hits" of intimacy through physical contact with a woman. It is in recognizing this emotional self-alienation that we can understand the darkest side of the male sex role (Dutton, 1995: 20).*

In his discussion of the cycle of violence and the abusive personality in general, and in relationship to the "tension-building" and "acute battering" phases as distinct from the "contrition" phase, Dutton (1995: 44) explains:

> *. . . over and over again in groups, rather than hearing, "I'm scared," "I feel like I'm falling apart," "I'm tense and anxious all over," I hear instead the externalization of blame for an inner state of unnamed anguish: "She doesn't dress the kids," "She doesn't keep the house clean," "She doesn't fix the meals." If she did, in the magical thinking of the abuser's mind, these strange bad feelings would disappear.*
>
> *At this stage, cyclical abusers repeatedly play what we call in group "the bitch tape," a mental cassette stuck permanently on auto reverse. Side one has some version of: "I feel bad. It's her fault." Side two says: "She's a bitch. She's always putting me down."*

Moreover, what the cyclical abuser never says is that he "desperately needs his wife to define him, finds himself irrevocably bound to her, and considers the prospect of being alone terrifying" (Dutton, 1995: 45). These batterers are said to be masking their dependency: "The abuse keeps the woman in place while allowing the man to overlook his own hidden dependency needs and maintain his illusion of detachment" (Dutton, 1995: 45).

In short, Dutton's analysis of the violence-prone borderline man weaves together an appreciation for the roles of the shaming father, the ambivalent attachment to the mother, and the history of the presence of violence in the home. Finally, in trying to answer the question why the male batterer becomes so angry and abusive in intimate relationships, Dutton explains that the answer lies, in part, in what intimacy means to him:

> *The borderline man asks his intimate relationships to do the impossible. They serve the unenviable task of gluing together, with relational chewing gum and piano wire, a*

*shaky ego. This flimsy arrangement—and with it, the man's very sense of integrity, his sense of himself as whole—threatens to fail at any time.*

> *Yet the relationship that the man needs so desperately is fraught with "dysphoric stalemates"—abandonment anxiety, extreme demandingness, and an incapacity to communicate intimacy needs. As the tension and malaise build, the borderline man unconsciously requires that his wife [or lover] take it away, to soothe him, to make him feel whole and good. He has trouble sleeping, he's depressed. But he does not express this because he is either unaware of it or doesn't want to reveal his weaknesses (Dutton, 1995: 154–155).*

## Gangbanging

The following excerpts come from *Do or Die* by Leon Bing (1991), a journalist and former fashion model. Bing has written cover stories on gang life for *L.A. Weekly* and *Harper's* magazines; portions of this book first appeared in *Rolling Stone*. Beginning in 1986, Bing started to explore the ghetto of South Central Los Angeles and was able to work her way into the world of the Crips and Bloods, two of L.A.'s most notorious teenage gangs, at a time when these gangs were doing some serious battling for supremacy in the streets. Keep in mind that what you are about to read is not meant to be representative of the behavior of the some 250,000 gang members across America, but is meant merely to contextualize the world of gangbanging violence from the perspective of a 17-year-old homeless "homeboy."

His name is Faro and he lives from couch to couch, or in a sleeping bag, or in the back seat of a parked car. A couple of days here, a week or two there. He does not remember the last time he went to school. Neither can he read or write. As Bing (1991: 39) writes, Faro "is as close to invisibility as it is possible to be." In spite of his invisibility, Faro wears his hair sectioned into a myriad of tiny braids with blue rubber bands at the tips. "He is wearing shabby sweats and busted-down Nike high-tops. He is very thin; the bones of his wrists stick knobbily out of the elastic cuffs of his hooded jacket, which is at least two sizes too small for him" (Bing, 1991: 39).

> *My mother, she died from a drug overdose. I got a grandmother, but she gonna go the same way—she just wanderin' the streets day and night, lookin' for handouts so she can fix herself a pipe. My brother got killed in a holdup three years ago.*
>
> *Most people think he was holdin' the gun . . . He wasn't but eight years old. He was lookin' at comic books in a 7-Eleven and some dude come in to rob the place . . . The homies give him a nice funeral. I used to have a picture of him, laid out, in my scrapbook. It got lost (Bing, 1991: 40).*

As Bing and Faro are cruising the "hood" he says to her, referring to two dudes driving in a car beside them, "I'm gonna look crazy at 'em. You watch what they do" (Bing, 1991: 41).

> *He turns away from me, and I lean forward over the wheel so that I can watch the faces on the two guys. The driver, sensing that someone is looking at him, glances over at my car. His eyes connect with Faro's, widen for an instant. Then he breaks the con-*

*tact, looks down, looks away. And there is no mistaking what I saw there in his eyes: it was fear. Whatever he saw in Faro's face, he wasn't about to mess with it.*

*Faro giggles and turns back toward me. He looks the same as he did before to me: a skinny, slightly goofy-looking kid. . . . I ask Faro to "look crazy" for me. He simply narrows his eyes . . . and everything about his face shifts and changes, as if by some trick of time-lapse photography. It becomes a nightmare face, and it is a scary thing to see. It tells you that if you return his stare, if you challenge this kid, you'd better be ready to stand your ground. His look tells you that he doesn't care about anything, not your life and not his.*

*I ask Faro what would have happened if the guy had looked crazy back.*

*"Then we woulda got into it . . . Never woulda happened. That was just some damn preppy out on his lunch hour."*

*"But if he had returned the challenge. What then?"*

*"Then I woulda killed him."*

*My eyes slide over his skinny silhouette. No way can he be hiding a weapon under that sweatsuit. He smiles slyly and pats the top of his right shoe. I peer down and there, unbelievably, is the glint of metal.*

*"Like there was this fool, this enemy nigger from our worst enemy set, and he was with his wife and his baby. They was walkin' down there near Vermont, where he had no business bein'. He was slippin' bad and we caught him. We was in a car, all homies, and I was like, 'Let's pop this dumb nigger, let's empty the whole clip [referring to an AK-47 automatic rifle]. . . . I just wanted to make him pay.*

*"For all our dead homeboys. For bein' our enemy. . . . You gotta understand— enemy got to pay just for being alive. . . . So I strapped it [the AK-47] to the seat . . . and we circled around and pulled up on this nigger from two blocks away, crept up on him slow like, and I just gave it to him . . .  Pah-pah-pah-pah-pah-pah- pah! You know, just let him have it. Just emptied the whole . . . I lit his ass up! I killed him—shot his baby in the leg—crippled his wife!"*

*We are silent for a moment; when Faro speaks again his voice is a fusion of bad feelings: despair, remorse, a deep, biting resentment.*

*"It was like, damn, Cuz—I killed him, that was my mission, but still—his whole family."*

*He shakes his head several times, as if he cannot will himself to believe his own story. Then he places the tip of one index finger on the glass next to him and taps it in a nervous, rhythmic beat.*

*"That's a crazy world out there, and we livin' it."*

*"Dying in it, too."*

*[The finger stops tapping.] "If you die, you die. Most gangbangers don't have nothin' to live for no more, anyway. That why some of 'em be gangbangin' . . . I tell you this—you see enough dyin', then you be ready to die yourself, just so you don't have to see no more of death"* (Bing, 1991: 41–44).

In closing out this section in general and in relationship to black criminality and questions of fatalism in particular, Austin (1992: 1787) notes a truism about young African American male offenders that applies more or less to all of the male convicts that we have heard from: All of these lawbreakers "wind up with little control over their images and less control than they imagine over their lives and their own world views." For the most part, although these offenders are responsible for their own actions, on the one hand, they are weak and vulnerable human beings, on the other hand. They are materially unsatisfied or emotionally unfulfilled and very much "out of control," with the hope that their illegitimate activity will somehow make things better or tolerable.

## *An Inventory of Criminological Indicators*

At the risk of appearing to have adopted some kind of positivistic-medical model of crime production, complete with a diagnostic kit for discerning the relevant factors circumventing the commission of crimes by individual or groups of offenders, I would like to identify what might be called "an inventory of criminological indicators." These indicators are not meant to be suggestive of criminal profiles. Although such indicators may refer to attributes or characteristics of both people and environments, profiles refer only to potential or actual offenders. The ten indicators that I have identified refer to the specific manifestations of problems associated with the constitutive nature of crime production. These include:

- Physicality (biochemical conditions)
- Temperament (personality types)
- Cognition (analytical abilities)
- Ego/Identity (psychic development)
- Familiality (early socialization)
- Gender (sexism)
- Race/Ethnicity (discrimination)
- Class (inequality)
- Resources/Services (distribution)
- Social Ecology (environmentalism)

Stated differently, the production of crime and criminals is constitutive of these elements (indicators) in a state of non-homeostasis or imbalance. The point is that to reduce the production of crime and the reproduction of criminal behavior, public policy needs to adopt a comprehensive and integrative view of both, whereby the constitutive nature of particular crimes and criminals are taken into account. Hence, unlike policies of repressive crime control that focus primarily on retaliatory and punitive models of deterrence aimed solely at containing the transgressive behavior of individual offenders, the policies of nonrepressive crime prevention focus not only on the offenses as well as the needs (indicators) of offenders, but also on the noncriminal dimensions of unhealthy social ecologies aimed at reforming the reproduction of criminogenic environments, such as market societies.

As Ralph Taylor and Adele Harrell (1996: 24) have concluded, "The relevance of the physical environment appears contingent on a range of nonphysical factors and the type of crime or crime-related outcome in question." Once again, consistent with constitutive criminology, the physical and the nonphysical dimensions of crime production in relationship to each other are dynamically and recursively situated. Hence, just as the production of crime is interactively integrated, policies of crime reduction should also be interactively integrated. In other words, the inventory of criminological indicators that I suggest to be consulted, whether in terms of legislation, codification, and social change or in terms of the application of the penal sanction in the case of a particular offender, are viewed as constituting the entire field or etiology of crime.

By consulting these factors of criminality, it is possible to derive policies of social control grounded in a constitutive approach to crime reduction because all the causes of crime and criminal behavior have been rationally accounted for. This integrative approach to crime control attempts to come to grips with difficult and pending questions about the relationships between the physical and nonphysical and between the individual and social or environmental. For example, what are the effects of a market society's social, political, and economic environments on the risks of crime? Or, how do social, cultural, and organizational features of U.S. society contribute to the successes or failures of crime reduction? And finally, which of these relations or indicators of crime production were diagnostically present in the particular cases of individual offenders?

In the final chapter, I offer a constitutive-integrative approach to crime and social control as an alternative to the cultural, political, and economic responses to crime that dominate contemporary practice. As such, this constitutive model challenges the dominant discourses on crime and justice as it brings together the complementary practices of shaming and reintegration envisioned by Braithwaite (1989), of peacemaking (Pepinsky and Quinney, 1991), feminist (Gelsthrope and Morris, 1990), and newsmaking (Barak, 1994) criminologies, and of critical legal-race theory (Cook, 1990; 1992).

## *Summary and Conclusions: Overcoming Cultural Hegemony*

Crime and criminal behavior are cultural productions inseparable from developing political economies and social ecologies as these are experienced by the isolated individual and the individual as group member, as each makes his way in ultramodern and consumptive U.S. society. Crime emerges within the relationship of a cultural hegemony that assimilates differences of mass society and yet commodifies their marketization while struggling against counterhegemonic ideologies (e.g., "cultural wars"). The argument explicit here and implicit throughout *Integrating Criminologies* has been that criminologists should take into account the full range of criminological indicators as these relate to individual offenders, groups of criminals, and types of crime and crime control as these interact with the development and realization of individual identities as these are, in turn, shaped by the dynamically interdependent variables of race, gender, and class as these are, in turn, informed by changing political economies and mass systems of communication, *ad infinitum*.

## Discussion Questions

1. What are the connections between the "culture of consumption," the "consumer personality," and the expressions of crime in contemporary America?

2. How do Russell's "racial inequality hypothesis" and her argument advance our understanding of the relationship between race and crime?

3. Using Joe and Chesney-Lind's study of gangs, discuss the gang's attraction to both genders.

What are the differences in the attractions for boys and girls?

4. Citing various studies noted in this chapter, compare and contrast white-collar and blue-collar crime.

5. What is Dutton's explanation for why certain men batter and abuse their spouses or lovers?

## References

Alvarez, Alexander. 1995. "Adjusting to Genocide: The Techniques of Neutralization and the Holocaust." Paper presented at the annual meetings of the American Society of Criminology, Boston.

Anderson, Margaret L., and Patricia Hill Collins, eds. 1992. *Race, Class, and Gender: An Anthology.* Belmont, CA: Wadsworth.

Austin, Regina. 1992. " 'The Black Community,' Its Lawbreakers, and a Politics of Identification." *Southern California Law Review* 65:1769–1817.

Barak, Gregg. 1991a. *Gimme Shelter: A Social History of Homelessness in Contemporary America.* New York: Praeger.

———, ed. 1991b. *Crimes by the Capitalist State: An Introduction to State Criminality.* Albany, NY: SUNY Press.

———, ed. 1994. *Media, Process, and the Social Construction of Crime: Studies in Newsmaking Criminology.* New York: Garland.

Benson, Michael L. 1996. "Denying the Guilty Mind: Accounting for Involvement in a White-Collar Crime." In Paul Cromwell, ed., *In Their Own Words: Criminals on Crime.* Los Angeles: Roxbury.

Berger, Bennett M. 1995. *An Essay on Culture: Symbolic Structure and Social Structure.* Berkeley: University of California Press.

Bing, Leon. 1991. *Do or Die.* New York: Harper-Collins.

Bloland, Harland G. 1995. "Postmodernism and Higher Education." *Journal of Higher Education* 66(5):521–559.

Bottoms, Anthony, and Paul Wiles. 1994. "Crime and Insecurity in the City." Paper presented at the annual meetings of the American Society of Criminology, Miami.

Braithwaite, John. 1979. *Inequality, Crime and Public Policy.* London: Routledge and Kegan Paul.

———. 1989. *Crime, Shame and Reintegration.* Cambridge: Cambridge University Press.

Cerroni-Long, E. L. 1996. "Ethnic Expressive Style and American Public Opinion: The O. J. Simpson Case." In Gregg Barak, ed., *Representing OJ: Murder, Criminal Justice, and Mass Culture.* Albany, NY: Harrow and Heston.

Chambliss, William. 1989. "State-Organized Crime." *Criminology* 27:183–198.

Coleman, Richard P., and Lee Rainwater. 1978. *Social Standing in America.* New York: Basic Books.

Colvin, Mark, and John Pauly. 1983. "A Critique of Criminology: Toward an Integrated Structural-Marxist Theory of Delinquency Production." *American Journal of Sociology* 89:513–551.

Cook, Anthony E. 1990. "Beyond Critical Legal Studies: The Reconstructive Theology of Dr. Martin Luther King, Jr. *Harvard Law Review* 103:985–1012.

———. 1992. "The Spiritual Movement Towards Justice." *University of Illinois Law Review* 4:1006–1019.

Covington, Jeanette. 1985. "Gender Differences in Criminality Among Heroin Users." *Journal of Research in Crime and Delinquency* 22(4):329–353.

Cromwell, Paul, ed. 1996. *In Their Own Words: Criminals on Crime*. Los Angeles: Roxbury.

Currie, G. David, Robert J. Box, Richard A. Ball, and Darryl Stone. 1992. *National Assessment of Law Enforcement Anti-gang Information Resources: Draft 1992 Final Report*. West Virginia University: National Assessment Survey.

Currie, Elliott, 1996. "Market Society and Social Disorder." In B. MacLean and D. Milovanovic, eds., *Thinking Critically about Crime*. Vancouver: Collective Press.

Daly, Kathleen. 1994. *Gender, Crime, and Punishment*. New Haven: Yale University Press.

Davis, Mike. 1992. *City of Quartz: Excavating the Future in Los Angeles*. New York: Vintage Books.

Derber, Charles. 1992. *Money, Murder and the American Dream*. Boston: Faber and Faber.

Dines, Gail, and Jean M. Humez, eds. 1995. *Gender, Race and Class in Media: A Text-Reader*. Thousands Oaks, CA: Sage.

Dutton, Donald G., with Susan K. Golant. 1995. *The Batterer: A Psychological Profile*. New York: Basic Books.

Friedrichs, David O. 1995. "White Collar Crime and the Class-Race-Gender Construct." Paper presented at the annual meetings of the Academy of Criminal Justice Sciences, Boston.

Gelsthorpe, Loraine, and Allison Morris, eds. 1990. *Feminist Perspectives in Criminology*. Milton Keyes: Open University Press.

Giddens, Anthony. 1983. *The Constitution of Society: Outline of the Theory of Structuration*. Cambridge: Polity Press.

Granovetter, Mark. 1985. "Economic Action and Social Structure: The Problem of Embeddedness." *American Journal of Sociology* 91:481–510.

Gunderson, John G. 1984. *Borderline Personality Disorder*. Washington, D.C.: American Psychiatric Press.

Hall, Stuart. 1995. "The Whites of Their Eyes: Racist Ideologies and the Media." In Gail Dines and Jean Humez, eds., *Gender, Race and Class in Media*. Thousand Oaks, CA: Sage.

Harer, Miles D., and Darrell Steffensmeier. 1992. "The Differing Effects of Economic Inequality on Black and White Rates of Violence." *Social Forces* 70(4):1035–1054.

Harris, Anthony. 1991. "Race, Class, and Crime." In *Criminology: A Contemporary Handbook*. Belmont, CA: Wadsworth.

Hawkins, Darnell F., ed. 1995. *Ethnicity, Race, and Crime: Perspectives Across Time and Place*. Albany, NY: SUNY Press.

Hickey, Eric W. 1996. "An Interview With a Serial Murderer." In Paul Cromwell, ed., *In Their Own Words: Criminals On Crime*. Los Angeles: Roxbury.

Hollinger, David A. 1995. *Postethnic America: Beyond Multiculturalism*. New York: Basic Books.

Huff-Corzine, Lin, Jay Corzine, and David C. Moore. 1991. "Deadly Connections: Culture, Poverty, and the Direction of Lethal Violence." *Social Forces* 69(3):715–732.

Jensen, Robert. 1995. "Men's Lives and Feminist Theory." *Race, Gender and Class: An Interdisciplinary and Multicultural Journal* 2(2):111–126.

Joe, Karen, and Meda Chesney-Lind. 1993. " 'Just Every Mother's Angel': An Analysis of Gender and Ethnic Variations in Youth Gang Membership." Paper presented at the annual meetings of the American Society of Criminology, Phoenix.

Kellner, Douglas. 1995. "Cultural Studies, Multiculturalism and Media Culture." In Gail Dines and Jean M. Humez, eds., *Gender, Race and Class in Media*. Thousand Oaks, CA: Sage.

Lasch, Christopher. 1979. *The Culture of Narcissism*. New York: Norton.

Lynch, Michael J., and E. Britt Patterson., eds. 1991. *Race and Criminal Justice*. Albany, NY: Harrow and Heston.

Mills, C. Wright. 1951. *White Collar*. New York: Oxford University Press.

Messner, Steven F., and Rosenfeld, Richard. 1994. *Crime and the American Dream*. Belmont, CA: Wadsworth.

Muwakkil, Salim. 1993. "Ganging Together." *In These Times* (April 5): 6–8.

Pepinsky, Harold E., and Richard Quinney, eds. 1991. *Peacemaking Criminology*. Bloomington, IN: Indiana University Press.

Pfohl, Stephen. 1993. "Twilight of the Parasites: Ultramodern Capital and the New World Order." *Social Problems* 40(2):125–151.

Roberts, Dorothy E. 1993. "Crime, Race, and Reproduction." *Tulane Law Review* 67(6):1945–1977.

———. 1995. "Consumption and Crime: An Institutional Inquiry." Paper presented at the annual meetings of the Academy of Criminal Justice Sciences, Boston.

Rothstein, Michael. 1992. "Who are the Real Looters?" *Dissent* (Fall): 429–430.

Russell, Katheryn K. 1994. "The Racial Inequality Hypothesis: A Critical Look at the Research and an Alternative Theoretical Analysis." *Law and Human Behavior* 18(3):305–317.

Sampson, Robert J., and John H. Laub. 1993. *Crime in the Making: Pathways and Turning Points Through Life*. Cambridge, MA: Harvard University Press.

Semmes, Clovis E. 1992. *Cultural Hegemony and African American Development*. Westport, CN: Praeger.

Shover, Neal, and David Honaker. 1996. "The Socially Bounded Decision Making of Persistent Property Offenders." In Paul Cromwell, ed., *In Their Own Words: Criminals On Crime*. Los Angeles: Roxbury.

Simon, David R., and D. Stanley Eitzen. 1993. *Elite Deviance*. 4th ed. Needham Heights, MA: Allyn and Bacon.

Simon, David R., and Frank Hagan. 1995. "The Criminology of Scandal." Paper presented at the annual meetings of the Academy of Criminal Justice Sciences, Boston.

Simpson, Sally S. 1991. "Caste, Class, and Violent Crime: Explaining Difference in Female Offending." *Criminology* 29(1):115–136.

Sklar, Holly. 1995. *Chaos or Community? Seeking Solutions, Not Scapegoats for Bad Economics*. Boston: South End Press.

Sulton, Anne T. 1996. *African-American Perspectives on Crime Causation, Criminal Justice Administration, and Crime Prevention*. Newton, MA: Butterworth-Heinemann.

Surette, Ray. 1992. *Media, Crime, and Criminal Justice: Images and Realities*. Pacific Grove, CA: Brooks/Cole.

Taylor, Ralph B., and Adele V. Harrell. 1996. *Physical Environment and Crime: A Final Summary Report Presented to the National Institute of Justice*. Washington, D.C.: U.S. Department of Justice.

Veblen, Thorsten. [1899] 1953. *The Theory of the Leisure Class*. New York: Macmillan.

Walker, Lenore E. 1979. *The Battered Woman*. New York: Harper and Row.

———. 1984. *The Battered Woman Syndrome*. New York: Springer.

Walker, Samuel, Cassia Spohn, and Miriam DeLone. 1996. *The Color of Justice: Race, Ethnicity, and Crime in America*. Belmont, CA: Wadsworth.

Walters, Mary. 1990. *Ethnic Options: Choosing Identities in America*. Berkeley, CA: University of California Press.

West, Cornell. 1989. "Black Culture and Postmodernism." In Barbara Kruger and Phil Mariani, eds., *Remaking History*. Port Townsend, Washington: Bay Press.

Williams, Patricia. 1991. *The Alchemy of Race and Rights*. Cambridge, MA: Harvard University Press.

Wilson, James Q., and Richard Herrnstein. 1985. *Crime and Human Nature*. New York: Touchstone.

Wilson, William J. 1987. *The Truly Disadvantaged*. Chicago: University of Chicago Press.

Wright, Richard A. 1995. "Women as 'Victims' and as 'Resisters': Depictions of The Oppression of Women in Criminology Textbooks." *Teaching Sociology* 23:111–121.

*Chapter* **12**

# Integrating Crime and Social Control: An Interdisciplinary Approach to Crime Reduction

Samuel Jackson and John Travolta in *Pulp Fiction*, 1994.

On a typical news day, the average number of crime stories carried by one of the three major networks is two. In 1995, ABC, NBC, and CBS combined to produce a record number of 2,574 crime stories on their evening newscasts. During the same year, however, "the proportion of those under 30 who say they regularly watch network TV news [had] dropped by more than one-third" (Editorial, 1996: 3). A growing percentage of those both younger and older than 30 prefer watching and getting their knowledge about crime and its control from programs such as *NYPD Blue* and *Law and Order* than from the nightly news. By now, the readers of this textbook should know that neither crime nor its control is fundamentally about the collection of media-generated images. Rather, both are representative of social relations among people, mediated by images of crime and justice as these are constituted in everyday life.

Unfortunately, in an ultramodern society such as the United States, the realities of the street, of the corporate boardroom, and of the mass media are typically conflated into contemporary versions of crime and crime control that are consumed by popular culture. These homogenized renderings of crime control reflect the premises of the rich and powerful worlds of corporate America rather than the premises of the academic and scientific worlds of criminology. In this final chapter of *Integrating Criminologies*, I argue, among other things, that to successfully reduce crime in U.S. society there has to be a change in the public discourse that permeates the relationship between the mass consumption of American cultural values in general and of crime and crime control in particular.

When it comes to mass media inclusive of newspapers, books, magazines, films, radio, and television, we are living in an age dominated by the National Entertainment State (NES; Miller and Biden, 1996: 23–26). For example, Ted Turner, founder of the Cable News Network, once informed an audience of foreign journalists: "The more complex, the more forward-looking the story is here in the United States, to a large extent the smaller the ratings are" (quoted in Editorial, 1996: 3). In short, as entertainment came to trump "pure" news, the latter increasingly presented itself as the former (e.g., ABC's *20/20*, CBS's *60 Minutes*; and NBC's *Dateline*). In early 1996, Turner decided to switch rather than fight, and he agreed to fold his all-news CNN into the magazine, book-publishing, and entertainment conglomerate Time Warner in a $7.5 billion deal. Besides another mega financial take over, one might say that, in terms of the production of mass culture, a homogenization of news and entertainment is marching into the future.

Today, the NES consists of four corporate conglomerates that virtually monopolize the majority of images of crime and social control consumed by the general public. These include: (1) *General Electric*, which in addition to its interests in transportation, turbines, electrical equipment, motors, communications, plastics, lighting, appliances, retail, medical services, music, financing, insurance, and software, also owns television and cable stations, not to mention NBC network news; (2) *Disney/Cap Cities*, which in addition to its interests in multimedia, home video, book publishing, motion pictures, magazines, retail, athletic franchises, newspapers, theme parks/resorts, insurance, and oil, also owns television, cable, and radio stations, not to mention ABC network news; (3) *Westinghouse*, which in addition to its interests in communications and information, insurance, financing, banking, managing, electricity, nuclear power, and refrigeration, also owns television, cable, and radio stations, not to mention CBS network news; and (4) *Time Warner*, which in addition to its interests in liquor (Seagrams), electric utilities, coal, motion pictures, book publishing, magazines, multimedia, entertainment/resorts, athletic franchises, retail, television programming, home video, now owns Turner Broadcasting and its assorted interests, not to mention CNN, TNT, and TBS.

The point is that these conglomerates no longer conform, if they ever did, to the Marshall McLuhan truism that "the medium is the message." Instead, when it comes to producing mass cultures or responses to crime, these corporate media giants as part of the NES act more as censors and buffers of social reality as they characteristically "omit the message, suppress the message, homogenize the message, sensationalize the message or convert the message into entertainment—or worse, 'infotainment' " (Editorial, 1996: 3). In sum, the NES is the contemporary equivalent of a "user friendly" Big Brother.

The corporate culture that owns the media and the media that control mass culture help to infuse a system of news coverage that is selective at best. This is certainly the case when it comes to the representation of crime and crime control. For example, media pundits rarely, if ever, come close to examining, let alone criticizing, corporate monopoly and its relationship to crime. As Morton Mintz, an award-winning investigative journalist for the *Washington Post*, now retired, has argued about media coverage of the pervasive abuses of corporate power in general and of corporate murder, manslaughter, and environmental destruction in particular, there has always been a chronic tilt distorting its lack of presentation. Mintz (1992: 72) contends that

> *the media tilt is the net result of a gamut of causes and motives, including bias, boosterism, careerism, cowardice, libel risks, economic imperatives, friendships, ignorance, lack of resources, laziness, protection of news sources, retreats from investigative reporting, stupidity, suppression, survival instincts, and the pro-business orientation of owners and of the managers these owners hire.*

A similar argument can be made about the value-clarification folks and the virtue marketeers leaving out the ethical relationships between employer and employee, not to mention between the economy and the society as a whole. As Ellen Goodman (1995: A7) argues, "What's missing in the morality business is business." The "only time we put a moral grid over corporate behavior is when some company, TV network, or media mogul is mucking about in popular culture" (Goodman, 1995: A7). Otherwise, when it comes to discussing corporate responsibility to consumers, workers, and communities, there is a virtual silence regarding the moral obligations to upgrade worker skills, to fully fund pension plans, to provide health care, and to improve human services in general.

As part of the NES, these conglomerates have formidable power and influence over the social construction of crime and its control. They participate regularly in the formation and distribution of crime control as the conscious and unconscious producers of corporate news. By the late 1980s, prime-time viewing audiences had experienced the blurring of crime news with crime entertainment resulting frequently in crime infotainment (Barak, 1994). For example, the war metaphors used daily against persons thought to threaten the well-being of America, such as the War on Welfare, the War on Crime, the War on Drugs, and the War on Youth as well as the various social policies attached to these "wars," have generally proved themselves to be inadequate, inappropriate, or irrelevant to the production of crime (Messner and Rosenfeld, 1994). However, as metaphors they are quite successful. Over and over, the playing out of these law-and-order themes as crime and justice news in the form of mass entertainment serves to establish a common mentality or cultural hegemony about the nature of crime and its control.

In the next section of this chapter, I will examine and critique the thematic War on Youth and Youth Violence as an example of how the cultural dominance of corporate America inappropriately problematizes crime and social control in general. After this discussion, I will divide the rest of the chapter into three sections: (1) the discourses and modes of social control; (2) the nonintegrated modes of formal and informal means of crime control; and (3) the integrated models of crime reduction. Following that, I will conclude with a summation that binds together the themes of this chapter and book.

## The War on Youth and Youth Violence

By 1996, curfews for minors had been established in a number of cities throughout the United States. Different state courts had reached different conclusions regarding the right of local governments to impose such restrictions. However, as long as such laws do not inhibit youth from running errands for their parents or going to work, if and when necessary, then they will probably remain on the books. Similarly, in a suburb of Detroit in 1996 a local ordinance was passed holding parents responsible for the criminal acts of their children and subject to fines, if not incarceration, for failure to pay. Within a few months, this law had been once enforced and had yet to be legally challenged as to whether it violates the civil rights of those to whom it is applied. Acts like the curfew law passed in Atlanta in 1990, which hold parents responsible for their under-age children going out after 11:00 P.M., have also been viewed as targeting African American populations (Smothers, 1990).

Writing specifically about the cultural politics of "youth in crisis," Charles R. Acland (1995: 135–136) contends that the war against kids "combines the popular images of television as monster corrupter, the delinquent child, and the absent parent." To those politicians and advocate groups responsible for the passage of such laws, it makes little, if any difference whether there is any infringement on the lives of African Americans specifically or youths more generally, nor does it matter that there is no evidence that curfews have ever been successful instigators of parental responsibility. According to the prevailing rhetoric, youths are out of control and the rates of violent crime by youths are rising. Therefore, youths need to be better controlled; youths need to be increasingly under the surveillance of people or technology.

Censorship of gratuitous violence in films and on television, for example, combines neatly with the movement to survey the entertainment habits of youthful audiences as those are spuriously linked to increased rates of violence among teenage youths and young adults. Regardless of whether millions and millions of young viewers are not engaging in violent behavior, we bring on the electronic technology that will keep an eye on the viewing habits of children; restricting what they watch, where they watch, when they watch, and, of course, how much they watch. An implicit assumption is that by restricting their intake of television, this will, in turn, increase the number of hours spent doing homework or some other productive activity. The problem, in a nutshell, is not, however, the fact that by the time the average child leaves grammar school in this country he or she will have witnessed 8,000 murders and who-knows-how-many acts of violence in the mass media. The problem is the rarely examined and less-than-effectively addressed fact that millions of children in this country experience actual rapes and beatings while still in grammar school. It is estimated, for example, that, excluding spanking and whipping, 7 million children per year are subjected to severe violent acts by their parents, including being punched, scalded, burned, and threatened with a knife or gun (Cockburn, 1996). These data are more disturbing and threatening to the well-being of youth than are the data reflecting the relative increase in the usage of marijuana experimentation among youth, still down from the rates of experimentation from over a decade ago.

Alexander Cockburn (1996: 7) helps to place the issue of youth violence in perspective, when he emphasizes that young people are primarily victims rather than perpetrators.

> *With films like* Kids *making the rounds, we're now back in William Golding country, with youth depicted as feral in essence. Yet Golding did at least concede in a commentary on his novel* Lord of the Flies *that "... adult life appears, dignified and capable, but in reality is enmeshed in the same evil as the symbolic life of the children on the island."*
>
> *Even this statement elides the connection between adult and juvenile evil. Notoriously, murderers and other violent criminals are almost invariably abused as children. Violence is handed down in the form of blows, sexual predation, and punishment inflicted by adults on the young. The U.S. Advisory Board on Child Abuse and Neglect ... reported in April 1995 that violence, mostly by parents and caretakers, kills 2,000 children and seriously injures 140,000 more per year.*

This is not to deny the fact that between 1985 and 1995 the homicide rates doubled, and violent crime rates rose 70 percent among 13- to 19-year-olds and that there were some 135,000 school kids toting guns in America. During the same period, Cockburn also noted in passing that the doubling of homicides was paralleled by the doubling of youth poverty, not to suggest that one necessarily causes the other. However, a public policy to reduce the rates of children living in poverty certainly makes as much, if not more, sense than the efforts to reduce televised violence as a way of decreasing kid violence. At the same time, for example, in 1993, thirty-one suburban and rural California counties, with a population of 2.5 million, including 250,000 teenagers, had no teenage murders. As Cockburn (1996: 8) further notes,

> *Yet in a state with 4,000 murders that year, these kids saw the same movies, heard the same music, possessed as many guns as those central Los Angeles census tracts with the*

*same youth population, but with more than 200 youth murders. One difference: The youth poverty level of those thirty-one suburban and rural counties is tiny in comparison with central L.A.*

Looking a bit more critically at the War on Youth and its relationship to images of crime, control, and stability, Acland (1995: 136) reveals how "youth's complex relationship with popular culture as a lived and expressive domain is menacing because the uses of culture cannot be policed completely." Without trying to oversimplify, although there is an increase in teenage violence in certain areas, there is a strong tendency in mediated portrayals to extend the problem too inclusively as all youths are presented in danger of becoming out of control. In the context of a generalized fear of youth, there is an overflexing of rhetorical energy to survey and control the activities of youth. For example, the "evils of delinquency" (e.g., musical taste, youth style, subcultural membership) transcend the behavior of individual offenders. These representations are used because the imagery has the viewer believing that all youth in general are threatened with contamination.

In one sense, there is something familiar here. Historically, one can go back to antiquity where the dangers of the "evils" of youth are well known. In the United States, teenagers have been the subject of public scrutiny at least since the end of World War II. In another sense, as part of the more recent criminalization of youth, the traditional conception of the essential innocence of childhood has been joined by the newer contradictory relation of the essential guilt of youth. After all, as the contemporary argument goes, television introduces the young to all of those previously and allegedly hidden topics, including sex, violence, and other so-called adult topics. And if teenagers and even younger children have access to the same knowledge and are perpetrating adult crimes, well, then they should be treated like adults, and they should be removed from the more empathetic environs of the juvenile justice system.

Acland argues further that not only has youth been demonized by mass culture, youth has also been democratized as well. In the demonic state, "style as an expression of youth culture becomes one way to identify affiliations with 'subcultures' and, by implication, with crime" (Acland, 1995: 136; see also, Ferrell, 1993). For example, in the early nineties, there were "links among Raiders gear, black style, and black crime [which] immediately inspire[d] worry that as Raiders gear proliferates, so, too, will the possibilities of youth crime" (Acland, 1995: 136). The hysteria about youth includes not only a preoccupation with violence, but also with "babies having babies," with teenagers contracting AIDS/HIV or some other sexually transmitted disease, or with children as simply more reckless, more stupid, and in more need of tough controls than adults. Once again, the "just say no" mentality to drugs and life as a teenager belies the data that those groups with the greatest risks of contracting a sexually transmitted disease are not teenagers, but rather people in their twenties and thirties.

Youth represents many states of being, including, but not limited to crisis, spectacle, affectation, and the sublime, as they become social agents from beyond the ideological confines of the dominant or hierarchical structures of power. In short, "there is currently a consensual moment of crisis concerning youth, one that is met with the affective responses of despair, desire, and fear and with the material changes of increased surveillance and discipline" (Acland, 1995: 140). On the other hand, youth and youthfulness are presented in the mass media as having so much fun that in a consumptive or market society they set the styles or identities for those older generations that came before. In this sense, there is also a "democratization of youth" that is open to and can be experienced by the aging population.

Nevertheless, with all the concern about youth in crisis, the real threats to youths at risk, such as the increasing levels of childhood poverty, the lack of proper day care, health care, or education, for example, seem to all take a back seat to the issue of controlling violent crime. This kind of political confusion over the ideological struggles concerning questions of contemporary youth, families, race/ethnicity, class, gender, and sexuality was exemplified in the article "Growing Up Scared" by Karl Zinsmeister (1990) that appeared in *The Atlantic*. The cover of the magazine depicted a child's lunchbox adorned with brightly colored pictures of animals and riddled with bullet holes. The theme of the essay was about the growing crime in the educational systems across the United States, especially within African American communities. These incidents were linked to broken homes without male authority figures, drugs, gangs, and even feminism. Disregarding the dysfunctionality and presence of violence in many of the families involved, the solution advocated was for the reinstallation of the nuclear family through an agenda of policing the home, without any thought or discussion given to the economic or social prospects of the affected people. Such policy proposals exhibit a simple confusion that equates parental responsibility and policing.

What is missing, once again, from these discussions is often more important than what is addressed. Like Zinsmeister, the mass media generally pay inadequate attention to the much more common and persuasive forms of violence and abuse of children related to a market society. In the process, the media help to reproduce the relations of growing inequality that negatively affect the lives of youth, especially impoverished ones. A similar point was made by bell hooks, when she analyzed misogyny, gangsta rap, and the movie *The Piano*, all in relation to the treatment given these topics by the mass media. As hooks (1994: 26) wrote to the white-dominated media,

> *The controversy over gangsta rap makes a great spectacle. Besides the exploitation of these issues to attract audiences, a central motivation for highlighting gangsta rap continues to be the sensationalist drama of demonizing black youth culture in general and the contributions of young black men in particular.*

She continued to argue that these contemporary remakes of *Birth of a Nation* encourage us all "to believe it is not just vulnerable white womanhood that risks destruction by black hands but everyone" (hooks, 1994: 26).

In other words, the outcome was that gangsta rap, rather than being viewed as a reflection of the dominant culture, was instead viewed as an aberrant pathology. In the process, rape and male violence against women, which are part and parcel of patriarchy, became deflected from their source; in its place stood young black males who were forced to accept the blame for all the violence. As hooks (1994: 27) argued at the time, gangsta rap was part of the contemporary anti-feminist backlash, and its expression by young black males had far less to do with their manhood than it did with their "subjugation and humiliation by more powerful, less visible forces of patriarchal gang-sterism." In brief, hooks wanted to locate gangsta rap in the center, rather than at the margins, of what this country is fundamentally all about.

hooks also wanted people to examine such questions as: Why were huge audiences, especially young white consumers, so turned on by the music, the misogyny and sex-ism, and the brutality? Where was the anger and rage at females expressed in this mu-sic coming from? Why was there the glorification of violence, death, and destruction? Avoiding these tough questions, then, the mass media turn to the simpler task of at-tacking gangsta rap and of vilifying the musicians, rather than confronting the culture that produced the need for such "trash" in the first place.

As a final comment on this discussion of the War on Youth, it is interesting to note that youth are regarded as socially threatening and disruptive, the unfortunate prod-ucts of mass media and moral decline, and yet, they are also viewed as consummate consumers as well as the successors of advanced capitalism. These kinds of contradic-tions are merely suggestive of the complexity of matters involved in social control.

## Social Control: A Conceptual and Practical Overview

Nearly two decades ago, Jack P. Gibbs (1982: 9) observed: "The term 'control' could become central for the social and behavioral sciences because it can be used to describe virtually any type of human behavior, be it the modification of inanimate things, the domestication of plants and animals, or social interaction." The contemporary study of control—"social" or "self"—remains marginal to the social and behavioral sciences in general and, ironically, to criminology in particular. Gibbs (1982: 245) has suggested that the aversion to examine the manipulation (control) of human behavior can be traced back to the bourgeois period and its preoccupation with human liberty that reached an apex in the West in the eighteenth and nineteenth centuries.

> *With the advent of democracy, both the idea of being controlled and controlling came to be distasteful, so much so that social or behavioral scientists are seemingly reluctant to recognize that benign behavior (e.g., inviting a friend out for lunch) can be control.*

Hence, the traditional practices have been to equate control with "evil" or vested in-terests, and with things reserved for the "other" or "dangerous." At the same time, over the past decade or two, the scope of social control has opened up in the academy. As Stanley Cohen (1994: 63) has commented, "Although it originated in the narrow con-fines of criminology and the sociology of deviance, it has spread to virtually every area of modern life—not just crime and madness, but also family life, education, welfare, the body, the market, gender, sexuality and mass culture." This underscores the fact that formal modes of social control, traditionally and narrowly thought of as either "control through intervention" (i.e., juvenile detention) or "control through preven-tion" (i.e, drug education), have conceptually broadened their views to include the in-formal modes of social control in everyday life.

Nevertheless, theoretically and empirically speaking, there has not been much development since Edward A. Ross's seminal work *Social Control* in 1901. Most sociologists, anthropologists, and criminologists, following Ross and later the Chicago and functionalist schools, have treated the concept of social control as referring primarily, if not exclusively, to norms and social order. In other words, any sociocultural phenomenon or human institution that allegedly maintains or contributes to social order was regarded as social control. Equating social control with normative consensus was and is tautological. More specifically, this kind of reasoning

> *ignores or belittles not only social conflict but also the conscious and deliberate manipulation of human behavior. When sociologists speak of norms, they rarely suggest that norms are created to manipulate behavior; rather, norms are commonly described as unplanned or beyond human control. Sociologists do recognize that some norms are created (as in the case of laws), but they often express doubts as to whether such norms effectively control behavior. Even the "internalization of norms" is presumed to be somehow automatic, meaning that it need not be promoted consciously and deliberately (Gibbs, 1982).*

In reality, social control operates at both the conscious and unconscious levels. Social control also involves elements of consensus and conflict. Moreover, "since control itself gives rise to a conflict of interests, and power is best defined as the perceived capacity to control, control is the central notion rather than power" (Gibbs, 1982: 246). At the same time, however, social control is also about actual power or the real abilities of some to control others. In this sense, control is the basis of power. All of this raises the fundamental questions of who should exercise control (power) over whom, how, and to what end?

A related problem is that, too often, social control is not viewed as encompassing all of society, including the shaping of self-control and everything that it entails, from psychoanalytic theories to theories of moral development as these are played out in the individual worlds of socialization. Typically, social control has been confined to theories of social learning and operant conditioning. Similarly, social control has essentially been identified with two particular institutions, government and law. Analytically, the meaning of social control has been restricted, for the most part, to the activities of the criminal justice system as it counteracts the presence of deviance (crime) in order to reproduce (reestablish) stability. However, there are also other institutions, for example, the family and the economy, that control members and workers, on the one hand, and that are subject to corporate monopolistic control, on the other hand. Once again, the reference is to social control as inclusive of both formal (legal) and informal (extralegal) means of regulation.

Over the past two decades, certain visible trends in social control have occurred in advanced Western societies generally and in the United States specifically. First, there has been an *expansion, dispersal, and intensification* of the formal control systems. In the United States, this has involved not only the internal organizational growth of the public and private spheres of criminal justice enforcement, but also the widening of the processes of criminalization, which have included, for example, male sexualized violence and harassment, family violence, corporate and business crime, environmental crime, and crimes of the state or violations of human rights. Second, the expansion of formal social control has been accompanied by *managerialism*, or the ascendancy of administrative and technocratic styles of crime control, so that contemporary prisons are as likely to be governed by "moral accountants" as the early-nineteenth-century ones governed by "moral architects," or the mid-twentieth-century ones governed by "moral therapists." Third, and consistent with the first two trends, has been the movement away from positivism and psychodynamic models of crime production/reduction and toward neoclassicism and reasoning criminals with the latter's emphases on *behaviorism, risk management, and population control.*

As we move into the twenty-first century, the discourse is such that the objects of crime prevention have become specific groups of offenders rather than individual perpetrators. In the process, the older disciplinary regimes of individualized punishments are being replaced by the newer regimes of actuarial justice, surveillance, and compliance (Cohen, 1994). However, discussions of social control cannot be limited to humans and their behavior. As Gibbs (1982: 133) notes, "One need not be a Marxist to appreciate the possibility that the character of social control over nonhuman objects (material technology and inanimate energy sources especially) in a society at least partially determines the character of social control in that society." Hence, the continuing substitution of inanimate energy for human energy constitutes an expansion of social control in its own right as it, at the same time, transforms the relations governing the control of a displaced worker. As Gibbs (1982: 133) concludes, "Whatever the causal direction, social control and the control of nonhuman things appear so interrelated that a treatment of one without reference to the other is grossly unrealistic."

The rest of this section is divided into a discussion of the discourses and modes of social control. In the case of the discourses, I am particularly interested in the conceptual rather than popular meaning. In the case of the modes, I am particularly interested in the practical rather than the theoretical significance. From an integrated perspective, both levels of discussion have theoretical and practical implications.

### *Discourses of Social Control: Conceptual Implications*

Stanley Cohen has identified three discourses of social control. He has claimed that there are essentially "three different traditions of thought about social control, each with its own literature, style and set of problems" (Cohen, 1994: 64). Cohen characterized the discourses of social control as revolving around politics, anthropology, and deviance and crime.

Of these three discourses of social control, the oldest tradition is the *political*, which emerged with the birth of the modern state and the discourse of *Leviathan* in the seventeenth century. The political tradition reflects the classic concerns of philosophy and of social and political theory. "It deals with order, legitimacy, and authority. It confronts the central problem in the liberal democratic tradition: how to achieve a degree of order, regulation and stability not inconsistent with the suppression of individual liberty" (Cohen, 1994: 64). This model of social control is state centered in its orientation and emphasizes the importance of justice, rights, or legality.

The tradition of an *anthropological* discourse is inclusive of a cultural approach that encompasses social and behavioral science discourses more generally. These might reflect, for example, the Chicago School of the 1920s and the subsequent development of functionalism, inclusive of the narratives of both Freud and Parsons. More recently, anthropological models of control have included Lasch's "culture of narcissism," Elias's "civilising process," and the postmodernists' "spectacle." The common threads that connect in the anthropological tradition have been the emphases on socialization, conformity, internalization of norms, value consensus, and so forth.

Although the *deviance and crime* tradition can be traced back to the classical and positivist schools of criminology, the revisionist chronology beginning in the mid-1960s with the emergence of the "new deviance theories" and the "new criminology" ushered in a broader framework within what had been a fairly narrow tradition. Influenced first by labeling, interactionist, and conflict theories, then by Marxist state-centered theories of law and crime, and finally by Foucauldian notions of surveillance and discipline, the grids of the deviance-and-crime tradition widen to include other areas of social life; hence, housing as social control, welfare as social control, education as social control, psychiatry as social control, and so on. What brings the mainstream and revisionist traditions of deviance and crime together is a common interest in

> *first, the emerging state monopoly over social control through criminal law, policing and criminal justice; second, the development of grand styles of categorization, expertise and professional power/knowledge; third, the segregation and incarceration of deviants into special institutions (Cohen, 1994: 65).*

Although the three discourses in general and the deviance and crime discourse in particular have their own traditions complete with separate ways of thinking and talking, it gradually appears that these different approaches to social control have begun to interface. Such a state of development is to some extent a by-product of postmodernism. What, then, are the practical implications of the convergence of discourses in social control? To answer this question, it is necessary to turn to a discussion of the modes of social control.

## *Modes of Social Control: Practical Implications*

Although there are numerous ways to classify modes of control, for example, formal versus informal, public versus private, and coercive versus consensual, I believe that such distinctions are misleading because all of the above dichotomies constitute the field of social control. Perhaps a more useful classification is the one that Cohen has used to describe four common styles of social control: punitive, compensatory, conciliatory, and therapeutic. Before distinguishing between these ideal types or modes of social control, two things should be noted: First, these modes overlap with each other, and, second, they are not mutually exclusive in practice.

The *punitive* style of control is embodied in the entire criminal and penal law. Although, relatively speaking, it is an extremely special and rare style of control, it is perhaps the most familiar, not just to lawyers and criminologists, but to mass consumers of images of crime and justice. Because of its dominance in such fields as jurisprudence, philosophy, law, and political science, Cohen (1994: 67) argues that many folks have "mistakenly taken" the punitive model "to be paradigmatic of social control itself." Elements of this style of control include: (1) the infliction of pain (loss, harm, suffering); (2) the identification of a legally responsible (guilty) party; (3) the presence of a morality lesson; and (4) the use of coercion and the transfer of social control to a third party.

The *compensatory* style of control entails the repayment of debt from the offender to the victim. Restitution is sought to compensate the victim for his or her damage or harm. Once compensation has occurred, the matter is theoretically over and settled. The emphasis is on the consequences (or harmful outcomes) of the act rather than on the intentions (or mental state) of the actor. As Cohen (1994: 68) explains,

> *This stress on damage rather than guilt should make this style of control less moralistic, more restorative. Sanctions are grounded not on the violation of abstract moral rules, but on a network of mutual obligations. This mutuality is further emphasized in systems of restitution which are collective, rather than individual.*

Nevertheless, the outcomes of this kind of social control are still rather one-sided affairs where the offended reaps most, if not all, of the compensation.

The *conciliatory* style of control involves both parties working with or without a third party to negotiate a mutually acceptable outcome: "The eventual solution is arrived at through mutual bargaining and is not coerced by imposing external sanctions. The point is to reconcile people to each other" (Cohen, 1994: 68). Under this model, nobody necessarily has to be defined as the offender and the victim. Blame is either shared or it is not even allocated. Focus is less on the intent, (as in penal law) or even on harm (as in compensatory or tort), than it is on the problematic relationship or situation. The outcome is less about winners and losers and more about compromise.

The *therapeutic* style of control is very different from the other styles. The emphasis is neither on the act or actor of the penal law nor the situation (compensatory) or the relationship (conciliatory). Instead, the emphasis is on helping to change a deviant person, "either, in the psychodynamic model, to change internal psychic states or, in the behaviorist model, to produce external behavioral conformity" (Cohen, 1994: 69). Hence, the process is not viewed in moralistic terms as in the punishment of the guilty (or evil), nor is it viewed as the repair of a damaged relationship or the fulfillment of an obligation.

Generally, the nonintegrative approaches to crime control tend to overuse one mode of social control, usually the punitive mode. By comparison, an integrated approach to crime reduction aspires to incorporate the full range of modes, not merely in terms of the disputing parties, but also in terms of the larger social ecologies and the cultural production of crime. The next two sections provide, respectively, overviews of the nonintegrative and integrative modes of crime control.

# Nonintegrated Modes of Crime Control

Since the 1980s, the nonintegrated modes of crime control have focused their policies of crime prevention and control on "target hardening," "proactive policing," "judicial restraint," and the "new penology" (Hagan, 1994; Messner and Rosenfeld, 1994; DeKeseredy and Schwartz, 1996). Revolving almost exclusively around the formal agencies of the criminal and juvenile justice systems, these policies neglect or ignore altogether, for example, the social ecologies of crime or the cultural adaptations to restricted opportunities for the redistribution of wealth (Sullivan, 1989). As Hagan (1994: 80) has argued, many of the inner-city illegal economic strategies that include muggings, robberies, and other forms of theft and drug-related activities have been "subcultural adaptations [that] represent investments for short-term economic gains." Put another way, "these youth have substituted investments in subcultures of youth crime and delinquency for involvements in a dominant culture that provides little structural or cultural investment in their futures" (Hagan, 1994: 80). Compared to other industrialized countries, the United States both collects less taxes and spends less dollars per capita, for example, in terms of protecting mothers and children in the areas of maternity leave, health insurance, and programs to aid the unemployed and poor (Bok, 1996). By contrast, an integrated approach to crime reduction incorporates modes of social control whose policies address elements of crime production that go well beyond individual offenders to include the social ecologies of crime and market society.

*Target hardening*, also referred to as "situational crime prevention," is aimed at taking steps to reduce crime by lowering the vulnerability of potential victims. Influenced by routine activities theory, the objective is to reduce criminal opportunities by focusing on social and environmental factors that contribute to criminal victimization such as never remaining alone in an apartment, laundry room, mailroom, or parking garage; never hitchhiking alone; when babysitting, being escorted home after dark, and so forth. This approach to crime control is directed at offenses committed primarily in public and by strangers. This does nothing, for example, to protect women from intimate, heterosexual violence, which is committed far more frequently by men they know at home than by those they do not know away from home. Target hardening also places a major responsibility on the victims—the responsibility to avoid their victimization. Potentially, this may have a chilling effect on individual freedom because it asks potential victims to curtail or change their routine activities. Women, especially, are asked to restrict their freedom by venturing out only in crime-free and safe environments. At the same time, these situational crime prevention strategies have a tendency to increase rather than decrease fear of crime. In turn, people then perceive that the problem is getting worse when that may not be the case at all. They invest in costly technology, if they can afford to, even though the real danger of this type of crime is typically displaced to the street and to nonaffluent areas of marginal society. Finally, these strategies typically ignore the factors that motivate persons to commit crimes in the first place (DeKeseredy and Schwartz, 1996: 445–448).

*Proactive policing* as a policy either on an intermittent basis or as a steady diet has a long history in the United States. Perhaps the best example "involves the periodic attention paid by the criminal justice system to drug law enforcement and its punitive concentration on minorities through most of this century" (Hagan, 1994: 145). Whether we are discussing the criminalization of heroin at the turn of the century or the more recent crack down on crack cocaine, the results have been the same: the unequal or selective enforcement and punishment of people of color, especially African Americans. More generally, proactive policing (and prosecuting) differs from the loosely coupled and reactive systems of justice in that the former aggressively seeks out crime rather than simply responding to citizen complaints. In the process, enforcement activities are organized or concentrated around initiatives identified as important in the War on Crime. Police, in short, have to tighten up their organizational actions, for in the absence of complaints, they must develop other sources of information and assistance in developing cases. For example, as Jerome Skolnick (1966) pointed out some time ago in relationship to narcotics enforcement, three proactive strategies exist: going undercover, using techniques of entrapment, or developing informants. All these approaches are labor intensive and costly and reduce the possibilities for other means of social control.

*Judicial restraint* refers to the changes in sentencing policies and guidelines that limited the discretionary authority of judges in handing out punishment. Beginning in the 1970s with the demise of indeterminate sentencing and the introduction of determinate sentencing (e.g., flat time, life without parole, three strikes), punishments using the classical model were once again supposed to fit the crime or the act rather than the criminal or actor. Numerical conceptions of equality, emphasizing that punishments should or must correspond in fixed ways to specific crimes, have become the order of the day. By contrast, those proportional and subjective conceptions of equality, reminiscent of positivism's rehabilitative ideal, which had taken into account both the objective and subjective characteristics of offenders and their circumstances, became irrelevant. The results of fixed sentences coupled with proactive drug enforcement have resulted in escalating prison populations containing disproportionate numbers of young people of color in this country. As part of "taking back the streets," for example, the War on Gangs calls for "mounting all-out efforts to place as many gang members as possible in prison—often in the same prisons" without any consideration of the consequences for the individual gang members, the prison system, or the society at large (DeKeseredy and Schwartz, 1996: 450). As most gang researchers are quick to note, placing gang members in prison is no solution. In fact, it only tends to exacerbate the problem because gang membership and involvement are even more important in prison than on the street. The outcome of such policies is to actually strengthen rather than weaken the gangs (Hagedorn, 1988).

*"New" penology*, a throwback to classical criminology, is the prevailing ideology and practice of corrections today. It has successfully shifted the emphasis away from rehabilitation and treatment to an emphasis on incapacitation, deterrence, and retribution. To put it simply, punishment is the name of the game, and the results have been staggering: "In 1979, the United States ha[d] an imprisonment rate that probably more than doubled any country in Western Europe, at 230 per 100,000. . . . A decade later, in 1989 . . . the U.S. rate increased to 426, about four times the highest Western European figure" (Hagan, 1994: 161). By 1994, the U.S. prison population exceeded 1 million for the first time while the jail population was just under 500,000. Again, young

African American males have been disproportionately impacted by such policies as the total number under the control of the criminal justice system in 1994 rose to 609,690, a figure that significantly passed the 436,000 African American men of all ages enrolled in college as of 1986 (Irwin and Austin, 1994).

The new penology is allegedly concerned with efficiency as it targets subgroups or aggregates of individuals who are viewed as constituting "high-rate offenders" or "career criminals." Like the estimated 1 million welfare recipients who have been displaced en masse by President Clinton signing the Welfare Reform Act of 1996, when it comes to regarding the individual offender, his or her reasons (causes) for criminal involvement are of little, if any, importance. Prescriptive sentencing and selective incapacitation have accomplished something besides expanding U.S. prison populations; they have also helped to institutionalize a permanent underclass or dangerous class in America. Removing persons from the welfare rolls, without concern for the reasons, may also contribute to the "truly disadvantaged" (Wilson, 1987).

Although the nonintegrative modes of crime control characterize both conservative and liberal approaches to crime prevention, the two conventional approaches can be distinguished. The former mentality has been captured by the language of a War on Crime, the latter mentality by the language of a War on Poverty. As a prelude to the next section, I will briefly discuss these dominant metaphors of crime prevention and their deficiencies. In general, whether one is talking about the policies of conservatives or liberals, neither has stemmed the tide of high levels of serious crime in the United States. Both have failed, as Messner and Rosenfeld (1994: 94) suggest, because their "strategies reinforce the very quality of American culture that leads to high rates of crime in the first place."

According to the conservative War on Crime, the function of crime control is to recapture the streets from criminals and to make them safe for the rest of us.

> *The police will act swiftly to remove criminals from the streets; prosecutors will vigorously bring their cases to court without plea-bargaining them to charges carrying lesser penalties; judges and juries will have less discretion in determining the penalties imposed; and more criminals will serve longer sentences for their crimes. Corrections officials will thus keep offenders in prison for longer periods of time, both because offenders are serving longer sentences and because officials will have less discretion in granting parole to offenders. The cumulative effects of these "get tough" actions will be lower crime rates brought about by increases both in deterrent effects of punishment and in what criminologists term the incapacitation effects of imprisonment (Messner and Rosenfeld, 1994: 94).*

Despite the logic of the conservative approach and its dominant position in criminal justice policies for the past two decades, no better proof of failure can be evidenced than in the epitome of the War on Drugs approach and an absence of appreciable change in rates of serious crime.

The predictable increase in jail and prison populations and the expanded apparatus of crime control have not only failed to reduce crime, but they also have tended to undermine or reduce the capacity of the system to uphold the U.S. Constitution by its increasing inability to deliver to criminal defendants their legal rights. For example, bowing to excessive case loads and the need to dispense with justice efficiently and quickly, the participants in the adjudication process of metropolitan areas—prosecutors, defenders, and judges—have been engaging in assembly-line justice since before the 1920s (Barak, 1980). Likewise, the new penology turns away from individualized treatment or punishment and focuses instead on the most efficient ways of risk managing dangerous populations.

The unintended consequences of the War on Crime extend well beyond the confines of the criminal justice system. As particular populations have been considered to be the most dangerous and as particular crimes and criminals have been targeted, minority communities such as Native and African Americans have been hit particularly hard. Incarceration rates of young black males, for example, have had negative impacts on the sex ratio of these communities and on their family relations. The large-scale removal of young black males from their communities depletes the supply of potential marriage partners for young females. "In so doing, expansive incarceration policies impede the formation of traditional families and thereby encourage, indirectly, higher rates of female-headed households and illegitimacy—precisely the types of family conditions that have been linked with high rates of crime" (Messner and Rosenfeld, 1994: 97; Wilson, 1987). Not only do the strategies of the War on Crime, unfortunately, tend to exacerbate the very problems that they are allegedly designed to improve, but the ideology of the war becomes that of a self-fulfilling prophesy wherein, rather than recognizing the futility of the effort at some point, conservatives simply intensify the War on Crime *ad nauseam*.

By contrast, recognizing the futility and the limitations of the definition (metaphor) of crime as war and criminals as enemies, liberals are, nevertheless, engaged in another war, a War on Poverty and on the inequality of opportunity. Liberals are going about the business of providing access to those locked out of the American Dream by creating means of success for those who lack opportunities. Liberals assume that the poor and disadvantaged want to conform but that they lack the legitimate means to do so. In addition to supporting such Great Society programs as Head Start and the Mobilization for Youth, liberal approaches to crime control emphasize rehabilitation and reform, from individual treatment and group counseling to job training and skill development.

Although a number of liberal defenders still maintain that the the War on Poverty was more rhetorical than real, even during its peak at the height of liberal social reform in the 1960s and early 1970s, crime rates increased markedly during these periods. Of equal importance—although certain forms of street crime are committed disproportionately by the poor—crime rates have not risen or fallen in direct proportion with poverty rates, unemployment rates, or other indicators of economic deprivation per se. In fact, there are certain historical periods, such as the Great Depression of the 1930s or more recently the economic recessions of the mid-1970s and early 1980s, when crime declined. Conversely, during the economic boom period of the 1960s, crime rates were soaring. Moreover, the liberal approach to crime prevention has virtually nothing to say about those individuals who engage in white collar or corporate crime despite their surplus of skills and the availability of legitimate opportunities.

In either case, the liberal approach fails to address the issue of relative deprivation and the fact that over the past three decades, the distances between the poor and the middle and rich have grown considerably as more and more persons have become vulnerable to the vagaries of a global economy and subject to the conditions of relative impoverishment. Like the conservative approach, the liberal approach has also failed to target the underlying cultural and structural causes of crime that are and are not related to questions of impoverishment. As a consequence of these omissions, the policies of both the War on Poverty and the War on Crime may have actually resulted in exacerbating rather than improving the crime problem in the United States.

> *We have been hurting ourselves with our fear of crime. We have decimated the African-American and Hispanic communities, robbed everything from road construction to university education to pay for more and more prison beds, created a never-ending politics based on racial polarization, and developed what purports to be a victim's movement but in fact seems to be a hotbed of hatred. Even worse, much of what we are doing about crime today has not been working and will not suddenly start working with still more funding. Prisons in particular have not succeeded in stopping crime, and individual treatment has been a dismal failure for the most part. Target hardening may have some positive effect for some people, but overall, it is not a solution to anything (DeKeseredy and Schwartz, 1996: 484).*

Again, if crime is a product of cultural pressures to obtain material wealth and the lack of a social control founded on a balance between economic and noneconomic institutions, then crime reduction must reflect policies that restrain the unbridled cultural accumulation of wealth (winners) and of poverty (losers). In the end, without more fundamental social change, policies of liberal reform tend to reinforce the commitment to the American Dream and to its criminogenic consequences. As Messner and Rosenfeld (1994: 101) have argued, "The failure of both liberals and conservatives to offer effective solutions to the crime problem ultimately reflects the inability, or unwillingness, of the advocates of either approach to question the fundamental features of American society." In the language of constitutive-integrative criminology, these policies have failed to deal with the co-responsibility in the production and reduction of crime. Hence, if effective policies of crime reduction and social control are to become a reality, then strategies must be developed that move beyond the self-defeating tenets of liberal and conservative crime prevention policies. These policies, which have essentially ignored the social ecologies of crime in both the street and the suite, have also disregarded social policies, which represent any kind of challenge to the historically and popularly cherished values of a market culture, such as the belief in and support for the radical individualism discussed in the previous chapter.

## Integrated Modes of Crime Reduction

As I have just described, the nonintegrated approaches to crime control in the United States have focused primarily, if not exclusively, on the formal mechanisms of punitive social control in relationship to selected populations or aggregated groups of offenders. These approaches have not only been limiting in their conceptions and practices of social control, but they have also been counterproductive in the War on Crime and more expensive than informal mechanisms of social control. By contrast, integrated models of social control would focus on the development of all human beings, from conception forward as they are caught up in various realities of institutional, structural, and cultural life in America. Integrated approaches to crime reduction assume that there is much more to crime control than the criminal justice system. The integrative strategies also take seriously the conditions of crime production and attempt to buffer their impact by: (1) challenging some of the culture's fundamental values, beliefs, and assumptions about crime, criminals, and American society; and (2) developing domestic policies within a global context that support interactive systems of individual and community development.

The integrated modes of crime reduction are inclusive of the cultural interactions of individuals, social ecologies, and institutional relationships. These integrated styles of crime prevention take a holistic, or epidemiological, view of the individual, the community, and the larger society, all within the context of developing political economies. Domestically, this means that the reduction of crime must be addressed not only with respect to the developments of the offender, community, and nation, but also with regard to the dynamics of social and political democratization or power sharing. In terms of social control, this means a greater emphasis on the informal mechanisms of social control or on the order of the inventory of criminological indicators rather than on the formal mechanisms dedicated solely to controlling convicted perpetrators. In terms of individual offenders, should the formal mechanisms become necessary, the criminal justice systems must be prepared not only to punish, but also to treat, train, counsel, develop, and support their clientele populations. After all, this is a service economy, and these convicted offenders, sooner or later, will be returning to the "free world," as the inmates refer to it.

Finally, integrated models of crime and social control also strive for balance between, on the one hand, the worlds of consensus and conformity and, on the other hand, the worlds of conflict and diversity. The balance comes from recognizing not only the strengths and weaknesses associated with formal versus informal systems of social control, but with how these modes of control respond to the cultural traditions of individualism versus communitarianism present in any society (Braithwaite, 1989). Historically, social control or sanctioning on behalf of community norms has become less dispersed and more concentrated superordinately, especially in the state. This does not imply that subordinate sanctioning by intermediate or peer intervention has to necessarily weaken. After all, because sanctioning occurs in social space and is a matter of human agency and political decision making, the potential always exists to fashion social control in a variety of ways (Bayley, 1985).

The late political economist David M. Gordon (1996) argued correctly that values matter, but that jobs and livable wages matter as much, if not more. Marian Wright Edelman (1996), president of the Children's Defense Fund and author of *The Measure of Our Success: A Letter to My Children and Yours*, has succinctly underscored the values problem: "Something is wrong with the values of a nation that would rather spend far more to lock up children than spend far less to give them a Healthy Start, a Head Start, a Fair Start, a Safe Start, and a Moral Start in Life." Nonintegrative criminologists, especially conservative ones, in their discussions of family values, for example, have tended to disassociate the economic and the noneconomic. For these criminologists, like conservative pundits and politicians more generally, values or virtues have become divorced from their social and economic realities. Instead, values have become abstract signifiers that are derived from cultural wars unrelated to material conditions of the real lives of millions of persons.

Thus, over the past twenty years or so, social problems, for example, have been attributed to corroding values and a shifting list of symbolic scapegoats, including teen pregnancy, lazy workers, ungrateful immigrants, violent movies, rap lyrics, welfare chiselers, gangsta teens, racial quotas, and so on, rather than to the role of deteriorating job opportunities and earnings for a growing percentage of the young adult population. Although conservatives tend to blame crime and deviance on bad people, and liberals tend to blame it on bad programs, "neither group entertains the possibility that the enemy comes from within, that the causes of crime lie within the dominant culture itself" (Messner and Rosenfeld, 1994: 101).

By contrast, integrative criminologists and integrative modes of crime (harm) reduction recognize the inextricable relationships between values and material conditions. Thus, it may very well be that what needs changing is the American Dream itself and the values of avarice, consumption, and exploitation on which that dream is partially and silently constructed. As Messner and Rosenfeld (1994: 102) argue,

> *Genuine crime control requires transformation from within, a reorganization of social institutions and a regeneration of cultural commitments. This is certainly a formidable task, given the powerful influence of existing cultural beliefs and structural arrangements. The task is not, however, an impossible one. Culture and social structure inevitably place constraints on human action, but these constraints are of a unique type. Unlike the limits imposed by the natural world, the social world is ultimately created and recreated by the participants themselves.*

The "reorganization of social institutions and a regeneration of cultural commitments," as Messner and Rosenfeld (1994) suggest, call for a bottom-up and top-down cultural reorganization that would affect corporate as well as marginal America. We are not talking here of merely making good on the promises of the Civil Rights movement and the Great Society programs, we are talking about a more fundamental understanding of inequality and hierarchy in all of its consequences. Therefore, if integrated strategies to reduce the excessive investment of energy in the power to control, deny, or injure others by offenders or enforcers are to be useful, they will have to include proactive responses to social control that are at the same time diverse and encompassing of the constitutive elements of crime that exist at the very core of the whole social structure.

In the end, the practices of an integrative social control are reflective or derivative of a concern for the relationship between crime and criminals and social, political, and economic justice. As for the visions of an integrated social control, there is a conscious desire to pursue the possibility of true freedom through the actualization of the self and the collective, and through an appreciation of the need to respect both individual rights and social obligations. As we are almost at closure with this textbook, I would now like to present an outline of both what needs to be confronted and what needs to be done

in order to reduce crime in the United States. The following integrative policy plat-
form, outlined and divided into four related parts, is what I believe to be necessary in
order to facilitate human and social development and to resist the coproduction of
crime as we have come to know it in the United States.

### Full Potential and Full Employment: Toward a Society Where Money Is Not the Principal Value of Personal and Social Worth

Hagan (1994) has called for a new sociology of "crime and dispute" that focuses on the
criminal costs of social inequality. His approach to crime and crime reduction is not
only consistent with the integrative-constitutive perspective advocated here, but it also
dovetails nicely with the integrative works of Braithwaite, DeKeseredy and Schwartz,
Henry and Milovanovic, Messner and Rosenfeld, Pepinsky and Quinney, Sampson and
Laub, and others. What all of these criminologists share in common is an appreciation
for the contextual relationship between the features of organizational society and the
offender, both as an individual agent and as a member of the collective group. Furthermore, they (we) are also concerned with revitalizing or energizing conciliatory
rather than punitive forms of social control. In other words, whatever specific interventions or policies of social control are devised, they should be incorporated within
the socio-historical or formative structural contexts. These formative contexts, of
course, are the political economies. Any transformation in the practices of social control, therefore, must deal with the reality of changing political economies. As Henry
and Milovanovic (1996: 15) have argued, unless "the existent totality of capitalist hier-
archies of order and control" are addressed, any alternative social policies to crime reduction remain utopian as their possibilities are simply absorbed by the prevailing
relations of the political economy.

Thus, crime reduction through replacement discourse begins with a deconstruction of or an assault on the cultural assumption that social inequality encourages individual initiative, and is, therefore, economically efficient. As Hagan (1994: 98) and
others have pointed out, "This belief is challenged by the last half-century of economic
development in the advanced capitalist nations, when declining social inequality accompanied economic expansion, and increases in social inequality were joined with reduced economic growth. Meanwhile, increased social inequality and reduced
economic growth are both associated with increases in crime, especially in America's
low-income minority communities."

Unfortunately, the erroneous beliefs and goals associated with the value of social
inequality are inseparable from the historical experience and consciousness of the
American Dream. Fortunately, however, as Messner and Rosenfeld (1994: 109) have
argued, a wholesale rejection of the American Dream is not called for in order to vi-
talize noneconomic institutions: "Instead, by moderating the excesses of the dominant
cultural ethos, and emphasizing its useful features, institutional reform can be stimulated." In other words, the positive values of the American Dream can empower everybody to dream about a brighter future, and the very vision of possibilities, of hope, can
be liberating. The Dream, of course, can also serve as a catalyst for helping to establish the structural contents of its reality. On the other hand, the negative values asso-

ciated with the Dream, such as the exaggerated reverence for monetary success and the individual pursuit of materialism without limits on the means or concerns for the consequences, must be curtailed in both rhetoric and practice:

> *Any significant lessening of the criminogenic consequences of the dominant culture thus requires the taming of its strong materialistic pressures and the creation of a greater receptivity to socially imposed restraints. To dampen the materialistic pressures, goals other than the accumulation of wealth will have to be elevated to a position of prominence in the cultural hierarchy. This implies greater recognition of and appreciation for the institutional realms that are currently subservient to the economy. More specifically, social roles such as parenting, "spousing," teaching, learning, and serving the community will have to become, as ends in themselves, meaningful alternatives to material acquisition (Messner and Rosenfeld, 1994: 110).*

More specifically, as I have argued in the case of homelessness and crime, for example, the solution to affordable housing and to ending homelessness and its associated harms in the United States, such as the predatory behavior and frequent assaults on the bodies as well as the dignities of the homeless, depends on the development of mixed economies more in character with the economies of Europe and Japan (Barak, 1991). In these nations, there have been a wide range of domestic policies and programs that guarantee not only that material well-being not be solely dependent on economic functions alone, but that noneconomic institutions receive substantive support from collective (state) resources. In short, there are conscious policies in place to resist the capitalist tendencies of economic and social inequality. In the name of reducing the costs of social problems in general and of crime in particular, these policies are also aimed at facilitating a broadened participation of citizens in work and in the production of goods and services.

Unfortunately, the United States' domestic policies have been in a state of confusion for the past twenty years or more, and the discernable trends that exist reveal an intensification of stratification throughout the society and an isolation and separation of the marginally nonproductive groups from the conventionally productive groups. In the distressed inner-city communities of America, for example, because of the workings of capital disinvestment, the crime problems have worsened. The interconnected processes of capitalist disinvestment, such as residential segregation, racial/ethnic inequality, and the concentration of poverty, are not resisted or altered in the name of investing in social or human capital. In fact, they are encouraged by the unsubstantiated belief that efforts to increase social equality are wasteful and that they diminish economic efficiency. Meanwhile, "capital disinvestment impairs the closure of social networks and the formation of social and cultural capital in distressed communities and families, and it indirectly encourages subcultural adaptation. These adaptations are in effect forms of recapitalization; that is, they represent efforts to reorganize what resources are available, albeit usually illicit, to reach attainable goals" (Hagan, 1994: 98).

The point is that U.S. domestic policy must recognize that the process of recapitalization in these communities, involving the development of ethnic vice industries, the formation of deviance service centers, and the establishment of "free enterprise zones" of crime as Hagan refers to them, is simply a spin-off of capital disinvestment. Hence, to alter or reduce the flow of drugs, sex, and other contraband in these communities, there will have to be social investments of capital into these communities. To accomplish this, a replacement discourse is needed that reflects the reality that overwhelming percentages of adults want to work.

One of the problems here has been in confusing joblessness with shiftlessness. The former refers to those who are either unemployed or out of the work force; the latter refers to those who are lazy, have opted out of conventional labor, and prefer other forms of support, even if these are grossly inadequate to maintaining a decent lifestyle. As Gordon (1996) has revealed, something like 5 or 6 percent of inner-city adults might reasonably conform to the notion of being able to but not willing to work. The percentages for unmarried African American men are a bit higher, but this is relatively small too. Studies in both Chicago's and Boston's inner cities, for example, revealed that willingness to work was the norm. In fact, the study in Chicago, contrary to popular stereotypes, revealed that black men appeared most willing and white men least willing to accept low-paying jobs: "The average wage rate expected by those who had worked and wanted a job was $5.50 an hour for black men, $6.20 for Mexicans and Puerto Ricans, and $10.20 for white men" (Gordon, 1996: 22). Thus, to abandon these communities in the name of efficiency, self-dependency, and family values is not only a cultural lie that serves to legitimate the further erosion of the average person's worth in this nation, but, at the same time, a highly costly and counterproductive approach to maintaining social control.

### Crime Reduction Through Institutional Reorganization: Supporting Social Ecologies of Crime Prevention

If criminal activities in the United States are located within a dominant ideology and practice of extreme individualism and privilege, and if crime generally flows from a combination of mass-mediated pressures to consume material success and a normative order with weak moral restraints to control the means employed to obtain that success, then it follows that "crime reductions would result from policies that strengthen social structure and weaken criminogenic qualities of American culture" (Messner and Rosenfeld, 1994: 103). Therefore, with respect to the latter policies, social changes are required that can reintegrate all types of criminal offenders and harmful inflicters; with respect to the former policies, social changes are required that can reintegrate informal institutions of social control such as the family, the school, the workplace, and the political system.

The essence of the crime control problem in individualistically oriented cultures like the United States has been described appropriately by Braithwaite (1989: 171) as ironic because "the ideology of the minimal state produces a social reality of the maximum state." In other words, "because sanctioning by peers and intermediate groups like schools, churches, trade unions and industry associations cannot work in an individualistic culture, the state responds (ineffectively) to perceived increases in crime the only way it can—by locking more people up, giving the police and business regulatory agencies more powers," and in the process, "trampling on the very civil liberties which are the stuff of individualist ideologies" (Braithwaite, 1989: 171).

Instead, all of the informal institutions of social control need to become more participatory in nature. The practice of workplace democracy, for example, which includes the representation of workers and community members reflective of different ethnic and gender backgrounds on corporate boards of directors, holds out the possibility that corporate decisions could be responsive to something else besides the "bottom line" (Messerschmidt, 1986). In addition to the economic considerations there would also be the social considerations, involving such broader issues as environmental hazards, plant locations, product safety, family planning, and so on (Simon and Eitzen, 1994).

With respect to families, the development of "pro-family" economic policies are called for that specifically provide for liberal family leave, job sharing for husbands and wives, flexible work schedules, and employer-provided child care. These policies and others like them allow for both the family and school to exert more informal control over children's behavior. At the same time, with respect to schools, there is the need to move beyond the market-oriented mentality of American education that was exemplified in the 1990s by the educational "choice" theme whereby allegedly bad schools were to be driven out of business by good ones, once the obstacles blocking open markets in schooling were eliminated. The point is that primary schools should be going about the business of providing formal education, not competing for students. And children's prospects for the future should be less closely tied to their economic resources and performance in school than to the abilities of policies to strengthen in concert both the family and the school as the two engage parents and teachers, as well as children and students, "in the distinctive goals and 'logics' of these institutions" (Messner and Rosenfeld, 1994: 104). This logic indeed makes sense if the family, school, and work are viewed as part of developing social ecologies that can be adequately fueled through a political commitment to full potential, full employment, and continuous lifelong educational opportunities.

As for the various political arenas, reference is made both to opening up the discourse (debate) on crime prevention and control so as to reform the formal, costly, and hyperpunitive systems of crime control and to incorporate broader patterns of social participation and social control beyond the criminal justice system. These institutional reforms in crime prevention call for the development of both formal and informal means of social control at the community level. Whether one is talking about intensive probation programs, corporate receiverships, or the national service corps, these intermediate interventions between total isolation and separation, on the one hand, and anarchy and law and disorder, on the other hand, emphasize changes within the polity that are directed at developing individual duty, collective obligation, and mutual trust. In short, these envisioned modes of social control not only deemphasize the practices of state-sanctioned punitiveness, but they also abandon the inappropriate metaphor of a War on Crime. Consequently, while aspiring for more freedom for all, adherents of integrated models of social control are in the liberated position of reducing crime through the processes of reintegration.

### Reintegrating Laissez-Faire Society: Reconstructing Mutual Support, Collective Obligations, and Coresponsibility for Crime

This is not some utopian call for returning to a simpler precapitalist existence where individualism had not yet emerged, the group's survival depended on its solidarity and collective well-being, and the informal modes of communitarian justice prevailed. On the contrary, this call simply recognizes as Braithwaite (1989: 154) suggests, "that there is neither an inexorable historical march away from communitarianism nor an inexorable trend toward it." It also recognizes the capacity of human agencies to mobilize collective actions on behalf of both mutual self-interests and a desire for social interaction. In fact, as Nils Christie (1981) has pointed out, the communitarian strategies of reintegration employ experiences whereby offenders, victims, and community members come to know each other as total personalities rather than as mere transgressors of state law. In the process, the responses to harmful behavior are less likely to criminalize and punish the offender than they are likely to stimulate a starting point for real dialogue.

Cohen (1985) and Braithwaite (1989) have made similar observations about the characteristics of social control. Whether formal or informal, the means of social control may facilitate a modern version of "banning" or they may facilitate a postmodern version of "forgiveness, tolerance, and understanding." Cohen has distinguished between inclusionary and exclusionary modes of social control. Braithwaite has distinguished between shaming that stigmatizes and shaming that reintegrates. They both favor modes of integration, yet both appreciate the value or necessity of status degradation ceremonies.

More specifically, Cohen has described the contradictory relations involved in such inclusionary modes of social control as assimilation, incorporation, and normalization. Although Cohen (1985: 233, 268) has been drawn to these approaches of reintegration, he also believes that the "inclusionary controls [have been] ill-equipped to foster social integration" because they have failed "to confront the moral issues of guilt, wrong-doing, punishment and responsibility." Moreover, without a moral edge, the rituals of blaming are difficult to sustain in a context of inclusiveness. On the other hand, in a context of exclusiveness, the rituals of stigmatizing are difficult to overcome. Hence, Cohen concluded that, until there was a conceptual alternative to stigma, he would prefer exclusionary control because of its symbolic richness.

Braithwaite (1989: 156) contends that his theory of crime, shame, and reintegration provides a way out of the dilemma described by Cohen:

> *Reintegrative shaming implies opposition to both a laissez-faire which renounces community responsibility for caring for weaker citizens (as decarceration has sometimes been used to justify), and opposition to therapeutic professionalism which uses inclusionary slogans to justify widening the net of coerced state control over deviants. Community moralizing is the anti-thesis of both professional technocracy and laissez-faire. It is both symbolically and instrumentally an alternative to conservative law-and-order politics.*

In terms of the constitutive perspective on the coresponsibility of crime and victimization, for example, take the case of controlling corporate crime where the consequences may adversely affect workers and consumers. There are difficulties in punishing corporations not only because of their vast economic resources and the availability of numerous legal technicalities, but also because of the direct consequences for workers who may have their salaries reduced or jobs eliminated or the indirect consequences for consumers who are likely to pay more as the costs of punishment are passed along. One alternative to the traditional modes of social control includes placing deviant corporations into receiverships where they become subject to the supervision and control of court-appointed management specialists. Whether simply monitoring the corporation's behavior or taking over control for a stated period of time, these receiverships would seem to hold out more promise for seeing that corporations comply with the law than by simply punishing one or two scapegoats while the organization returns to business as usual (DeKeseredy and Schwartz, 1996).

In the spirit of reintegrating the corporation (corporate offenders) and the community, an alternative to the traditional practice of so many hours of community service might be a reconstructed policy of corporate responsibility and obligation to the citizenry in general and to those communities in particular where the signs of capital disinvestment are most apparent. This reintegrative form of social control could involve an order for the corporation to reinvest some of its capital in social and human development. A policy of "penal recapitalization" would truly represent an innovation in creative crime prevention whereby the punishment of corporate offenders would serve to benefit those impoverished and devastated communities where high incidences of predatory crime exist.

To recapitulate as well as to continue: The integrative-reintegrative approaches to social control view the problem of crime reduction as part and parcel of the problem of constructive social change and structural transformation. Integrative strategies of social control, therefore, concentrate their efforts at both the macro and micro levels of intervention by emphasizing the constitutive relationships between crime and culture, on the one hand, and, between criminals and social ecologies, on the other hand. In order to resist, overcome, and ultimately change the dominant and counterproductive paradigm of nonintegrated crime control and in order to facilitate the emergence of a new paradigm of integrated social control, a replacement discourse of harm reduction must be substituted for the discourse of the war on crime. New metaphors of crime prevention reflective of the spirit of mutual trust, collective obligations, and coresponsibility are required to replace the outmoded metaphors of competition, individualism, and privilege. Finally, policies and practices consistent with these new metaphors must be implemented.

According to Henry and Milovanovic (1996: 219), replacement discourses in the prevention and reduction of harm provide

> *not just another package of ways to talk and make sense of the world, but a language of "transpraxis." A replacement discourse is a non-reificatory connecting of the way we speak with our social relations and institutions. Through its use, we are continuously aware of the interrelatedness of our agency and the structures it reproduces through our talking, perceiving, conceptualizing and theorizing. A genuine alternative replacement discourse envelops not just crimes as popularly understood but harms*

*that cause pain, regardless of whether these have been defined as criminal by the po-
litical process. It includes all the players in the construction of harm: the victims, the
offenders and the agencies of the criminal justice system. Here it captures not only the
declarations of policy but the ways its practitioners and policy makers distinguish their
reality from the totality that is the social order.*

The activist agenda of replacement discourse has become the practice of newsmaking
criminology (Barak, 1988; Fox and Levin, 1993; Greek, 1994; Henry, 1994). Although
I have defined newsmaking criminology as the "study of newsmaking crime and crime
control and its relationship with the ongoing development of criminal justice policy in
particular and of public consciousness concerning law and order in general" (Barak,
1994: xiv), the applied aspect of "newsmaking criminology consists of criminologists
actively challenging silences, identifiying omissions, and resurrecting the eliminated
through participating in the making of news stories" about crime and justice (Henry
and Milovanovic, 1996: 216).

Methodologically speaking, four basic styles of newsmaking criminology have
been identified and experimented with, including (1) disputing data: the criminologist
as expert; (2) challenging journalism: the criminologist as journalist; (3) self-reporting:
the criminologist as subject; and (4) confronting media: the criminologist as educative
provocateur (Henry, 1994). There are advantages and disadvantages to each of these
styles and these will vary according to the particular medium—print, television, radio—
and format—live versus taped. Lastly, the different styles of newsmaking employed will
also vary depending on the desired audiences and the political (or nonpolitical) agendas of the criminologists (Barak, 1996).

To transform the prevailing nonintegrated strategies of crime control, new
metaphors and interventions are called for that resist and redirect the constitutive energy
of the excessive investors in both the illegitimate (crime) and legitimate (punishment)
forms of violence. In the reality of power, these investors, whether they be offenders, victims, enforcers, or punishers, would be turned away from harm production and toward
reinvesting in positive connections with a relationally oriented community of fellow human subjects. For example, peacemaking criminologists have rejected the idea that violence can be overcome by the use of state violence (Pepinsky and Quinney, 1991).
Similarly, the death penalty and prison abolitionists (MacLean and Pepinsky, 1993) and
the postmodern adherents of peace studies (Scimecca, 1988) believe that the reduction
of crime will come neither from reactive nor proactive measures of crime control, but
rather from those societal transformations that reconnect people to each other.

Einstadter and Henry first introduced the "judo metaphor of crime control" in
1995. This metaphor refers to the philosophy behind judo and the other martial arts.

*Judo means "gentle way" and is based on the seeming paradox that the best defense is
non-fighting and that one gains victory over an opponent by yielding—gentle turns
away from the sturdy opponent. . . . It is a method whereby the energy of the violent
is redirected against the opponent to diffuse the violence. In a metaphorical sense this
is a model stance that might release us from the punitive trap (Einstadter and Henry,
1995: 315).*

Shortly thereafter, Henry and Milovanovic (1996) preferred the metaphor of "social judo" or that point in time when people act in concert to defensively reflect the strength and power of their oppressors/repressors back at themselves. Social judo

> *requires a minimal use of energy toward redirecting the considerable power of those seeking to exercise power over us. The object is that they are made abundantly aware that the more energy they expend in harming us the more that energy converts into constraining them, limiting their further ability to harm us (Einstadter and Henry, 1995: 221).*

### Reintegrating Ex-Convicts: Reconstructing Images and Stereotypes of Recovering Subjects

Practices of reintegration that are specifically aligned with those needs of offenders and victims caught up in the systems of criminal justice include, for example, developing communities of mutual respect, reconstructing images and stereotypes of recovering subjects, and incorporating narrative models of therapy. Each of these strategies for dealing with those individuals who have posed a physical danger or who have been adjudicated guilty of crime, and who are subject to jail or prison time, assumes that social control works better in the context of just or moral rather than punitive or repressive communities, both inside and outside of prison. For example, in one Connecticut women's prison in the early 1970s a democratic model of inmate internal discipline and control was established. Except for major felonies, all other prison offenses were referred to a "cottage community meeting" (Scharf, 1977). "Thus, instead of the traditional approach of coercive power and control that simply reproduces and reaffirms the reality of the excessive investor, inmates and guards had their conventional roles reconstructed toward a shared and democratic relationship" (Henry and Milovanovic, 1996: 222). This not only allowed for both of these groups to "de-identify" and "re-identify" in less antagonistic and more positive ways, but it also helped create alternative discourses and new ways of looking at those incarcerated criminals who, sooner or later, will need to return to the "free" community.

A reconstruction of the stereotypic ex-convict can also continue in the community. This reconstruction can help ex-offenders, especially those recently released from prison, adjust to the world as they become recovering subjects rather than menaces to society. Moving beyond traditional rehabilitation and individualized treatment, this form of social control dissipates guilt about the past while it focuses on shared responsibility and mutual respect as a means of participants learning to become self-reliant and self-confident. In place of the passive and reactive criminal, this approach, exemplified by the Delancey Street Project in San Francisco (a privately operated ex-offender program), adopts a philosophy of the ex-offender as an active human subject who can make a difference in his (her) own life and that of others. Over the past two decades, former offenders and Mimi Silbert, a criminologist and director of the project, have built Delancey Street into a multimillion dollar commercial center, complete with shops, restaurants, a moving company, and several other businesses, right in the middle of the prestigious Embarcadero district. In the process, Silbert and the Delancey Street Project have created a new discursive framework about the desired possibilities for ex-offenders.

Moreover, from a constitutive-integrative approach to crime reduction, the offender-victim relationship is viewed as a dynamic expression in which the two categories are not ever fully discrete. From a practical point of view, most criminals and victims are connected through the mutuality of doing and suffering (Schafer, 1976). And from a postmodern perspective, there are other kinds of connections, such as the interrelated nature of human subjects to become excessive investors either in controlling others or in being controlled by others. With respect to the categorization of criminals and victims and the relations of social control, there are at least three implications for the reproduction of post-crime (harm).

First, there are the reconstituted ideologies of treatment and the tendency to primarily blame, although in different ways, both victims and offenders for situations allegedly of their own making. Second, there are the reconstructed realities of recovering subjects that are common to both offenders and victims. Third, there are the overlapping tendencies of former victims to become subsequent offenders and of previous victimizers to become the victimized. Because these three conditions are interrelated both to each other and to the dominant policies of social control, I will briefly discuss them as one integrated configuration.

The tendency of nonintegrative modes of social control to respond in totalizing ways that stress the differences between the abusers and the abused rather than acknowledging their overlapping needs and similarities, for example, requires reconcep-

Delancey Street Project in San Francisco, California, 1992.

tualization. Instead of supporting practices of social control that exclusively vilify and stigmatize offenders, policies are needed that construct social realities (ecologies) that facilitate possibilities of individual transformation. Similarly, rather than supporting practices of social control that either dwell on the vulnerability of victims and the concomitant need to intensify the assault on criminals, or that dwell on the humiliation and stigmatization of the violation, policies are called for that empower these victims without giving into their retributive urges to simply "offender bash." A promising alternative to these nonintegrative practices of social control is the practices subsumed under the notion of the recovering subject. The activities of Denise Brown (sister of Nicole Brown Simpson who was brutally murdered in 1994) as an advocate for domestic violence awareness come immediately to mind as an illustration of this phenomenon.

Because criminals and victims are both subjects open to human "diversity and specificity, as well as being contingently formed so as to adjust to emerging renditions of subjectivity," they "can never be [fully] 'recovered' because this limit is only reachable under the delusion that allows some contingent constitutive elements to slip away" (Henry and Milovanovic, 1996: 12). Hence, strategies of social control are necessary to assist constitutive offenders and victims to become reintegrative subjects within their local communities. Models of reform, once again, are those self-help and local support groups that have included nontraditional forms of treatment such as the recent movement in narrative therapy (White and Epston, 1989).

In general, narrative therapies import into clinical practice the privileging of pluralistic discursive production while they take seriously the importance of the postmodern "narrative turn" (Parry and Doan, 1994). Moreover, narrative therapies have recently appeared in the family therapy business, for example, that have provided both a redirection of the constitutive energy of the excessive investors in marital conflict as well as affirmative mediums for their recovering subjects' authorship. These narratives have been important in helping intimate couples to regain their senses of personal authority or individual responsibility and to reconstruct life stories that move them from guilt to liberation. These same kinds of narratives should also be significant not only for criminals and victims who are trying to pull their lives together, but for the rest of us as well.

Narrative therapies, in other words, discover the untold stories through "revisioning," while they reconstruct the unspeakable. In the process, they challenge cultural values, stereotypes, and behavior. The deconstruction, for example, of traditional family therapy away from its central position of normalizing both the problem and the suffering of its clients, and toward the de-reification of both of these, enables participants to become fellow sufferers and compassionate empathizers of the human condition. As an alternative to the more traditional forms of punitive reactions to conflicting behavior, narrative therapies combined with the philosophy of recovering subjects help in efforts to (re)establish conciliatory relationships between people that have had their lives disrupted by cycles of violence, for example.

Lastly, the integrative-constitutive perspective on crime and social control contends that criminals and victims are similar in that they have both experienced harms comprising physical and emotional stress, conflict, tension, and pain. Therefore, from a criminal- or victim-oriented perspective, the critical question remains: How do they (we) best deal with the pain and associated anger of having been harmed in the past? The conventional responses have been to reestablish the past by a resurrection of the familiar. Whether they are dealing with criminals or victims, these nonintegrative reactions have tended to reproduce the status quo. These results have been directly related to the fact that these strategies of intervention have sought uncritically to restore both offenders and victims to their former positions within the prevailing systems of harming and privileging. By contrast, integrative approaches to crime reduction and social control share the view that the crime problem in the United States is indicative of the serious disturbance of its constituted political and economic arrangements.

Hence, rather than return offenders or criminals to their pre-offense or pre-victim statuses, the evidence suggests, instead, that what is really needed are new statuses and a more fundamental transformation of the U.S. social structure.

## Summary and Conclusions: Criminology as Interdisciplinarity

*Integrating Criminologies* has introduced a scholarly exegesis in the form of a call for an integrative criminology. This textbook has also provided a unique depiction of the discipline over the past two hundred years or more. These two intellectual tasks are traditionally kept separate and distinct. In bringing them together, I have introduced a new synthesis of criminological knowledges. This integration has also embodied a paradigmatic shifting in the rules of criminological practice.

In the world of academics, there have been essentially three audiences for which one can write: the scholarly, the textbook, and the popular. When it comes to a single writing, the academy expects authors to covet only one of these mentally constructed audiences. Of course, this rule of expository writing fits hand-in-glove with the book publishing business that counts on categorization and expects specialization in the distribution and marketing of knowledge. I have, of course, violated this rule by writing for both scholars and undergraduates in the same volume.

Without dwelling too much on textbook conformity and difference, allow me to elaborate just a bit more. With a few notable exceptions, most criminology textbooks have conformed to the format of providing an overview of the crime problem, of the ways of collecting data on crime, of the theories of crime/criminal causation, and of the criminal justice system. In addition, most of these textbooks have devoted some, if not an inordinate, amount of attention to assessing the value of the competing explanations of crime. These same books have devoted far less attention, if any, to appraising the impact of public policies on crime and social control. Hence, one might conclude that most criminology texts have been heavy on theory and light on practice.

Typically, questions of policy and exercises in practice have been left to the criminal justice textbooks. Most of the criminal justice texts, however, have provided little in the way of theory. Perhaps too simplistically, one might conclude that what we have are the contradictory relations of theory without practice in the case of criminology and practice without theory in the case of criminal justice. The prevailing rationale has been that because there is so much knowledge and discourse about criminology and criminal justice, textbooks devoted to either theory (criminology) or practice (criminal justice) are appropriate responses for managing the proliferation of information. I could not disagree more with this false dualism. Thus, in response to both the modern rationale of efficiency and specialization that has split the criminological atom into at least two parts and to the traditionally nonintegrative paradigms of criminology, which have preferred one or two disciplines, I have come forward and offered an alternative way of integrating criminologies.

The reader of this book will, I hope, understand by now that the integrative project or agenda in criminology views the fragmentation of knowledges (theories) and policies (practices) as antithetical to interdisciplinarity. Moreover, the assumptions underlying this interdisciplinary agenda share a common belief that the field of criminology cuts across most, if not virtually all, of the domains of knowledge. Thus, because of the ontological reality that there are too many depths of knowledge to consume, most criminologists have become relatively selective or reductive in their knowledge consumption. In order to keep the expansive knowledges of crime and justice manageable, these criminologists have become specialists of knowledge, of theory, of methods, of gangs, of corporate crime, of domestic violence, and the like. More generally, some are specialists of crime while others are specialists of crime control. But what is needed are integrative generalists of both crime *and* social control.

As specialists, most of the nonintegrative criminologists have come to prefer vertical over horizontal knowledge. As a result, they have typically ended up espousing one particular line of inquiry, or, even more narrowly, one particular theory from one particular domain of knowledge, as offering the "best" path to criminological action. Or even worse, they have cynically ended up concluding that one theory is as bad as the next theory because neither can account for most of the variation in deviance and criminality. Of course, this conclusion results in inaction on the parts of criminologists and in *de facto* support for the status quo. Whereas the latter groups of criminologists become distrustful of theory in particular and of the potential of human nature in general, the former groups of criminologists become overly invested in theory and lose perspective on its value in the larger schemes of criminological development. In either case, criminological practice suffers as criminological knowledges are placed on the back burners, and policies of crime reduction and social control are surrendered up to the counterproductive strategies of the War on Crime as they are served up by the pundits, politicians, and mass culture.

By contrast, *Integrating Criminologies* prefers horizontal over vertical knowledge and has argued throughout that what counts is breadth rather than depth of knowledge. Stated differently, criminological practice need not wait for criminological theories as long as the more bountiful criminological knowledges are informed by interdisciplinary frameworks. Interestingly, modern criminology has always required a blending of its knowledge bases derived as they were from philosophy, law, anthropology, and other disciplines. Now, more than ever, in the face of postmodernism and the information revolution, I believe that an integration or a synthesis of the expansive bodies of knowledge enacts the most useful criminological praxis.

Following the horizontal paths to criminological wisdom, I have argued for a plurality of disciplinary knowledges. I have also presented an integrative approach to the building of criminological knowledge that has attempted to balance the importance of nature, nurture, agency, and social structure. To have done anything less, at best, would have provided another incomplete understanding of crime and crime control in American society. In mass culture, as I have already shown, there is always a danger present that partial representations of the inventory of criminological indicators will produce unsuitable metaphors, such as the War on Crime or the War on Poverty. These metaphors, despite their inefficaciousness, have persisted for more than three decades, and they have helped to perpetuate inappropriate policies of crime reduction and social control. Clearly, the amelioration of crime in the United States requires the development of new metaphors, such as reintegration or recovery, that revolve around images and actions of peacemaking and collectivism.

To recapitulate for the very last time: At the center of the constitutive approach to integrating criminologies are cultures. Cultures are critical not only because customs and beliefs differ from place to place, but because these differences also exist within people themselves. Cultures, in other words, are the unitary mediums that permeate the individuals and the parts of societies that compose them. In turn, cultures provide the social glue that holds customs and institutions together. Moreover, cultures are both instrumental and expressive. They can be warm and personal or they can be cold and impersonal. Cultures are inclusive of all members and audiences, yet some are more socially oriented while others are more individually oriented. Globally speaking, the former cultures tend to have significantly less crime, less violence, and less punishment than the latter cultures. In this very objective sense, the rates of crime a culture gets are exactly the rates that it deserves. As the vegetarians say, "You are what you eat."

In the United States, the culture of laissez-fare and radical individualism has historically resisted most efforts to become more social and collective. Nowhere has this been more true than in the area of the reproduction of crime and criminals where the spirit of reintegration and recovery has essentially been repudiated. The results have been perfectly clear: The United States has the highest rates of crime and punishment in the postindustrial world. As for the future? Pessimistically, things may have to get even worse than they already are before public policies, for example, start to seriously address the social ecologies of destruction that are endemic to our political and economic arrangements. Optimistically, however, cultures are capable of changing, growing, and

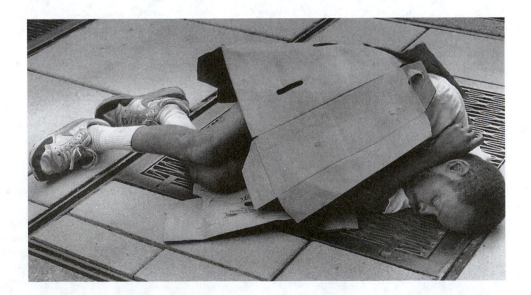

adapting. Perhaps, in the not too distant future, a real social contract with all the American people, reflective of substantive structural and cultural reform, will be established with a material ethic of individual and collective responsibility for crime reduction.

## Discussion Questions

1. Broadly speaking, what is social control and how has it changed over time?

2. Compare and contrast Cohen's three discourses of social control: political, anthropological, and deviance/crime.

3. What are the similarities and differences between the traditional (conservative and liberal) policies of social control advocated by mainstream politicians and nonintegrative criminol-

ogists and those policies advocated by constitutive-integrative criminologists?

4. Why does Barak argue that in order to reduce crime in America it is important to develop "nonrepressive" practices of social control?

5. Using Braithwaite's theory of crime, shame, and reintegration as a point of reference, what could the United States do to implement new and innovative polices of crime and social control?

## References

Acland, Charles R. 1995. *Youth, Murder, Spectacle: The Cultural Politics of "Youth in Crisis."* Boulder, CO: Westview Press.

Barak, Gregg. 1980. *In Defense of Whom? A Critique of Criminal Justice Reform.* Cincinnati, OH: Anderson.

———. 1988. "Newsmaking Criminology: Reflections on the Media, Intellectuals, and Crime." *Justice Quarterly* 5(4): 173–192.

———. 1991. *Gimme Shelter: A Social History of Homelessness in Contemporary America.* New York: Praeger.

———, ed. 1994. *Media, Process, and the Social Construction of Crime: Studies in Newsmaking Criminology.* New York: Garland.

———. 1996. "Media, Discourse, and the O. J. Simpson Trial: An Ethnographic Portrait." In G. Barak, ed., *Representing O.J.: Murder, Criminal Justice, and Mass Culture.* Albany, NY: Harrow and Heston.

Bayley, D. H. 1985. *Social Control and Political Change.* Research Monograph No. 49. Woodrow Wilson School of Public and International Affairs, Princeton University.

Bok, Derek. 1996. *The State of the Nation: Government and the Quest for a Better Society.* Cambridge, MA: Harvard University Press.

Braithwaite, John. 1989. *Crime, Shame, and Reintegration.* Cambridge: Cambridge University Press.

Christie, Nils. 1981. *Limits to Pain.* Oslo: Universitetsforlaget.

Cockburn, Alexander. 1996. "The War on Kids." *The Nation* 262(22, June 3): 7–8.

Cohen, Stanley. 1985. *Visions of Social Control: Crime, Punishment and Classification.* Cambridge: Polity Press.

———. 1994. "Social Control and the Politics of Reconstruction." In David Nelken, ed., *The Futures of Criminology.* London: Sage.

DeKeseredy, Walter S., and Martin D. Schwartz. 1996. *Contemporary Criminology.* Belmont, CA: Wadsworth Publishing.

Edelman, Marian Wright. 1996. "Blurb" on the back of *Search and Destroy: African American Males in the Criminal Justice System.* Jerome Miller. New York: Cambridge University Press.

Editorial. 1996. "Corporate Culture." *The Nation* 262(22, June 3): 3.

Einstadter, Werner, and Henry Stuart. 1995. *Criminological Theory: An Analysis of Its Underlying Assumptions.* Fort Worth, TX: Harcourt Brace.

Ferrell, Jeff. 1993. *Crimes of Style: Urban Graffiti and the Politics of Criminality.* New York: Garland.

Fox, James A., and Jack Levin. 1993. *How to Work with the Media*. Newbury Park, CA: Sage.

Gibbs, Jack P., ed. 1982. *Social Control: Views from the Social Sciences*. Beverly Hills: Sage.

Goodman, Ellen. 1995. "Virtue Marketeers Leaving Out Employer-Worker Relationship." *The Ann Arbor News* [*Dis. Washington Post*] (October 31): A7.

Gordon, David M. 1996. "Values That Work. *The Nation* 262(24, June 17): 16–19, 22.

Greek, Cecil. 1994. "Becoming a Media Criminologist: Is 'Newsmaking Criminology' Possible?" In G. Barak, ed., *Media, Process, and the Social Construction of Crime: Studies in Newsmaking Criminology*. New York: Garland.

Hagan, John. 1994. *Crime and Disrepute*. Thousand Oaks, CA: Pine Forge Press.

Hagedorn, John. 1988. *People and Folks: Gangs, Crime and the Underclass in a Rustbelt City*. Chicago: Lake View Press.

Henry, Stuart. 1994. "Newsmaking Criminology as Replacement Discourse." In G. Barak, ed., *Media, Process, and the Social Construction of Crime: Studies in Newsmaking Criminology*. New York: Garland.

Henry, Stuart, and Dragan Milovanovic. 1996. *Constitutive Criminology: Beyond Postmodernism*. London: Sage.

hooks, bell. 1994. "Sexism and Misogyny: Who Takes the Rap?" *Z Magazine* (February): 26–28.

Irwin, John, and James Austin. 1994. *It's About Time: America's Imprisonment Binge*. Belmont, CA: Wadsworth.

MacLean, Brian, and Harold Pepinsky. 1993. *We Who Would Take No Prisoners: Selections from the Fifth International Conference on Penal Abolition*. Vancouver, BC: Collective Press.

Messerschmidt, James W. 1986. *Capitalism, Patriarchy, and Crime: Toward a Socialist Feminist Criminology*. Totowa, NJ: Rowan and Littlefield.

Messner, Steven F., and Richard Rosenfeld. 1994. *Crime and the American Dream*. Belmont, CA: Wadsworth.

Miller, Mark C., and Janine J. Biden. 1996. "The National Entertainment State." *The Nation* 262(22, June 3): 23–28.

Mintz, Morton. 1992. "Why the Media Cover Up Corporate Crime: A Reporter Looks Back in Anger." *Trial* (November): 72–76.

Parry, Alan, and Robert Doan. 1994. *Story Re-Visions: Narrative Therapy in the Postmodern World*. New York: Guilford Press.

Pepinsky, Harold E., and Richard Quinney, eds. 1991. *Criminology as Peacemaking*. Bloomington, IN: Indiana University Press.

Ross, Edward A. 1901. *Social Control*. New York: Macmillan.

Schafer, Stephen. 1976. *Introduction to Criminology*. Reston, VA: Reston.

Scharf, Peter. 1977. "The Just Community." *New Society* (April 21): 104–105.

Scimecca, John A. 1988. "Conflict Resolution: Not Just for Children." *Peace in Action* 1: 20–23.

Simon, David, and Stanley Eitzen. 1994. *Elite Deviance*. 4th ed. Boston: Allyn and Bacon.

Skolnick, Jerome. 1966. *Justice Without Trial*. New York: Wiley.

Smothers, Roland. 1990. "Atlanta Sets a Curfew for Youths, Prompting Concern on Race Bias." *New York Times* (November 21): A1ff.

Sullivan, Mercer. 1989. *Getting Paid: Youth Crime and Work in the Inner City*. Ithaca, NY: Cornell University Press.

White, Michael, and David Epston. 1989. *Literate Means to Therapeutic Ends*. Adelaide, Australia: Dulwich Centre Publications.

Wilson, William Julius. *The Truly Disadvantaged: The Inner City, the Underclass, and Public Policy*. Chicago: University of Chicago Press.

Zinsmeister, Karl. 1990. "Growing Up Scared." *The Atlantic* (June): 49–66.

# Glossary

## Chapter 1
### Criminology and Crime: An Integrative Perspective

*Criminology*  An interdisciplinary study of the various bodies of knowledge, which focuses on the etiology of crime, the behavior of criminals, and the policies and practices of crime control.

*Deconstruction*  The examination of the heterogeneity of the discursive or textual conditions of theories in order to expose the fissures and ambiguities in their conceptual structures.

*Determinism*  The belief that human behavior results from the operation of forces beyond the control of the individual.

*Discipline*  An institutionalized body of knowledge or academic interest with specific sets of rules and assumptions that govern its methods of inquiry.

*Discourse*  The words, phrases, and thought processes that constitute a communicated representation of reality.

*Empiricism*  Deriving knowledge from observed facts.

*Interdisciplinary*  An integration of two or more bodies of knowledge (discipline), which captures a fuller approach to theoretical, methodological, and practical constructions than is the case for a single discipline (body of knowledge).

*Modern*  The historical period from the early Renaissance of the fourteenth century to the middle of the twentieth century, characterized by grand theories and meta-narratives of progress.

*Multidisciplinary*  A juxtaposition of two or more disciplines whereby the relationship created is mutual, cumulative, and additive.

*Paradigm*  A model of or orientation to theory and research, which includes its domain assumptions, appropriate methodologies, and issues to be addressed.

*Postmodern*  The historical period that began in the mid-twentieth century, characterized by nonessential, nonlinear, and pluralistic views of the universe.

*Rationalism*  Relying on reason to construct knowledge, and used as a basis for beliefs and actions.

*Textual Intersubjectivity*  Different meanings and interpretations that can be given to a text by its audiences.

*Transdisciplinary*  Approaches to understanding the universe that transcend disciplinary boundaries for the purpose of developing holistic models of human interaction.

*Utilitarian*  A principle dating back to eighteenth-century philosophy that public policies should provide "the greatest happiness shared by the greatest number."

## Chapter 2
### Crimes and Harms: A Comparative Perspective

*Aggravated Assault*  An attack with a weapon for the purpose of inflicting serious physical injury.

*Arson*  Willfully setting or attempting to set fire to another's property with the intent to inflict suffering or to one's own property with the intent to defraud.

*Burglary*  The unlawful entry or attempted entry of a structure with the intent to commit a felony or larceny.

*Corporate Crime*  Deliberate acts by large business enterprises to maximize profits at the expense of doing physical or economic harm to the environment, to workers, to consumers, and to the general public.

*Counterfeiting*  The creation or manufacture of imitations that are deceptively or fraudulently passed off as genuine.

*Cybercrime*  The use of computers, technology, and electronic communications to commit illegal acts.

*Embezzlement*  The misappropriation or misapplication of legally entrusted property with the intent to defraud the legitimate beneficiary or legal owner.

*Forcible Rape*  Sexual intercourse or attempted intercourse against the victim's will through the use of force or threat of force. Most states have redefined their statutes and refer to *sexual assaults* by degrees of aggravation that may or may not involve penetration of a body orifice.

*Forgery*  Making or copying something, such as a document or signature, with the intent to deceive or cheat.

*Fraud*  Obtaining money or property through false pretense.

*Genocide*  The systematic killing or extermination of a whole people or nation.

*Homicide*  The unlawful killing of a human being.

*Larceny Theft*  The unlawful taking, without force or deceit, of property from another person's possession with the intent to permanently deprive the owner of property.

*Motor Vehicle Theft*  The unlawful taking of a road vehicle with the intent to deprive a person of his or her property.

*Regulatory Offenses*  Behavioral violations of federal regulations involving such domestic areas as agriculture, food and drugs, motor carriers, labor law, and antitrust.

*Robbery*  The taking or attempted taking of anything of value from the custody of a person through the use or threat of force.

*White Collar Crime*  Illegal acts committed mostly by persons of middle class status, usually through their occupational endeavors, which involve concealment or guile in order to obtain financial, business, or personal advantage.

### Chapter 3
### Punishment and Criminology: A Historical Perspective

*Actuarial Justice*  An attempt to reduce the effects of crime by the redistribution of the aggregating patterns of criminal offenders in society.

*Collective Incapacitation*  The confinement of individuals based on their affiliation with a particular offending crime category (e.g., violent offender, drug dealer, child molester).

*Deterrence*  A philosophy of crime control dating back to the eighteenth century that calls for preventing crime through the actual (*specific*) punishment of offenders or the perceived threat of (*general*) punishment to any potential would-be offenders.

*Incapacitation*  The confinement of individuals for the purpose of preventing them from engaging in criminal acts that transcend their incarceration in jail or prison.

*Penality*  The cultural realities of punishment as a social institution.

*Penology*  The study of prison management.

*Punishment*  Any action that inflicts harm on a person for something that that individual has presumed to have done.

*Rehabilitation*  Changing a law-violating person into a law-abiding member of society through educational, vocational, or therapeutic intervention.

*Retribution*  The dominant justification for punishment as expressed in the biblical phrase of "an eye for an eye," or in the notion of "paying back" the offender with an equivalent degree of suffering.

*Revenge*  The enactment of punishment in a resentful or vindictive manner.

*Selective Incapacitation*  The incarceration of individuals based on their "predictive" likelihood of committing additional criminal acts upon release from confinement.

### Chapter 4
### Theory and Practice: On the Development of Criminological Inquiry

*Epistemology*  The study of the origins, nature, and limits of human knowledge.

*Essentialism*  A unitary perspective that views the diffuse bodies of knowledge as linked by some kind of common grounding.

*Nominalism*  A continuum of perspectives that view bodies of knowledge, to varying degrees, as both unique and overlapping in their groundings.

*Ontology*  The study of the nature of being and existence in the abstract, that is, separate and distinct from material, religious, and social existence.

*Phenomenology*  The scientific description of consciousness and its intentional objects or acts in their pure essences.

*Post-postmodern Synthesis*  An integration of bodies of knowledge across the domains of modernism and postmodernism for the purpose of developing inclusive or holistic models of social interaction.

*Science*  A branch of knowledge that arranges facts or truths systematically for the purposes of explanations, ranging from models that seek to describe particular phenomena to those that seek to prescribe specific ways of building theory about these phenomena.

*Pseudoscience*    A disparaging term used by those in the scientific communities to describe intellectual endeavors that employ questionable facts, theories, or methodologies.

*Veracity*    A concern for truthfulness, honesty, and accuracy.

### Chapter 5
### Contributions from Biology: "Body and Temperament"

*Adoptive Variables*    Comparison studies that center on persons who were adopted at, or shortly after, birth between groups of parents and the offsprings of known criminals with groups of parents and the offsprings of known noncriminals.

*Biochemical Variables*    Complex chemicals produced by an organism to regulate bodily functions, associated with the limbic system and studies of hyperactivity or impulsivity.

*Cellular Variables*    Self-contained carriers of a complete set of DNA that regulate biological activity, associated with genetic studies that examine and compare the human chromosomes and behaviors of fraternal and identical twins.

*Natural Selection*    A process in nature resulting in the survival and perpetuation of those living specimens having characteristics that best enable them to adapt to a specific environment.

*Neurotransmitter*    A chemical produced by the brain and stored in neurons that are released by electrochemical stimulations and that transmit information from one point in the organism to another.

*Phrenology*    Primarily a nineteenth-century system of personality and behavior based on the notion that the mental powers and characteristics of an individual consist of independent faculties, each related to different regions of the brain, supposedly indicated by the size and shape of the skull over that area.

*Physiognomy*    An analytical approach that allegedly connects the physical body types or features of individuals with their personality traits and behavioral actions.

*Somatotype*    The morphological shape or construction of the human physique generally, and specifically to the degree to which one may be classified as endomorph, mesomorph, or ectomorph.

*Systemic Variables*    Any combination of variables that regulate the functioning of specialized organs in the body.

### Chapter 6
### Contributions from Psychology: "Mind and Nurture"

*Attention-deficit Disorder*    A behavioral problem related to minor brain damage that may lead to antisocial personality traits.

*Antisocial-personality Criminal*    One who commits crimes for instrumental or emotive reasons. Often lacking a conscience or sense of guilt, this self-aggrandizing personality is typically intolerant of rules and seeks immediate gratification while avoiding responsibility. Such persons, often referred to as *psychopaths* or *sociopaths*, usually have difficulty establishing long-term relationships and empathizing with other people.

*Biopsychology*  A body of knowledge that links individual behavior with the chemical makeup and functioning of the brain.

*Differential Reinforcement*  A theory that argues that people commit illegal or nonconforming behaviors because they are more satisfying and rewarding than are legal and conforming behaviors.

*Ego*  One's self as conscious and distinct from others. According to Freud's "reality principle," the ego seeks to control or balance the needs of biology (id) with the needs of morality (superego) based on environmental experience.

*Humanistic Psychology*  A view of human beings that sees them as essentially moral and rational, and in control of their behavior through the possession of free will rather than determinism.

*Hyperactive Disorder*  A behavioral problem related to minor brain damage that leads to low cortical arousal, short attention spans, and the possibility of antisocial impulsivity.

*Id*  The Freudian term used to refer to that part of the unconscious containing an individual's inborn instincts, reflexes, and passions that seek gratification without concern for the consequences.

*Introjection*  The unconscious incorporation of the characteristics of another person or identity into one's own personality.

*Psychoanalytic Analysis*  A theory that states that all behavior, in addition to conscious thought, is motivated by the unresolved and unconscious tensions, conflicts, and struggles that exist within people.

*Psychotic Criminal*  One who commits crimes in response to delusions or hallucinations stemming from a functional psychotic disorder.

*Social Psychology*  A view of individual behavior as the end product of interactions between one's biopsychological traits and the structural and social factors of the immediate environment.

*Superego*  The moral basis of personality formation that embodies the values and control mechanisms of society. Freud used the term to denote the inner world of the individual's conscience and ideal expectations as transferred through introjection.

## Chapter 7
### Contributions from Sociology: "Environment and Structure"

*Alienation*  A condition typified by the lack or loss of relationships to others, and by feelings of powerlessness and meaninglessness. Marx emphasized alienation from self, from work, from community, and from society.

*Anomie*  The notion that normlessness occurs when there is a shifting of moral values and individuals lose sight of or are unable to express acceptable norms of behavior. Durkheim's emphasis was on the dissociation of the individual from the collective conscience whereas Merton's emphasis was on the contradictions between the culturally prescribed means and ends of society.

*Differential Anticipation*  The idea that crime occurs when expectations of gratification exceed those of learned conformity, perceived opportunities, and social bonds.

*Differential Association*    A theory that argues that criminal acts are learned behaviors resulting from an abundance of patterned interactions with criminals in combination with a lack of or isolation from patterned interactions with anticriminals.

*Differential Identification*    The idea that criminal acts occur when an individual identifies more with members of a criminal group than with members of a conformist group.

*Differential Opportunity*    A theory that argues that crime is the product of the relationship between legitimate and illegitimate opportunity structures as these intersect in the ways in which communities are organized (*differential social organization*).

*Marxist Criminology*    Theories of crime and crime control that emphasize the role of the political economy in the production of criminal and harmful behavior. For Quinney, there are essentially two kinds of crime: (1) the *crimes of domination and repression*, or those acts committed by the ruling classes and their agents in order to remain in power and maintain a position of privilege over the working classes; and (2) the *crimes of accommodation and resistance*, or the acts committed by the working and nonworking unemployed classes in order to survive under capitalism.

*Primary Deviant*    An individual who commits a deviant act before he or she has identified with any deviant label associated with the act.

*Secondary Deviant*    An individual who, having experienced stigmatization and the label of deviant, not only continues in the behavior but also identifies with the negative label as a badge of distinction.

*Social Disorganization (and Subcultural Theories)*    The conditions in which the usual controls over delinquency and crime are largely absent. Depending on the differential organization of communities, some are inclined to be primarily involved in expressive crimes of violence (conflict subcultures), some in instrumental crimes (criminal subcultures), and some in expressive crimes (retreatist subcultures) involving alcohol and drugs.

*Subcultures*    Groups of people with distinctive patterns of norms, beliefs, attitudes, values, and concerns that have evolved from the dominant society and its traditions. However, particular values to the exclusion of other values become exaggerated as a means of justifying nonconformity.

*Symbolic Interactionism*    The view that personality and social relationships are built up symbolically and rationally through language, images, and gestures.


### Chapter 8
### *Contributions from Law and Economics: "Reason and Rationality"*

*Classical Theory*    A framework that emerged during the Enlightenment, which assumes that people exercise free will and are, therefore, responsible for their actions. Classicism argues that all human behavior, including criminal behavior, is motivated by the desire for pleasure and the avoidance of pain. Hence, crime can be rationally controlled by manipulating the punishments (and rewards) that offenders rationally associate with violating different criminal laws.

*Due Process*    The rights of people suspected of or charged with crimes, specifically to those criminal procedures that are adhered to by the courts in ensuring that a defendant's constitutional rights are not violated.

*Free Will*    The ability to choose or control actions in one's own interests.

*Neoclassical Theory*    A modification of classical theory that recognizes individual differences (e.g., mental capacity) or factors (e.g., occasional versus habitual offenders) that inhibit the exercise of free will, and the reintroduction of discretionary as opposed to uniform punishments for the same act.

*Routine Activities Theory*    A model that argues that crimes are related not only to the motivation of individuals to commit criminal acts, but also to the presence of suitable targets and the absence of informal or formal constraints, all of which will vary not only by age, gender, and class, but also in relationship to the routinization of opportunities and conflicts presented by these variables.

*Social Contract*    An assumed consensus or imaginary agreement that individuals will sacrifice a minimum of loss of personal freedom in exchange for security and protection from anarchy, chaos, and disorder.

*Social Control*    The ways in which members of a group, community, or society punish deviance and attempt to induce others to follow the prescribed norms of conduct.

*Tort*    A private or civil wrong or injury, independent of the nation/state, resulting from a breach of a legal duty or obligation, not punishable by a criminal sanction of loss of liberty or life, but subject primarily to fine, restitution, or compensation.

**Chapter 9**
***Integrating Criminological Theory: A Critique***

*Conceptual Integration*    Combining concepts from various theories without formulating testable propositions.

*Dialectical Causality*    Also referred to as "codeterminist" causality, this model of crime may be thought of as a case of multiple interactive causality.

*End-to-End Integration*    or Sequential Integration    The specifying of the temporal order between causal variables, so that the dependent variables of one theory constitute the independent variables of another theory.

*Interactive Causality*    Also referred to as "reciprocal causality," this model of crime assumes that cause and effect influence each other, and that over time they form a spiral process.

*Linear Causality*    Also referred to as "interdependent" or "conditional" causality, this model of crime assumes a single, sequential, and linear chain of events.

*Motivated Deviance*    Conscious and unconscious desires to engage in nonconforming behavior.

*Multiple Causality*    A model of crime that assumes either many causal factors, any one of which may be sufficient for crime to occur, or some kind of combined causal factors that coproduce crime.

*Propositional Integration*    Formulating testable hypotheses for theories that have been conceptually integrated.

*Side-by-Side Integration*    or Parallel Integration    The partitioning of the subject matter of crime into cases that are explained by different theories.

*Unmotivated Deviance*    Nonconforming behavior whereby the conscious desires to conform are without the required resources or skills to do so.

*Up-and-Down Integration*    or Deductive Integration    The identifying of a level of abstraction that encompasses the conceptualizations of its constituent theories.

*Chapter 10*
*Integrating Criminological Knowledges: A Post-Postmodern Synthesis*

*Constitutive Criminology*   An integrated and critical analysis that recognizes crime as the coproduction of human subjects and the social and organizational structures that humans develop and endlessly (re)build.

*Hermeneutics*   The art or science of interpretation.

*Reconstruction*   The attempt to transform that which has been deconstructed into new alternative constructions.

*Textuality*   A mode of analysis that favors the constitutive over the causal or the communicative while it stresses an understanding of subjects' meanings in the context of the regulative principles of our social systems.

*Zetetics*   The totality of culturally produced and recorded systematized knowledges as these are related to methods of research, mental processes, psychological factors, and environmental conditions.

*Zetetic Studies*   The science of research and artistic activity or the study of human knowledge as a whole.

*Chapter 11*
*Integrating Cultural, Gender, and Media Studies: An Interdisciplinary Perspective on Crime Production*

*Consumer Personality*   The mass-produced need to identify through consumption.

*Corporate Restructuring*   The processes of automation and the reallocation of resources, through downsizing and the relocation of operations to cities, states, and nations that provide lower costs of labor.

*Cultural Kaleidoscope*   The idea that mass society is represented by multiple and ever-changing cultural realities.

*Culture of Consumption*   The expectations and obligations that motivate and shape acquisitive behavior in relation to dominant cultural values and goals.

*Cybernetics*   The comparative study of the control and communication systems in animals, humans, and computers.

*Domestic Violence*   The physical, psychological, or emotional abuse that occurs within primary living groups, usually involving husbands or male lovers as the primary offenders, and wives or female lovers as the primary victims.

*Ideology*   A doctrine used to justify a group's course of action.

*Ideologies*   Images, concepts, and opinions that are associated with different ways of understanding the world.

*Integrative-Constitutive*   An approach to crime and social control that incorporates an analysis of the recursive and interactive processes of socialization practices, structural organizations, and societal reactions to nonconformity.

*Market Society*   Any society, according to Currie, in which the pursuit of private gain increasingly becomes the organizing principle for all of life, and the balance between private and public shifts dramatically, so that the public retreats to a miniscule and unempowered part of social and economic life. In the process, the idea of common purpose and common responsibility steadily withers as an important social value.

*State Crime*   Illegal and harmful behavior engaged in by governments, which injures the interests of their own citizens or those of peoples of other nations.

**Chapter 12**
**Integrating Crime and Social Control: An Interdisciplinary Approach
to Crime Reduction**

*Conciliatory Social Control*   A style of informal control involving both parties working with or without a third party to negotiate a mutually acceptable outcome.

*Compensatory Social Control*   A style of formal control that entails monetary payment from the offender to the victim.

*Judicial Restraint*   The two-decade-long trend in sentencing policies that have limited the power and discretion of judges in their authority to distribute punishment.

*Narrative Therapies*   Therapies that are both reality based and engaged in reconstructing biographies rather than therapies that are subconsciously based in early childhood and psychoanalysis.

*New Penology*   The back-to-the-future ideological shift away from corrections and to punishment as expressed in a de-emphasis in rehabilitation and treatment, and in an emphasis on incapacitation, deterrence, and retribution.

*Punitive Social Control*   A style of formal control involving the infliction of pain, the identification of a guilty party, and the use of coercion.

*Social Capital*   The investment in human capital as a way of addressing social problems.

*Target Hardening*   Making physical property less vulnerable to criminal exploitation.

*Therapeutic Social Control*   A style of control that attempts to change nonconforming behavior by internal psychic alteration that results in external behavioral conformity.

# *Photo Credits*

Page 1, Steve LaVasseur/Courtesy of Social Justice; Page 3, 19, AP/Wide World Photos; Page 30, Reuters/Emil Vas/Archive Photos; Page 40, 56, AP/Wide World Photos; Page 64, UPI/Corbis-Bettmann; Page 72, Rick Browne/Stock, Boston; Page 81, Barbara Alper/Stock, Boston; Page 94, UPI/Corbis-Bettmann; Page 110, Christopher Brown/Stock, Boston; Page 119, Corbis-Bettmann; Page 126, AP/Wide World Photos; Page 128, UPI/Corbis-Bettmann; Page 135, Lyrl Ahern; Page 138, UPI/Corbis-Bettmann; Page 149, AP/Wide World Photos; Page 152, 161, Lyrl Ahern; Page 170, Bob Daemmrich/Stock, Boston; Page 177, AP/Wide World Photos; Page 186, Robert Harbison; Page 216, AP/Wide World Photos; Page 236, Photofest; Page 247, Miro Vintoniv/The Picture Cube; Page 253, Archive Photos/Miramax Films; Page 255, 269, Photofest; Page 296, Courtesty of the Delancey Street Foundation; Page 300, Shia photo/Impact Visuals.

# Author Index

# Subject Index